365
DAYS OF
GUTSY
WOMEN

Rosemary Roenfanz

365 Days of Gutsy Women
Copyright © 2021 **Rosemary Roenfanz**

ISBN: 978-1-7373347-0-5 (Paperback)
ISBN: 978-1-7373347-2-9 (Hardcover)
ISBN: 978-1-7373347-1-2 (E-book)

Library of Congress Control Number: 2021910968

Front cover image by Michelle Goodhew
Book formatting by Arjen Broeze, Black Bee Media

Printed by IngramSpark

First printing edition 2021.

DEDICATION

In memory of

Lenore Gaudin, who guides me from the stars.

For Jennifer Brooks, my shining light.

INTRODUCTION

Daily readings (devotionals) have been a way of life for many seeking emotional, intellectual, or spiritual growth. Nightstands are often covered with volumes consisting of 365 daily readings offering one easily consumed entry for each day of the year and are kept handy for either a hasty morning read or a nighttime browse.

365 Days of Gutsy Women is a secular compendium of the same tradition, a year's worth of daily readings that will inspire and fascinate as you discover extraordinary women who have come before us. For centuries, women's stories and their accomplishments have been ignored or forgotten. Too often left out of narrative, women need to be celebrated. And what better way than a daily glimpse of their lives?

Each woman in this book is drawn from a different category. Enjoy a mini-biography per day exploring each category once a week. What makes them different (or similar) to you and me? You're holding the answer in your hands.

365 Gutsy Women's biographies are divided into the following categories:

Monday—Activists/Rebels
Icons who fought for the nation's as well as women's freedoms, equality, and rights that *changed the world.*

Tuesday—Educators/Philosophers
Deep thinkers who taught, lectured, debated, counseled, and designed curriculums as they *helped change the world.*

Wednesday—Scientists/Innovators
Women whose brilliant minds and original thinking gave the world answers, cures, and businesses and *changed the world.*

Thursday—Authors/Poets
Writers who created art with words while protesting injustice or conserving Mother Earth while *changing the world.*

Friday—Leaders
From the beginning of time, women who have led nations or their communities and *changed the world.*

Saturday—Artists/Musicians
Female creative spirits who gave us visual beauty or lifted us to great heights with their voices *as they changed the world.*

Sunday—Goddesses
Ancient and revered women who continue to guide us with their blessings *as we change the world.*

Epigraph

Heal yourself with the light of the sun and the rays of the moon. With the sound of the river and the waterfall. With the swaying of the sea and the fluttering of birds. Heal yourself with mint, neem, and eucalyptus. Sweeten with lavender, rosemary, and chamomile. Hug yourself with the cocoa bean and a hint of cinnamon. Put love in tea instead of sugar and drink it looking at the stars. Heal yourself with the kisses that the wind gives you and the hugs of the rain. Stand strong with your bare feet on the ground and with everything that comes from it. Be smarter every day by listening to your intuition, looking at the world with your forehead. Jump, dance, sing, so that you live happier. Heal yourself, with beautiful love, and always remember ... you are the medicine."

María Sabina, Mexican healer and poet

"The young women of today, free to study, to speak, to write, to choose their occupation, should remember that every inch of this freedom was bought for them at a great price.... The debt that each generation owes to the past it must pay to the future."

Known as Oregon's "Mother of Equal Suffrage", Abigail Jane Scott Duniway (1834-1915) was a writer, orator, editor, pioneering feminist and a mother. "The pioneer Woman Suffragist of the Great Northwest" committed over forty years to working to further women's rights. In Idaho, Washington, and Oregon, Abigail traveled many miles during her important mission. Outspoken and controversial, her twenty-two novels centered around women's rights and were serialized in the papers she edited. Gutsy and strong-willed indeed.

Abigail was actually born in Illinois, traveling to the Oregon Territory with her family when she was seventeen. During her first year there, she taught school, and met her future husband, Benjamin Duniway. After he suffered a permanent injury in 1862, Abigail became the chief breadwinner.

Taking in boarders, teaching school, and running a millinery shop allowed the family to move to Portland in 1871. *The New Northwest*, a weekly publication, then became the family's enterprise, Ben handling business matters and their older sons helping out with the printing.

With her signature line "Yours for Liberty" and led by her paper's motto of "Free Speech, Free Press, Free People", Abigail exposed and fought against social injustices. Mainly self-taught, with less than a year of formal schooling under her belt, she resolved to make *The New Northwest* a voice not only for women's suffrage but for all social injustices. Her human rights newspaper published weekly and edited by Abigail, ran for sixteen years.

In the Idaho Territory, Abigail celebrated a victory for women's suffrage in 1896. Early successes were overturned in Washington Territory, until finally in 1910 women were given the right to vote. And in Oregon, where women's suffrage was defeated five times, the right to vote was passed in 1912.

DID YOU KNOW?

1. Abigail also spoke up against poor treatment of Chinese Americans and Native Americans.
2. Oregon's women's suffrage was defeated five times before the right to vote
3. Was passed in 1912.
4. She died four years shy of the passing of the nineteenth Amendment.

An American educator, Adelina Otero-Warren (1881-1965) fought for women's rights as a writer, businesswoman and a politician. She created a civil service heritage through her work in education, public health, and politics. As one of New Mexico's first female government officials, she served as Santa Fe Superintendent of Instruction (1917-1929). Otero-Warren was also the first Latina to compete for a Congressional seat in 1922.

Adelina began working with the woman's suffrage campaign in New Mexico with Alice Paul's Congressional Union. She quickly rose in rank because of her commitment. Believing she had an even greater calling advocating for Hispanics, particularly in education, Adelina began a progressive campaign for a seat in the U.S. House of Representatives. She advocated strongly (speaking out in Spanish to reach fellow Latinos) for education, health care and welfare services, also hoping to be able to preserve Hispanic heritage and culture. Controversy evolved when news of her divorce came out during the election, as did concerns about her stance on Spanish-language instruction in schools and employment of Hispanic teachers; she ultimately lost the national election.

While serving as school superintendent, she made several substantial changes repairing dilapidated school buildings and improving teachers' salaries. Adelina increased the school year's duration and created county high school and adult education programs. She amended the curriculum to emphasize bilingual and bicultural education as well. As an inspector in Indian schools, Adelina continued her attempt at integrating ethnic cultures and languages into public school curriculums. She advocated against sending Native children to boarding schools and sought to further opportunities to learn about Native culture, history and tradition.

Her contributions to her community were not just in politics and education. Adelina worked to preserve the historic structures of Santa Fe and Taos. She also worked closely with the arts community and was instrumental in renewing interest in and respect for Hispanic and Indian culture.

DID YOU KNOW?

1. There are currently seventeen Latina women serving in the 117th U.S. Congress. Yay!
2. At age sixty-six, Adelina began a Santa Fe real estate career that kept her busy until her death. (Never too late to start over, right?)

ADA LOVELACE

Considered to be the first computer programmer, Augusta Ada King-Noel (1815-1852), Countess of Lovelace, was an English analyst, mathematician, and mother of three. She wrote an algorithm for a computing machine in the mid-1800s, the "Analytic Engine." Ada's father, poet Lord Byron left their home only months after her birth, never to return. Her life became a struggle between sentiment and reason, poetry and mathematics, illness and energy surges—enduring migraines and years of paralysis from measles as an adolescent. What a trooper she was.

Lady Byron encouraged Ada's gift for mathematics and language. Certainly not the standard for women at the time, Ada was educated by tutors in history and geography, sciences and the arts, as well languages. Insisting on rigorous studies, Lady Byron hoped to prevent her daughter from acquiring her father's moody and unpredictable temperament.

At the age of seventeen, Ada met Charles Babbage, a Cambridge mathematician and inventor who became her mentor and life-long friend. He introduced her to his mathematical machine. Ada published a translation of Luigi Menebrea's 1842 *Notions sur la machine analytique de M. Charles Babbage.* She added her own set of appended notes to it; entitled *Translator's Notes,* Ada explained in easily understood words and diagrams exactly how the engine worked.

Signing her notes A.A.L., Ada theorized a method for the machine to repeat a series of instructions, known as looping in today's world. The translation with her appended notes was published in 1843. She described how codes could be created for the machine to handle letters, symbols and numbers.

DID YOU KNOW?

1. Because Ada's notes were not published separate from the translation, she received no recognition for her contribution. (Jeez.)
2. It wasn't until the 1980s that Ada Lovelace and the importance of her work was recognized.

"All books are either dreams or swords, you can cut, or you can drug, with words."

An American poet, Amy Lowell (1874-1925) won the Pulitzer Prize posthumously for her poetry in 1926. As an editor, translator, biographer and critic, she dedicated her life to modern poetry. Amy wrote and published over 650 poems before her untimely death, flouting convention with her pro-feminist poetry and public persona which included smoking cigars. (I love her outrageousness!)

Born on the family estate in Brookline, Massachusetts, Amy was first tutored at home by her mother, later attending private schools in Boston, and was encouraged to write from an early age. At seventeen she secluded herself in the 7,000-book library at the family estate to study literature.

Around 1902, she decided to devote her energies to poetry. Amy, through strong will and determination, became a major force in American poetry at the critical moment of the birth of modernism. Though lacking the advantages of a first-rate education, her energy and passion for the genre was boundless. She became the leading speaker for the modernist movement known as Imagism (a movement that uses precise imagine and clarified speech).

She had a lifelong love for Keats, whose letters she collected. Amy's vivid and powerful personality along with her independence and zest made her conspicuous, as did her scorn for convention. Lowell was notorious for her huge pack of pedigreed Old English sheepdogs. She was both beloved and despised for her outspoken manner and her challenge to gender conventions.

In addition to her poetry and books of criticism, Amy lectured frequently and wrote critical articles for periodicals. In 1918, she was the first woman to deliver a lecture at Harvard University. She has led the way for our generation of female poets.

DID YOU KNOW?

1. Her final publication was not poetry but a biography of John Keats.
2. Amy Lowell was considered the "most important American woman of letters" at the time of her death.

Queen Ahmose Nefertari (1570-1530 BCE) was the Royal Wife of Ramesses II the Great and first Egyptian queen of the 18th dynasty. A Nubian and mother of six, she was often referred to as "the most beautiful woman in the world". She played an important role because of her religious and economic influence in the cult of Amun-Re. Queen Nefertari had the right to endow lands and goods, as well as choose her own successors. She is arguably the most venerated woman in Egyptian history. As we gaze at her picture, we are reminded how *powerful* female leaders were in ancient times. (!)

Nefertari was highly educated and able to read and write hieroglyphs—a rare talent. As queen, she also played an active role in foreign politics. She was also involved in the king's building projects, unusual for the time. Said to be an excellent military woman, Nefertari was the first female military leader in the history of mankind. She showed great superiority and power in training. As such, Nefertari was considered a national hero and one of the outstanding figures in African history.

When the king died, Nefertari ruled the land as regent for Prince Merneptah, the king's 13thson by another wife. She is credited with restoring temples and official cults throughout the land after decades of neglect by the Hyksos dynasty, which she and the king had defeated.

Queen Nefertari was the first Egyptian queen to hold the title of "God's First Wife of Amun". She was deified as the patron of Thebes. Upon her death, she became "Mistress of the Sky" and "Lady of the West".

DID YOU KNOW?

1. She was the mother of at least six children.
2. Some historians believe she was the half-sister to her husband, Ramses II.
3. Nefertari's tomb is considered the most exquisite of all tombs and is located in the Valley of Queens near Thebes. The walls are covered with paintings and the ceiling painted dark blue with stars.
4. Her tomb is named QV66 and is referred to as the Sistine Chapel of Ancient Egypt.

"It has happened more than once that a composition has come to me, ready-made as it were, between the demands of other work."

> American composer and pianist, Amy Cheney Beach (1867-1944) was the first successful American female composer of large-scale art music—her *Gaelic Symphony* premiered by Boston Symphony Orchestra in 1896. Amy was also one of the first U.S. composers recognized in Europe. Her courage to follow her dream was extraordinary.

Born in New Hampshire, Amy showed every sign of being a child prodigy. She was able to sing forty songs accurately by age one, and at two-years-old was already capable of improvising counter melody. She taught herself to read at age three and began taking piano lessons at age six, although she had been composing simple melodies on the keyboard since she was four. Amy gave her first public recital at Boston Music Hall. Several more successful recitals followed, and in March 1885 she played Chopin's *Piano Concerto in F Minor* with the Boston Symphony Orchestra.

She married Henry H.A. Beach, an eminent surgeon and Harvard University professor, the same year. He encouraged her to concentrate on composition, so Amy began curtailing her public performances and undertook a rigorous course of self-instruction in Music theory and composition.

In February 1892, she heard the Boston Symphony and the Handel and Haydn Society perform her *Mass in E-flat* (written 1890), her first major work (numbered Opus 5). Amywas the first woman composer to be performed by those organizations. After her husband died in 1910, Amy continued composing and returned to performing. She toured Europe playing her own compositions. Europeans were not used to American composers or female composers meeting their high standards for classical music, and she gained considerable attention for her work on the continent—as well she should.

Did you know?

1. In total, Amy composed more than 150 numbered works, nearly all of which were published.
2. As generous in death as she was in life, Amy donated her royalties from her works to the MacDowell Colony, an artists' haven in New Hampshire.

Greek Goddess of divine retribution, Adrestia is believed to have become an independent deity developing from many supernatural beings. Known as "She whom none can escape," Adrestia is venerated as a Goddess of revolt, just retribution and the sublime balance between good and evil. Her symbols are the scales (balanced), a blindfold (representing impartiality of revolution as a natural force), a sword and a shield. Adrestia reminds us to seek justice for the downtrodden, holding our community and its leaders accountable.

Of the seven children of Ares and Aphrodite, Adrestia is the only girl who is most like Her father, joining Him (Ares) and His brutal men on the battlefield. She is estranged from most of Her siblings, especially her own twin sister *Harmonia,* and often keeps to herself. She feels responsible to aid humanity in small struggles against injustice, sometimes entering schools to stick up for the bullied.

As the times and tides shifted on the planet, Adrestia scoured the world to find wrongdoing and injustice, seeking to undo them for the good of the people. Adrestia was known by many names and many faces throughout her journeys, but none knew of her godly origin.

As a Goddess, Adrestia is armed with a myriad of supernatural powers, including agelessness, enhanced speed, strength, stamina, and physical allure—a 'godly' form whose presence killed mortals, and accelerated healing. Like Her mistress, Nemesis, Adrestia is able to manipulate reality to the point where Her selected targets (those overcome by their inner vices) are punished fittingly. Her retribution thus upholds the cosmic balance.

DID YOU KNOW?

1. She is able to manifest a pair of black wings so she can fly.
2. The feathers of these wings are tipped with a venom that forces those who ingest it to relive their wrongdoing against another. (I advise avoiding them.)

Russian revolutionary Alexandra Mikhailovna Kollontai (1872-1952) was a feminist, stateswoman, the world's first female ambassador, a student of Marxism, and a mother. She was the socialist behind paid child-care and parental leave. A champion for women's rights, Alexandra helped liberalize divorce, gave women access to their own earnings, and advocated for women's rights to sexual autonomy. As a socialist and an early advocate of sexual freedom for women, Alexandra was written out of many histories concerning global feminism.

Alexandra's emphasis on providing public services for women and children pervaded the key international United Nations treaty on women's rights, *The Convention on the Elimination of All Forms of Discrimination Against Women*. This treaty has been ratified by 187 countries, but sadly, not by the United States.

After WWII, Eastern European nations began implementing her reforms in order to help mobilizing women into the labor force. Her feminist ideas spread across the globe long before they became part of a U.S. presidential campaign. Alexandra served as the Soviet ambassador to Sweden throughout WWII. She was nominated twice for the Nobel Peace Prize in 1946 and in 1947 for brokering the Finnish-Soviet ceasefire.

Alexandra recognized that the institutions of marriage and traditional family contributed to the oppression of women. She also realized household labors continued to prevent women and girls from advancing educationally and professionally. Aleksandra promoted radical ideas about women's sexuality when Victorian prudishness was the norm. Hounded by the czarist police, she spent years in exile, returning from the West in 1917 when Lenin named her minister of social welfare.

She spearheaded drastic changes in Russian family law and organized the socialization of women's domestic work through a vast organization. The *1918 Family Code* reversed centuries of ecclesiastical and patriarchal power over women's lives. This made her an international pariah to nervous male leaders in the West. (Figures.) In spite of her accomplishments, Alexandra Kollontai's name and work have been overlooked.

DID YOU KNOW?

1. Alexandra was deemed dangerous by the U.S. government and called a *national security risk* because of her progressive thinking on women's issues.
2. The 1970s feminist movement garnered new interest around the world in her writings and her life.

ALBERTINE NECKER DE SAUSSURE

Swiss educator and mother, Albertine Adrienne Necker de Saussure (1766-1841) wrote an influential study on the education of women. She was an early women's rights advocate, believing women's education was a necessity more than a way to create proper wives. Albertine authored a large three-volume work on the importance of education, *L'Education Progressive* (1828), which is still considered an educational classic today.Ignoring her deafness, Albertine learned four languages before influencing the world view of women and education. Because of her efforts, we women can realize our academic dreams.

The daughter of a Genevan scientist and Alpine explorer, Albertine was educated at home. She learned four languages plus the sciences. Her religious views were liberal and unprejudiced. Encouraged by her father, the young girl began keeping a diary of scientific observations at age ten. Later on, she became active in experimenting, even burning her face quite badly during an attempt to prepare oxygen. Albertine also went on geological and botanical expeditions with her father.

Marrying a botanist, Louis Necker, she initially wrote her husband's botany lectures for him. Albertine went on to teach her own children a wide range of subjects including science. Much like Mary Wollstonecraft, Albertine believed single women must maintain themselves through education, not simply to please a man.

Her literary works were written later in life, after her children were grown. L'Education Progressive or Etude du Cours de la Vie was divided into two parts, originally in three volumes. The first two volumes are an examination of general education from childbirth to fourteen. The third volume focuses on the education of women, encouraging them to learn how to make independent judgments.

DID YOU KNOW?

1. Albertine believed that historically, social attitudes had been damaging to women, to their dignity and their *sense of self*.
2. She was compared to Mary Wollstonecraft who also believed single women ought to bolster themselves up through education.

The first woman and first African American woman to receive a master's degree from the University of Hawaii, Alice Augusta Ball (1892-1916) was an American research chemist who discovered an effective treatment for Hansen's disease also known as leprosy She was also the first female African American chemistry professor at the same University. Known as the "Ball Method", Alice developed a way to effectively use chaulmoogra oil, making it water-soluble, therefore, easier to dissolve in the bloodstream. Unfortunately, Alice died before being able to publish her discovery. Arthur L. Dean (a chemist and president of the University) finished writing her papers and took all credit for Alice's discovery!

Alice began studying chemistry at The University of Washington in Seattle. She earned a bachelor's degree in pharmaceutical chemistry in 1912 and another one in the science of pharmacy in 1914. She then published an article in the *Journal of the American Chemical Society*. A woman being published in a respected scientific journal, an African American woman, was an extraordinary accomplishment.

Alice went on to attain her master's degree in Hawai'i. Dr. Harry Hollman of Hawaii's Kalihi Hospital reached out to her regarding the cure for leprosy. Chaulmoogra oil had previously been used but it was discontinued due to mixed results and severe side effects. Injecting it was an ideal solution, and it took Alice less than a year to develop a water- soluble solution for efficacy.

Alice died tragically, some say from a laboratory accident, before publishing the results of her work. In the 1970s, two Hawaiian professors began investigating her research. It wasn't until the year 2000 that papers were uncovered bringing to light the injustice done to her.

Alice Ball overcame racial and gender barriers to develop the only pain-free leprosy treatment that lasted thirty years until sulfone drugs became available.

DID YOU KNOW?

1. Ninety years after her discovery, Alice was finally honored by the University of Hawaii.
2. She was only twenty-three when she became a chemistry professor at the University of Hawaii.

"It was a time when only the dead smiled, happy in their peace."

Regarded as the greatest female poet in Russian literature, Anna Akhmatova (1889-1966) also wrote memoirs, autobiographical pieces and literary scholarship on other Russian writers. She also translated Italian, French, Armenian and Korean poetry. Can you imagine doing that in early twentieth century Russia?

Anna Andreyevna Gorenka was born near the Black Sea. She began writing verse at eleven, but when her father found out about her aspirations, he told her not to shame the family name by becoming a "decadent poetess". He forced her to take a pen name, and she chose the last name of her maternal great-grandmother, Akhmatova.

Anna's writing was stamped with elegant colloquialism and the psychological sophistication of a young cosmopolitan woman. The smallest detail could evoke a large gamut of emotions. Her collections brought her fame and made her poetic voice a symbol of the experiences of her generation. The artistic and emotional integrity of her poetic voice garnered great enthusiasm. Anna's principal motif is that of a frustrated and tragic love expressed with intense femininity.

Even with her broadening themes of patriotism and religious motifs during war time, Anna's poems were frequently ostracized and castigated by the Soviet government and the Central Communist Party— though the Russian people continued to love and adore her. At times she was expelled from national writing groups, called names ("half-nun-half harlot") and her published books destroyed. Anna's reputation was shattered.

Despite her family members' imprisonment, Anna continued to write, and began publishing again in 1958. She also translated other poets, including works by Victor Hugo, Rabindranath Tagore and Giacomo Leopardu. Anna's own works were widely translated and her international stature continues to grow even after her death.

DID YOU KNOW?

1. During her son's imprisonment, Anna wrote praising Stalin in order to gain Lev's release from prison to no avail.
2. She requested those poems not appear in her collected works.

CARTIMANDUA QUEEN OF BRIGANTES

> Cartimandua was a 1st century queen of Brigantia from around 43-69 CE. As the first documented queen to rule part of Britain in her own right, Cartimandua reigned over the Brigantes, a Celtic people of Northern England living in what is now Yorkshire. Territorially they were the biggest tribe in Britain.

Around the time of the Roman invasion and conquest, Cartimandua came into power. The Roman historian Tacitus has given us most of what we know about her. His writings tell us Cartimandua she was a very strong influential leader. In order to retain her throne, Cartimandua and her husband, Venutius, were pro-Rome. They made several deals and agreements with the Romans. Tacitus described her as loyal to Rome and "defended by our [Roman] arms".

In 51AD Cartimandua's allegiance to Rome was tested. The British king, Caratacus, leader of the Catuvellauni tribe of Wales, was defeated and sought sanctuary along with his family, with Cartimandua and the Brigantes. Instead of giving him shelter, Cartimandua chained him up, giving him to the Romans—who then showered her with great wealth and favors. However, her own people turned against her for this traitorous act.

Divorcing Venutius in favor of his armor-bearer Vellocatus further angered the Celts. Scorned, Venutius incited a riot against the queen. Cartimandua was eventually defeated in 69 CE. She fled, abandoning Brigantia to Venutius. The once mighty queen simply vanished— her fate unknown. Cartimandua remains a mystery to all generations, but we can recognize how our actions have far reaching consequences by reading her story.

DID YOU KNOW?

1. Cartimandua most likely inherited her power as she was "born of illustrious birth."
2. Her life story is fictionalized in the book *Daughters of Fire.*

A Swiss neo-classic painter, Angelica Kauffman (1741-1807), was the go-to paint-er for the British aristocracy. The most famous portraitist in 18th century Europe, male or female, Angelica was often plagued with allegations of being a 'plaything' for famous male artists. Despite her talent and *avant-garde* status, she has generally received less attention than her male Neoclassical colleagues. Philosopher Johann Gottfried Herder once called her "possibly the most cultivated woman in Europe".

Maria Anna Catharina Angelica Kauffmann was a precocious child, a talented musi-cian and painter by her 12th year. Her parents came from a noble family, allowing Kauffman to glean the best parts from both of their respective worlds in order to form her own identity. She took those "best parts" and funneled them into her art. We can emulate Angelica by discovering our inherited talents and utilize them—even if it's just for our own pleasure.

A child prodigy who was producing commissioned portraits in her early teens, Angelica was trained by her father, the muralist Johann Joseph Kauffman. During the early 1760s, she traveled through Switzerland, Austria, and Italy working as her father's assistant.

During a three-year stay in Italy, she garnered a reputation as a painter of portraits; she also produced historical paintings. In 1766, Angelica moved to London where she achieved immediate success as a portraitist. Over the next 16 years, she exhibited regularly at the prestigious Royal Academy and worked for a glittering array of aris-tocratic and royal patrons. Gender did however remain an on-going obstacle in her career.

During her lifetime she was one of the highest paid and most sought after portrait art-ists, second only to her great friend and colleague, Sir Joshua Reynolds. Angelica chal-lenged contemporary perspectives on gender from the very center of the art world, cleverly using the most elite and respected form of art at the time, history painting—paintings of mythology and classical history. She was charming, financially indepen-dent, and internationally acclaimed.

DID YOU KNOW?

1. Angelica was nearly forgotten by historians despite her magnificent talent.
2. She was one of the founders of the Royal Academy in London.

AINE

An Irish Goddess of summer, love and fertility, Aine (Awn-ya) rules over wealth and sovereignty and is the protectress of women and animals. Also known as a Faery queen and Love Goddess, She is called "The Lady of the Lake" and "Goddess of the Earth and Nature". In Her role as Moon Goddess, She guards livestock, crops and cattle. As SunGoddess, Aine takes the form of a red mare. Her name is thought to mean brightness, glow, radiance, splendor, glory and fame.

Associated with midsummer and summer solstice, Aine has sacred days following *Lughnassadh* (a festival that falls halfway between the summer solstice and the autumn equinox, *Mabon).* She is among the most revered and powerful of Irish Goddesses.

Because Aine is also known as the "Love Goddess", people worshiped Her hoping to be endowed with fertility, sexuality, abundance and prosperity. She was believed to have given the gift of grain to people of Ireland. Legends tell of royal ceremonies held at *Cnoc Aine* (Knockainey, Co. Limerick). It is there while sheep quietly graze that mythological Irish kings were crowned and a sacred marriage was held. The *Oenach* festival (honoring the dead, proclaiming laws and funeral games) was continued here until the twentieth century.

Traditions and legends grew about the hill where Aine is celebrated as the "people's Goddess". At *Samhain,* on November 1st, it is said Aine emerges from the side of the hill where a cairn is located. The locals light bonfires on all the surrounding hilltops in Her honor. She is also celebrated at midsummer's festival on June 23rd. The local men march around the summit and run through their cattle and fields to bestow good luck on them for the upcoming year.

DID YOU KNOW?

1. Aine is associated with air, the direction southwest, and a sacred herb of the Druids—Meadowsweet.
2. Aine is part of the triple Goddess group with her two sisters—Fenne and Grianne.

A Finnish social activist, Baroness Alexandra van Gripenberg (1857-1913) was an author, editor, newspaper publisher, and legislator. A pioneer of the Finnish feminist movement, she founded the first women's rights organization in Finland, the Suomen Naisyhdistys (Finnish Women's Association) in Helsinki in 1884. Her book, *A Half Year in the New World*, was inspired by her tours of England and the United States, absorbing the women's movements there. She was known as Finland's most prominent women's rights activist.

As a leader of the *Suomen Naisyhdistys*, Alexandra headed a campaign for educational, professional, and political equality. She strongly advocated feminist reforms of property rights, divorce laws, and the abolition of state-regulated prostitution. (Lucina Hagman, another feminist, was campaigning for women's suffrage at the same time.)

In 1883 Alexandra attended the Women's Congress in Washington, D.C. organized by Susan B. Anthony. The formation of the International Council of Women in 1889 led to her becoming its vice-president from 1893 to 1899. The Council organized national bodies in eastern and southern Europe, read papers at congress, as well as writing and giving interviews.

Alexandra concentrated on educating women to be wise political participants after they won the vote in Finland in 1906. (Finland was the first European country where women gained full political rights.) Elected to the membership of the *Finnish Diet* (the Parliament of Finland) in 1909, she was known as a female conservative.

DID YOU KNOW?

1. She argued *against* legislation of protection for women, believing that total equality between the sexes would not be achieved if either of them received special protection.
2. Her collection of nearly 300 books, periodicals, newspapers, and ephemera is stored in the National Library of Finland.

Alice Freeman Palmer (1855-1902) was known as the "New Woman" of the 19th century. An American educator and a wife, Alice was an outspoken advocate of higher education for women. She was the first female college president of Wellesley College (1881) at age twenty-six. Later, the founding Dean of Women at the University of Chicago, Alice also co-founded and became president of the Association of Collegiate Alumnae (later known as the American Association of University Women). She was one of the most influential people expanding women's education in the US and we can be grateful to her for leading the way.

Alice had an inherent desire to advocate for women and children's rights. Gaining acceptance at the University of Michigan, she quickly rose to the top of her class. After graduation, she accepted a position as principal of a high school in East Saginaw. Accepting Wellesley's offer in 1879, she distinguished herself and was named acting president two years later. Alice was elected president of Wellesley after the death of Henry Durant and the first woman to be college president of a well-known national school.

By raising admission standards and adding honored faculty members, Alice improved the general image of higher education for women. She overhauled Wellesley's academic program, turning it into a premier college for women. In America's early years, people believed that if women were educated, it would have an adverse effect on their health and their femininity. Alice's efforts proved that women deserved to be educated.

Marrying Harvard professor George Palmer in 1887, she resigned from Wellesley and began touring the country speaking on the importance of higher education for women. Later on, The University of Chicago offered her a position as Dean of Women, which she accepted in 1895. Her solid administrative experience helped create an appealing intellectual and social environment for women in the new University.

DID YOU KNOW?

1. Alice chose both marriage and a successful career—quite unusual for the late 19th century.
2. She died of a heart attack after undergoing surgery in Paris at the age of 47.

A nationally recognized, self-taught ornithologist, Althea Rosina Sherman (1853-1943) was a teacher and an artist. She was the first to observe and document chimney swifts. Althea published over 70 different articles for technical and ornithological journals. Her illustration of the American Goldfinch spurred the Iowa Legislature to choose it as its state bird. Instead of killing birds to study them, Althea began studying individual species on her family farm, calling it her "Acre of Birds", she started her ornithological career at age 50 drawing on her skills of observation, illustration and writing. She embodied a life grounded on the natural world—we should do the same.

Mirroring my own childhood, Althea grew up on an Iowa farm with a love for nature, She would later write about the animal and plant life that disappeared from it as her father developed the land for agriculture. Graduating from Oberlin College in 1875, Althea started teaching art before returning to the same school for her master's degree in 1882. While teaching full-time, she attended additional art classes to hone her artistic skills until her parents' health decline.

After her mother's death in 1902. Althea began studying birds full time. The family farm became a living laboratory allowing her to seek out natural nesting sites. She loved adding bird houses, piles of brush, and nesting platforms to the property—anything that would organically attract more avian life.

Althea began writing meticulous notes in her journal, making reports of all her observations. In 1915, she built a twenty-eight-foot wooden tower near her home to attract and study nesting chimney swifts. In total, Althea studied 38 individual bird species copiously.

She then started submitting articles and field notes giving accounts of bird activity to numerous ornithological and scientific journals. Althea also struck up correspondence with leading avian researchers. Utilizing her artistic talents, she began creating realistic illustrations of her birds. Traveling throughout Europe, Asia, and the Middle East, Althea produced a monograph, *Birds by the Wayside,* bringing her international praise.

DID YOU KNOW?

1. One of her students was Margaret Morse Nice, a notable ornithologist and child psychologist.
2. Her chimney swift tower has been revamped and stands today at Garnavillo, Iowa.

"It isn't for the moment you are struck that you need courage, but for the long uphill climb back to sanity and faith and security."

> Overshadowed by her famous husband, Anne Spencer Morrow Lindbergh, (1906-2001) was a passionate author, aviator, environmentalist and the mother of six children. As co-pilot to Charles, she operated the radio and navigated his flights. When Anne penned *North to the Orient* in 1935, she was among the first to receive a National Book Award. Her book, *Gift from the Sea*, is an inspirational book for women that has foreshadowed the green movementand made her a feminist figure. It sits on my personal library shelf. Already famous for exploratory flights with her husband, the kidnap and murder of their oldest child shocked the world. How does a person ever recover from that?

Anne graduated from Smith College in 1928 with writing awards tucked under her cap. She had met her future husband the previous year in Mexico City; they married in 1929. The following year, Anne was the first woman awarded a glider pilot's license. By 1931, she had not only given birth to their first child but was flying from Africa to South America and exploring polar routes from North America to Asia and Europe as well as writing and publishing.

Twenty-month-old Charles Jr. was kidnapped March 1st, 1932; an extensive investigation and search led to the recovery of a baby boy's body two months later. The ever-present hounding by the media, along with the public's obsession and threats, forced the Lindberghs to relocate to England.

In Europe, Charles began supporting Nazi beliefs. Anne felt strongly that fascism "was the wave of the future". Returning to the U.S. in 1939, she began rebuilding their reputation. With the publication of the best-selling *Gift from the Sea,* Anne gained respect and admiration.

DID. YOU KNOW?

1. Her husband's illicit affairs, fathering seven other children by three different women in Germany, was not made public until after Anne's death.
2. Anne was honored by her alma mater, Smith College, with both a master's and doctor of letters degrees.

ARTEMISIA I, QUEEN OF HALICARNASSUS

> Artemisia (520-460 BCE) was the queen of the Anatolia region of Caria (south of Lydia in modern day Turkey). She is most famous for her role in the naval Battle of Salamis in 480 BCE. She fought for the Persians, gaining notoriety for her conduct in battle as well as her advice to Xerxes, despite losing the battle. Artemis I was definitely courageous and fierce!

She was the daughter of the king of Halicarnassus, who named her after the Greek Goddess of the hunt, Artemis. When she grew up, she married the governor of Caria, and after his death, Artemisia assumed the throne of Caria as regent for her under-aged son. Ancient reports depict her as a courageous clever commander of men and ships.

Artemisia inherited her throne from her husband, whose name is not known, during the rule of the Persian emperor Xerxes I, also known as Xerxes the Great (ruled 486–465 BC). Her kingdom included the city of Halicarnassus and the nearby islands of Kos, Calymnos, and Nisyros. She was the ruler of the city of Halicarnassus at the time of the Persian Wars (499–449 BCE).

As a Carian colony of Persia, Halicarnassians fought against the Greeks. When Xerxes went to war against Greece (480–479 BCE), Artemisia was the only woman among his commanders. She sent five ships into battle, and those five contained forces with a reputation for ferocity, Herodotus (an ancient Greek historian) suggests that Xerxes selected Artemisia to lead a squadron to embarrass the Greeks. When they heard about it, the Greeks offered a reward of 10,000 drachmas (about three years wages for a workman) for capturing Artemisia. No one succeeded in claiming the prize.

Even though you and I may not command battleships, the sisterhood of women continues to show ferocity and valor when we advocate for justice on every issue close to our hearts in the 21st century.

DID YOU KNOW?

1. Herodotus, the Greek historian, held Artemisia in good opinion, despite her favoring of Persia.
2. Several modern ships in Iran are named after Artemisia.

ANNA PAVLOVA SATURDAY, WEEK 3

"....work transforms talent into genius."

Anna Matveyena Pavlova (1881-1931) was a world-famous Russian prima ballerina and choreographer. One of the most celebrated and influential ballet dancers, Anna created her own touring company in 1911 as well as redesigning the pointe shoe to aid her highly arched feet. The Imperial Russian Ballet designated her their principal artist as did the Ballet Russes. Anna was most famous for her portrayal of *The Dying Swan.* She was the first ballerina to tour around the world, dancing in Europe, Asia, Australia, and Central and North America. She overcame poverty and rejection to achieve world-class status in ballet.

Born into poverty near St. Petersburg, Russia, Anna spent her early years with her grandmother. Rejected at her first attempt to enroll in ballet school, Anna was successful the second time, accepted by Marius Peptiva at the St. Peterburg's Imperial Ballet school. It was there she would practice eight hours a day at dance, as well as taking singing lessons because of her perfect pitch.

Anna's training years were difficult. Her feet were extremely arched, she had thin ankles and long legs—physical characteristics which went against the small, compact body type that was favored in the late nineteenth century. Her unusual body frame led to taunts by fellow students who called her names. She persisted, practicing daily and taking extra lessons. Graduating in 1899, Anna was selected to enter the Imperial Ballet as a *coryphee*, dancing in a small group instead of the *corps de ballet.*

Anna danced with the Mariinsky Ballet (1899-1907), first performing the role of the *Dying Swan.* In 1908, she was contracted with the *Ballet Russes* (Russian Seasons) in London and Paris. After she married Victor D'Andre in 1911, they formed a ballet touring company; her troupe would grow to sixty dancers, managed by D'Andre.

DID YOU KNOW?

1. Between 1913-1925, Anna gave over 4,000 performances. Can you imagine that kind of endurance?
2. She adopted fifteen girls into her home near Paris supported by her performances and donations, including small amounts given by American Camp Fire Girls.

Airmid (also known as Airmed, Airmeith, or Airmedh) is the Celtic Goddess of healing, especially herbal healing. She is a member of Tuatha De Danann, the most ancient race of deities in Ireland and has great magical powers. Proclaimed one of the wisest Gods, Airmid is associated with gardening, nature, family and loyalty. Her legends tell of a generous Goddess who was knowledgeable and empathic. According to Irish mythology, She was one of the "enchanters" whose verbal charms sung over the well of Slaine was able to resurrect the dead. Her colors are green, blue, purple and brown. Her animal is the snake.

While Airmid was grieving at Her brother's gravesite, She suddenly saw hundreds of plants with healing powers growing amongst the flowers. Her tears watered all the healing herbs growing there. Legend tells us Her jealous father abruptly scattered all the herbs Airmid had gathered to the wind, which She was never able to gather again in order to complete her work. Today we have some knowledge of plant and herb healing properties, but many are still unknown.

Pictures of Airmid show her dressed in a green cloak and with long, flowing red hair. She carries a medicine pouch filled with healing herbs. Beltane, May 1st, is her holiday, and Her seasons are summer and fall. She is celebrated in today's world by appreciating nature and the gift of plant medicine—which we all unknowingly use today.

DID YOU KNOW?

1. Airmid is the daughter of the divine physician, *Dian Cecht.*
2. Airmid is often represented by a mortar and pestle, by wells and running water and dried herbs.

Aqualtune Ezgondidu Mahammud da Silva Santos (c. 16ᵗʰ century) was a Kongolese princess (modern day northern Angola, the Republic of Congo) who was captured and sold as a breeding slave to the Portuguese. After arriving in northeast Brazil, she organized a runaway plan with other enslaved individuals. Aqualtune then founded one of the most important Maroon settlements in Brazil, The Palmares.

In 1665, Aqualtune was a military leader with a force of ten thousand men in the Battle of *Mbwila*. The Kongolese were defeated which ultimately led to the scattering of the Kingdom of Kongo and to the enslavement of warriors, ordinary people and nobles. Aqualtune was then transported to the Port of Recife (Brazil). She was purchased as a breeding slave and later sold to a mill in Porto Calvo, and already pregnant.

In her last months of pregnancy, she organized an escape to *Palmares*, leading one of the *mocambos* (village-sized communities mainly populated by runaway slaves in colonial Brazil during the Portuguese rule) that received her name. She gave birth to Ganga Zumba and Ghana Zona, who became heads of two of the most important mocambos of Palmares (or *Quilombo dos Palmares*). Palmares was located in the current state of Alagoas.

Later on she gave birth to Sabina, who would be the mother of Zumbi—the great leader of the Palmares, and also Zona. Aqualtune (the village) with its political, organizational and war strategy knowledge, was the foundation for the consolidation of the Black State, the Republic of Palmares. A warrior, leader and a mother—what an indomitable combination.

DID YOU KNOW?

1. Aqualtune died a mysterious death in 1675.
2. She is considered the patron saint of Brazil's blacks.

"The cause of freedom is not the cause of a race or a sect, a party or a class—it is the cause of humankind, the very birthright of humanity."

Known as "the Mother of Black Feminism", Dr. Anna Julia Haywood Cooper (1858-1964) was born enslaved in North Carolina. Becoming a preeminent African American scholar in the U.S., Anna was an author, educator, lecturer, sociologist and a pioneering Black feminist. An eloquent forthright advocate for gender and race equality, she published *A Voice from the South by a Black Woman of the South* in 1892. The book is recognized as one of the earliest voices of Black feminism. As president of Frelinghuysen University in Washington DC, she helped provide continuing-education courses for working African American adults. Anna earned her Ph.D. in history from the *Sorbonne,* and her Ph.D. in philosophy at age sixty-five.

Anna's academic distinction led her to start teaching in 1883. The income from teaching the classics, modern history, English, and both vocal and instrumental music enabled her to begin her studies at Oberlin College, earning her M.A. in mathematics in 1888. Later, moving to Washington DC, she helped found the Colored Women's League in 1892.

While teaching and administrating at M Street High School, Anna wrote her first book, *A Voice from the South by a Black Woman of the South,* advocating the view that it was the duty of highly achieving Black women to support their disadvantaged sisters. Anna felt the violent natures of men ran counter to higher educational goals, thus female scholars brought more discernment to education. Her views were criticized as fueling the "19th century cult of true womanhood."

In 1915, while furthering her doctoral studies at Columbia University, Anna adopted her late half-brother's five children. Returning to school in Paris, the Sorbonne awarded her a Ph.D. in philosophy. From slavery to acquiring two doctorates—Anna's life was remarkable, don't you agree?

Did you know?

1. Anna lived for 105 years, born before the Civil War began. Incredible, isn't it?
2. She was the first female student permitted to enter Oberlin College.

Antonia Caetana de Paiva Pereira Maury (1866-1952) was an American astronomer, the first to detect and calculate the orbit of a spectroscopic binary. A teacher and astrophysicist, Antonia invented a system of star classification, the stepping-stone to discoveries that constitute the foundation of modern stellar astrophysics. Antonia was a woman ahead of her time but not fully recognized for her work until late in her life.

After graduating from Vassar in 1887, Antonia went on to work at the Harvard College Observatory as one of the so-called "Harvard Computers" for twenty-five cents an hour. While there, Antonia was asked to determine the orbit of *Urasae Majoris*, which she did. In 1889 she discovered a second spectroscopic binary, *Beta Aurigae*. When the paper was published on these findings and calculations, only a small mention of Antonia's name was included.

Antonia continued her work at Harvard until 1891, when she left the observatory because of unacknowledged work. She began teaching in Cambridge, Massachusetts. Edward Pickering asked her to complete her work, which she did from a distance in 1893 only after expressing her desire for full credit for her previous work.

In 1897, Antonia's name appeared in the title of an observatory publication. It presented results of her examination of 4800 stellar photographs with her own system classification and an analysis of 681 bright northern stars in detail. Pickering's name was also placed in the title as the director of said observations.

Between 1896 and 1918, Antonia taught physics and chemistry at a suburban school for girls in New York. She also lectured on astronomy at Cornell. Returning to Harvard College Observatory in 1918 as an adjunct professor, Antonia began working with Pickering's successor, Harlow Shapley. Given credit for her work and publishing under her full name, she remained there until retirement in 1948.

DID YOU KNOW?

1. Antonia, an accomplished ornithologist, was also passionate about conservationism.
2. She was known as one of the Harvard Computers—a group of women skilled in gathering astronomical data.

Aphra Behn (1640-1689) was one of the first English women to earn her living as a writer. A poet, novelist, dramatist, political spy and translator, Aphra broke cultural barriers and became a literary role model for later generations of women authors. As a spy, her code name was Astrea, which she sometimes used as a pseudonym when writing. Her literary works were repeatedly dismissed by 18th and 19th century writers. In the mid-twentieth century, her writings have been re-evaluated as the first abolitionist and humanitarian novels. Since the 1970's, Aphra's works were discovered by feminists which led to a rebuilding of her reputation and reprintings of her many works. Her poetry focused on gender, sexuality, femininity, pleasure and love—a radical concept for 17th century writers.

Aphra's claim that her reputation as a writer of scandalous plays "would not have been improper if a man had written them" is documented and affirmed by many. As a woman, she was excluded from institutions such as Oxford, Cambridge, and the Inns of Court. Biographical information is difficult to recover as she was not a man, an aristocrat, or a nonconformist. Little is known of her life other than being a spy for Charles II in Antwerp as a young woman.

When Aphra returned to London, King Charles II refused to pay or reimburse her—thus leading her to write for a living to avoid debtor's prison. Her plays, written for the Duke's Theatre, became increasingly political. As the public's appetite for drama decreased, she began writing fiction, poetry and translations.

Heralded as a successor to Sappho, her reputation as a poet was no less remarkable than her notoriety as a dramatist. Frequently her poems addressed enlightened members of the community. Homoeroticism was standard in Aphra's verse, breaking boundaries in writing as she had in living her life. How gutsy was that for a 17th century woman?

Did you know?

1. Aphra is also suspected of spying in South America for King Charles.
2. She used those experiences in *Oroonoko,* a story of a kidnapped West African prince.

BORTE UJIN

> Borte Ujin (c.1161-1230) meaning mistress, was the first wife of Genghis Khan,
> married to him at seventeen. She was a skilled archer, mother of nine children, her
> husband's most trusted advisor and beloved by the people. Known as the Grand
> Empress of the Mongolian Empire, Borte also served as head of the first Court of
> Genghis Khan.

While Genghis Khan went about expanding his empire, Borte Ujin stayed behind to manage the lands and family. She was given authority to rule over and control most of the Kherlen River, which had been previously owned by the Tatars. An amazing leader in her own right, Borte Ujin was a skilled archer who ruled with the wisdom of a true empress.

Even though her fate had been decided by her father and brothers, she stepped into the role advising her husband on many issues and conflicts. He even relied on her wisdom when making tough decisions—for it is said she advised Genghis Khan to separate from Jamuka when Mongolian tribes were seeking to unify.

Mongolian women, in general, raised cattle, rode horses and shot arrows alongside the men in the tribe. But in a nomadic society, a woman had the status of a continuer of human-kind, mother and guardian of the hearth. Some sources describe Borte as a beautiful woman and a wise *Khansa* (hidden treasure), she wore a white silk dress with golden coins in her hair.

As her husband's advisor, she was a key figure in history, though her name is not mentioned in history books. Her husband's greatness was due in part to Borte's counsel and voice of reason.

Once again, that old saying holds true, Behind every good man is a great woman.

DID YOU KNOW?

1. Borte was senior and first wife of Temujin—who later became Genghis Khan.
2. Her marriage was arranged by her father when she was ten-years-old.

Augusta Holmes (1847-1903) was a French composer of Irish descent. She had her greatest success with choral works and wrote over 130 songs. A mother of five children, Holmes preferred to write about epic themes on classical or mythological subjects, including dramatic symphonies and symphonic poems as well. She was a dominant figure in French musical circles and also in literary salons. Wagner and Cesar Frank were her greatest influencers.

Augusta had to fight for the right to become a musician because her mother actively discouraged it. Only after her mother's death was she able to take music lessons, beginning at age eleven. By 1875, Augusta had become a celebrity in Parisian cultural circles.

Feeling a need to compete in a male dominated profession, she was very entrepreneurial and an excellent self-promoter. Highly developed emotional intelligence helped her promote and produce grandiose works when women were expected to write songs and salon pieces. Augusta did publish some of her earliest works under a male pseudonym (Hermann Zenta) because women in European society at that time were not taken seriously as artists and were discouraged from publishing anything.

A true feminist, Augusta lived her life in ways that society did not condone. She lived openly as the mistress of a prominent literary figure having five children with him. Augusta published her works under her own name and was their official owner. Her compositions were often characterized as 'masculine' and 'virile' by the men she competed against. Many of the pieces supported patriotic or humanistic causes. Holmes was commissioned to write *Ode Triomphale* for the 1889 *Exposition Universelle* in Paris.

Though popular during her life, she has since fallen out of favor. Augusta wrote twelve symphonic poems, four operas and well over one hundred songs. Perhaps her hidden music will once again be admired by those of us in the 21st century.

DID YOU KNOW?

1. Augusta was a brilliant pianist.
2. She became a naturalized French citizen in 1871.

A Hindu Goddess, Akhilandeshwari is known as "She Who Is Never Not Broken". Her powers are both universal and cosmic: *Akhila,* meaning Universe, Anda— Universe, *Ishwari,* Sovereign or Ruler. *Akhilanda* means "never not broken" or "infallibly broken". The double negative spotlights the reality of Her brokenness. It's strange to think of a Goddess as broken but She represents our broken-ness, the world's broken-ness. Though not a well-known Goddess, She is a treasury of knowledge, bringing us closer to wisdom and the arts. Akhilandeshwari also gifts liberation from death to both gods and humans. One of Her many gifts is to remind us of the potential found in our "cracks"—our brokenness and losses. We can find power in our fears and anguish.

Dark in complexion, Akhilandeshwari owns a serene smile and carries a trident. She rides a crocodile through the rivers of life. Her crocodile assists her with her prey. She can help us move through challenging difficulties, reminding us to find the light of our essence through the cracks of chaos.

It is indeed hard to feel unbroken with today's crises, wars, catastrophes and destruction happening everywhere. Every day we are bombarded with the media's pictures and sounds of cruelty, suffering and terror. Fear can rattle us to our core, paralyzing us. We try to understand and rationalize the many losses and atrocities. A sense of powerlessness overcomes us. Our broken hearts and spirits try to understand as we seek a connection that will heal our thoughts and search for solutions.

Unlike other Goddesses who marry, Akhilandeshwari, the "Never Not Broken" sovereign becomes more powerful. She teaches us that by resting with our own fears and intense energies we can bring more peace to the world and ourselves. Isn't She wonderful?

DID YOU KNOW?

1. Akhilandeshwari is often compared to a spinning prism which splinters light yet produces beauty.
2. Crocodiles also represent our reptilian brain where we feel fear—reminding us to ride on top of our fears, embracing our emotions.

"No one can claim to be called Christian who gives money for the building of warships and arsenals."

Leading the way for other female politicians, Belva Ann Bennett Lockwood (1830-1917) was the preeminent female U.S. presidential candidate in 1884. An activist, educator, feminist, attorney, author and mother, Belva blazed the way for women to practice law in front of the United States Supreme Court in 1879. She jumped over many personal and societal hurdles due to her gender. An activist for women's rights, their suffrage and world peace, Belva's name graces four U.S. towns and a WWII Merchant Marine ship.

Married at eighteen, Belva lost her first husband to tuberculosis in 1853. With a young daughter to support, furthering her education became essential. Determination led to her acceptance at Genesee in New York State. Graduating with honors garnered her a position as headmistress of Lockport Union School. Whether teaching or administrating, Belva soon discovered she was being paid half what men earned in similar positions. She began studying under a local law professor but was yearning to learn more.

Belva began changing curriculums wherever she Administered classes, but she realized she needed a law background to achieve more. After being refused admission at Columbia because her presence was thought to distract male students, Belva was finally accepted at George Washington University Law School. Moving to Washington D.C. with her daughter in 1866, Belva opened a private co-ed school while she continued to study law.

Upon finishing the coursework in 1873, the school declined to award her a diploma because she was a woman. The bias was unbelievable. Undeterred, Belva wrote to President Ulysses S. Grant for his help. In less than a week, 43-year-old Belva was granted her diploma. Then the uphill struggle of a woman being taken seriously amplified exponentially. Some of us, all around the world, still fight that same battle.

DID YOU KNOW?

1. Meeting Susan B. Anthony broadened Belva's views of women's education.
2. She was the first woman to argue before the U.S. Supreme Court.

"Confidence is a plant of slow growth."

> Ann Harriette Emma Edwards Leonowens (1831- 1915) was an Indian-born British author, educator, lecturer, mother and social activist. She became famous as the British governess to the wives and children of the King of Siam (Thailand) in the 1860's. Later in life, she was known as the "dean of Halifax Feminists". Anna also founded the Nova Scotia College of Art and Design in 1887. Her life, in reality, was much different from the famous movie, *The King and I*.

In her books, Anna hid her social class and ethnic background. When she and her family moved to Singapore, her husband, Thomas, worked as a hotel keeper until his death. As a widow, she opened a school for the children of British officers in Singapore. In 1862, King Monghut of Siam let it be known that he desired a governess for his wives and many children. Anna accepted the position and sailed to Bangkok with her son, Louis.

The king instructed Anna to "do your best endeavor for knowledge of English language, science and literature and not for conversion to Christianity". In addition to her teaching duties, Anna acted as an informal secretary to the king, whom she thought was "as fickle and petulant as he was suspicious and cruel" to his wives but an able and virtuous leader.

After King Monghut's death in 1868 Anna was dismissed and emigrated to the United States where she worked as a teacher, lecturer, author and a journalist. She wrote two books about her time in Siam, exaggerating her influence at the Siamese court. Moving to Halifax, Nova Scotia in 1878, she assumed a leading role in the social and cultural life there. She began advocating for women's suffrage in Canada at all governmental levels. Anna also held leadership positions in women's organizations.

DID YOU KNOW?

1. *The King and I* is banned in Thailand because of its negative portrayal of the King of Siam and the Siamese people.
2. The word Siam in Sanskrit means dark or brown—referring to native skin color.

Barbara McClintock (1902-1992) was an American scientist and cytogeneticist whose discovery in the 1940s and '50s of mobile genetic elements, or "jumping genes", won her the Nobel Prize for Physiology or Medicine in 1983. She was the first American woman to win an unshared Nobel. Her discovery had an effect on everything from genetic engineering to cancer research. Barbara was always cognizant of what she had achieved, and recognized her role as an example for other women. She refused to put up with men's arrogance, encouraging us today to persist despite male chauvinism.

After receiving her B.S. from Cornell's College of Agriculture in 1923, Barbara stayed on and completed a PhD in botany in 1927, then continued her research as an instructor at Cornell. Awarded a Guggenheim Fellowship in 1933 to study in Germany, she left Europe early because of the rise of Nazism. McClintock returned to Cornell for several more years until, in 1936, she accepted a position as an assistant professor at the University of Missouri at Columbia from the influential maize geneticist, Lewis Stadler.

Believing she would not gain tenure at Missouri, Barbara left her job in 1940. In December of 1941, she was offered a one-year research position at the Carnegie Institution of Washington's Department of Genetics at Cold Spring Harbor on Long Island, New York. This job turned into a full-time staff position the following year.

Barbara's work was ahead of its time and was for many years considered too radical — or simply ignored — by her fellow scientists. Deeply disappointed with her colleagues, she stopped publishing the results of her work and ceased giving lectures, though she continued doing research. Not until the late 1960s and '70s did members of the scientific community begin to verify her early findings. When recognition finally came, Barbara was inundated with awards and honors, most notably the 1983 Nobel Prize for Physiology or Medicine. Finally.

DID YOU KNOW?

1. In 1970, Barbara was awarded the National Medal of Freedom by Richard Nixon.
2. She was most intolerant of ignorance — especially men's.

"It is not our differences that divide us. It is our inability to recognize, accept, and celebrate those differences."

Daughter of Caribbean immigrants, Audre Geraldine Lorde (1934-1992) was a Black feminist poet whose writings challenged and spoke against racism, sexism, classism and homophobia. She described herself as "black, lesbian, mother, warrior, poet" to all as she lived her life dedicated to confronting fear and injustices. Recognized internationally for her activism and artistry, Audre was awarded many honors including New York State's Poet Laureate for 1991-1992. An educator and prolific writer, she authored many influential books, essays and articles traveling around the world as a lecturer and an activist.

Audre grew up during the late Depression period. Her difficult relationship with her mother is the premise of her later poems. Learning to read and write at a very young age, she penned her first poem at age of twelve. Because she felt like an outcast, Audre used poetry to communicate and express her feelings. Even as an adult, she felt unaccepted. Believing people thought "she was crazy and queer but would grow out of it", Audre began speaking up for herself and her beliefs.

She wrote during her times lecturing, teaching and working as a librarian. While living on Staten Island, Audre co-founded Kitchen Table: Women of Color Press. She traveled to the Caribbean, South Africa and Germany where she not only lectured but helped found many organizations like the Women's Coalition of St. Croix—dedicated to helping women who have survived intimate partner violence and sexual abuse.

Audre described herself as a continuum of women with a concert of voices inside herself. During her later years, Audre fought breast cancer. She delved into the disease by writing and publishing an award-winning book, *The Cancer Journals.* May we all learn from Audre's courage and determination as we continue the battle against sexual violence and gender bias.

DID YOU KNOW?

1. In *Sister Outsider: Essays and Speeches,* Audre declares the necessity of speaking out for marginalized groups to make their struggles visible.
2. Her writings tell of her belief that the category of women is full of subdivisions.

> Boudicca (30-60 CE), a warrior queen of ancient Celtic Iceni tribe, is regarded as an epic hero in British history. She led an uprising against the conquering forces of the Roman Empire. You will find a statue of her and her daughters on the north side of the western end of Westminster Bridge in London.

Boudicca (or Boudica) was born in South East England. It is believed that she came from a royal family. Boudicca was described as a very tall woman with thick long reddish-brown hair that hung below her waist. A Roman historian claims she had a harsh loud voice and one would feel as if they were being stabbed by her piercing glare. (I imagine it was a man that said that.)

Around 48 CE, she married *Prasutagus*, the head of the Iceni tribe in South East England. They lived in Norfolk and, during his lifetime, were given semi-independence from their Roman occupiers. Upon *Prasutagus' death,* Roman law required the majority of his possessions be given to the Roman Emperor. However, the local Roman commanders took this as a pretext to confiscate all of his property and that of other leading Iceni tribe members.

Tacitus (a Roman historian) wrote that Boudicca was flogged and her two daughters raped. Other tribes were subject to similar treatment, leading to growing feelings of rebellion amongst the native Britons. It was Boudicca who was able to unite the various warring tribes of Briton and lead them in revolt against the Romans in 61CE.

At the battle's end, four hundred Romans had died while around 200,000 Britons were foundslaughtered. Reports vary about how Boudicca died. Some historians claim she poisoned herself after the unsuccessful uprising, while others claim she died of shock or illness. Regardless, we can only stand in awe of Boudicca's strength to stand up and fight back, especially her leading an uprising after the personal assault on herself and her daughters.

DID YOU KNOW?

1. Boudicca sacrificed captured Roman Women to the Goddess Andraste.
2. She was only thirty-one when she died.

AUGUSTA SAVAGE

"I have created nothing really beautiful, really lasting, but if I can inspire one of these youngsters to develop the talent I know they possess, then my monument will be in their work."

> Augusta Savage (1892-1962), an American sculptor, educator and mother was the first African American to open her own art gallery. She played a significant role in the Harlem Renaissance and consistently battled racism as she secured a place for African American women in the art world.

Augusta Christine Fells Savage was born in Florida. Her father, an impoverished Methodist minister, strongly opposed Augusta's early interest in art. Around 1915, she married James Savage, a carpenter, whose surname she retained after their divorce in the early 1920's.

Despite poverty and sexism, Augusta retained her burning desire to become a sculptor. By the mid 1920's she had moved to New York City where she quickly found a job and enrolled at the Cooper Union School of Art. Completing the four-year course in three years, Augusta worked in a small studio apartment where she earned a reputation as a portrait sculptor. You and I can learn from Augusta—it doesn't take a large space to become creative. I've personally known artists who created their works in the laundry room. Learn to create with what you have wherever you are.

In 1929, Augusta was awarded a Julius Rosenwald Fellowship to study in Paris. Returning to New York three years later, she established the Savage Studio of Arts and Crafts, becoming an influential teacher in Harlem. During the Depression, she helped persuade the WPA to include black artists in its Federal Art Project.

She was appointed the first director of the Harlem Community Art Center. Leaving the art world in 1940 after a lifelong battle with racism and sexism, she moved to a farm in the Catskill Mountains of New York. For twenty years Augusta lived in relative obscurity, supporting herself by teaching art locally.

DID YOU KNOW?

1. Augusta was the first African American to be elected to the National Association of Women Painters and Sculptors.
2. Augusta grew up with 13 siblings, creating her first sculptures from Florida's clay soil.

The Eastern Nigerian Earth Goddess, Ala (meaning earth, ground) rules over the *Igbo* people. She is the most eminent Alusi, or deity, of the Igbo Gods. As "Mother Goddess" of the earth, Ala is responsible for creativity, ethics and fruitfulness. All ancestors are stored in Her womb. Ala is guardian of the harvest and ruler of the underworld. She is a law giver who shows people how to live a just life, emphasizing good morals such as honesty. She is also known as Ani, Ana, Ale and Ali depending on the varying Igbo dialects. Present at the beginning of the cycle of life, Ala is there at the end of life to receive the souls of the dead. Her living messenger is the python, her symbols are yams and the crescent moon. She is both productive earth and harvest's empty fields. All ground is considered "holy land" as it is Ala Herself. Perhaps we should consider Mother Nature and all that surrounds us sacred.

As the Goddess of morality, Ala is a judge of human actions and is in charge of Igbo law and customs known as *Omenala*. Army ants who serve the Goddess attack those who break such rules. Ala is usually depicted as a gorgeous black queen wearing a gilded crown with lights. Sometimes She is pictured squatting as if giving birth to Africa, Her legs entwined with gold bangles while She wears a gilded necklace with attached golden feathers hanging over Her breasts.

Her shrine sits at the center of a village, where people can easily offer sacrifices at times of planting and harvest. *Mbari* (shrines) are large square unoccupied houses with open sides. People build life-sized figurines of Her with a child on Her knees, holding a sword painted in bright colors like red and yellow. Around Her are other sculptures representing other Gods and Goddesses.

DID YOU KNOW?

1. Ala sends a snake or a bee's nest to indicate where Her shrines are to be built.
2. She is often shown with a thick neck and elongated torso—features that represent the Igbo's ideal of feminine beauty.

A Quaker teacher, Bertha Lillian Bracey OBE (1893-1989) was a British aid worker before, during and after World War II. An educator who organized safety and comfort for thousands of Jewish refugees, she is known as a "British Hero of the Holocaust." Bertha was the driving force behind England's Germany Emergency Committee. It was that delegation of Quakers and Jews that was able to convince the Home Secretary Sir Samuel Hoare to evacuate Jewish children from Germany. The operation, called Kindertransport, began in December of 1938, one month after *Kristallnacht*. Bertha also helped found Stoatley Rough School for England's Jewish refugee children. If only we all could emulate Bertha's determination.

After five years of teaching, Bertha joined the Quakers (often called Friends) to begin work at the Quaker center in Vienna. While there, she provided necessities for comfort and reconstruction as well as established numerous youth clubs. Bertha then moved on to Nuremburg setting up a station for needy families before going to Berlin. Returning to London in 1929, she became secretary of the Germany and Holland Committee of Friends Service Council where they practiced the Quaker vision of peace and reconciliation.

Their work changed quickly when Hitler came into power in 1933. Bertha then began organizing help for persecuted Jews in Germany, Czechoslovakia, Austria and Paris. Helping them flee these countries, in addition to finding them shelter and a vocation in Britain became urgent. Because Bertha was fluent in German and had considerable experience in both Austria and Germany, her large network of friends became invaluable. By 1938, her staff had grown to fifty-nine people.

Because of Bertha's influence in the church and Britain and Germany, the British Friends were able to exert pressure for the release of political prisoners. She also played a predominant part in developing Kindertransport bringing between 9,000 and 10,000 Jewish children out of Nazi hands.

DID YOU KNOW?

1. Bertha helped found the Stoatley Rough School in 1934 for German refugees in Haslemere.
2. She was awarded the Order of the British Empire in 1942 for her help with refugees.

A pioneering children's librarian, Anne Carroll Moore (1871-1961), was known as "The Librarian Lion." An American educator, literary agent and critic, writer and advocate, she tirelessly worked as head of the New York Public Library system's children's library services from 1906 to1941. She worked endless hours to see that children were treated as individuals believing they should be taken seriously. Forced to retire at seventy, Anne remained writing and teaching until near death. Recognized as one of the "100 most important leaders we had in the 20th century", she was dubbed the "Grande Dame of Children's Services". Her biographer, Frances Clarke Sayers, noted Anne "was obsessed by the knowledge of what excellence in books could mean to children". We owe much to Anne's advocacy for children.

Anne initially wanted to follow in her father's footsteps and practice law. Life happened, plans changed, and she enrolled in Brooklyn's Pratt Institute. When asked to lead the institute's new children's department, Anne jumped in. While there, she began storytelling hours and developed conceptual ideas, using the children's library as an educational tool. She became the driving force of the American Library Association's "Club of Children's Librarians."

Moving on to the NYPL, Anne established its first children's division. Within two years, she had advocated for and achieved professional status for children's librarians in the NYPL. Going forward, Anne once again instituted storytelling hours and cancelled age limits that stopped children from entering some of its branches. Delivering lectures on children's literature, Anne began reviewing for *The Bookman* and *the New York Herald Tribune*. Anne also scheduled celebrations that were planned around special subjects.

We need to remember that all this was accomplished at a time when children were to be *seen* but *not heard*. Anne traveled New York City's ethnic conclaves listening to children's interests and desires, and then chose books to improve their minds. (What a cool lady!)

DID YOU KNOW?

1. Anne started an annual "Children's Books Suggested as Holiday Gifts" list, which continued until her retirement.
2. She hired Pura Belpre, the first Puerto Rican Librarian in New York City.

Caroline Lucretia Herschel (1750-1848) was a pioneering German astronomer. She catalogued stars and nebulae, as well as discovering comets. Caroline was the first woman astronomer to earn a salary, acquire honors and be accepted into scientific organizations. The first woman to discover a comet (1786), Caroline spotted another seven comets in the following eleven years. Despite severe childhood illness, and the misogyny she faced as a woman scientist, Herschel was able to accomplish much and receive recognition for her achievements. I admire her spunk a great deal.

Caroline was assisting her brother William, an amateur astronomer, when he discovered Uranus (1781). As part of the research team, they became employed at the royal court by King George III. Alongside her brother, she made astronomical observations and constructed new telescopes.

By day, Herschel made lengthy calculations on her brother's nightly observations with remarkable accuracy. It was only when he was away that she was able to spend time on her own research. After they moved to Slough in 1786, Caroline discovered her first comet, bringing her some fame and well-deserved recognition. Her comet became known as "the first lady's comet."

In addition to discovering fourteen nebulae, Caroline compiled a catalogue for star clusters and nebulae. She also created an Index to Flamsteed's *Observations of Fixed Stars* adding a list of 560 stars previously omitted.

After her brother's death in 1822, Caroline focused on helping with her nephew's education as well as her own independent research. She began producing a catalogue of nebulae to assist her nephew (John Herschel) in his work. The reformulated catalogue of 2500 nebulae was completed in 1828, solidifying Caroline Herschel as a celebrity. What makes her contributions so unusual is that they were publicly acknowledged in her own time—quite a feat in the 19th century.

DID YOU KNOW?

1. Her four-foot three-inch height was caused by typhus she contracted when she was ten years old. The disease that stunted her physical growth certainly didn't stop her from achieving world recognition in astrology.
2. She was two months shy of her 98th birthday when she died.

"Thank goodness I was never sent to school; it would have rubbed off some of the originality."

Helen Beatrix Potter (1866-1943), born in London, was a British botanist, artist, author, farmer and conservationist. Her Beatrix Potter books sell over two million per year worldwide. A staunch supporter of the National Trust, she endowed her fifteen farms and over four thousand acres upon her death to this wonderful cause. Her early activism of caring for Mother Earth is a path we should all heed.

Instead of practicing law, her father devoted his time to photography and art. Her mother was a skilled watercolor artist. And as a result, Beatrix got to know several influential artists and writers through her parents.

Demonstrating a talent for sketching as a child, with animals being her most favorite subjects, she began studying at the National Art Training School in the late 1870s. Although Beatrix had sold some of her artwork for greeting cards and illustrations in the early 1890s, she devoted most of her energy to the study of natural history – archaeology, geology, entomology and, especially, mycology—fungi. She became a skillful scientific illustrator, even submitting a paper to the Linnean Society. Her drawings and paintings are displayed at the Armitt Museum and Library and the Perth Museum and Art Gallery in Scotland.

In 1901 she wrote her first book, *The Tale of Peter Rabbi*. Frederick Warne published it in 1902. Twenty-two little books followed at the rate of two or three a year. We now recognize her as one of the most beloved children's authors of all time.

In 1905, with proceeds from *The Tale of Peter Rabbit*, Beatrix purchased Hill Top Farm in the England's Lake District. Four years later, she purchased Castle Farm, a second property in Sawrey just across the road from Hill Top. Her ambition to preserve land and protect it from being overdeveloped continued through the rest of her life, as she worked closely with the National Trust.

DID YOU KNOW?

1. Beatrix was unofficially engaged to Norman Warne until his death from pernicious anemia—a disease where the body cannot make enough red blood cells.
2. She was a generous sponsor of the Girl Guides.

"If you hold your hand closed, nothing good can come in. The open hand is blessed, for it gives in abundance even as it receives."

> Bridget "Biddy" Mason (1818-1891) was a Mississippi-born slave. A nurse, mother, real estate entrepreneur as well as a philanthropist, Bridget became one of the first landowners and prominent citizens in Los Angeles in the 1850s and 1860s.

At the age of thirty, Biddy walked 1,700 miles behind a three hundred wagon caravan to the Salt Lake Valley in Mexico (present day Utah). Her owner, Robert Smith, made her responsible for setting up and breaking camp; cooking all meals; herding cattle and being a midwife. She also took care of her owner's three young daughters.

Smith then set out with his family and slaves for San Bernardino, ignoring warnings that slavery was illegal in California. Along the trek, Biddy met the Rowans, free blacks who encouraged her to legally contest her slave status upon reaching the new state. Afraid of losing his slaves, Smith and his family headed to Texas, a slave state. A posse apprehended them along the way, preventing them from leaving California.

Biddy petitioned the court in 1856 for her freedom and that of her extended family of thirteen women and children. She was granted her freedom three days later. Biddy then moved her family to Los Angeles where she worked as a midwife and nurse, saving up her money to purchase two plots of land in what is now downtown Los Angeles.

Biddy was soon known by everyone in Los Angeles, as the population numbered only two thousand at the time. Encouraged by friends, she began to invest in real estate. Biddy continued working as a mid-wife, crossing class and color lines. She became a shrewd businesswoman, at the time of her death, she had amassed approximately $300,000 (about $6 million today). A successful nurse and pioneer of real estate, she never learned to read or write. But man, did she have guts.

DID YOU KNOW?

1. Biddy founded the First African Methodist Episcopal Church in L.A.
2. She was buried in an unmarked grave until the mayor and church members held a ceremony and placed a headstone there in her honor.

BARBARA STROZZI

Born in Venice, Italy, Barbara Strozzi (1619-1677) was an Italian virtuoso singer and composer of vocal music during the Baroque period. Barbara was one of the few women in the 17th century to publish her own compositions. She was a progressive, independent woman whose ingenuity shone throughout her life and her music. A single mom with three children and publishing under her own name, it's incredible Barbara accomplished what she did in the 17th century.

Barbara Strozzi was the adopted daughter—and likely illegitimate child—of the poet Giulio Strozzi. Only twelve-years-old, Barbara had already begun to develop as a musician and started to demonstrate virtuosic vocal talent along with being able to accompany herself on the lute or the orbo. Guilio Strozzi used his connections in the intellectual world of Venice to showcase his daughter and to advance her career. In 1637, he founded his own academy, *Accademia degli Unisoni*, where her talents as a singer and an instrumentalist (and her beauty) were important attractions.

Known for her intellect, learning, and wit, Barbara presided over academy meetings, naming the subjects to be debated during the evening. In 1644, she issued the first of her eight publications, a volume of madrigals on her father's texts. Barbara issued a second publication of cantatas, ariettas and duets, in 1651.

Often writing her music as the result of a challenge by members of the academy, Barbara also penned love poetry. Her use of musical form is very flexible, adapting to the demands of the text, moving easily between recitative, *arioso*, and *aria* in the longer works of cantatas. Barbara created an intimate relationship between her song texts and its music, but her harmonies were thought by some "to be wacky". I'm sure many contemporary composers pen dissonances that we may find hard on the ears. She was simply ahead of her time.

DID YOU KNOW?

1. During her lifetime, she published eight volumes of her own music and was recognized as the most prolific composer of her era.
2. She was a professional musician during a time when few women could accomplish that.

Japanese Sun Goddess Amaterasu (also known as Ohirume-no-Muchi-no-Kami) is the most important deity of the Shinto religion and ruler of Takama (the High Celestial Plain), which is the domain of the *kami* (spirits). Amaterasu possesses the conventional powers of a superhuman— strength, stamina, vitality, resistance to injury, and an immortality comparable to that of Olympian Gods. The highest deity in Japanese mythology, we can emulate Her strength and stamina, always "keeping on." Amaterasu means "that which illuminates the Heavens".

The most celebrated myth concerning Amaterasu is when She blocked herself in a cave with a rock following an argument. When Amaterasu disappeared, the earth was shrouded in darkness and evil spirits ran amuck. She remained in the cave until She was overcome by curiosity hearing laughter and seeing an eight-sided mirror placed outside the cave's entrance. Fascinated with the reflection of Her light, Amaterasau stepped out of the cave. The world was instantly bathed in sunlight.

People of Japanese nobility claim descent from this ancient Goddess. In art, She is most often depicted as being good-natured and seated back-to-back with Her brother, the moon God. Cocks are associated with Her as they herald the rising sun, and the raven is believed to be Her messenger.

Her myths are the most revered of the indigenous Japanese faith—remaining unchanged over past millennium. Aamaterasu is credited with inventing the cultivation of rice, wheat, the use of silkworms, and weaving with a loom. Amaterasu is represented as an octagonal mirror, one of the three Japanese Imperial regalia. She is celebrated every July 17th with street processions all over Japan. Festivities on December 21st, the winter solstice, celebrate Her coming out of the cave. From Amaterasu, we are reminded of the light always within us.

DID YOU KNOW?

1. Her most important shrine, the Grand Shrine of Ise, is located in western Honshu.
2. She is usually depicted as a virgin Goddess and never participates in sexual relations.

"Sooner or later the white races must disgorge some of their spoils and give a place to the other races of the world. We stole land--whole continents...."

> An American leader of women's suffrage, Carrie Lane Chapman Catt (1859-1947) was an educator, principal, superintendent, writer, lecturer and political strategist. Reorganizing the Iowa Woman Suffrage Association led her to begin working nationally in 1890 with the National American Woman Suffrage Association (NAWSA). Recognizing the relentless bias against women, her earlier bigotry against immigrants and Blacks evolved as she became more involved with the suffrage movement. Retiring after the nineteenth Amendment passed, she focused attention on child labor and world peace. Later, Carrie worked as a spokesperson for German Jewish refugees.

Growing up in 19th century rural Iowa, Carrie learned not only the value of hard work but absorbed the bigotry surrounding her. Defying her father's wishes, she attended Iowa State University. Working as a teacher, dish washer and librarian to support herself, she graduated at the top of her class in 1880. Three years later, she rose from principal to superintendent of schools at Mason City, Iowa.

Widowed in 1886, Carrie joined the Iowa Woman Suffrage Association working as a certified writer, lecturer and state organizer. Gaining national attention, she spoke at the NAWSA convention in Washington D.C.

Elected to the presidency of NAWSA and championed by her new husband, she steered campaigns for women's suffrage in Colorado, Tennessee, South Dakota, New Hampshire and New York. Carrie also helped organize the International Woman Suffrage Alliance (IWSA) in 1902. Laboring diligently, she planned campaigns, wrote speeches and assembled women while acquiring political shrewdness. Unveiling her "Winning Plan" in 1916, Carrie proposed a campaign to "lock in" women's suffrage in a minimum of thirty-six states making it enough to ratify a federal amendment. Voting at the state level, women could then pressure Congress to pass the amendment.

DID YOU KNOW?

1. Carrie was active in anti-war causes during the 1920s and 1930s.
2. She is buried next to her long-time companion, Mary Garrett Hay, in the Bronx.

"You're not a mess, you're brave for trying."

> Anne Jemima Clough (1820-1892) was a British educator and woman's suffragist. A pioneer in women's education, she was educated at home. Determined to create public educational opportunities for young women, she opened her own school in 1841 and started another one when she moved to Ambleside in the Lake District. Clough helped found the North of England Council for Promoting the Higher Education of Women in 1876. Later, she was asked to be the head of a women's house of residence in Cambridge which evolved into Newnham College in 1875.

When her father went bankrupt in 1841, Anne took the opportunity to set up a small day school. In this way, she could contribute financially to the family and fulfill her personal interest in education. Because she had been educated entirely at home, which was standard for middle-and-upper class English families, Anne developed a passionate lifelong concern for the teaching process. A legacy she had received from her brother's early death removed financial anxieties but added additional burdensome family responsibilities—both parents being deceased.

Her educational schemes were encouraged by influential educated friends and the Langham Place Circle (a feminist activist organization). In order to raise standards and mobilize resources economically, Anne advocated sharing specialized teachers between schools.

Anne and friends founded the North of England Council for Promoting the Higher Education of Women. The council developed a scheme of lectures as well as a university-based exam for women who wanted to teach. Newnham, a residence for women attending lectures at Cambridge University, was established in 1871 with Anne taking charge. Seven years later, Newnham College was fully established with its own staff. She also helped found the Women's University Settlement in Southwark two years later.

DID YOU KNOW?

1. Anne helped found the Cambridge Training College for Women in 1885.
2. She also helped form London's Society for Women's Suffrage in 1907.

DOROTHY CROWFOOT HODGKIN

"I was captured for life by chemistry and by crystals."

Born in Cairo, Dorothy Mary Crowfoot Hodgkin (1910-1994) was a Nobel Prize winning British chemist, botanist, humanitarian and mother of three. She was the third woman and first Englishwoman to receive the Prize in Chemistry. Working in X-ray crystallography, Dorothy's research determined the structures of steroids, penicillin and Vitamin B12. She later determined the structure of insulin alongside Chinese scientists and helped scientists in India and Africa with their research as well. Involved in a wide range of peace and humanitarian causes, Dorothy was especially concerned about the welfare of scientists and people living in nations considered adversaries of the U.S. and UK.

Dorothy put up a fight to be allowed to study science beside the boys and succeeded. In 1928, she was accepted at Somerville College, University of Oxford, to study for a degree in chemistry. As an under-grad, Dorothy was foremost in studying the structure of organic compounds by using X-ray crystallography.

In 1932, she began attending the University of Cambridge to carry out doctoral research with John Bernal, a British physicist. Offered a temporary research fellowship at one of Oxford's few colleges for women, Somerville, Dorothy returned there in 1934 and remained until her retirement in 1977.

Her insulin research was put aside in 1939 when Howard Florey, an Australian pathologist, asked Hodgkin to map out the structure of penicillin which he and his colleagues had isolated. By 1945 she had succeeded, making the drug much easier to manufacture.

As her fame grew, Dorothy was increasingly asked for help getting people, mainly scientists, released from imprisonment in the USSR. Hodgkin dedicated her later years in to helping the cause of scientists in developing countries and nuclear disarmament.

DID YOU KNOW?

1. By determining the structure of insulin Dorothy made the mass production of it possible, saving many lives.
2. At twenty-four, Dorothy was diagnosed with Rheumatoid Arthritis which crippled her over time. Astonishingly, she was able to continue her research. Those of us with this terrible disease can take heart from her perseverance.

Betsey Guppy Chamberlain (1797-1896) was a woman of Native American descent who not only worked long hours in Massachusetts textile mills but wrote for local publications while she raised her children. She published some of the first criticisms of the US government's treatment of Native Americans. In her short stories, Betsey advocated the radical ideas that Native Americans deserved to be treated well and women deserved to be paid the same as men. Quite radical ideals for the early 1800s, don't you agree?

Born somewhere in New Hampshire, Betsey was part European and part Abenaki or Narragansett. She was widowed young and forced to sell their farmland. Betsey was able to find employment in textile mills to support herself and her children.

The Lowell Massachusetts mill owners, while forcing employees to work seventy hours per week, established educational and cultural Occasions through local lectures, concerts and libraries. The mill girls also requested and received the magazine published in Lowell, *The Lowell Offering,* its name was later changed to the *New England Offering.* The paper was initially organized by the local Universalist minister Rev. Abel C. Thomas.

Betsey Chamberlain wrote over thirty poems and stories for both publications. In her writings, she espoused themes of Native American gods and spirituality while satirizing Christian hypocrisy. She penned essays about class and gender injustices stating rules that dealt with women's education equality, eight-hour workdays and equal wages for women and men.

While Betsey lived in Lowell, she worked in the textile mills and ran a boarding-house. Thirty-three prose works were published by her between 1841-1848.

DID YOU KNOW?

1. Betsey sometimes used the pseudonyms Tabitha, Jemima or B.C.
2. Her writings were characterized by humorous incidents and sound common sense.

"I don't think there has ever been a man who treated a woman as an equal and that's all I would have asked, for I know I'm worth as much as they."

> Berthe Morisot (1841-1895) was a French Impressionist painter and mother who portrayed a wide range of subjects—from landscapes and still lifes to domestic scenes and portraits. Celebrated in her time as one of the founding members of the Parisian avant-garde group called Impressionists, she exhibited at seven of their eight shows beginning in 1874. Unfortunately, her works remain under-recognized. Morisot was often described as a visual poet of womanhood and the female experience. A feminist, she believed in the capabilities of all women.

In 1874, Berthe was invited to exhibit with the *Société Anonyme des Artistes-Peintres, Sculpteurs, Graveurs*—a landmark event that would become known as the first exhibition of the Impressionists. That same year, she married Eugene Manet, writer and political activist who greatly supported her throughout her career.

Berthe explored a range of themes from modern life that came to define impressionism. The intimacy of contemporary bourgeois living and leisure activities, the importance of fashion and the toilette, even women's domestic work, she blurred the lines between interior and exterior, public and private, finished and unfinished.

Berthe was celebrated for the loosest, least finished-looking technique of all the Impressionists. She created a full spectrum of color and light, demonstrating her remarkable mastery of capturing fleeting shades and shadows. Renowned artists such as Edgar Degas, Claude Monet and Pierre-Auguste Renoir accepted her as an equal. Berthe led the way for female artists around the world. Discover her beautiful artwork for yourself.

DID YOU KNOW?

1. Berthe missed the 1878 Impressionist exhibition to give birth to her daughter.
2. She often posed in her brother-in-law's (Edouard Manet) paintings.

"What a noble gift to man are the Forests! What a debt of gratitude and admiration we owe to their beauty and their utility!"

The first American woman to publish nature writing, Susan Fenimore Cooper (1813-1894) was more than just a famous author's daughter. An author, philanthropist, amateur ornithologist and nature artist, Susan was one of the first environmental-ists concerned with preservation of forests and our birds. Her written works were largely forgotten until just recently, overshadowed by her famous father—James Fenimore Cooper. Susan founded an orphanage in Cooperstown, New York, and then founded "The Friendly Society"—a group whose female members mentored orphans.

Fortunate to have been well educated in Europe, young Susan quickly learned to assist her father by documenting and organizing his notes. Despite having devoted much of her life to him, she also published a great number of her own books.

Susan is best known for her nature writing. Taken from her acute observations scrib-bled down in journals, *Rural Hours* was published in 1850. By publishing her book anonymously, Susan "was following a tradition of female authors, being modest and not claiming authorship." Her book, admired by Thoreau and published four years before *Walden*, offered the reader a close picture of plant and animal life in Cooper-stown.

More than a century before Rachel Carson penned *Silent Spring*, Susan focused a bright light on environmental pollution and warned of overexploitation of natural resources. She also talked of dwindling bird species, some of which are extinct in today's world. As a philanthropist, Susan gave her time and monies to help the under-privileged. She considered the "Orphan House of the Holy Savior" in Cooperstown her life's mission.

DID YOU KNOW?

1. One thing I especially admire about Susan—the home she shared with her sister was built with materials and bricks from Otsego Hall ruins. Was she one of the first recyclers? An ecofeminist?
2. She became a naturalist during a time when opportunities for women to publish written works or art were slim. Indeed, another woman ahead of time.
3. A quick search on the internet will bring you face-to-face with her artwork.

Aphrodite is the ancient Greek Goddess of love, beauty, desire and all aspects of sexuality. The Greek word *aphros* means sea foam and Aphrodite was born from the white foam produced by the severed genitals of Uranus *(Heaven) after His son* Cronus *threw them into* the sea. However, a different source is presented in Homer's *Iliad*. Aphrodite is always depicted or is referenced as being born as an adult, nubile and infinitely desirable. Additionally, She is honored as a protector of courtesans and prostitutes, and of those who travel by sea. Aphrodite's symbols are myrtles, roses, doves, sparrows and swans.

Worshipped by men, women, and city-state officials, Aphrodite played a role in the commerce, warfare, and politics of ancient Greek cities. She was especially worshipped in Paphos and Amathus on the island of Cyprus—a geographic location which hints at her eastern origins as a fertility goddess. The two areas of Greece and the Near East witnessed intense cultural exchange prior to the 8th-century BCE. Greek historian Herodotus states that the most ancient cult site to Aphrodite was at Ascalon in Syria.

Aphrodite was associated with the brightest planet, Venus. She also represented unity and harmony as well as mingling. This may explain the Goddess' wide range of associations such as warfare and politics. As we spy Venus in our heavens, let's remember Aphrodite and her unbounding love.

The Greek poet, Hesiod, describes the Goddess as quick-glancing, foam-born, smile-loving, and most often as the golden Aphrodite. She is usually clothed in archaic and classical art and wears an elaborately embroidered band or girdle across Her chest which held Her magic powers of love, desire and seductive allurement.

DID YOU KNOW?

1. Aphrodite's eyes are said to originally be ocean blue.
2. The red rose and red anemone are sacred flowers to Her.

"No one should have to buy justice in a land that boasts that justice is free."

A pioneering American lawyer, Clara Shortridge Foltz (1849-1934) was a suffragist leader, teacher, publisher, mother of five children and founder of the public defender movement. The first female lawyer on the West Coast, Clara was also the first woman admitted to the California bar, dubbed "Portia of the Pacific." She was the first woman deputy district attorney (1911-1913) and the first woman to argue before the California State Supreme Court. This gutsy woman raised five children on her own after her husband's abandonment while she studied law!

She first studied law in the office of a local judge (1879). Clara supported herself and her five children by giving public lectures on women's suffrage. Unable to take the bar because California law only allowed "white males" to do so, Clara authored a state bill, known as the "Woman Lawyer Bill" which replaced the wording *white males* with *white persons*. In September of 1878, she passed the exam and became the first female in California admitted to the bar.

Clara practiced law for fifty years continuously, always regretting her lack of formal training. Starting the Portia Law Club in San Francisco, she prepared women for the bar. Clara also taught law classes for women in her office.

Her greatest achievement as a law reformer was conceiving the idea of a public defender. Her compelling presentation was given as the representative of the California bar at the Congress of Jurisprudence and Law Reform held at the Chicago World's Fair (1893). Clara's several law review articles on the subject were convincing in their formulation of the notion that the government should pay for the defense of the criminally accused. The "Foltz Defender Bill" (1921-California) was a clear success of her lobbying efforts.

DID YOU KNOW?

1. Clara practiced law in San Francisco, San Diego, New York and Denver.
2. The Criminal Courts Building in downtown L.A. was renamed The Clara Shortridge Foltz Criminal Justice Center in 2002.

Belle Aurelia Babb Mansfield (1846-1911) became the first female lawyer in the United States in 1869. Despite Iowa state law restricting the bar exam to only white males, Arabella (Bella) took the exams. Scoring high marks, she challenged the courts and was admitted to the bar—Iowa became the first state in the Union to admit women to the bar. Bella made her career as a college educator, administrator and activist in the women's suffrage movement.Every female attorney in America is beholden to Bella Mansfield.

Bella entered Iowa Wesleyan University in the fall of 1862, graduating valedictorian in 1866. Her brother, Washington, graduated the same year as salutatorian. She accepted a position teaching at Des Moines Conference Seminary, now known as Simpson College.

After a year of teaching, Bella returned to Iowa Wesleyan to pursue her master's degree. She married John Mansfield, a Wesleyan graduate and professor of natural history in 1868. Upon completing her master's degree, she began lecturing on women's rights, becoming one of the founders of the Iowa Woman Suffrage Society.

Bella completed a second B.A. in law at Iowa Wesleyan and became a professor of English Literature at the school. Maintaining her interest in legal proceedings throughout her lifetime, she joined the National League of Women Lawyers in 1893.

Relocating to Greencastle, Indiana, the couple taught for the next eight years at Indiana Asbury University, presently known as DePauw University. Bella lectured around the country, served as principal of Mount Pleasant High School and taught mathematics at Iowa Wesleyan during the 1885-1886 school year. After her husband's death in 1894, Bella returned to DePauw University where she became a tutor of the Ladies Hall, a registrar for three years and dean of the School of Art and dean of the School of Music from 1893 to 1911.

DID YOU KNOW?

1. Bella did not attend law school before she sat for and passed the law exams?
2. She chaired the Iowa Women's Suffrage Convention in 1870 and worked alongside Susan B Anthony.

"So long has the myth of feminine inferiority prevailed that women themselves find it hard to believe that their own sex was once and for a very long time, the superior and dominant sex."

Dr. Elizabeth Gould Bell (1862-1934) was not only a brilliant doctor but also a feminist. An advocate for women's rights in Ireland, she became one of the first women doctors ever to graduate from Queen's University after trying to gain entrance for fifteen years. Against all odds, this working single mother ignored social conventions and set up a surgery (medical practice) in Ulster, Northern Ireland. Exposed to the hard life of the most vulnerable females led her to become involved in the women's suffrage movement.

Elizabeth worked long hours at the Women's Maternity Home in Belfast and at the Belfast Babies Home. Keeping close to her values, helping those most in need, she was also the Medical Officer at the Malone Place Hospital which gave unwed pregnant mothers refuge. Through her work, she was exposed to the difficult lives of Ireland's most vulnerable females.

This led Elizabeth to become very active in women's suffrage, believing the right to vote would give them some control over their lives. Not just a bystander in the women's movement, Elizabeth was arrested for throwing rocks at a demonstration in London. She then found out about life behind bars at Holloway Prison in 1911.

Returning to Belfast, she became the doctor for suffragette prisoners in the Crumlin Road Jail. When WWI broke out, Elizabeth began serving with the Royal Army Medical Corps (RAMC). She promptly left to work at St. Andrews Medical Hospital in Malta.

DID YOU KNOW?

1. It wasn't until 1928 that Great Britain enacted the Equal Franchise Act that gave voting rights to *all* women over twenty-one, regardless of property ownership, marriage, or social class.
2. About one thousand Irish women participated in the Ulster suffrage movement.

Cai Yan (c. 178- c. 249 CE) was a poet, musician and mother who lived during the late Eastern Han dynasty of China. She was a longtime calligrapher and her works were often praised. Her poems were noted for their sorrowful tone, which mirrored her hard life. Cai Yan is the first Chinese female poet whose life and writings are documented. Celebrated as one of China's most talented poets, she is revered for the hardship she endured and survived. During the Jin dynasty, her "courtesy name" was changed to *Wenji*.

Wenji was the daughter of a famous Eastern Han scholar and poet. Her poetry was often compared to his. Married and widowed before being captured, she was taken north by the Huns. Held captive for twelve years, she gave birth to two sons by a Hun chieftain. Thus, the stories Wenji wrote reveal much sorrow. That same sorrow spurs poets and writers today, including me.

Wenji's family finally was able to locate her and paid a ransom to have her returned, but without her sons. This heartbreak and her brutal experience while being held captive is believed to be described in *Eighteen Verses*, where she talks of "war, barbarism and grief." Upon Wenji's return from captivity, she married Dong Si, a local government official from her hometown. She inherited some four thousand volumes of ancient books from her father's vast collection. However, they were destroyed in a war.

Many artists have portrayed her return to Han territory, various painters doing so from the Tang dynasty. There have also been renderings in the traditional Beijing opera.

DID YOU KNOW?

1. Wenji was able to recite four hundred volumes of ancient books by memory and wrote them on paper. That's impressive.
2. Craters on both Mercury and Venus are named for her.

Catherine II (1729 – 1796) was the longest-serving female Russian monarch, reigning from 1762 to her death in 1796. An absolute monarch and mother of four, she westernized Russia by championing the arts and reorganizing Russia's code of law. She significantly expanded Russian territories and created a greater integration of Russia within Europe. Catherine was a patron of literature and a writer. She established literary reviews, encouraged the sciences and founded schools. Catherine also created one of the world's most impressive art collections held in St. Petersburg's Winter Palace, now the Hermitage Museum. Isn't it amazing that you and I can view her 18th century art collection at the Hermitage?

Catherine was born Sophie von Anhalt-Zerbst in Stettin, then part of Prussia (now modern Poland). Accepted into the Russian Orthodox Church in 1745, she changed her name to Catherine and married Grand Duke Peter, heir to the Russian throne.

Initially viewed with suspicion because of her foreign roots by the Russian court, her lack of Russian culture and liberal attitudes also caused concern. Once Catherine threw herself into Russian culture, she became adept at forming relationships within the court. Her foreign birth became less important over time; she was seen as more capable than her husband – Tsar Peter III –a weak, childish and incompetent leader. Little love was lost between Catherine and Peter.

Shortly after her husband's ascension to the throne, he was deposed and Catherine put in his place. Peter was killed shortly afterward. Once she secured the throne, Catherine proved to be a clever leader, gradually increasing Russia's sphere of influence.

DID YOU KNOW?

1. Despite being a strong ruler, Catharine's participation in foreign wars made her unpopular with ordinary Russians.
2. It is unknown whether Catharine had any knowledge or involvement in her husband's death.

"I've been poor and I've been rich, and rich is better."

Known as the "Empress of Blues," Bessie Smith (1894-1937) was among the highest paid Black performers of her time. Her music stressed independence, fearlessness, sexual freedom and respect for working women. A black feminist, Bessie's recordings expressed the frustrations and hopes of a whole generation of Black Americans.

In 1906, Bessie began performing as a busker (a street singer/dancer) accompanied by her younger brother, Andrew, on guitar. Six years later, she began dancing with a minstrel show which eventually led to her meeting Ma Rainey. Rainey took the young singer under her wing, and over the next decade, Bessie performed at various theaters and on the vaudeville circuit. By the early 1920's, she was living in Philadelphia.

In 1923, a representative from Columbia Records heard Bessie sing, and offered her a contract. Among her first recordings was "Downhearted Blues" which sold over 2,000,000 copies. She began touring extensively becoming very successful because of her rich and powerful contralto voice. The subject matter of Bessie's songs was classical blues —poverty and oppression, love and stoic acceptance of defeat in a cruel and indifferent world.

Perhaps Bessie's most popular song was her 1929 hit "Nobody Knows You When You're Down and Out." However, at the height of her success, her career began to flounder due in part to the financial chaos of the Depression and the advent of sound in movies. By 1931, Bessie had stopped recording for Columbia Records. Ever diligent, she continued to tour.

Tragedy hit in 1937. En route to a show in Memphis, the vehicle in which she was riding side-swiped a truck and lost control. Bessie was thrown from the vehicle and sustained critical injuries. She died without regaining consciousness. You can discover her soul-filled voice on YouTube.

DID YOU KNOW?

1. Bessie made 160 recordings in her short life.
2. That fateful night, her Packard was hit a second time by an oncoming car while she lie on the side of the road.

Artemis is the Greek Goddess of the Moon, the hunt, the wilderness, vegetation and chastity. She is regarded as a patron of girls and young women *(particularly brides-to-be)* and a protectress during childbirth. Among the rural population, Artemis is the favorite Goddess. Her character and function vary greatly from place to place, but behind all forms lay the Goddess of wild nature who dances accompanied by nymphs in mountains, forests and marshes. Artemis embodies the sportsman's ideal, so besides killing game She also protects it, especially the young. Her symbols include a bow and arrow, a quiver and hunting knives. Deer and cypress are sacred to Her.

Many of Artemis' local cults preserved traces of other deities, often with Greek names. This suggests upon adopting Her, the Greeks identified Artemis with nature divinities of their own. The virginal sister of Apollo is very different from the many-breasted Artemis of Ephesus, for example. Dances of maidens representing tree nymphs (dryads) were especially common in Artemis' worship as Goddess of the tree cult.

Throughout the Peloponnese, bearing such epithets as *Limnaea* and *Limnatis* (Lady of the Lake), Artemis supervises waters and lush wild growth, attended by nymphs of wells and springs (naiads). In parts of the peninsula, Her dances are wild and lascivious. She reminds us to embrace our wild side in the same way you and I embrace animals. Though our dances aren't always crazy, we can at least twirl around barefoot under the full moon's embrace.

Outside the Peloponnese, Artemis' most familiar form is "Mistress of animals." Poets and artists usually picture Her with the stag or hunting dog but the cults show considerable variety. Early representations also emphasize Her role as Goddess of animals and show Her winged with a bird or animal in each hand.

DID YOU KNOW?

1. Artemis is known to have perfect aim with the bow and arrow.
2. As She is associated with chastity, Artemis has eternal virginity.

"But while Ireland is not free I remain a rebel, unconverted and unconvertible."

> An Irish Sinn Fein and Fianna Fail politician, Constance Georgine Gore-Booth Markievicz (1868-1927) was a suffragist, revolutionary nationalist, socialist, artist and mother. Known as Countess Markievicz, she was an officer in the Irish Citizens Army during the "Easter Rising." Though she didn't take her seat, Constance was the first woman elected to the British House of Commons (1918). The first woman in Europe to hold a cabinet position as Minister of Labor of the Irish Republic (1919-1922), she spent much of those years in jail. The "people's Countess" is best known for her compassion and strength shown during Ireland's struggle for independence.

Born in London, her father (Sir Henry Gore-Booth) was a compassionate Anglo-Irish landowner. His actions during the Irish Famine (1879-80) inspired Constance to develop a deep concern for the poor.

Studying at the Slade School of Art in London, Constance became politically active joining the National Union of Women's Suffrage Societies (NUWSS). After moving to Paris, she married Kazimierz Dunin-Markiewicz and became Countess Markiewicz. After settling in Dublin in 1903, Constance helped found the United Artist Club. Meeting many patriots and future political leaders, she eventually read some revolutionary journals which spurred her to action.

In 1908, Constance became actively involved in Ireland's politics. Despite being an aristocrat, her feminine compassion for the forgotten ones gained her a reputation as being a friend to the workers and the poor. She joined Sinn Fein and *Inghinidhe nah Eireann* ("Daughters of Ireland"). Constance founded *Fianna Eireann* (1909)—a para-military organization instructing teenage boys in the use of firearms.

Imprisoned by the British three times between 1911- 1918 and twice during Ireland's struggle for independence (1919-21) she proved a woman could fight alongside men honorably. She returned as an MP (member of Parliament) in 1923, and again in 1927.

DID YOU KNOW?

1. Constance retired as a colonel from the IRA in 1923.
2. She was the lone female cabinet member in Irish history until 1979.

Ban Zhao aka Ban Huiban (45 CE-117 CE) was a renowned Chinese scholar and historian, poet, writer, teacher, philosopher and politician. She was the first known female Chinese historian and China's most famous female scholar. Called the "gifted one", Ban wrote about "Confucian feminism" in her text *"Lessons of Women."* Simply amazing for a female in the first century.

Ban was taught Confucianism and the more traditional Chinese belief system, Taoism, which stresses man's place within nature. Because she was born at a time of great reform in China, Ban witnessed the replacement of the ancient feudal system with the imperial system. In a Chinese feudal society, women had often been powerful influences in politics, sometimes even rulers. Later on, women became distinctly inferior to men in the eyes of Confucians, who believed the father or husband was the absolute authority in the family and thecore of Chinese society. In contemporary Asian society, gender equality is more prevalent than the interpretations of ancient Confucianism.

The Han court had adopted Confucianism as its central value system. The new system was beneficial because, unlike feudalism, it provided a degree of social mobility. Learning and scholarly accomplishment were greatly rewarded under the Confucian system. Thus, the incentive to become highly educated was quite strong.

Married at fourteen, Ban moved in with her husband's family. Reports are that her husband was quite frustrated with his young wife's desire to "write all day long". Nonetheless, along with regular household chores, Ban continued to study and write.

After her brother's death in prison, Ban was summoned to court in order to continue as imperial historian. She was apparently put in charge of the royal *Tan Kuan Library and* appointed teacher of the ladies of the court, including all concubines. Later, she became a lady-in-waiting. Known in the court as "Mother Ban", she retained much influence within the royal family.

DID YOU KNOW?

1. Ban Zhao was China's first poet laureate.
2. She was the teacher of Taoist sexual practices for the royal family.

"Prejudice is more violent the blinder it is."

> Born in England, Elizabeth Blackwell (1821-1910) was the first woman in America to receive a medical degree when she graduated in 1849 from New York's Geneva Medical College. In 1857, she established the New York Infirmary offering a practical solution to women who were rejected for internships elsewhere. Dr. Blackwell also published several important books on the issue of women in medicine.

Once she became determined to become a physician, Elizabeth applied to twelve schools in the northeast and was accepted by Geneva Medical College in western New York in 1847 accidentally. The faculty assumed the all-male student body would never agree to a woman learning alongside them, so they allowed them to vote on her admission. As a joke, the male students voted in her favor and Elizabeth gained admittance.

Not surprising, her months there were extremely difficult. Townspeople and much of the male student body ostracized and harassed her. Blackwell was, at first, even barred from classroom demonstration. Persevering, in January 1849, Blackwell became the first woman in the United States to graduate from medical school—even ranking first in her class!

In April, having become a naturalized U.S. citizen, Dr. Blackwell traveled to England to seek further training and in May she went on to Paris. After working at London and Paris clinics for two years, Blackwell then studied midwifery at *La Maternité*.

She returned to New York City in 1851. After applying for a physician's spot at the women's department of a large city dispensary, Dr. Blackwell was turned down. In 1853, with the help of friends, Blackwell opened her own dispensary, seeing patients three afternoons a week. She was soon joined by her sister, Dr. Emily Blackwell, and together with *Dr. Marie Zakrzewska*, opened the New York Infirmary for Women and Children in 1857.

DID YOU KNOW?

1. Elizabeth lost sight in one eye—having to set aside her dream of becoming a surgeon—when she contracted purulent ophthalmia from a young patient.
2. In 1874, she and four others worked alongside Florence Nightingale to create the first medical school for women in England.

"Tread softly! All the earth is holy ground."

> Christina Rossetti (1839-1894) was an English Victorian poet who wrote romantic, devotional and children's poems. She was much influenced by romantic stylistic elements. Best known for ballads and mystical lyrics, Christina wrote some of her works under the pseudonym Ellen Alleyne. Throughout her life, she suffered bouts of depression and Grave's Disease, and yet persisted to become a world-renowned poet. She must have had great courage and determination to persevere.

British poet Christina Rossetti received all of her education from her mother, who had been trained as a governess and was committed to cultivating intellectual excellence to her children. Christina wrote her first poem *To my Mother on her Birthday* when she was eleven. She went on to become one of the Victorian age's finest poets. Isn't that extraordinary for someone educated at home?

Christina's faith in her life and art cannot be overstated. Half of her poems are devotional in nature, and her later works in both poetry and prose are almost exclusively so. The fleetingness of human love, individual unworthiness, the vanity of earthly pleasures, and divine love's perfection are recurring themes in her poetry.

Christina had bouts of serious illness throughout her life. The morbidity that readers have so often noted in her poetry was attributable to her ill health and the ever-present prospect of early death. By her sixteenth birthday, Christina had written more than fifty poems that were transcribed into a notebook by her sister.

In 1848 she had her first taste of fame when she submitted two of her poems, *Death's Chill Between* and *Heart's Chill Between* to *The Athenaeum*, a prestigious literary periodical. Their acceptance made her a nationally published poet at seventeen. Today, *Goblin Market,* published in 1862 when she was twenty-three, remains Christina Rossetti's most discussed poem.

DID YOU KNOW?

1. Those of us who sing regularly will recognize her words published in 1872, "In the bleak mid-winter frosty wind may moan; Earth stood hard as iron, water like a stone…"

CLEOPATRA VII

Cleopatra VII Thea Philopator (c. 69-30 BCE) was the last ruler of Egypt *before it was* annexed as a province of Rome. Although arguably the mostfamous Egyptian *queen,* Cleopatra *VII was actually Macedonian-Greek. She was a lover of* Julius Caesar, and wife of Mark Antony. Cleopatra VII was a powerful queen before her interaction with either man and a much stronger monarch than any of the later Ptolemaic Dynasty. Egypt flourished under her reign.

Debate continues to surround Cleopatra's ethnicity, as she may have been partly descended from Black Africans. She ruled jointly with her father, Ptolemy XII Auletes. She inherited the throne when her father died—Cleopatra was eighteen. Egyptian tradition held that a male must accompany a female to reign. Ptolemy XIII, her twelve-year-old brother, was ceremonially married to her. Cleopatra soon dropped his name from all official documents, however, and ruled alone.

In an era when women rarely or never asserted political control over men, Cleopatra was able to maintain an independent Egypt. As long as she sat on the throne, she never forgot what was due the Egyptian people. Fluent in a number of languages, Cleopatra was extremely charming, an effective diplomat and administrator.

After a crushing defeat by Roman rival Octavian, Mark Antony killed himself believing Cleopatra was already dead. She then followed suit, committing suicide. Though the truth is unknown, stories are told of her being bitten by an asp. Thirty-nine years old at her death, Cleopatra had ruled for twenty-two of those years.

DID YOU KNOW?

1. Cleopatra tried to maintain the concept of *ma'at* –balance and harmony–during her reign.
2. Almost fifty Roman historians mention Cleopatra, only referring to her suicide and gossip about her negative attributes.

"If I'm going to sing like someone else, then I don't need to sing at all."

> Born Eleanora Fagan Gough (1915-1959), Billie was a legendary American jazz singer and songwriter whose evocative voice and style made her a jazz icon. In 1957, Lady Day was awarded a Grammy Lifetime Achievement Award. She lost her battle with addiction in 1959. Her 1957 autobiography, *Lady Sings the Blues*, tells of the many abusive and destructive relationships in her life.

Billie Holliday had a tough life, giving rise to an emotionally intense voice—a gift to our world. When Billie sang, she poured her heart and soul into the music by her unique phrasing. Growing up on Baltimore's streets in the 1920s, she worked alongside her mother in a brothel. Raped at the age of ten, Billie soon dropped out of school. As a teenager, she made her way to New York City and began singing in Harlem's nightclubs. By 1937, Billie had joined Count Basie's Orchestra and became a force to be reckoned with.

In 1939, she recorded "Strange Fruit"—a poem's telling of a horrific lynching set to music. It became an instant hit, though banned by some radio stations. Garnering the attention of Federal Bureau of Narcotics commissioner Harry Anslinger, a notorious racist, Billie was *forbidden* to perform it. When she refused, Anslinger concocted a plan to frame her for using drugs.

Imprisoned for eighteen months, Billie was refused a cabaret performer's license when released. She persisted, performing in Carnegie Hall to sold-out concerts. In 1959, Billie lay in a hospital bed suffering with cirrhosis of the liver along with heart and lung problems. Anslinger, dead set on ruining her, had his men handcuff Billie to the bed. He also ordered doctors to stop treating her. (Can you imagine such hate?) She died shortly thereafter.

DID YOU KNOW?

1. Her recording of "Strange Fruit" was named by *Time Magazine* as the Song of the Century in 1999. You can find her heart-wrenching recording on the internet.
2. Billie's lifelong friend and mentor was Lester Young.
3. She had a passionate, life-long love for dogs.

Athena (Athene) is the Olympian Goddess of wisdom and war and the adored Patroness of the city of Athens. A virgin deity, She is associated with peace and handicrafts, especially spinning and weaving. Majestic and stern, Athena is also Goddess of courage, inspiration, law, justice and mathematics. Athena's symbols are owls, the olive tree, snakes, the Aegis (goatskin shield), armor, helmets, the spear and the Gorgoneion (an amulet showing the Gorgon head). The colors purple and blue are most often associated with Her.

Athena is one of the most important Olympian gods and has many functions. Ancient Greek heroes asked for Her advice. As a war Goddess, She fought alongside Greek heroes in Homer's *Iliad*. Her moral and military superiority derives in part from the fact that She represents the intellectual and civilized side of war with the virtues of justice and skill. We can all learn much from Athena's attributes, especially those of us in leadership positions.

Her superiority also comes in part from the immense variety and importance of Her functions, and from patriotism of Homer's predecessors. In the *Iliad*, Athena is the divine form of the heroic, martial ideal: She personifies excellence in close combat, victory and glory. In Aeschylus's dramatic tragedy *Eumenides*, She founded the *Areopagus* (*Athens's* aristocratic council). By breaking a deadlock of the judges in favor of Orestes, the defendant, She set the precedent that a tied vote signified acquittal.

Known as Parthenos, Athena was perpetually a virgin. Her most famous temple, the Parthenon, on the Athenian Acropolis, takes its name from this title.

DID YOU KNOW?

1. Athena usually lacks emotion and compassion.
2. She is considered the most intelligent and wisest of all Greek Gods.

"No man or woman who tries to pursue an ideal in his or her own way is without enemies."

An African American civil rights activist, Daisy Lee Gatson Bates (1913-1999) was a journalist, publisher and lecturer. The desegregation of Little Rock's Central High School (1957) was achieved by her efforts. Daisy's role as mentor to the "Little Rock Nine" was vital. Her home became headquarters for the integration battle of schools in Arkansas. Her life was dedicated to ending racial injustice, her mother had been raped and murdered by three white men when Daisy was only three. Fighting gender inequality as well as racial prejudice, many of us have never heard of Daisy Bates—our loss. She was relentless in her activism.

Born in Arkansas and raised in a foster home, Daisy and her husband, L.C. Bates, settled in Little Rock. *The Arkansas Weekly,* the newspaper the couple immediately started, was the only African American paper dedicated solely to the Civil Rights Movement. Daisy also became president of the Arkansas chapter of the NAACP. It was her efforts that helped transformed the Civil Rights Movement.

When the Supreme Court ruled segregated schools unconstitutional in 1954, Daisy began enrolling African American students in white schools. She used her newspaper to make everyone aware of which schools were allowing black students. Although many Arkansas schools rejected the court's mandate, Daisy persevered, working tirelessly for the safety of the students. She mentored the first nine students allowed into white schools, driving them to school and protected them from violent crowds. Daisy even joined the school's parent organization.

Because of her role in integration, Daisy's life was often threatened. She and L.C. were forced to shut down their newspaper but she continued her life's work, raising the status of African Americans in the South. Daisy's influential work with school integration gave her national recognition.

DID YOU KNOW?

1. Daisy was the only woman to speak at the "1963 March on Washington."
2. In 1999, she was posthumously awarded the Medal of Freedom.

Catharine Esther Beecher (1800-1878) was an 19th century American educator, activist and author who promoted equal access to education for women. She co-founded the innovative Hartford Female Seminary (1823). Catharine led a women's movement to protest Andrew Jackson's "Indian Removal Bill"—which was the first national campaign on the part of women in the United States (1829-1830). Her marvelous example, leading that first national campaign, motivates us to take action against today's injustice.

Catharine acquired her education primarily through independent study, becoming a schoolteacher in 1821. In 1823, she co-founded the innovative Hartford Female Seminary, training for mothers and teachers was priority.

While Catharine did not advocate a radical change in women's roles, she did fight for increased recognition of the value of the work women did in managing homes, raising families and teaching. She felt women should expand their place in society by teaching nurturing skills and moral conscience in a profession (teacher).

Catharine founded schools and organizations devoted to training women to become teachers, believing that the basis for a well-ordered and moral society began with women. This theme contributed to a growing feminist attitude that women were strong, not passive creatures, that could be contributing members of society. She believed women should be given more responsibility and respect outside the home. Catharine saw the field of teaching as the perfect professional arena for women— allowing them independence and giving them an important "feminine" role outside the home.

She opened the Western Female Institute (early 1830s) in Cincinnati. Catharine was not well-liked in the city—thought to be a cultural elitist—and her abolitionist views gained her no support. The school closed in 1837. This did not stop Beecher, as she began printing tracts calling on women to unite against slavery. When she published *Treatise on Domestic Economy* (1841) she finally reached a wider audience. The book's incredible success earned her fame across the nation.

DID YOU KNOW?

1. Catharine went undercover in Massachusetts textiles mills to expose the poor working conditions of women.
2. She founded The American Woman's Education Association in 1852.

The first Native American to earn a medical degree, Susan La Flesche Picotte (1865-1915) was a late 19th century social reformer and mother. Campaigning for public health issues, she also fought for the formal and legal allotment of Omaha tribal lands. Susan diligently worked to discourage drinking on the reservation and championed prevention and treatment of tuberculosis.

Born on Omaha Nation land (present day Nebraska), Susan's father was the last recognized Omaha chief. Because their lands were ceded to the U.S. government, the Omaha people were moved to a reservation. Susan spoke English, French and her native tongue. She learned Omaha traditions before being sent to boarding schools off reservation. Hampton Institute, a traditional Black school, welcomed Native American students like Susan. After graduation, she attended Women's Medical College of Pennsylvania. Needing monies for tuition, Susan asked for assistance from the Connecticut Indian Association. Her request was granted, she is considered the first U.S-born person to receive financial assistance for a professional education.

Assimilating herself to white classmates, Susan began dressing and wearing her hair as they did. Graduating valedictorian in 1889, she applied at the Omaha Agency Indian School for the position of government physician. Her main responsibilities were teaching students good hygiene and keeping them healthy. She soon found herself caring for community members as well. For many years Susan traveled the reservation treating the sick and translating legal documents. After resigning her position, she continued her medical practice on the reservation and in the surrounding community, treating people of all races.

Susan championed preventive medicine by giving lectures on alcohol abuse and lobbying local governments to ban alcohol on the reservation. She advocated for food sanitation and school hygiene, and was relentless about stopping the spread of tuberculosis, it had killed hundreds on the reservation (including her husband). After his death, Susan became more outspoken against TB. She also began fighting for her inheritance, South Dakota lands left to her and her children by her husband.

DID YOU KNOW?

1. Susan struggled with chronic illness her entire life. She eventually became deaf.
2. She succeeded in receiving her inheritance.
3. Susan died from bone cancer in 1915 before she could be administrator at the new reservation hospital.

CHRISTINE DE PIZAN

"Just as women's bodies are softer than men's, their understanding is sharper."

A prolific, versatile French scholar and poet, Christine de Pizan (1364-1430) produced diverse writings including numerous poems of <u>courtly love</u> plus a <u>biography</u> *of France's* Charles V. Christine was the first female professional writer of the Middle Ages and is best remembered for her revolutionary works about women.

Christine de Pizan (aka Christine de Pisan) was the first woman of letters in France. She was born in Venice but her family soon moved to France when King Charles V appointed her father as court astrologer. Losing her husband after only ten years of marriage, Christine took up writing to support herself and three small children. She also had to care and provide for her mother and a niece. While Christine had offers to join the royal courts of England and Milan, she was committed to staying in France. Can you imagine a woman trying to earn a living while caring for three children, her mother and a niece in the late 14th and early 15th century?

There is no denying that Christine embodied the values and principles of feminism. Specifically, women were the equals of men in every regard and should be accorded the same rights, opportunities and respect as any male. The works of Christine de Pizan were very influential during her lifetime. Her books' popularity remained through the early part of the Renaissance when, for unknown reasons, they fell out of print.

Christine de Pizan was rediscovered in the 19th century and has steadily regained a following primarily because of feminist interest in *The Book of the City of Ladies* and *The Treasure of the City of Ladies*—both regularly taught in Women's Studies classes at universities.

DID YOU KNOW?

1. She published forty-one poems and prose during her lifetime.
2. With her pen, Christine defended women and is recognized as the first writer to do so.

Eagle Woman That All Look At (1820-1888), also known as Matilda Picotte Galpin, was a Lakota peace activist, diplomat, trader, translator and mother of seven children. Also known for mediating conflicts between the U.S. government, the Sioux and white settlers, she was a strong advocate of the Teton (Western Sioux) people. Her courage and diplomacy earned her great respect from both Native American and white settlers. Eagle Woman was especially known for her generosity. She was regarded as the only woman recognized as a Chief among the Sioux, dedicated to the tribes' independence.

Eagle Woman's early diplomacy efforts were focused on peace, her later efforts, after reservations were relocated, focused on convincing the Sioux to adapt to the new era of change and compromise. She helped support the Sioux materially when the U.S. government forced tribes to sustain themselves on barren reservation lands.

Eagle Woman was in part responsible for the party of leaders sent to sign the 1868 Second Treaty of Fort Laramie, though she was against the1876 Standing Rock Treaty. She became the first woman to sign a treaty with the U.S. government.

She and her daughter, Louise, organized the first day school at Standing Rock Indian Reservation. Once peace was achieved, Eagle Woman continued to give material aid as the tribes adjusted to reservation life, until her death. Speaking out frequently against cruelty of any kind by whites or Indians, Eagle Woman was committed to peace. She and her second husband, Charles Gilpin, established trade operations during the post-Civil War economy, resolving many conflicts between settlers and tribes in their area.

DID YOU KNOW?

1. In 1865, Eagle Woman protected a wounded white soldier after he had been ambushed.
2. She began traveling alone in 1866 speaking at many Sioux councils to negotiate peace.

CECILE CHAMINADE

"Not just a woman who composes......but a composer who is a woman." - Ambroise Thomas

A Parisian born composer, Cecile Louise Stephanie Chaminade (1857-1944) was also a pianist.She was the first female composer to be awarded the *Legion d'Honneur* (1913). Her music is described as tuneful, highly accessible and mildly chromatic—typical characteristics of 'Romantic French music'. The late 20th century depreciation of Romantic French music meant that interest in her compositions nearly died.

Cecile began composing at age seven. An accomplished performer, she was giving recitals of her own music by 1878. Over the next ten years, these recitals turned into international concerts in Vienna, Belgium and Britain—where she was a favorite of Queen Victoria.

When Cecile toured the U.S., she performed in Carnegie Hall, Symphony Hall and at the Academy of Music alongside the newly formed Philadelphia Orchestra. President Teddy Roosevelt invited her to play at the White House as well. Performing throughout the Midwest inspired hundreds of women to found musical societies, *Chaminade Clubs.*

Despite her international fame, Cecile found herself marginalized by the musical world of Paris. Even though her shorter compositions were favored in Britain and the U.S., Parisian critics labeled them *salon music,* stating they were marked by "gushing sentimentality and empty virtuosic flourishes best consumed at home for the light entertainment of women."

Contrarily, Cecile's concert works faced criticism as being "fraudulently masculine." Blatantly sexist critiques from across the ocean were actually quoted in the *New York Evening Post* (after a 1908 Carnegie Hall performance) stating, "while women may someday vote, they will never learn to compose anything worthwhile." How sad and misogynistic is that?

DID YOU KNOW?

1. Cecile favored her character pieces when performing.
2. The prolific woman composed over four hundred pieces of music covering a wide range of forms. Extraordianry!

Worshipped as the Goddess of Spring and flowers in Wales, Blodeuwedd is often depicted with owls—signs of Her inherent wisdom. Created by magicians, Blodeuwedd was formed from nine different blossoms: primrose, hawthorn, meadowsweet, oak, cockle, broom, nettle, chestnut and bean. As the White Goddess of both life and death, She reminds us of the fragility of relationships. Blodeuwedd's main message is that beauty is only skin deep. She demonstrates to us that in order for spring blooming to occur, there must be death in autumn and winter. The natural world always goes full circle; birth and death in plants, animals and humans is simply part of the circle of life.

An ancient tale reveals that Blodeuwedd was created to become the wife of Lleu Llaw Gyffes— whose mother had cursed Him preventing Him from ever taking a wife. Blodeuwedd was not only an unfaithful wife but treacherous. She and Her lover killed the unprotected Lleu Llaw. The same magicians that created Her punished Her, transforming Blodeuwedd into an owl.

When first creating the Goddess, the magicians blew oak pollen into Her for breath. Instilled with faithfulness and long life, She failed, choosing the wrong path. This lesson teaches us to be cautious of the decisions we make during our lives, for there are consequences. Broom flower instilled life and vitality to Blodeuwedd. We can recognize this basic symbol of resourcefulness, reminding us of basic and simple values, making do with what we have instead of jumping on the consumerism merry-go-round.

Her transformation to the white owl symbolizes the change of light to darkness. She lived in light but then was changed into a nocturnal creature. When this happened, Blodeuwedd's vision was greatly expanded, helping Her to see all aspects of life and death. This reminds us we can bear our difficulties as we go through life by seeing through different eyes, remembering with broader vision comes wisdom.

DID YOU KNOW?

1. Blodeuwedd actually means "flower face."
2. Her most important aspect is the Triune Goddess—the Maiden, the Mother and the Crone.

"I have learned to live each day as it comes, and not to borrow trouble by dreading tomorrow."

An American social reformer, Dorothea Lynde Dix (1802-1887) advocated for the mentally ill and indigenous people. It is because of her relentless lobbying of state legislatures and the United States Congress that we have safe facilities for people who suffer from mental illness. A writer, activist and prison reform advocate, Dorothea was instrumental in creating first-generation mental institutions in Massachusetts, New Jersey, North Carolina and Illinois. Thank goodness for her understanding and compassion.

Though not much is known about Dorothea's childhood, there is evidence her parents were alcoholics and her father was abusive. She and her brothers moved to Boston to live with her well-to-do grandmother. While there, she took classes as well as taught lessons. Dorothea established an elementary school around 1821, and then a secondary school in 1831 which was attended by wealthier students. At the same time, she taught poor and neglected children, holding classes in her grandmother's barn.

Her grandmother's connections allowed her to associate with brilliant influential people like Ralph Waldo Emerson and William Channing—the "Father of Unitarianism." During 1824-1830, Dorothea wrote and published children's stories and devotional books. Ill health soon halted Dorothea's teaching activities. It is speculated that she suffered from bouts of severe depression. On a doctor's recommendation, Dorothea traveled to Europe. While there, she began meeting with social reformers who advocated for prison reform and the mentally ill.

Returning to the States, Dorothea began investigating the inhumane treatment of mentally ill patients. She also began volunteering in prisons. Determined to improve the conditions of prisoners and patients, Dorothea traveled throughout the U.S. lobbying for more humane treatment of the most vulnerable, while promoting higher education for women. She believed "moral treatment" should be the standard for treating mentally ill people. Her tireless testimonies of horrific conditions advanced the merit of "compassionate care."

DID YOU KNOW?

1. During the Civil War, Dorothea served as Superintendent of Army nurses.
2. While in Italy, Dorothea met with Pope Pius IX who was shocked at conditions the two of them found in a Roman mental asylum.

"Never be within doors when you can rightly be without."

> Charlotte Maria Shaw Mason (1842-1923) was a British educator, lecturer and reformer at the turn of the 20th century. She proposed to base children's education on a wide liberal curriculum. The 'Charlotte Mason Method' is based on her firm belief that a child is a person, and that we must educate the 'whole' person, not just the mind. "Education is an Atmosphere, a Discipline, a Life"—her theory is three-pronged. Charlotte had begun an educational revolution!

In a world becoming increasingly oriented to machines and data, the Charlotte Mason method is the only educational style that affirms each child's humanity. There are seven characteristics to the Charlotte Mason theory: Habits, Style of lessons, Living Books, Narration, Dictation, Art and Music study, and lastly, Nature study.

When Charlotte talked about 'Living Books' she was not referring to classroom textbooks crammed full of dry facts and information. Living books should be written by one author who is enthusiastic about his subject and shares that in a book.

Children gain their knowledge through their own efforts with living books. They discover facts and information clothed in literary language, narrating their learning either orally or in writing. Their thinking is personal, follows a train of thought, and isn't stunted by an offered page of multiple-choice questions.

Children educate themselves by narrating from the author's words. Charlotte believed true education is self-education, and her method created that ability. With living books, children are motivated by a curiosity, a love of learning rather than stimulated by prizes, competition and grades. It helps retain the child's natural curiosity. Children apply their minds in the morning to learning lessons. Afternoons are about recreation, especially in the out-of-doors- running, climbing and yelling. I believe adults can learn from this method, as well.

DID YOU KNOW?

1. The educational principles she developed in 19th century England are still used today.
2. Charlotte was the first person to recognize the educational opportunities of *Scouting*—which led to the formation of the *Scouting* movement.

An early 19th century British fossil collector, amateur paleontologist and artist, Elizabeth Philpot (1780-1857) gathered fossils from Lyme Regis' cliffs in Dorset on the southern coast of England. She is well known today for her collaboration and close friendship with the fossil hunter Mary Anning. Renowned in ecological circles for her fossil fish expertise as well as her extensive collection of specimens, Elizabeth was often consulted by leading geologists and paleontologists of the time, including swiss scientist Louis Agassiz.

Born in 1780, Elizabeth moved to Lyme Regis around 1805 when her London solicitor brother, John, rented a house in Silver Street for his four sisters. At Morley Cottage the sisters became heavily involved in fossil collecting. As the Philpots' collection grew, it became known within the geological community.

One familiar visitor was William Buckland (1784-1856), Reader in Geology at Oxford. Since Buckland's student days, he had often spent vacations around Lyme. Apparently he examined the Philpot collection regularly. His earliest published reference to the Misses Philpots is in his 1829 paper on the pterosaur found at Lyme Regis by Mary Anning.

In 1826, Mary Anning—another Lyme resident and dear friend of the Philpots—discovered a chamber holding dried ink within a belemnite fossil. She showed it to her friend Elizabeth Philpot. Elizabeth was able to revivify the ink by mixing it with water and used it to illustrate some of her own ichthyosaur fossils. Other local artists were soon doing the same as more such fossilized ink chambers were discovered.

DID YOU KNOW?

1. Elizabeth's collection contains around four hundred fossils, mostly from Lyme Regis, including more than forty types of specimens: a remarkable total for any collector.

2. Her collection along with her letters are now in Oxford University Museum of Natural History. You and I can actually wander through her early 19th century discoveries.

Dorothy Noel 'Dorf' Bonarjee (1894-1983) was an Anglicized Indian poet, artist, lawyer and mother. She was Indian by birth, English by upbringing, French by marriage and Welsh at heart. The perpetual outsider, she was the first woman and first non-European to win acclaim in Wales as a bard and went on to become the first woman to get a law degree from the University College of London. Despite racial prejudice, she was a trailblazer at Eisteddfod College (and UCL) and now has the distinction of a place in the Dictionary of Welsh Biography—the only person of Indian origin among nearly five thousand entries. An active supporter of women's right to vote, Dorothy deserves recognition for overcoming racial and gender issues.

I Having a mother who was a strong advocate of women's education, Dorothy had the rare privilege of getting an education that was as good as her brothers. Coming from an upper-caste Bengali brahmin family, she was sent to London (1904) along with her brothers at age ten for schooling.

Finding London "too snobbish", Dorothy and her older brother opted for the University College of Wales in *Aberystwyth*, which had a progressive reputation of welcoming "all religious persuasions and cultural backgrounds." The college also had an impressive record of gender equality.

Her popularity among students and faculty was evident when Dorothy was enthusiastically awarded the coveted "hand-carved oak chair" at the college's annual *Eisteddfod*. Dorothy, the first woman to earn an internal law degree (internal meaning that while women pursued their studies, they could not formally enter the legal profession) from UCL Faculty of Laws in 1917, doing so when other universities did not even admit women to earn degrees.

DID YOU KNOW?

1. The Eisteddfod pageant is a celebration of music and competition of poetry in the traditional Welsh style still held today.
2. As a suffragist, Dorothy signed the Indian Women's Franchise Address—which called for women's right to vote while Colonial India remained under British rule.

Brazil's foremost female conductor, Francisca Edwiges Neves Gonzaga (1847-1935) was better known as Chinquinha. A pianist, composer, abolitionist, suffragist and mother of three, she did many things considered scandalous in 19th century Brazil. Her music was extremely popular with Brazilians, she introduced "choro" music to them.

Chinquinha's mother was the daughter of a slave, her father a white nobleman. Mixed marriages were taboo at the time, nonetheless her father wanted her educated to become a lady. She learned to read, write, play piano and do mathematics. Music became her most important reason for living. By eleven, Chinquinha had composed her first musical song for a Christmas celebration.

Nineteenth century women in Brazil were most often seen as slaves, any girl defying her parents was sent to a convent or a reformatory. Marriages were arranged. At sixteen years old, against her wishes, Chinquinha was married to an official of the Imperial Navy. It's no surprise she was unable to withstand the trials of life raising a family on a ship where she was psychologically and physically abused. Humiliation was standard fare for the young and talented wife. When her husband made her choose between music and him, Chinquinha left and requested a divorce. She was only allowed to take her eldest son with her. Because of the scandal, her father declared her dead and she was shunned by her family and community.

Determined to pursue a musical career, which was also scandalous for a Brazilian woman at the time, her compositional debut of "Atraente" in 1881 was wildly successful. Her arrangement combined different musical styles of ragtime, polka, waltz and Afro-Brazilian rhythms and became known as "Choro".

By the end of her incredible career, Chinquinha had composed music for seventy-seven operettas and had over two thousand compositions of tangos, waltzes, mazurkas, polkas, Fado, Choros and serenades.

Her life example helped to demolish societal walls and empowered women personally and professionally. I hold great respect for Chinquinha's ability to overcome marital abuse and ignore societal norms.

DID YOU KNOW?

1. There is a sculpture in *Rio de Janeiro's Passeio Publico* honoring Chinquinha.
2. She founded the Brazilian Society of Theatre Authors which put in place copyright protections for Brazilian artists.
3. Grave's Disease is an immune disorder that causes hypothyroidism, an overproduction of thyroid hormones affecting nearly every organ in your body.

"Talent works, genius creates."

Clara Josephine Wieck Schumann (1819–1896), was a talented German pianist, composer, piano teacher and mother of eight children. As a child prodigy, she practiced violin, piano, singing, music theory, harmony, composition, and counterpoint daily. She was one of the first pianists to perform from memory, becoming one of the leading European virtuosos. Her piano playing has been described as "feisty and passionate." Schumann's work has been marginalized by people claiming her husband, Robert, was the *real* composer. Nonetheless, Schumann's pieces were more popular than her husband's; she was also the bread winner of the household. You can listen to this extraordinary woman's compositions on the internet.

She met Robert Schumann when he came to study with her father in 1830. Despite strong objections from her family, she married Schumann in 1840 and they had eight children between 1841 and 1854—during which time she toured and continued to compose. Slowly Clara watched her sensitive husband lose his mind. The couple at first lived in Leipzig, where both taught at the University. The couple performed in Germany, Russia, Vienna and the Netherlands. But by 1854, Robert was institutionalized.

Clara wrote some sixty-six pieces over the course of her lifetime, but the focus of her career was performing and touring. Setting new standards of performance that we use to this day, she played her recitals and concertos from memory. Over the years, Clara Schumann gave 238 concerts with violin titan Joseph Joachim throughout Germany and England, during which they became especially celebrated for their performances of Beethoven's violin sonatas.

Clara composed little in the years following Robert's death in 1856, leaving us with just twenty-three published works. After briefly returning to Berlin in 1873, she took a teaching post at the *Frankfurt Hoch Konservatorium* in 1878. She continued to perform until 1891.

DID YOU KNOW?

1. Clara was the 19th century's most important female pianist.

1. She was the first piano teacher and only woman on staff at *Dr. Hoch's Konservatorium*.

Boann (Boinn) is the Celtic Goddess of water, fertility, poetry, inspiration, creativity and knowledge. She is associated with the Boyne, a river in Northeast Ireland, and its source, the Well of Segais. Folklore tells us that Boann walked counterclockwise around some stones, causing water underneath the earth to spring up with great force and rush down to the sea. Salmon of wisdom swim in the waters of the hidden pool, and sacred hazelnut trees—whose nuts impart knowledge when eaten—have grown up around the pool. She is honored mid-winter at Imbolc, the February 1st festival that marks the beginning of spring. Her colors are green, blue, aqua and silver. Her crystal is amethyst.

Cows are sacred and associated with water in many ancient cultures. Milk and water were the substances of life flowing from Boann's breast. The Milky Way is also called the Way of the White Cow. Boann either becomes or rules over the river of heaven.

Boann lives at *Brug na Boinne,* an ancient Gaelic name for the site known since the 14th century as *Newgrange.* It has been carbon dated to around 3000 BCE, making it 1000 years older than Stonehenge and five hundred years older than the Egyptian pyramids. Amazing, yes? The ancient Gaelic site offers great hospitality to spiritual travelers. It was a mysterious structure full of passageways and chambers, some of which housed Fairy-folk. Boann rules poetry and writing in general. It is said She gave birth to three strains of music: lamentation, joy, and sleep.

In the same way that flowing waters clear debris in its path, Boann clears your mind of mental chaos and negativity. Our unique gift from Her is that we must learn to experience through *all* of what we are, each of our five senses being open. Only then can life flow through us fully.

DID YOU KNOW?

1. Some scholars associate Boann with the heavens.
2. The Dindesenchas, ancient Irish writings, tell of Boann creating the river Boyne.

"Patriotism is not enough. I must have no hatred or bitterness towards anyone."

> Executed by a German firing squad in Brussels, pioneering British nurse Edith Louisa Cavell (1865-1915) needs remembering for her fearlessness, selfless acts of healing and *maitri* –the Sanskrit word for loving-kindness and clear-seeing. Simply a "nurse who tried to do her duty," most people outside of Britain today have never heard of Edith. Credited with saving the lives of both Allied and Nazi soldiers without bias, she also helped over two hundred Allied soldiers escape from German-occupied Belgium.

Edith became a nurse at thirty, traveling the countryside as she treated patients in their own homes. In 1907, Dr. Antoine Depage recruited her as "matron" of a newly founded nursing school in Brussels. By 1910, she was publishing a professional journal, *L'infirmiere.* Within twelve months, Edith was training nurses for three different hospitals, twenty-four schools and thirteen Belgium kindergartens. Wow.

When the German occupation of Belgium began, Edith started sheltering and channeling British soldiers to the neutral Netherlands. Wounded soldiers as well as British and French citizens were hidden, given false papers and money, then provided guides to the Dutch border. Edith's outspokenness brought suspicion down on her by German authorities.

Arrested on August 3, 1915, she was charged with harboring Allied soldiers. Edith was held in custody at Saint-Gilles prison for ten weeks, the last two of which were in solitary confinement. Admitting to her guilt of funneling both soldiers and civilians of military age out of Belgium, she was prosecuted and found guilty of treason—which makes no sense. Edith was not a German citizen.

Sentenced to death, world governments pleaded for her pardon. Sadly, Edith was executed October 12, 1915. Outrage at her execution was immediate, swaying neutral countries—including the U.S.—to join the war.

DID YOU KNOW?

1. Edith was recognized in Belgium as a pioneer of modern nursing.
2. Her quote is inscribed on a memorial to her in Trafalgar Square in London.

"Everybody's business is nobody's business, and nobody's business is my business."

Clarissa Harlowe Barton (1821-1912), better known as Clara, was not only founder and first president of the American Red Cross, but also an educator, humanitarian, author, patent clerk and a pioneering nurse. Risking her life to supply and support fighting soldiers on Civil War battlefields, she is one of the most honored women in America's history. Clara overcame many of society's inequalities while taking abuse and slander from men.

Painfully shy as a child, Clara received her teaching certificate at age seventeen and began teaching the following year. She first founded a school for mill workers' children, and then moved on to Bordentown, New Jersey, where she established the first free school in 1852. When Clara discovered the schoolboard hired a man to take over running the school at twice the salary she was being paid to do the same work, she left—determined to never work for less money than a man.

Hired as a recording clerk in the US Patent Office (1854), Clara was the first woman ever appointed to that post. When government higher-ups heard of her position and salary, they quickly reduced her to a copyist with lower pay. Again she left, but returned after President Lincoln was elected. With the Civil War breaking out in 1861, Clara felt her skills would be needed there. Leaving her position at the Patent Office, she began bringing supplies to Union soldiers, which started a life-long career helping people during times of disaster and need.

Receiving official permission to transport supplies to battlefields in1862, the "angel of the battlefields" began tending to the wounded. Officially named head nurse of General Butler's units (1864) would eventually lead her to start the American Association of the Red Cross in 1881. With the help of Frances Gage, she prepared slaves for living life freely. Clara also helped locate missing soldiers and mark graves.

DID YOU KNOW?

1. After the Civil War ended, Clara ran the Office of Missing Soldiers in Washington D.C. helping to locate over 22,000 missing men.
2. The building where the office was located is now the Clara Barton's Missing Soldiers Office Museum at 437 ½ Seventh Street Northwest, Washington, D.C.

A pioneering U.S. cryptologist, Elizebeth Smith Friedman (1892-1980) was also a writer, mother, Shakespeare enthusiast and America's first female cryptanalyst(codebreaker). A hidden figure until recent years, books and documentaries are now making people aware of her great accomplishments. Virtually unknown, Elizebeth was a codebreaker employed by the U.S. government during both World Wars. She alone uncovered a Nazi spy ring (1943) operating in South America—J. Edgar Hoover (FBI) taking full credit for her work. (Why am I not surprised?)

After graduating college (1915), Elizebeth's keen linguistic skills caught the attention of George Fabyan, his Riverbank Laboratories honed Elizebeth's cryptology competence. It was there she met William Friedman, whom she would marry in 1917. Elizebeth had an intuitive skill that quickly recognized patterns while her husband's skill was interpreting them. Radio transmission during WWI meant that those skills were especially needed as America did not have a codebreaking unit as such.

Fabyan volunteered the services of the Riverbank team. After the war, the Friedmans were employed by the U.S. government. Elizebeth was in charge of a cryptanalytic unit of the U.S. Guard monitoring smuggling rings, resulting in 650 prosecutions. She testified as an expert witness in thirty-three cases.

During WWII, Elizebeth was transferred to a Navy unit which did not allow civilians to be in charge of a unit. Frustrated by her situation and irritated at the FBI's sloppiness, she felt taken advantage of by a system that demanded her help but treated her in a sexist manner. Fabyan observed, "She was always fixing messes men had created or solving problems they could not solve." Nonetheless, Elizebeth decrypted German messages that exposed an entire spy ring in South America headed by Johannes Siegfried Becker.

DID YOU KNOW?

1. She was responsible for breaking the codes of narcotics and alcohol runners during Prohibition, incriminating mob-run rings.
2. Once the South American spy ring was pulverized, Argentina, Chile, and Bolivia sided with the Allies—all due to Elizebeth's diligence.

" Of course I talk to myself. I like a good speaker, and I appreciate an intelligent audience."

Dorothy Parker (1893-1967) was a journalist, prolific critic, screenwriter and civil rights activist. She was most famous for her scathing wit, savage put-downs and drinking Scotch. (I wish I could have known "Dottie" Parker—what fun conversations we'd have had!)

Despite never receiving a high school diploma, by twenty-one Dottie had sold her first poem to *Vanity Fair*. In the 1920s, Parker came to fame writing book reviews, poetry and short fiction for a fledgling magazine, *The New Yorker*. When the *New Yorker* debuted in 1925, Parker was listed on its editorial board.

Over the years, she contributed poetry, fiction and book reviews as the "Constant Reader." During the 1920s, Parker traveled to Europe several times. Despite having one of the most successful writing careers of any woman of her time, Parker suffered from depression, severe self-criticism and alcoholism. Nonetheless, she persisted.

In 1934, Parker married Alan Campbell, an actor and writer, in New Mexico; the couple relocated to Los Angeles and became a highly paid screenwriting team. At the height of their career, they were blacklisted by Hollywood because they were named in the pamphlet *Red Channels,* a right-wing compilation of Communist sympathizers. Having been active in the political scene since the *Nicola Sacco Bartolomeo Vanzetti* trials, Parker championed numerous causes from unionizing to civil rights. Her FBI file contained over one thousand pages. Despite no affiliation with the Communist party and no credible evidence, she was called before the notorious McCarthy-era House on Un-American Activities committee in 1955.

DID YOU KNOW?

1. A firm believer in civil rights, she bequeathed her literary estate to Dr. Martin Luther King, Jr.
2. When he was assassinated some months later, the estate was turned over to the NAACP.

"The best therapist has fur and four legs."

An Australian social reformer, politician and mother of five, Edith Dircksey Brown Cowan OBE (1861-1932) was a women's activist who worked for the rights and welfare of both women and children. She is best known as the first Australian to serve as a member of Parliament. A founding member of the Karrakatta Club, Edith was well known for her pragmatism, strong will, her skill, intellect, untiring energy and indomitable courage. Edith was the first woman to be elected to a British legislature anywhere in the world.

Edith's remarkable ability to overcome obstacles was born of personal tragedy. She lost her mother at age six, was separated from her siblings and sent to a boarding school in Perth. At age sixteen, her father was charged with the murder of his second wife and sentenced to hang. Good god—talk about trauma.

She watched her new husband, James Cowan, by studying the sad cases that walked through his courtroom daily. She recognized the injustices created by poverty and lack of education, especially for girls and women and was determined to do more. Edith raised her four daughters to be autonomous and capable, emphasizing economic independence and their higher education.

She became a founding member of the Karrakatta Club in 1894. The Club's name became synonymous with women's suffrage in Western Australia. For forty years she championed social-reform, fought against domestic-violence, drunkenness and women's legal disadvantage. Edith also spoke out about sexual diseases, prostitution, contraception, illegitimacy and sex crimes long before it was polite to do so.

Edith believed in enlightened and rational self-control and self-determination, arguing the *need* for women in public life rather than just their right to it. She ran for a Parliamentary seat of West Perth (1921) and won, refusing to toe the party line by amending legislation that would benefit women and children.

Did you know?

1. Edith was appointed an officer of the Order of the British Empire in 1920.
2. Her likeness adorns Australia's 50 dollar note.

DAME ETHYL MARY SMYTH DBE

"I feel I must fight for [my music], because I want women to turn their minds to big and difficult jobs; not just to go on hugging the shore, afraid to put out to sea."

A British composer, Dame Ethyl Mary Smyth DBE (1858-1944) was a writer and suffragette. Her compositions include songs, piano works, chamber music, orchestral works, operas and choral works. She wrote no less than six operas. Despite being marginalized by mainstream male composers, Dame Ethel was the first female composer to be granted "damehood".

Ethyl's *Mass in D* (1893) brought notoriety her way. *The Wreckers* (1906), her best-known work, was the most praised English opera of its time. She became interested in the Women's Social and Political Union (Suffragette movement) as a result of her friendship with Emmeline Pankhurst. Suspending most of her musical activities for two years, she devoted her energies to assisting and promoting the Suffragettes.

In 1912, following a large-scale Suffragette protest, Ethel was sentenced to three months in Holloway prison for smashing the window of an anti-suffrage politician's office. Her uncompromising spirit and boundless energy led her to be the eminent motivator in the women's movement. When she wrote "The March of the Women", it became a battle song sung by suffragettes throughout London and elsewhere.

A remarkable woman—Ethel Smyth even trained as a radiographer during WWI and was attached to the XIIIth Division of the French Army at a large military hospital in Vichy. It was then that she commenced writing her memoires; it was impossible to compose music under the wartime conditions, she said. She often wrote of the difficulty of getting works by female composers published and performed.

DID YOU KNOW?

1. Ethyl turned to writing as her hearing faded.
2. An adoring dog lover, sheepdogs were her favorite.
3. Ethyl was made a Dame Commander of the Order of the British Empire in 1922.

> The flame-haired Goddess, Brigid, comes to us from Ireland. A Goddess of wisdom and healing, She oversees poetry, blacksmithing and domesticated animals. Her name means "power, strength vigor and virtue." She is known as the "exalted one." Another Goddess full of contradictions—exactly as you and me—She was not only the Goddess of healing, fertility, and motherhood, but fire and passion, serenity and water as well. When Brigid was not protecting newborn babes and their mothers, she inspired poets and writers.

Many legends are told of strangers who came to Brigid seeking inspiration and asking for Her blessings. She freely heals all who are pure of heart and have good intentions, and those who are clever and cunning. For people who lack those virtues, Her blessing comes with a caveat—a lesson that teaches them what they really need in order to become a better person.

Serving as the Water Goddess, She controlled both rivers and wells. Her most famous wells are "Brigid's Well in Kildare" and "Brigid's Well in County Clare." The well in Kildare is the most renowned of the wells, its water is said to heal any wound or illness. Brigid's cross is Her symbol, usually made of grass or rushes. The geometric cross is still used today, found hanging above doorways of homes as well as businesses. The cross has different three-armed variations.

Brigid's holiday is *Imbolc* (the beginning of Spring), with celebrations taking place in Ireland on February 1st. Offerings of food and coins are brought to rivers, canals or wells. People come to celebrate and ask for protection for their household, children and livestock. Requests for inspiration are also popular, especially for poets and writers like me.

DID YOU KNOW?

1. Brigid is patroness of the hearth.
2. She often appears with fiery hair and cloaked in sunbeams.

Wane Roonseraw (c. 1754-1838) also known as Edy (Edie) Turner, was chief of the Nottoway people of Virginia in the eighteenth and nineteenth centuries. She not only owned a prosperous farm but was fluent in English and Nottoway. A Renaissance woman, Wane was active as an advocate for and foster mother of Nottoway children, successfully petitioning white trustees to return four children to the reservation. One of the last three speakers of the Nottoway language, she did her best to preserve it before it became extinct around 1900. An astute businesswoman, Wane taught Nottoway children their tribal traditions and also how to exist in a white-dominated society.

Wane's level of self-sufficiency was considerable taking in account the fact she was a woman of her time and place. Her compassion for *Nottoway* children made her an exceptional figure. At the age of seventy-six, she still looked after two children in her home as she led the struggle to keep children on the reservation. Highly intelligent and a skilled conversationalist, she dictated to a William and Mary professor (dispatched by Thomas Jefferson) over two-hundred words from the Nottoway language. It was later determined that the language was from Iroquoian language stock (parental language).

Strong willed though she was, Wane faced many disturbing issues — such as providing safe haven for Nottoway orphans. She also fought for treaty rights to maintain the children's stay on the reservation, not to serve as apprentices or indentured servants to Caucasian planters in nearby communities of Southampton County.

As a social activist, politician and businesswoman, Wane was a progressive thinker. Her fighting Iroquoian spirit lives on in the twenty-first century Nottoway people. They believe it is their right and duty to speak the truth, to tell of their rich, historical past, present and future.

DID YOU KNOW?

1. Today, only about fifteen acres of tribal land are owned by a direct descendant of the Nottoway tribe. How sad is that?
2. Wane was so ahead of her time that when she married William Green, she retained her last name. Very cool, especially in the eighteenth century.

The United States first female dean, Edith Abbot (1876-1957) was appointed in 1924 at the University of Chicago. An educator, author, economist, statistician, and prominent activist in social reform, she believed humanitarianism was an essential part of education. In charge of graduate level social work studies, Edith fought for and achieved her curriculum changes to social reform and was then elected dean of the graduate school (School of Social Service Administration). A leading immigration expert, she also championed reforms to end the exploitation of immigrants.

Edith was fortunate to have an abolitionist mother who was also a leader of women's suffrage, her father was the first Lieutenant Governor of Nebraska. She grew up with civic minded parents who were actively involved in public welfare and the social problems of the state.

Edith started her teaching career in her hometown of Grand Island, Nebraska, while still studying at the University in Lincoln. She then began her studies at the University of Chicago where she earned her Ph.D. in economics (1906).

Returning from England, Edith ended up back in Chicago residing at Jane Addams' Hull House. She was working with Sophonisba Breckinridge, making waves to reform Chicago's social welfare issues. Hired again at the University in 1920, Edith became a professor at the Graduate School of Social Service Administration, then was elected dean in 1924. She was called upon to study many social issues plaguing Chicago. Edith published ground-breaking books on immigration, the tenements and social welfare. She also co-founded, and was longtime editor, of the *Social Service Review*—a celebrated publication (1927).

Did you know?

1. In 1950, Edith was appointed a single case on the California Supreme Court, becoming the first woman to sit on the state's highest court.
2. Edith helped establish the Cook County Bureau of Public Welfare and assisted in designing the Social Security Act (1935).

"The desire for liberty has also made itself felt as struggle against domestic tyranny or arbitrary rule."

Emily Green Balch (1867-1961) was an American economist, sociologist, teacher, writer, political scientist and pacifist. During and after WWI, Emily became a leader of the women's peace movement. She received the Nobel Prize for Peace in 1946 (jointly with John Mott). Emily was well known for her sympathetic and complete study of Slavic immigrants in the U.S. She also co-founded the Women's International League for Peace and Freedom, setting up and organizing the WILPF's international office in Geneva.

After graduating with honors from Bryn Mawr College (1889), Emily pursued further studies in Paris, Berlin, the University of Chicago and was then trained in social work. Her interest in social settlements (community centers) grew and she helped found Denison House in 1892, the first settlement house in Boston. Modeled on Jane Addams' Hull House in Chicago, Denison House provided the poor and largely immigrant residents of the South End with educational and recreational activities and facilities, including a library and clinic. They also provided emergency programs when times grew tough.

Emily then began her teaching career at Wellesley College in 1896, becoming a full Professor of Political Economy, and of Political and Social Science in 1913, and later dean. She remained there for twenty-two years. When WWI broke out, there was a major shift in Emily's career. A pacifist since the Spanish-American War, she began focusing all her energies on world peace. Taking a leave of absence from teaching, Emily attended the International Congress of Women in the Netherlands.

Returning home, she worked against the draft, defended the rights of conscientious objectors, the foreign born and unsuccessfully campaigned for the U.S. to remain neutral. Her anti-war views cost Emily her career at Wellesley. She went on to promote lasting peace by attacking the underlying social, economic and political conditions that cause conflict to manifest itself.

DID YOU KNOW?

1. Emily was a leader of the Women's International League for Peace and Freedom based in Switzerland.
2. She donated her share of her Nobel Prize winnings to the WILPF. (She put her money where her mouth was; I admire that greatly.)

"It's not true that life is one damn thing after another; it's one damn thing over and over."

An American poet and playwright, Edna St. Vincent Millay (1892-1950) won the Pulitzer prize in 1923. One of the most respected poets of the twentieth century, she was best known for captivating readings and feminist views.

In 1912, at the suggestion of her mother, Edna entered her poem "Renascence" into The Lyric Year's poetry contest. She won fourth place and publication in the anthology. This brought her immediate acclaim and a scholarship to Vassar where she continued to write poetry. In 1917, the year of her graduation, Edna published her first book, *Renascence and Other Poems*.

After graduation, Edna moved to New York City's Greenwich Village. She published poems in the *Forum*, *Vanity Fair* and others. She wrote short stories and satire under the pen name, Nancy Boyd. Her popularity as a poet had at least as much to do with her persona. She was known for her gripping readings and performances, her progressive politics and her honest portrayal of both hetero and homosexuality. Above all, her embodiment and description of new kinds of female experience and expression were spellbinding.

Her popularity grew, and she went on to win the Pulitzer Prize in 1923 for her fourth book, "The Ballad of the Harp Weaver". That same year, St. Vincent Millay married Eugen Boissevain, a Dutch businessman and self-proclaimed feminist. Unusual at the time, her husband gave up his career to manage St. Vincent Millay's. He set up the readings and public appearances she was so famous for and took primary care of domestic responsibilities. How many men out there are feminists like Eugen Boissevain? I hope many.

DID YOU KNOW?

1. She was the first woman to earn a Pulitzer Prize for poetry.
2. Edna inspired a generation of women with her subversive poetry and persona.

"Do what you feel in your heart to be right- for you'll be criticized anyway. You'll be damned if you do, and damned if you don't."

An American political figure, Anna Eleanor Roosevelt (1884-1962) was also an activist, diplomat and mother of six (one dying in infancy). She fought for expanded roles for women in the workplace, African Americans' and Asian Americans' civil rights and the equitable treatment of WWII refugees. Beloved by many, she was one of the most revered women of her generation. She is one of my personal heroines.

Shy and awkward as a child, Eleanor grew into a woman with great sensitivity to the underprivileged of all races, creeds and nations. Marrying her handsome distant cousin, Franklin in 1905, she became his political helpmate after they moved to Albany where he was serving in the State Senate.

With FDR stricken with polio in 1921, Eleanor not only attended to him devotedly, but became active in the State Democratic Committee to keep his interest alive. She became his eyes and ears, a trusted and tireless friend/reporter. Arriving in the White House in 1933, Eleanor understood social conditions better than any of her predecessors, thus transforming the role of First Lady. She broke precedent by holding news conferences herself and traveled to all parts of the country giving lectures and radio broadcasts.

Eleanor expressed her opinions candidly in a newspaper column entitled *My Day*. A target for political enemies, she was able to endear herself to many by her integrity, graciousness, and sincerity of purpose. Friends, heads of state and servicemen abroad held Eleanor in high esteem because of her truthfulness and loyalty. Even after the President's death in 1945, she continued her service as an American spokeswoman in the United Nations. Eleanor kept a vigorous pace until around 1962.

DID YOU KNOW?

1. She was the longest serving First Lady throughout her husband FDR's four terms of presidency.
2. At the time of her death, Eleanor was regarded as "one of the most esteemed women of the world."

"The Dancer believes that his art has something to say which cannot be expressed in words or in any other way than by dancing."

> A pioneer in American modern dance, Doris Humphrey (1895-1958) was an innovator in technique, choreography and theory of dance movement. She was a talented dancer authoring *The Art of Making Dances* which remains an important document for choreographers and dancers even today. Doris founded the Julliard School of Dance in 1955, personally choreographing ninety-seven dances during her career.

Despite her short height of 5'3", Doris Batcheller Humphrey was an avid talented dancer. After graduating high school in 1917, she helped support her family by teaching dance for four years. She joined the Denishawn Dance School and Company in Los Angeles. Doris soon became a leading soloist, by 1920 she was experimenting with choreography.

After a two-year tour of Asia, Doris and fellow Denishawn dancer Charles Weidman directed the Denishawn House in New York City until 1928. The two dancers left to form the Humphrey-Weidman School and Company, which was active until 1944. During the next four years, they created more than forty dances. Doris spent much time studying the theory of movement developing her own concepts.

Most of her choreography is based on the theory of *fall and recovery*—or as she put it, the "arc between two deaths." This technique utilized the rhythm of inhale and exhale to emphasize the momentum of a movement. Swing, suspensions, leaps, turns—all these gave the simplest steps moments of off-balance and eventual stability.

Doris retired in 1944 because of an arthritic hip, but as artistic director for José Limón's company, she choreographed a number of successful pieces. Extremely influential as a teacher, she conducted classes not only at her own school but also at Bennington College in Vermont (from 1934) and hosted various summer workshops.

Did you know?

1. Doris developed a *movement* vocabulary based on rhythms.
2. Middlesex University in the UK is a center for *Humphrey* training.

Changing Woman (Asdzaa Nadleehe)

> The most respected Goddess of the Navajo people, Changing Woman represents all the changes of life and each season. She is both nurturing and kind-hearted, their treasured personification of earth, sky, abundance, fertility, vegetation and ideal womanhood.

The Navajo are a matrilineal society, which means the owners of land are the women. The daughters receive the land from their mothers. When the Navajo introduce themselves, they initially name their mother's clan. Stories handed down in their sacred ceremonies speak of how women were revered. Sadly, in today's culture, rape and violence against women are common and we find very few female council delegates.

The legend of Changing Woman tells us She was born of First Man and First Woman. Sprouting from a medicine bundle, She is meant to become the inner form of the earth. Growing from infancy to puberty in four days, you can understand where Her name comes from. Dressed in jewels of abalone, turquoise and white shells for Her "first puberty ceremony", She is blessed with pollen from the dawn and twilight, jewels and fabrics, symbolizing Her authority over these objects. She runs toward the dawn and returns, repeating this each night of the four-day ceremony. As she runs, songs are sung—the same songs sung today at puberty ceremonies.

Changing Woman eventually meets a young Sun God. Twins are born and named Monster Slayer and Born for Water. She eventually leaves Her home, heading toward the Pacific Ocean. Her loneliness triggers Her to create the Navajo people from skin rubbed from Her body. Changing Woman grows old during winter months and is a young woman again in the spring, demonstrating Her qualities of strength, endurance and creativity. You and I can learn much from Her willingness to change and renew Herself.

Did you know?

1. All ceremonies of the Navajo must include a song dedicated to Changing Woman.
2. In the American Southwest, She is also known as Whiteshell Woman.

"The best protection any woman can have... is courage."

Elizabeth Cady Stanton (1815-1902) was an author, lecturer, abolitionist, human rights activist and one of the first leaders of the woman's rights movement. She was also the mother to seven children. At the Seneca Falls Convention in 1848, Elizabeth drafted the first organized demands for women's suffrage in the United States. That convention launched the U.S. women's suffrage movement.

Coming from a privileged background, she decided early in life to fight for women's equal rights. Elizabeth burned with an inner passion that hoped to remedy laws unjust to women. In 1851, she met Susan B. Anthony. Together, they formed a decades-long partnership that was crucial to the development of women's rights. They even started a newspaper, *The Revolution*, in 1868 that advocated women's rights.

Elizabeth helped write the Declaration of Sentiments, a document modeled after the Declaration of Independence that laid out what the rights of American women should be—namely, equality of all men and women; both genders with "unalienable rights to life, liberty and the pursuit of happiness". The Declaration of Sentiments highlighted how men oppressed women— as follows:

- preventing women from owning land or earning wages.
- preventing women from voting.
- compelling women to submit to laws created without their representation.
- giving men authority in divorce and child custody proceedings and decisions.
- preventing women from gaining a college education.
- preventing women from participating in most public church affairs.
- subjecting women to a different moral code than men.
- aiming to make women dependent and submissive to men.

DID YOU KNOW?

1. In the early 1880s, Elizabeth co-authored the first three volumes of *The History of Woman Suffrage*.
2. In 1895, she and a committee of women published *The Woman's Bible* to point out the Bible's bias towards women and challenge its stance that women should be submissive to men. Extraordinary women, indeed!

German educator and resistance fighter against Nazism, Elisabeth Abegg (1882-1974) was one of the first German women to receive a university education. Criticizing Hitler, Elisabeth was forced to retire from teaching history and then proceeded to build a rescue network for refugees. She personally helped shelter around eighty Jews during the Holocaust. She also supplied food, funds and forged papers for Jewish friends, former students and complete strangers.

Luise Wilhemine Elisabeth Abegg was born in Strasbourg (Germany). Studying history, classical philology and Romantic studies, she received a doctorate from Leipzig University in 1916. Two years later she moved to Berlin to begin teaching. At the same time, Elisabeth became associated with the Quakers and began providing food and medical assistance to Germans following the 1918 signing of the WWI Armistice.

Elisabeth's career at the prestigious *Luisenschule* all-girls' school began to suffer as Hitler's rise to power increased. She openly criticized the Nazi regime and refused to fly the swastika. By 1933, she was transferred to another school because of her outspoken criticism and conflicts with the new Nazi-appointed headmaster.

In 1940, Elisabeth was denied the right to teach and was questioned by the Gestapo. Three years later, she had built a rescue network of Quaker friends and former students. Elisabeth turned her 3 1/2 room apartment, where she cared for her disabled sister and eighty-six-year-old mother, into a temporary shelter and assembly point for Jews who had gone underground.

Despite Nazi neighbors who kept vigil, Elisabeth provided meals, financial aid and clothing to refugees. She also forged IDs and other papers. Spending all of her savings and selling her jewelry, Elisabeth helped some of the most endangered exiles to flee to Switzerland. How many of us would have made the same kind of personal sacrifice?

DID YOU KNOW?

1. Her activities, lying to the Gestapo and helping Jewish refugees, were never discovered.
2. Elisabeth was awarded the "Order of Merit of the Republic of Germany" in 1957.

Etheldred Benett (1776-1845) was an English geologist. Credited as the "First Female Geologist", she started studying and collecting fossils in South West England about 1810. Quite different from Mary Anning who earned her living excavating and selling her finds, Ethelred was able to devote her life to the Earth Sciences because her family was well-connected and were independently wealthy.

Ethelred's contributions to geology lie in four areas. First, she ordered the first recorded measured section of the Upper Chicksgrove Quarry, Tisbury in Wiltshire. Signed by her in 1815, the papers were donated to the Geological Society of London Library. Second, Ethelred was recognized as an expert concerning Wilshire's fossil mollusks and sponges, as attested to by her contributions to Sowerby's publication. Third, the Czar of Russia gave her a medal for her contribution to his fossil collection—because he thought she was a man!

Finally, Ethelred pushed forward the boundaries of biostratigraphy. She published an authoritative volume in 1831, *Organic Remains of the County of Wiltshire* with extensive drawings, which she herself produced. When she died, her substantial collection of thousands of labeled Jurassic and Cretaceous fossils was so valuable a resource that most of it was purchased by former Englishman Thomas Wilson of Newark, Delaware and shipped to America.

Ethelred was a vanguard of paleontology and biostratigraphy at a time when many people still believed fossils were deposited from catastrophic religious acts such as Noah's flood and that scientific investigation should solely be done by men. (Thank goodness we've evolved beyond that kind of thinking.)

DID YOU KNOW?

1. Ethelred never married but instead devoted her life to her fossil collection until she died at the age of sixty-nine.
2. Scientists now believe she under-estimated the value of her discoveries and knowledge.

ELIZABETH BARRETT BROWNING

"Light tomorrow with today."

A Victorian poet, Elizabeth Barrett Browning (1806-1861) used her poetry to speak out against traditional Victorian roles for women. Because her British family had gained their wealth from Jamaican sugar plantations relying on slave labor, she spoke out against slavery and for social justice—particularly for Italy's struggle for independence. Elizabeth is best known for her *Sonnets from the Portuguese* (1850) which are considered the finest love poems ever written.

Elizabeth Barrett Browning, though born in England, was part creole. Educated at home, she began writing verse at age four. By the age of twelve, Elizabeth (called 'Ba' by family and close friends) had written her first epic poem. Something of a child prodigy, she was highly intelligent, dedicated and determined to become a poet. She could soon read in the modern languages of French, Italian and Portuguese.

Anonymously published by Elizabeth in 1826, *An Essay on Mind and Other Poems* was well received. Gaining attention for her work in the 1830s, she continued to live in her father's London home under his tyrannical rule. In 1840, both of her brothers died. Elizabeth became an emotional invalid and recluse, spending most of the next five years upstairs at her father's home.

Her 1844 volume, simply named *Poems,* made her one of the most popular writers in England. It is now considered an early feminist text. This volume gained the attention of Robert Browning and he wrote her a letter. Their romance was bitterly opposed by her father, Edward—who did not want any of his children to marry. But marry they did, eloping and settling in Florence, Italy. Her father never spoke to her again.

DID YOU KNOW?

1. Biographers now believe Elizabeth suffered from hypokalemic periodic paralysis—when potassium is trapped in muscle cells triggering weakness and paralysis.
2. She also endured chronic pain from a spinal injury due to a horse fall in her adolescence.

"When I first met Thea, we danced all night. I danced a hole through my stockings."

Edith Windsor (1929-2017) is best known as the lead plaintiff in the 2013 case of the United States v. Windsor. An LGBTQ rights activist and IBM technology manager, she was victorious as the court ruled to strike down the "Defense of Marriage Act". Her campaign led her to become an icon for LGBTQ community which she dearly loved. The "grand dame of gay rights" received many awards for her lifetime efforts.

Edith Windsor and Thea Spyer, partners for nearly a half century, were eventually legally married in Toronto in May of 2007. An announcement of their marriage was placed in the *New York Times.* But when Spyer died in 2009, the federal government left Edith with a $350,000.00 estate tax bill because they did not recognize her marriage. Had federal law recognized their marriage, Edith would have qualified for the unlimited spousal deduction, thereby paying no estate tax.

Filing a lawsuit against the federal government in 2010 in New York's southern District, she requested a refund because of "differential treatment compared to other married couples." In 2012, Judge Barbara Jones ruled DOMA unconstitutional, ordering the federal government to refund Windsor's money.

Hearing oral arguments of the case in March of 2013, the US Supreme Court affirmed the lower court's decision (in June) that Section 3 of DOMA was indeed, unconstitutional. When, in 2015 the Supreme Court declared same-sex marriage legal nationwide, President Obama stated, "It was a victory for families, and for the principle that all of us should be treated equally, regardless of who we are or who we love."

"I thought about Edie that day," he continued, "I thought about all the millions of quiet heroes across the decades whose countless small acts of courage slowly made an entire country realize that love is love — and who, in the process, made us all more free. They deserve our gratitude. And so does Edie."

DID YOU KNOW?

1. She was runner-up to Pope Francis in 2013 for *Time Magazine's* person of the year.
2. "Sometimes," President Obama said in 2015, "there are days like this when that slow, steady effort is rewarded with justice that arrives like a thunderbolt."

"It formed me, guided me, instructed me, helped me, and humiliated me," she said of her disability.

Famous for her "photographic documentation" of the Depression, Dorothea Margaretta Nutzhorn Lange (1895-1965) was an American photographer on a mission. Encouraging people to better understand themselves by looking closer at ourselves through photography was her lifelong dream. Dorothea was so good at it that, at one point, the U.S. Army impounded her photos of Japanese American internment camps. Holding them captive for twenty years, Dorothea was not even allowed access. Believing a photograph was "an act of love", she was an activist against poverty and injustice through her photographs. Dorothea wanted the world to see the reality of social and economic turmoil. She certainly accomplished that, and more.

Another gutsy woman, Dorothea had a tough life. Polio at age seven left her with a shrunken lower right leg along with a twisted, cramped foot. Her disability meant that she was unable to use her right heel as she walked. When her father abandoned the family, Dorothea was traumatized a second time. Nonetheless, her ability to face reality and persevere as a child led her to overcome difficulties as an adult, earning world-wide recognition for her art.

Studying photography at Columbia University fueled her desire to become a photographer. Settling in San Francisco, she met and worked with other photographers. After finding a financial investor, Dorothea opened a portrait studio. When the Depression hit in 1929, she stepped outside and began taking photos of the tough life on San Francisco's streets. Married with two sons, Dorothea traveled the highways and rural areas with her camera, becoming the first "documentary photographer."

Published anonymously, her heart-wrenching photos soon began making headlines. In 1935, Dorothea began documenting the poverty and exploitation of sharecroppers and migrant workers. Later, she documented the cruelties and hopelessness of the Japanese Internment camps. Her genius has influenced millions.

DID YOU KNOW?

1. In later life when Dorothea's health began fading, it was due to post-polio syndrome.
2. Her 1936 photograph of a mother surrounded by her seven hungry children is entitled *Migrant Mother*. It spurred the U.S. government to rush aid to the starving migrant camp in Nipomo, California.

Circe was a Greek Sorceress (Goddess of magic/Witch) who was skilled in the magic of transmutation, illusion and necromancy (communicating with the dead). She lived on the mythical island of Aiaia (Aeaea), and was best known for Her vast knowledge of potions and herbs. Through the use of these and a magic wand or staff, Circe transformed Her enemies or those who offended Her into animals. Despised by her Divine family for her skills and beauty, Circe had the ability to manipulate mystical forces in the universe. Her sacred animal was the pig and Her sacred plants were alders, junipers, enchanter's nightshade and mandrake.

Since the beginning of humanity, witchcraft has always been important. People have searched for solutions through magical practices. Therefore, *Circe (or Kirke)* became one of the most magnetic women in Ancient Greece. *Circe* lived in a stone mansion on *Aeaea* located in a forest clearing. She had her own throne and was surrounded by nymphs. Some people believe wild beasts that behaved as domesticated animals lived with Her.

Her personality and attributes include all the key ideas related to witchcraft. *Circe* was an herbal specialist using them for magic and healing. She created many different recipes for ancient potions to be used in rituals.

Homer's depiction of Her in the *Odyssey* shows Her great knowledge and grasp of morality, understanding the powers of magic and the fear of deities in Ancient Greece. He also pictured Her to be one of the most attractive female figures in ancient mythology.

During medieval times, Circe became an important symbol in moral stories. Today, She is one of the most popular figures of ancient witchcraft and mythology, still casting Her magic spells and terrifying men. Perhaps we can call upon Circe when the men in our lives need some outside influence!

DID YOU KNOW?

1. Circe is regarded as the most powerful of Greece's three female sorceresses.
2. According to legend, Her ability to craft supernatural events led to her exile on her remote island, *Aeaea*.

"None of us are perfect, for which reason we should heed the voice of charity when it whispers in our ears, "Do not magnify the imperfections of others.""

> Elizabeth Hobbs Keckley (1818-1907) was a former slave who became a successful seamstress, civil activist, author, mother and philanthropist. She is best known as First Lady Mary Todd Lincoln's confidante and personal seamstress. Elizabeth established the Contraband Relief Association in 1862 to aid the camps of runaway slaves flooding the nation's capital city. She also penned a memoir *Behind the Scenes* in 1868 which, sadly, ended the remarkable friendship of two very different women.

Born enslaved, Elizabeth learned to read and write despite it being illegal for slaves to do so. Learning to sew from her mother, she became an accomplished seamstress. In 1842, Elizabeth was given to her owner's daughter, Ann Garland, with whom she moved to St. Louis. There, she became a dressmaker and supported Garland's entire house for over two years. Can you imagine? Unable to raise $1200 the Garlands required for her and her son's freedom, she turned to sympathetic customers. It takes a lot of courage to ask for and accept help—usually pride stops people from reaching out.

She and her son moved to Washington, D.C. in 1860 where she set up a dressmaking shop. Elizabeth's clients were the wives of influential politicians. The day following Lincoln's inauguration, she was hired by Mary Todd Lincoln as her personal seamstress. Her position and close relationship with the first lady provided Elizabeth with a unique perspective of domestic life in the White House.

After the President's assassination, Elizabeth published her memoir *Behind the Scenes or Thirty Years a Slave and Four Years in the White House* in 1868, hoping to alleviate some of Mrs. Lincoln's financial troubles. Elizabeth did not foresee the overwhelming public disapproval for publishing personal details about White House private life; it led to the loss of many customers as well as condemnation from the Lincoln family. She left Washington in 1892 after accepting a teaching position at Wilberforce University in Ohio.

DID YOU KNOW?

1. The dresses Elizabeth created for Mrs. Lincoln were much more sophisticated than those the President's wife had previously worn.
2. Both Elizabeth and Mrs. Lincoln had lost sons creating a bond between the two women.

Elizabeth Cabot Cary Agassiz

> Elizabeth Cabot Cary Agassiz (1822-1907) was an American educator, naturalist, philosopher, writer, co-founder and first president of Radcliffe College (the all-female college that later merged with Harvard University).

Educated at home, Elizabeth Agassiz conducted a school for girls, which, in addition to providing a needed supplement to family income, was a pioneering effort in women's education. She firmly believed that women should be taught the same subjects and by the same instructors as men. In 1879, because Harvard would not allow women to attend its schools, Elizabeth became chair of the Committee of Seven Lady Managers. Was it because she had no opportunity for public education available that Elizabeth advocated for it so strongly?

With the approval of Harvard's president, the group put forth a plan to provide education equal to a Harvard College degree to qualified young women ready to pursue a course of study in Cambridge. Called the Private Collegiate Instruction for Women, the ensuing organization was named the "Harvard Annex." Incorporated in 1882, the Annex became known as the Society for the Collegiate Instruction of Women, and Elizabeth became its first president. Agassiz's social and Harvard connections and experience in education made her well suited for the position.

The Harvard Annex was successful from the start, offering college instruction by Harvard professors. After ten years of Agassiz's presidency, during which the College had grown to more than two hundred students, the Annex tried to merge with Harvard for a second time, offering Harvard all of its real estate and $150,000. Fearing coeducation, Harvard refused once again. (Always afraid of the women, yes?)

In 1894 Radcliffe College was chartered. The institutional mission set forth included not only instruction by Harvard professors, but also "authorized [the College] generally to furnish instruction and the opportunities of collegiate life to women and to promote their higher education."

Did you know?

1. *Finally*, 120 years after the first attempts for women to attend Harvard, Radcliffe College and Harvard University merged in 1999.
2. Elizabeth remained president of Radcliffe College until 1899.

Florence Nightingale OM, RRC, DStJ

Florence Nightingale (1820-1910) was not only a trailblazing figure in nursing, but a true pioneer in the graphical representation of statistics. A British nurse, social reformer and statistician, Nightingale is known as the foundational philosopher of modern nursing. Her famous night rounds to aid the Crimean War's soldiers established her image as the "Lady with the Lamp." She was the first woman ever to be awarded the British Order of Merit, as well as the first recipient of the Royal Red Cross (RRC). Florence was also the first female member of the Royal Statistical Society. In 1904, she was appointed *A Lady of Grace* by the Order of St. John (DStJ).

As a child, Florence was provided with a classical education, including studies in mathematics along with German, French and Italian. Despite her parent's objections, she was determined to pursue her true calling. Florence eventually enrolled as a nursing student in 1850 at the Institution of Protestant Deaconesses in Kaiserworth, Germany.

When the Crimean War (1853) broke out, more soldiers were dying from infectious diseases like cholera and typhoid than from injuries sustained in battle. Florence made it her mission to improve hygiene practices, she and her nurse corps significantly lowering the death rate from 40% to 2%. As a result of her war efforts, a fund was set up for her to continue training nurses in England. In 1860, she funded the establishment of St. Thomas' Hospital and within it, the Nightingale Training School for Nurses.

Did you know?

1. By age thirty-eight, she was homebound (never fully recovering from Crimean Fever), routinely bedridden and would remain so for the rest of her life.
2. Despite her confinement, Florence did pioneering work in the field of hospital planning.
3. Florence published *Notes on Nursing: What it is, and What it is Not* in 1859.

"The dearest ones of time, the strongest friends of the soul—BOOKS."

One of America's ultimate and most unique poets of all time, Emily Dickinson (1830-1886) was not published until four years after her death. She changed how poetry was written and is best known for her innovative form and syntax. Writing almost eighteen hundred poems, Emily's honest and uninhabited voice made her an early feminist; her subversive poems are widely read, taught and studied even today. Emily was sometimes referred to as the "Belle of Amherst." She is now considered one of the towering figures of American literature.

Emily's education reflected the 19th century love of sciences. That emphasis reappeared in her poems and letters through her fascination with naming, observing and the cultivation of flowers. She refused to be confined by social expectations. Emily was fascinated not with religion, but with poetry and its process of making metaphor and watching the meaning emerge.

As early as 1850, Emily's letters speak of a mind turning over the possibility of her own work. Using opposition to frame meaning in her poetry, the reader knows what something is by what it is not. Emily crafted a new first-person characterization. The speakers in her poetry are sharp-sighted observers who see the inescapable limitations of their societies as well as their escapes—both real and unreal.

Emily created in her writing a distinctively elliptical language for expressing what was possible but not yet realized. Like the Concord Transcendentalists—whose works she knew well—she saw poetry as a double-edged sword. While it liberated the individual, it readily left him or her ungrounded.

DID YOU KNOW?

1. Thanks to a discovery by her sister, Lavinia, Emily's remarkable work was discovered after her death and published by Lavinia.
2. "Skies in Bloom," featuring her nature poetry is one of my favorites holding a special place on my bookshelves.

"Grief is not very different from illness; in the impetus of its fire....it does not respect or spare anyone, not even itself."

> Eleanor of Aquitaine (c. 1122-1204 CE) was one of the most magnificent and powerful individuals of the High Middle Ages – male or female. Her influence shaped the politics, art, literature and perception of women in her era. Eleanor of Aquitaine would eventually become the queen of France, the queen of England and lead a crusade to the Holy Land. Mother of ten children (yes, ten) she was fiery, highly ambitious and intensely involved in power-politics. Can you imagine trying to run a nation(s) and keep track of ten children at the same time?

Born in what is now southern France, Eleanor was well educated, thoroughly versed in literature, philosophy and languages. She was also a passionate horse woman. Eleanor was trained to the rigors of court life when she became her father's heir presumptive at the age five. She led an active life until inheriting her father's crown and substantial lands upon his death. She was just fifteen.

In one stroke, Eleanor became Duchess of Aquitaine and by far the most eligible single young woman in Europe. The same year, Eleanor was married to Louis, heir to the throne of France. She became Queen of France shortly thereafter. The marriage was unhappy and they were divorced four years later. Eleanor then married Henry of Anjou, who became king of England in 1154 CE. The couple had five sons and three daughters. As Queen of England, Eleanor played an active role helping Henry run the empire as they traveled back and forth between England and France.

After Henry's death in 1189 CE, newly crowned King Richard I (Richard the Lionhearted) ordered his mother's release from prison—where Henry had placed Eleanor in 1173 CE. The king also entrusted her with the governance of England while he secured his continental realms.

DID YOU KNOW?

1. Eleanor counseled Henry, Richard and John—three of her sons that became kings.
2. She and Henry are the main characters in "The Lion of Winter".

The first sculptor of African American and Native American descent, Edmonia Lewis (1844-1907) achieved both national and international fame with her marble artworks. Known as 'Wildfire', she worked most of her career in Italy. Lewis shattered expectations about what female and minority artists could accomplish. Yay! This woman had guts.

Mary Edmonia Lewis, fulfilling a promise to her dying mother, lived among the Chippewa (*Ojibigwe*) throughout her early years. Her older brother financed her schooling in Albany, as well as helped her to attend Oberlin College in Ohio in 1859. While there she shed her Chippewa name and became Mary Edmonia Lewis. Her studies at Oberlin ended abruptly when she was accused of poisoning two of her white roommates. She was later acquitted of the charge but had to endure a highly publicized trial and a severe beating by white vigilantes. Subsequently accused of stealing art supplies, Edmonia was not permitted to graduate from Oberlin. How unfair is that? Her persistence is astounding.

Lewis left for Boston in 1863. There she met sculptor Edward Brackett and began limited sculptural studies with fierce determination to succeed. Through her sales of portrait busts of abolitionists, she was able to finance her first trip to Europe.

Lewis decided to settle in Rome after visiting Paris, London and Florence. She quickly learned the Italian language and became acquainted with many American female sculptors and stone-carvers. Lewis was unique among sculptors as she completed most of her works without assistance. Her work over the next several years danced between African American themes to subjects influenced by her devout Catholic faith. One of her most prized works was "Forever Free" sculpted in 1867 depicting a Black man and woman coming up from the bonds of slavery. Another masterpiece, "The Arrow Maker" comes from her Native American roots and depicts a father teaching his young daughter how to fashion an arrow.

DID YOU KNOW?

1. Neoclassicism declined in popularity and her fame diminished.
2. Edmonia had lost both parents by the age of nine.

An "all-embracing Mother Goddess", Devi represents Sakti—the female energy or power.Her name means "heavenly, divine, exalted, shining one." She manifests as the highest ranking in power, the optimum truth. Her worship began in the ancient Indus Valley (c. 3300 BCE) of northwestern South Asia. She rules the world, blesses Her followers with good fortune and positive outcomes and instills the inner self or spirit in every soul. Devi takes on many contrasting forms, being both a kind Goddess as well as a fierce one.

For many of Devi's worshippers, Her greatest strength is Her embodiment of all the different aspects of womanhood. Just like us, She can be quiet and nurturing but there are other times when She is a protectress of people. Devi has a wild and robust femininity, Her power quite startling to many. She reminds all women of our potential power, proving to us that all our characteristics are divine. Devi is especially worshipped by Shaivism and Shaktism, Hindu denominations. A statue of the Goddess stands where the Ganges meets the Vindhyas Mountains.

Devi's two opposite sides are represented by Uma, the benevolent, and Durga, the fierce protector against evil. There are many other names representing Devi's aspects, including Kali—the fearsome Black Goddess. Both Durga and Kali represent Devi's dark side. As Durga, She is most often depicted with yellow skin and riding her lion. Kali, the Black Goddess, is shown wearing garlands of skulls and snakes—powerful and fierce. You and I can learn to embrace all of our sides, both light and dark, as Devi does—though I think I'll skip the garland of snakes.

DID YOU KNOW?

1. In medieval literature, Devi is acknowledged as the Supreme Power.
2. The earliest shrine to Her is found at Cidambaram dated in the 12th century CE.

> Elizabeth Key Grinstead (1630-1665) was the first African woman in the American colonies to successfully sue for her freedom. She won her freedom as well as that of her infant son in the Virginia colony based on the fact that her father was an Englishman and she was baptized Christian. She was intelligent and certainly ahead of her time!

An illegitimate child of an enslaved black mother and a white English father, Thomas Key, Elizabeth was born a slave. Her father made arrangements for Elizabeth to be freed at age fifteen. Upon Key's death, Higginson (her godfather) sold the ten-year-old child to Colonel John Mottram, requiring her to serve another nine years. At Mottram's plantation, Elizabeth met and fell in love with William Grinstead, a young white English indentured servant and had a son.

After Mottram's death in 1655, the heirs of his estate classified Grinstead and her infant son as Negro slaves, thus property of the estate. William Grinstead, now an attorney, brought suit against the estate, claiming Elizabeth was a free woman and an indentured servant with a freeborn son, arguing she had been illegally kept in servitude ten years beyond her term.The court ruled in favor of Elizabeth and her child, granting them freedom according to longstanding "English common law." This court decision was upheld by the Virginia House of Burgesses having appointed a special committee to investigate.

Unfortunately, in 1662, the Grinstead case prompted the Virginia Assembly to codify laws regarding racial slavery, making it impossible for Blacks held in indentured servitude to gain their freedom. They eliminated the Christianity prohibition and also declared the legal status of a child to follow its mother's line, not the father's, as well as establishing the principle which made slavery multigenerational. Thus, any child born to a slave, regardless of its paternity, would remain a slave for life unless explicitly declared free. (The cruelty of government never ceases to dismay me.)

DID YOU KNOW?

1. Virginia's passing of their new law that included *partis sequiter ventrum* freed white fathers from all responsibility toward their biracial children.
2. Johnny Depp is an eighth great-grandson of Elizabeth Grinstead. Lucky man!

"Children are to be guided to make a beginning in all arts and sciences without interference with their spontaneity....without constraining them."

An American educator who opened the first English-language kindergarten in the United States, Elizabeth Palmer Peabody (1804-1894) was also a writer and lecturer. As a prominent figure in the Transcendentalist movement as well as an advocate for Native American rights to education, Elizabeth was known as "the grandmother of Boston reform".

Elizabeth opened a school in Lancaster, Massachusetts in 1820. She next opened a school in Brookline, Mass., where she met Dr. William Ellery Channing, who became her Socratic mentor. Together they explored philosophers, poets and the emerging theology of Unitarianism.

After her Brookline school closed in 1832, Peabody supported herself mainly through writing and private tutoring. Two years later, Peabody opened a bookstore at 13 West Street which became a sort of club for Boston's intellectual community. She published three of Nathaniel Hawthorne's books on her own press. Publishing and writing articles the next two years for *The Dial,* the literary monthly of the Transcendentalist movement. Peabody was one of the first female book publishers in the U.S.

Closing the West Street Bookstore in 1859, Peabody taught school, wrote and worked to promote public education for the next ten years. She learned of Friedrich Froebel's kindergarten work in Germany and in 1860 opened the first publicly funded kindergarten. It continued for the next seven years until she decided to visit European kindergartens to learn more of Froebel's thinking and methods. In 1873 she founded *the Kindergarten Messenger,* which she edited for its initial two years. From 1879 to 1884, Peabody lectured at the Concord School of Philosophy. She continued to speak out for the rights of Native Americans, against slavery and for women's suffrage.

DID YOU KNOW?

1. Following Froebel's methods, Elizabeth organized and became first president of the American Froebel Union.
2. Elizabeth could read and understand ten (!) languages.

"The Medicine Man, taking his music with him, is passing quietly into the Great Silence, where the old songs were 'Received in Dreams' by inner-plane communication."

Frances Theresa Densmore (1867-1957) was an American anthropologist, ethnologist and musician. The foremost authority of her time on songs and music of Native American tribes, Frances also published books on their culture and lifestyle.

Known as a "song catcher," Frances Densmore grew up in the Mississippi River town of Red Wing, Minnesota. As a child, she developed an appreciation for music by listening to the drums of nearby Dakota Indians at night. During the early years of her research into Native American music, Densmore continued her career as a professional performing musician. She was active in St. Paul and Red Wing as a church choir director, church organist, piano teacher and professional lecturer on various musical subjects to local clubs.

In 1903, Frances began her long and prolific career of writing on Native American music, as she had been lecturing on the subject since 1895. Two years later, she made her first visit to a Minnesota tribe in a Chippewa village near the Canadian border, publishing her observations in the *American Anthropologist* (April-June 1907). Later that year, Frances wrote to the Bureau of American Ethnology at the Smithsonian Institution, relating events she had observed at *Onigum* and asking for financial support of her efforts to record Indian customs before they disappeared forever. She was granted $150 to support her efforts, thus beginning her professional work and association with the Bureau of American Ethnology.

While serving with the Smithsonian Institution, Frances traveled throughout the country to remote Indian reservations and villages, recording on wax cylinders nearly 2,500 songs of the *Sioux, Yaqui, Cocopa, Pawnee, Yuma, Northern Ute*, and various other tribes whose cultures were already jeopardized by possible extinction. A simple box camera and a cylinder phonograph were her tools.

DID YOU KNOW?

1. In all, Frances recorded the songs of some thirty tribes.
2. She collected Native American songs for over fifty years. Remarkable.

The earliest known poet recorded in the history of the world is Enheduanna (2285 -2250 BCE). She was a princess, priestess, poet and a writer; she authored several works of literature, including three hymns to the Mesopotamian love Goddess Inanna. Enheduanna penned the myth of *Ebih* and Inanna, and a collection of 42 temple hymns. As high priestess of the Goddess Inanna and the moon god, Nanna, she lived in the Sumerian city-state Ur (present day Iraq, Syria). Enheduanna was the first known woman to hold the title of "EN", a role of great political importance often held by royal daughters. A Mesopotamian feminist, she helped lay the psychological foundations for the first well-balanced multi-lingual and multi-cultural empire in the world.

Enheduanna was a peacemaker, smoothing over differences between the north and the south—which is how she was given the position of high priestess of Ur and Uruk. Her importance is even more appreciated in modern times for the richness and beauty of her poetry, which often employed sexual imagery as a means of expressing love and devotion.

In addition to her longer works, Enheduanna wrote forty-two shorter poems on a wide range of themes; everything from religious piety and the effects of war to personal frustration and hope flowed from her pen. Her literary contributions are so impressive that one forgets the true reason she was sent to Ur—to help blend the different religious traditions and cultures.

History tells us that "she made an enormous impression on generations of scribes after her lifetime; her works were copied and read centuries after her death." Archeologists tell us Enheduanna's works were written in cuneiform, an ancient writing form using clay tablets. Written much later, only copies of the tablets survived. Enheduanna touched millions of lives and "helped to shape whole civilizations for thousands of years" to come.

DID YOU KNOW?

1. Enheduanna is most likely the earliest known woman to be called a feminist— nearly 5000 years ago!
2. A crater on Mercury has been named in her honor.

ELIZABETH I

"I would rather be a beggar and single than a queen and married."

> Known as the Virgin Queen, Elizabeth I (1533-1603) ruled England *during a period often* called the Elizabethan Age, when England vigorously proclaimed itself as a major European power in politics, commerce and the arts. Elizabeth I established Protestantism in England, defeated the Spanish Armada in 1588, maintained peace inside a previously divided country and created an environment where the arts flourished. Because she stayed in power so long, England was able to have a lengthy period of stability and relative prosperity.

When Elizabeth was a child, she came down with smallpox and nearly died. Scarred from the illness, she covered her facial pockmarks with heavy white makeup consisting of vinegar and white lead—slowly poisoning her over the years. At the death of Queen Mary (her older half-sister) on November 17th, 1558, Elizabeth came to the throne amid bells, bonfires and patriotic demonstrations. At the age of twenty-five, however, she was better prepared than most women to inherit leadership over men.

Elizabeth had survived the palace revolutions of her brother's reign and her sister's Roman Catholicism. As a child with a "Renaissance education", she grew to learn the need for strong secular leadership devoid of religious bigotry. Also Elizabeth possessed her father's charisma without his self-centeredness or ruthlessness.

Elizabeth was also her mother's daughter, and as the offspring of Anne Boleyn, she had no choice but to reestablish royal supremacy and once again sever ties with Rome. She quickly made it abundantly clear that she intended to rule in her own right and would not be subservient to any one individual or faction.

DID YOU KNOW?

1. Elizabeth I ruled for forty-four years.
2. She was the final monarch from the House of Tudor.

ELLA FITZGERALD

SATURDAY, WEEK 16

"It isn't where you came from, it's where you're going that counts."

> Ella Jane Fitzgerald (1917-1996) was the most popular jazz singer in America for over fifty years. Known as "The First Lady of Song" and the "Queen of Jazz", she was loved by people of every nationality, age and socio-economic background. Ella earned thirteen Grammy awards and sold over forty million records. An actress, humanitarian and philanthropist, she recorded over two thousand songs during her 60-year career.

By the time Ella was discovered at the Apollo theater in Harlem, she had already endured many hardships, that's putting it mildly. Her parents had split up shortly after her birth. Ella and her mom, Tempie, moved to Yonkers in New York to live with Tempie's long-time boyfriend. Ella took on small jobs to help support the family. When her mother died, fifteen-year-old Ella moved away from her abusive stepfather into her aunt's home. Ella's unhappiness increased, her grades decreased and after getting into trouble with the police she was sent to a reform school.

Living there was even more unbearable, she had to put up with beatings. Ella was able to break free but found herself alone and broke during the Depression. She somehow persisted through the dark times, then was lucky enough to win a lottery to sing at the Apollo. Once on stage and in the spotlight, Ella lost her shyness and found her "home."

By the mid 1930s, Ella had made her first recording with Decca Records. Shortly there-after, she began performing "scat", turning it into an art form as she astounded the crowds. By the time she turned twenty-one, Ella had a "million-dollar record" singing a jazzed-up version of "A Tisket, A Tasket". She was famous and never looked back. Ella toured the world singing for kings and presidents, but still found bigotry every-where she went in the U.S.

DID YOU KNOW?

1. Ella was arrested in Houston in 1955 for singing to a "mixed" audience. Taken into custody, the jailers actually requested her autograph!
2. In 1992, Ella was awarded the Presidential Medal of Freedom by President George H. W. Bush.
3. If Ella Fitzgerald married DarthVader she'd be Ella Vader. Get it?

111

One of the most powerful Goddesses of the Hindus, Durga came to kill the asuras (demons) that the male Gods had failed to control. Depicted as a warrior woman with eight hands carrying weapons of different kinds, She has the powers of all the male Gods combined. Durga symbolizes the divine forces (positive energies) known as the Divine Shakti (feminine energy/power) that are used against the negative forces of evil and wickedness. It is believed She was created as a warrior goddess to protect good people. Durga represents the power of a Supreme Being that preserves moral order and righteousness in creation.

Riding on a lion or a tiger, the image of Her symbolizes Her unlimited power to protect virtue and destroy evil, Her red sari symbolizing action to protect mankind from pain and suffering. The "Universal Mother", we can ask Her to remove our physical, mental and worldly problems in this life. The lion She rides is a symbol of uncontrolled animalistic tendencies such as anger, arrogance, jealousy, selfishness, desire to harm others, jealousy, greed, etc. Durga sitting on the lion reminds us to have courage and control these qualities, so that we are not controlled by them.

Holding a conch for happiness in one of Her eight hands, She holds a trident for courage in another. An arrow and bow for character, a lotus for detachment, a sword for discrimination, a chakra for righteousness—all are held in separate hands. Durga is the embodiment of a Supreme Being, including forgiveness, loyalty and love.

DID YOU KNOW?

1. *Durga-puga*, one of the great festivals of northeastern India, is held annually to honor Her.
2. Durga is recognized as Mother Goddess Devi's principal aspect.

A Union spy during the American Civil War, Elizabeth Van Lew (1818-1900) was an abolitionist, activist and a postmistress. As a Southern Unionist, she created an underground network to work against the Confederacy. Her network initially gave food and comfort to captured Union soldiers in the infamous Libby Prison. Elizabeth's mission then turned into a proficient intelligence gathering enterprise. I don't think I would have had the courage to be a Union spy let alone set up an underground spy network! Would you?

Born in Richmond to Quaker parents, Elizabeth and her family were part of Richmond's high society. Her northern education gave root to her abolitionist views before she returned to Richmond to be presented as a Southern belle. Though the progressive family had slaves, the workers were allowed to live elsewhere and work for an income.

When the Civil War broke out, both Elizabeth and her mother, Eliza, carefully walked the line between appearing to support the Confederacy while feeding and comforting imprisoned Union soldiers. Elizabeth helped pass messages to and from prisoners. In February of 1864, she helped 109 Union officers escape from Libby Prison at great personal financial and social cost.

Union General B. Butler heard of Elizabeth's accomplishments and recruited her as a Union spy in 1863. From the prison, she would gather information about Confederate troop numbers and movement. Elizabeth passed on the information via couriers to both General Grant and Colonel George Sharpe, his intelligence officer. The winter of 1863-64 found the Van Lew mansion turned into Richmond's center for an underground network. Elizabeth oversaw and positioned operatives (spies) using code names, invisible ink and messages hidden in clothing and shoes. The couriers furnished General Grant with critical information for the Union.

DID YOU KNOW?

1. Much later, the Confederacy investigated Elizabeth but she was not charged—the men simply couldn't believe a woman clever enough for such extensive activity. (Oh, really?)
2. Dying penniless, Elizabeth was inducted into the Military Intelligence Hall of Fame posthumously.

Esther Martinez aka P'oe Tsawa

A linguist and storyteller, Esther Martinez (1912-2006) was known for her commitment to preserving the Tewa (native American people of New Mexico) language. As an author, translator and teacher, she almost single-handedly saved the Tewa language which is spoken by six Pueblo Indian tribes. In 2006, the Esther Martinez Native Languages Preservation Act was signed into law to authorize funding for the prevention of loss of heritage and culture of the six tribes.

Named Blue Water by her father, Esther spent her childhood growing up in the southwest. She began her career as a linguist and storyteller relatively late in life. At fifty-four, Esther began taking linguistic classes at the University of North Dakota and at St. John's College in Santa Fe.

In collaboration with Randy Speirs, Esther helped compile the San Juan Pueblo Dictionary, student curriculum guides and storybooks, all in Tewa. She served as the Bilingual Education Program director as well as teacher for the San Juan Pueblo Day School from 1975 to 1985, and as co-director of the Tewa Language Project from 1995 to 1998. She traveled many miles on New Mexico's roadways and occasionally to other states telling her stories and becoming known as the "San Juan storyteller." In 2004, the University of Illinois published *My Life in San Juan Pueblo*—a collection of autobiographical stories detailing Esther's personal experiences, as well as Tewa stories.

As her reputation grew, Esther received dozens of awards recognizing her role as a educator, storyteller and advocate for the preservation of indigenous languages and cultures. The Indigenous Language Institute Award for "Those Who Make A Difference" was given to her in 1999. An honorary Bachelor of Arts in Childhood Education from Northern New Mexico College was awarded to her in 2006. What a difference Esther Martinez made to our American culture.

Did you know?

1. Esther was awarded The New Mexico Governor's Award for Excellence and Achievement in the Arts in 1998.
2. A New Mexico State Historic Marker was dedicated to her in November of 2008.

Dr. Gerty Theresa Radnitz Cori (1896-1957) was an Austro-Hungarian American biochemist who won a Nobel Prize in Science—the first woman to be awarded that prize in Physiology or Medicine. Her significant role in the discovery of the course of catalytic conversion of glycogen (a derivative of glucose) was only one of her accomplishments. Gerty, along with her husband, also identified the catalyzing compound –the "Cori ester"—as well as clarified carbohydrate metabolism.

At age sixteen, Gerty decided to study medicine. She graduated with a medical degree in 1920. While at school, she met and married Carl Ferdinand Cori. They both subsequently accepted positions at the University of Vienna and decided to do research rather than have a medical practice.

The couple immigrated to the United States in 1922 in order to pursue medical research at the State Institute for the Study of Malignant Diseases (now known as Roswell Park Memorial Institute) in Buffalo, New York. While there, they were discouraged from working side-by-side (they did so anyway) analyzing how sugar glucose is metabolized in the human body.

In 1929, they proposed the theory that bears their name, and later won them a Nobel Prize. The Coris left Roswell and headed for St. Louis after publishing their work on carbohydrate metabolism (energy moving from muscle to liver and back to muscle). Their move brought opportunity to Carl; he became the chair of the pharmacology department at Washington University School of Medicine—but not Gerty. Despite her accomplishments, Gerty was only offered a research assistant position. Promotion to full professorship came only after her husband was made head of the biochemistry department in 1947.

DID YOU KNOW?

1. The Coris were awarded the Nobel Prize in Medicine and Physiology (along with Dr. Houssay of Argentina) in 1947.
2. After Gerty's death in 1957 due to myelosclerosis, Edward R. Murrow eulogized her "dedication, intellectual integrity, courage and professionalism in her biochemistry pursuits".

Frances "Fanny" Burney, aka Madame Frances d'Arblay (1752-1840) was an English novelist, letter writer (diarist) and satirical playwright. Crowned "the mother of English fiction" by Virginia Woolf, Fanny was a master of social courtship novels. At just twenty-six, she published *Evelina or A Young Lady's Entrance into the World.* Fanny laid the groundwork for all female novelists. Her novels depict female heroines realistically. One of the most accomplished British writers of the late 18th and early 19th centuries, Fanny was an inspiration for Jane Austen, William Thackery and many more.

Born to an English father and French mother, Fanny was self-educated by reading books in her father's collection. Some scholars suggest she had a form of dyslexia, which makes it more remarkable that she became a writer. Precocious and ambitious, Fanny began writing journal letters to a family friend, Samuel Crisp, who encouraged her endeavor. A cultivated *litterateur,* Crisp was retired and often visited the Burney family.

Fanny's first novel, *Evelina,* was published anonymously in 1778. Her father had not given his permission nor did he have knowledge of what Fanny was doing. Because she worked as his literary assistant, Fanny was afraid her penmanship would be recognized by either him or the publisher. Thus, she wrote the pages out in a "disguised hand." Her elder brother posed as the author and negotiated a price of twenty guineas for the manuscript.

The novel was a critical success—praised for its comical view of English society and realistic depiction of working-class London vernacular. Her father, not realizing his daughter was the author, read the reviews before discovering her true authorship. Impressed by the favorable reaction, Charles Burney began supporting her efforts, seeing social advantages of having a published author in the family. She then published *Cecile (1782)* and *Camilla (1796).*

DID YOU KNOW?

1. Today's scholars are impressed with Fanny, she drew attention to the difficulties women endured in the 18th century.
2. Fanny's wide-awake account of her mastectomy is brutal reading but can be found on the internet.

Also known as "The Red Nun", Elvia Carrillo Puerto (1878-1968) was a socialist politician, a mother and feminist activist from Mexico. Married at thirteen, and widowed by twenty-one, Elvia founded Mexico's first feminist leagues, promoted women's rights and worked actively developing better lives for Mexico's women. Promoting progressive social reforms throughout the Yucatan region, the leagues fought against prostitution, drugs, alcoholism and superstitions. The longest lasting campaigns were for birth control and family planning. Elvia believed large families were a handicap to uplifting society. She propelled feminism to Mexico's political forefront in the early 20th century.

Born in the Yucatan, Elvia founded the first resistance league for women in *Motul* in 1912. She then traveled to organize farming women, launching campaigns for literacy and birth control. In 1918, a conference granted women the right to vote. The following year, Elvia created her most important league, *Liga Rita Cetina Gutierrez*. (Gutierrez was a prominent educator and mentor to Elvia.) The league held talks on child care as well as economics and hygiene. They also inspected schools and hospitals.

By 1923, Elvia and two other women had won the election to the state legislature. An uprising and revolt, led by Adolfo De La Huerta the following year, killed seven thousand Mexicans as well as the governor (her brother Felipe). Afterwards, many of the reforms put in place by Felipe were rolled back. This included women's rights — blocking the three women who had just been elected from serving. Damn.

After being physically assaulted twice, Elvia fled the Yucatan. While campaigning for Federal Deputy in San Louis Potosi (1925), she was shot at eight times. Arriving in Mexico City, the Chamber of Deputies refused to seat her. Undaunted, Elvia moved to Mexico City where she continued to fight for women's rights. In 1953, women gained full voting rights in Mexico.

DID YOU KNOW?

1. Since her childhood, Elvia recognized the inequalities between Mexico's social classes.
2. She lived to age 90 — long enough to see all Mexican women gain their voting rights.

"So still were the big woods where I sat, sound might not yet have been born."

> A pioneering Canadian artist, Emily Carr (1871-1945) was a teacher and writer. A preeminent Canadian painter of the first half of the 20th century, she was one of the only major female artists in either North America or Europe during that period. Inspired by Indigenous peoples of the Pacific Northwest, Emily, a "Canadian icon", did not receive much recognition until she changed from painting Aboriginal themes to landscapes. Influenced by the' Fauves', she painted in a bold, colorful post-impressionist style.

Growing up in Victoria, Emily had a special interest in Aboriginal peoples, their traditional culture and especially their totem poles and masks. Indigenous culture was thought to be dying under white encroachment. Their lands, languages and cultural practices were disappearing. When Emily returned from France in 1912, she announced her intentions to make a visual record of Aboriginal totem poles in their village settings. A six-week trip north to Charlotte Islands and Skeena River provided Emily's source material for one of her great painting themes, Aboriginal cultures of the past.

Her adventurous trips north led to her discovery of her second theme, Canada's distinctive west coast. But the sales of the eccentric Emily's paintings were not enough for her to make a living. Her reputation today rests on the work she painted later in life that was triggered by the discovery of her early paintings by an ethnologist in 1927. He brought her paintings of Aboriginal themes to the attention of curators in Ottawa.

While attending the National Gallery of Canada's art exhibit, she met Lawren Harris and other members of the *Group of Seven.* Impressed with their landscape paintings and no longer feeling isolated, Carr began painting again after a fifteen-year hiatus. After 1928, recognition and exposure began to come her way from the National Gallery of Canada as well as the American Federation of Artists.

DID YOU KNOW?

1. "The Forest Lover," an historical fiction penned by Susan Vreeland, tells us of Emily's life and her struggles. It sits on the top shelf of my personal library.
2. After 1937, she began writing and publishing, even winning the coveted Governor General's Award in 1941.

Eostre, also known as Ostara, is the Germanic Goddess of spring and dawn (or renewal) who is celebrated during the spring equinox. April is the month Her celebrations are held. Eostre's sacred animal is the rabbit, a sign of fertility and the egg is Her symbol of fertile purity. She is associated with flowers and Her name gives us the word Easter. Eostre is linked with serpent or dragon energy in some mythologies. Her colors are bright green, yellow, and purple.

Interestingly, Eostre does not appear anywhere in Germanic mythology. Her stories may have been passed down through oral tradition amongst Germanic areas. She is most likely a localized Goddess worshipped by Anglo-Saxons in Southeastern England.

Eostre is related to other deities and Goddesses of the dawn. Scholars do not know everything about Her existence, but She is certainly connected to Ostara (Easter). Eostre is thought to be the ancient word for spring. And there are also links to the name Eostre and East, the direction of the sky where the sun first rises—which gives Eostre the name "Eastern Star."

She is connected with growth, renewal, abundance, new beginnings, fertility, as well as the full moon. Eostre represents the transitional time between childhood's innocence and adult passion, reminding us that life is full of unknown possibilities and adventures.

Sacred to the Goddess, the hare is the totem animal of lunar Goddesses—thus a symbol of the moon in Celtic tradition. Both the moon and the hare were thought to die daily, thus they became a symbol of immortality. Over the centuries, the symbol of the hare at Ostara has become the Easter bunny who brings eggs to children on Easter morning.

DID YOU KNOW?

1. Her name means shine.
2. The hare is also a major symbol for fertility and abundance, the European brown hare can conceive while pregnant.

"We who believe in freedom cannot rest."

> Ella Josephine Baker (1903-1986) was an African American civil rights and human rights activist. She was a major force in shaping the Civil Rights Movement in America, becoming a respected and influential leader. Co-founder of the Southern Christian Leadership Conference (SCLC—1957) headed by Dr. Martin Luther King, Jr., Ella was the creative force behind the Student Non-Violent Coordinating Committee (SNCC).

Throughout her childhood in North Carolina, Ella developed her sense for social justice early, listening to her grandmother's tales of slavery life. She went on to study at Shaw University in Raleigh, as a student she challenged school policies she felt were unfair. Moving to New York City's Harlem after graduating as class valedictorian (1927), Ella joined the Young Negroes Cooperative League in 1930, believing in their purpose to develop black economic power through collective planning. Economic justice for all people was Ella's strongest commitment; she stated, "People cannot be free until there is enough work in this land to give everybody a job." Her legacy continues today at the *Ella Baker Center for Human Rights.*

Ella began her association with the NAACP in 1940, working as field secretary and serving as director of branches from 1943 to 1946. The SNCC was born in 1960 after a Greensboro sit-in.Believing voting was the one key to freedom, she helped create Freedom Summer—an effort to not only register black voters but also to gain national attention to Mississippi's racism. Ella co-founded In Friendship in 1955—an organization to raise money to fight against Jim Crow Laws in the deep South.

An organizer, strategist and mother to the Civil Rights Movement, Ella mentored Representative John Lewis of Georgia, Marian Wright Edelman and social activist Julian Bond among others. Her legacy runs deep indeed.

Did you know?

1. She was nick-named "Fundi"—a Swahili word meaning a person who teaches a craft to the next generation.
2. Ella left the NAACP in 1946 believing their strategies no longer held a "transformative impact against Jim Crow."

"....social evils are dangerously contagious."

> African American scholar Fannie Barrier Williams (1855-1944) was a powerful orator. Best known as an American educator, political and women's rights activist, Fannie was the first black woman to gain membership of the Chicago Women's Club (a prestigious philanthropic group dominated by well-to-do white women that, in Illinois, largely ushered in the first juvenile court in the U.S.). Fannie was also the first woman to serve on the Board of the Chicago Public Library.

Fannie Williams became the first African American to earn a degree at State Normal School in 1870 (now known as SUNY Brockport). After graduation, she traveled to the South hoping to help the *freedmen.* Her experience there was eye-opening, exposing her for the first time to intimidation, humiliation and physical assault—experiences common to Southern black people.

Eventually moving northward to Washington D.C., Fannie taught in public schools. She then moved to Boston intending to study piano at the New England Conservatory of Music. After Southern white students objected to her presence, Fannie was asked to leave. Departing from the conservatory, she returned to D.C. to teach. There she met Samuel Laing Williams, whom she married in 1887. The couple relocated to Chicago where they became friends with reformer Jane Addams.

Fannie became active in the local community, becoming the first woman to serve on the Board of the Chicago Public Library. (How about that?) In 1894, she was nominated for membership in the prestigious Chicago Woman's Club, but she was accepted only after a contentious fourteen-month battle. As the club's first black member, Fannie was its only black member for thirty years!

DID YOU KNOW?

1. Fannie helped found the National League of Colored Women.
2. She also assisted W.E.B. Dubois in founding the NAACP in 1909.

A pioneer in the study of archaeological textiles, Grace Hood Crowfoot (1877-1957) was a botanist, archaeologist, textile historian, trained midwife and activist campaigning against female genital mutilation (FGM). A mother of five daughters, she avidly wrote, photographed and drew pictures of her findings on textiles and culture in the Middle East and North Africa. Known as "Molly" to family and friends, she trained a generation of textile archaeologists in Britain and helped establish a new field of study, ensuring textile remnants found at any site were henceforth preserved for analysis.

Grace (Molly) had a grandfather who collected Egyptian antiquities. This family interest put her in contact with many archaeologists. Her earliest venture into archaeology was when she excavated prehistoric remains in a cave at *Tana Bertrand* on the Italian Riviera in 1909. Grace did not attend university but had a keen interest in medicine. She studied midwifery at the Clapham Maternity Hospital in London. The contacts made there proved invaluable later when she was living in the Sudan and Egypt.

In 1919, while living with her husband in *Khartoum,* a midwife invited Grace to attend a Sudanese childbirth. There, she was shocked to see what it meant for a Sudanese woman to be "circumcised" according to the local practice of infibulation. This entailed the excision and suturing of the external female genitalia and the near closure of the vaginal opening.

In 1921, as Crowfoot continued to write scientific papers and examine and analyze textile samples from excavations, the British colonial regime agreed to start a midwifery training program in Khartoum. Even after retirement, she attended the House of Commons to inform leaders of her Sudanese experience and of the careful work by the Midwives' School to reduce the incidence and harmful effects of FGM.

DID YOU KNOW?

1. Many of Mary's drawings of North Africa and Middle East flora are housed at Kew Gardens in London.
2. In her last years, Mary was often bed-ridden with childhood tuberculosis and leukemia.

FRANCES ELLEN WATKINS HARPER

"Slavery is dead, but the spirit which animated it still lives. ..."

> A poet and writer, Frances Ellen Watkins Harper (1825-1911) was an educator, abolitionist, suffragist, public speaker, reformer and mother. She was one of the first African American women to be published in the United States. Her collection *Poems on Miscellaneous Subjects* (1854) was a commercial success and made Frances the most popular African American poet before Paul Laurence Dunbar. She helped found the National Association of Colored Women (1896).

Born free in Baltimore, Frances Watkins Harper was orphaned at age three. Raised by her maternal aunt and uncle, the Watkins gave her their last name. He would be a major influence on Frances, as he was a civil rights activist, abolitionist, as well the minister of an African Methodist Episcopal Church.

Harper began working as a seamstress at age thirteen while working as a governess for a white family that owned a bookshop. Using her spare time to read and practice writing, by the time she was twenty-one she published *Forest Leaves*. This, her first book of poetry, was considered lost until rediscovered by a doctoral student in the 2010s. By age twenty-six, she had moved from Baltimore to teach domestic science at Union Seminary (an AME-affiliated school for black students in Columbus, Ohio). She was the school's first female teacher.

Harper's writing career began in 1839 when she published pieces in antislavery journals. While living with family friends who helped support her, she began writing poetry for antislavery newspapers, earning herself a reputation as the "mother of African American journalism".

Within a few years, Harper was traveling across the U.S. and Canada as a lecturer. In addition to her antislavery lectures, she was also committed to the struggle for women's rights. She then began publishing novels, short stories and poetry that focused on issues of racism, feminism and classism.

DID YOU KNOW?

1. Frances, a prolific writer, continued to speak out for equal educational opportunities and civil rights.
2. Her first novel was published when she was sixty-seven.

A Chinese empress of the *Manchu Yehe Nara* clan, Empress Dowager Cixi (1835-1908) becamedowager (king's widow) and regent—defacto supreme ruler of China in the late Qing dynasty for forty-seven years. Her modernizing accomplishments include the banning of foot-binding, reforming the legal code and education system, and outlawing certain barbaric punishments. Cixi sought to transform China into a constitutional monarchy, her efforts were cut short by her death. She is the most important woman in Chinese history and seen today as a feminist.

At age sixteen, she was brought to the *Forbidden City* to join emperor *Xianfeng's* harem—a posh role for Chinese women at that time. She quickly rose to the top of the concubine ranks when the emperor overheard her singing. She soon bore him a son, earning her the title *Tzu Hsi* meaning "empress of the western palace"—today spelled Cixi. When Xianfeng died, Cixi's five-year-old son was his only male heir, thus becoming emperor *Tongzhi,* making her "empress dowager" and regent ruler.

When her son turned seventeen, Cixi relinquished the regency. Tongzhi died two years later making Cixi a regent again, this time for her three-year-old nephew, *Guangxu.* Historians point to this as proof of Cixi's political shrewdness because it defied tradition. Questions also arose about the convenient deaths of *Alute* (Tongzhi's concubine) and her unborn child who died during the debate for succession.

In 1898, Emperor Guangxu launched the Hundred Days Reform, his poorly implemented attempts of modernization nearly caused a civil war. Cixi regained the regency with the support of conservatives who opposed the reforms. She stayed in power until her death in 1908, though her reputation had been tarnished when the leader of the failed reform spread slanderous rumors about her.

DID YOU KNOW?

1. She was the longest ruling woman in China's history.
2. Cixi encouraged modern education for women and founded an institute of higher education for them.

German composer and pianist, Fanny Mendelssohn (1805-1847) composed over five-hundred pieces of music. Musicologists now believe she pioneered the form "Songs Without Words." Mendelssohn was the older sister and confidante of Felix Mendelssohn. The majority of her works were piano pieces and lieder (German art songs) which were performed at the evening concerts held at the Mendelssohn home. Overshadowed by her famous brother, (due to societal norms), her beautiful but forgotten compositions have only lately been brought back to life.

As talented musically as her brother, the two children were given the same music teachers. Felix quickly admitted his sister was the better pianist. Fanny remained his chief musical adviser until he left home. She is said to have memorized J.S. Bach's complete *Well-Tempered Clavier* by age thirteen! Both Mendelssohns made striking progress in their musical and general studies, astonishing those who heard them perform by their prodigious musical technique.

Social conventions of the time regarding a woman's *place* as well as her family's reservations prompted a number of Fanny's works to be published under her brother's name in his Opus 8 and 9 collections. Felix often referred to his older sister as «Minerva,» the Roman Goddess of wisdom, for her intellectual insight and highly developed musical talent.

Upon her mother's death in 1842, Fanny took over the direction of the Mendelssohn family home in Berlin. Subsequently, she settled into the acceptable domestic roles prescribed by society of the time. Her musical creativity continued to manifest itself in the prolific creation of smaller scale genres. Stylistically her music is similar to that of her brother's.

Did you know?

1. Most of her remaining works exist only in manuscript.
2. Fanny lived to witness changing attitudes towards women in the musical professions, which resulted in a handful of her works appearing in print.

Erzulie Freda, of Haitian Voodoo, is the Haitian African spirit of love, beauty, jewelry, dancing, luxury and flowers. Her symbol is the heart, her colors are pink, blue, white and gold. Erzulie Freda's favorite sacrifices include jewelry, perfume, sweet cakes and liquors. Flirtatious, fond of beauty and finery, She is femininity and compassion embodied. Erzulie Freda is envisioned as a stunning, mixed-race woman and a wanton virgin. She envisions the world to be nothing but kindness and grace, with no racism, sexism or poverty. When harsh reality sets in, Her tears flood the entire world. Her all-encompassing acceptance makes her an easy patron saint (Goddess) for the LGBTQ community.

Erzulie Freda is the spirit of heartbreak, hope and disappointment. Life never fulfills Her expectations. In spite of her tears, She is never cynical. She stimulates and epitomizes "love that transcends death." She sends prophetic dreams and is often asked to interpret them. Sometimes during a ritual possession, Erzulie Freda enters the body of either a male or a female.

As a Great Goddess, due respect must be paid Her or one can expect demonstrations of power. Nonetheless, Erzulie Freda is very generous. Her devotees often invoke Her assistance in financial and romantic matters.

A golden fair-skinned woman, She is always stylish and impeccably dressed. Her emblems are a heart pierced with a dagger or a sword. Her element—water. Days associated with Her are Tuesdays and Thursdays. Erzulie Freda's sacred bird is the flamingo, her sacred animal is the snake and Her favored plants are basil, the fig tree and bay laurel.

DID YOU KNOW?

1. Erzulie Freda also has a dark side, being prone to jealousy, laziness and is somewhat spoiled.
2. She is thought of as never being able to achieve her heart's desire.
3. Her three wedding rings symbolize each of Her husbands.

EMMELINE PANKHURST

"Justice and judgment lie often a world apart."

> A British activist and mother of five, Emmeline Goulden Pankhurst (1858-1928) used militant tactics to agitate for women's suffrage. She founded the Women's Franchise League as well as the Women's Social and Political Union (WSPU). Imprisoned many times for her activism and forcefully fed when on a hunger strike, Emily persevered for forty years before British women obtained full equality to vote.

After marrying Dr. Richard Pankhurst in 1879, she continued her ardent support for the suffrage movement while having five children. His unexpected death (1898) left Emmeline with new responsibilities and significant debt. She became a paid Registrar of Births and Deaths in Chorlton. Her new women-only group, created in 1903, focused solely on voting rights, the Women's Social and Political Union.

At first the WSPU's militancy consisted of buttonholing politicians and holding rallies. These tactics led to members of Emmeline's group being arrested and imprisoned. She was first put behind bars in 1908. Her group was soon dubbed "Suffragettes." Because progress was slow, protests escalated. By 1913, militant actions by WSPU members included window-breaking and vandalizing public art and arson. By 1909, the women had begun to engage in hunger strikes while in prison. After their violent force-feeding, the hunger strikes also led to a quick release for many of the suffragettes.

Because of WWI, Emily decided to halt their militant acts and demonstrations. The government released all the WSPU prisoners and Emmeline encouraged her women to join the war effort and fill factory jobs so men could fight on the front. The women's wartime contributions helped convince the British government to grant them limited voting rights—for those who met a property requirement and were thirty years of age (the voting age for men was twenty-one)—in 1918.

DID YOU KNOW?

1. It wasn't until 1928 that the British government gave all women over twenty-one the right to vote.
2. A statue of Emmeline stands in London's Victoria Tower Gardens gesturing toward the Houses of Parliament.

"There is too much repression and suppression in schools."

The first Black teacher at Oberlin College, Fanny Marion Jackson Coppin (1837-1913) was a lifelong advocate for women's higher education. An American educator, lecturer, principal, superintendent, writer and African missionary, Fanny spent over thirty-seven years teaching. Born a slave, Fanny grew to be a "model of academic excellence" motivating her students to dream and achieve more than they ever thought they could. She was the first African American to become a school principal and was then promoted to Superintendent of the school district (another first for an African American in the United States).

Born enslaved, Fanny's freedom was purchased by an aunt when she was twelve. As a teenager, she became a domestic servant for an author and grabbed onto learning anything she could. At the age of twenty-three, Fanny enrolled in Oberlin College (Ohio) where she would become the first Black student to be asked to teach college prep classes. During her senior year, she was teaching college prep classes, privately instructing sixteen students in music, and still taking courses. (Wow.)

With the Civil War ending, Fanny developed an evening class to teach newly freed people how to read and write. She was then offered a teaching position at Philadelphia's Institute for Colored Youth. Soon Fanny was offered the position of principal at the Institute. She saw a need for Industrial Education and began soliciting for funds from local households. Fanny also lectured, raising awareness of the shortage of Black employment.

After raising thousands of dollars, the Industrial Department unfolded. The school began training seamstresses, woodworkers and bricklayers as well as teachers. In addition to teaching African American students, Fanny established homes for working and poverty-stricken women. She was also a prominent columnist who championed the rights of women and Blacks in Philadelphia.

DID YOU KNOW?

1. After retirement, Fanny was a missionary for ten years cofounding The Bethel Institute with her husband.
2. She opened a home for destitute young women in 1888, providing them shelter after having been refused by other charities.

"I grew up with a fierce hatred of devastating forest fires..."

Hallie Morse Daggett (1883-1964) was the first woman ever to be employed by the U. S. Forestry Service as a fire lookout (field officer). She held that position for fourteen seasons. Hallie worked at Eddy's Gulch Lookout Station at the top of Klamath Peak in the Klamath National Forest in Northern California. She broke down the barrier for women to enter the field of Natural Resource Management.

Educated in San Francisco, her deep love for her childhood home at the Black Bear Mine in the Klamath Mountains drew her back to the area. Hallie learned how to ride, hunt, trap, fish and shoot early in life – skills that were needed at the lookout high above the Salmon River.

In 1913, Eddy's Gulch Lookout Station in Klamath National Forest, California, was without a fire lookout for the approaching fire season. Assistant fire ranger, M.H. McCarthy stated that, though she was "no gentleman, [she] would make a first-class Lookout". At age thirty, Daggett became one of the most effective "forest guards" in the Klamath National Forest. Of the forty fires she reported in her first season, less than five acres burned.

Following Daggett, there is an account of another woman employed to do field work during WWI. Helen McCormick of Eugene, Oregon was given the position of *patrol-woman* to cover the Willamette National Forest in Oregon. Then again during WWII, a surge of women were employed as lookouts in the national forests of Oregon and Washington.

For many years, District Rangers' wives and other district employees served as unpaid employees (volunteers). They were considered a convenient, necessary source of free labor in forest districts short on money and staff. In fact, wives who balked at doing such free work were thought of as being unloyal to their husbands and the Forest Service. I'm glad we have moved beyond using women as free labor! (Or have we?)

DID YOU KNOW?

1. The elevation of Hallie's lookout station at Eddy Gulch was 6,444 feet.
2. It took her three hours of hard climbing from the base to reach her station.

Frederika Bremer (1801-1865) was a Swedish novelist, feminist, socialist and mystic. She is recognized as the Swedish Jane Austen, conveying the realist novel to the forefront of literature. Frederika successfully petitioned King Charles XIV for emancipation from her brother in her late thirties. Bremer wrote *Hertha* prompting a social movement that granted all unmarried Swedish women legal majority at age twenty-five. She also established the Royal Advanced Female Teachers' Seminary (teacher's college)—the first public institution of higher learning for women in Sweden (1861). Posthumously, she became the namesake of the Frederika Bremer Association, the first women's rights organization in Sweden.

Moving to Sweden with her family when she was three, Frederika was well educated and traveled widely despite having her activities being limited because she was a woman. Under the law, she was not allowed to make her own decisions regarding her family inheritance, though Frederika could control monies she earned from her writing.

Publishing her first novels anonymously, Frederika earned a gold medal from the Swedish Academy. In the 1830s, she studied philosophy and theology under *Boeklin Kristianstad*. She grew to become a Christian mystic/ Christian socialist. Frederika traveled to the U.S. in 1849 to study both culture and women's position. Grasping the issue of enslavement, she became an abolitionist.

After returning to Sweden (1850s), she became involved with the international peace movement and began working toward civic democracy. Later on, Frederika traveled to Europe and the Middle East to study their cultures. She published her travel diary about life in the Old World (1860-62) in six volumes.

DID YOU KNOW?

1. When she published *Hertha* (1856), Frederika risked her popularity as she depicted a woman free of the traditional female role.
2. As a result, the largest women's organization in Sweden adopted the name Hertha in honor of her novel.

EMPRESS WU ZETIAN

> Empress Wu (624 CE-705 CE) was empress regent of the Zhou dynasty of China. As the only female monarch in the history of China, she was one of the most controversial monarchs in China's history. Empress Wu was the power behind the throne from her husband's death (638 CE) until she proclaimed herself openly as emperor in 690 CE ruling until 705 CE. Believing women were equal to men, she didn't ask for any man's permission to act.

Wu Zetian was encouraged by her father to read and write, developing intellectual skills that were traditionally reserved for males. She also played music, wrote poetry and could speak well in public. Selected as concubine by Emperor *Taizong* at age fourteen, he named her *Mei-Niang,* meaning "beautiful girl." Taking care of laundry was how her court life began. One day, she began speaking to the emperor of Chinese history, and he was, of course, quite fascinated that his newest concubine could read and write.

Taizong was so impressed with Wu that he took her away from the laundry and installed her as his secretary. In her new position, she was constantly involved in affairs of state at the highest level, quickly becoming Taizong's favorite. In 660 CE China, Wu was essentially the emperor. Though she did not hold the title, she was the power behind the throne taking care of imperial business even when pregnant.

After taking back the rule from both her sons, Wu began to implement changes. She first changed the name of the ruling dynasty from *Tang* to *Zhou.* Wu reduced government spending and increased sufficiency, and appointed intellectuals and talented bureaucrats without regard of family status. She improved public education systems. She also improved the lives of peasants by reforming taxation methods, surveyed land, built irrigation systems and redistributed land so everyone had equal shares. Wu re-opened the Silk Road and expanded China's borders.

DID YOU KNOW?

1. Empress Wu practiced Buddhism.
2. Her reign was harshly criticized by Confucian histories until 1950 when they changed their attitude toward her.

An African American classical composer, Florence Beatrice Smith Price (1887-1953) was a pianist, organist, educator and mother of three. She was the first black woman to have her music performed by a major symphony orchestra. Not until the last few years have her compositions gained the notoriety they deserve.

A child prodigy, Florence performed her first piano recital at the age of four and had her first composition published at eleven. How about that? Following her college graduation, she taught school before becoming active in composition in 1912. After a move to Chicago in 1927, Florence's career began to flourish. Her songs, piano music and instructional pieces for piano were published and she began teaching music from her home.

Florence composed more than three hundred works at this time, including symphonies, organ works, piano concertos, arrangements of spirituals, art songs, works for violin and vocal chamber works. She and other African American classical musicians who flourished during the Harlem Renaissance faced nearly insurmountable challenges finding commercial success. It has only been within the last few years that Florence's compositions have become celebrated with publication and performance.

In 1931, she completed her *Symphony in E Minor* which garnered first place in the 1932 Rodman Wanamaker Prize Competition. Originally subtitled the *Negro Symphony*, it was selected to premiere at the Chicago World Fair in June of 1933. Florence gained national recognition with her performances throughout the 30s. She became friends with Marian Anderson who began performing her arrangements. Anderson's performance of Florence's original setting for Langston Hughes' poem cycle *Songs to a Dark Virgin* was an immediate hit. Published in 1941, other leading black vocalists began to sing Florence's songs.

DID YOU KNOW?

1. Many of her compositions were thought to be lost until approximately two hundred manuscripts and other papers were discovered at Florence's former summer house in a Chicago suburb.
2. That run down summer house is a strong symbol of how America has forgotten its cultural heritage.

Frigga (Frigg) is considered "queen" of the Nordic Gods, Her name meaning *beloved*. She was the Goddess of fertility, motherhood, marriage, the household and is possibly Friday's namesake. She is one of the preeminent Norse Goddesses. Famous for Her fondness of love, fertility, beauty and fine material possessions, She is considered to be something of a "party girl".

A practitioner of *seidr* (the most organized form of Nordic magic), it was Frigga that first brought art to the Gods and humans. She is regarded as the archetype of the *volva*—a traveling sorceress. Her knowledge and power are almost without equal. She also presides over the afterlife. Frigga is worshipped as a sky Goddess and is believed to be responsible for weaving the clouds. She is often called upon by Her worshippers for aid in the domestic arts and cottage industries, particularly in the spinning of wool.

Often depicted sitting on a throne or holding a commanding pose, Frigga is in charge of peace and the maintenance of social order. As Patroness of diplomacy, She is called upon by leaders in matters that deal with the community, especially feasting. She dwells in *Fensalir,* a water realm that is most likely a wetland, marsh or bog.

Frigga treasures a cloak of falcon feathers that Gods and Goddesses use to shapeshift into bird form. Her symbols and signs include wetlands, ponds, swamps and marshes as well as clouds, mist and vapor. The winter solstice, Christmas eve and the full moon are associated with Her, as are birch and linden trees, mistletoe, Fairy Godmothers and Mother Goose.

DID YOU KNOW?

1. Additional symbols representing Frigga are water-wading birds, sheep, cows and falcons.
2. Spinning, weaving, fabric and textiles are more signs of the Goddess.

"Nobody's free until everybody's free."

> Fanny Lou Hamer (1917-1977) was a leader in the civil rights movement, a community organizer, voting rights activist and mother. A civil rights hero, she taught black Mississippians to read and write so they could pass discriminatory voter tests designed to stop Black Americans from their right to vote. Fanny helped organize Mississippi's Freedom Summer—a volunteer campaign assisting African Americans to register to vote. Enduring horrific circumstances, Fanny persisted.

Walking with a limp and sustaining a blood clot behind her eye, both of which were results of being severely beaten by police in a Mississippi jail, Fanny rivaled Martin Luther King Jr. with her command of audiences. The youngest of twenty children born to Mississippi Delta sharecroppers, Fanny worked picking cotton until she was fired for trying to register to vote. After marrying in 1944, Fanny worked as the plantation's timekeeper as well as picking cotton until 1962.

In 1961, Fanny had been given a hysterectomy by a white doctor *without her consent* while having surgery to remove a tumor from her uterus. (That makes me sick to my stomach.) Forced sterilizations of Black women as a way to reduce Black population was so widespread it was dubbed a "Mississippi appendectomy." No longer able to have children of her own, she and her husband adopted two girls.

Fanny was incensed by efforts to deny Blacks the right to vote, so she became an SNCC organizer and led 176 volunteers to register to vote in August of 1962. Denied their right to vote, the group was harassed on their way home, police stopping their bus and fining them $100 because they said the bus was "too yellow." What bullshit! In 1963, Fanny was beaten so brutally by police she sustained permanent damage to her kidneys. A televised speech by Fanny in 1968 gave poignant descriptions of personal and brutal racial prejudice in the South.

DID YOU KNOW?

1. President Johnson gave a televised speech at the same time as Fanny's trying to take away her air-time.
2. Fanny was posthumously inducted into the National Women's Hall of Fame in 1993. What an extraordinary woman she was, and so unrecognized.

"The earth is the very quintessence of the human condition."

A German-born Jewish political theorist, Hannah Arendt (1906-1975) caused a revolutionary stir in political philosophy. She is widely recognized as one of the most important political philosophers of the 20th century. Hannah is best known for two works, *The Origins of Totalitarianism* published in 1951 and *The Human Condition* published seven years later.

Joanna (Hannah) Cohn Arendt received a doctoral in philosophy from the University of Heidelberg in 1928. Upon completing her education, Hannah tied the knot with Gunther Stern, becoming involved in political activism and agitations. (Their marriage lasted only 3 years.) She began collecting evidence of anti-Semitic practices by the Nazi regime. However, the narrow and pain-staking Nazi Party noticed her activities and Hannah began encountering disruptions. Her difficulties increased and in 1933 was forced to flee her homeland.

In Paris, Hannah married again, this time to Heinrich Blucher. She and her husband were sent to concentration camp in *Gurs,* France. Fortunately, they managed to escape from the camp and in 1941 left for the U.S. Hannah settled in New York City and was appointed research director of the Conference on Jewish Relations (1944–46). She was chief editor of Schocken Books 1946–1948 and from 1949–1952 she was the director of Jewish Cultural Reconstruction, Inc., which sought to salvage Jewish writings dispersed by the Nazis. She was naturalized as an American citizen in 1951.

Hannah's reputation as a major political thinker was established by her 1951 *Origins of Totalitarianism*, which also explores 19th-century anti-Semitism, imperialism and racism. She published another groundbreaking philosophical masterpiece in 1958, *The Human Condition,* which was intent on critically inspecting boundaries and limitations of the modern world.

DID YOU KNOW?

1. Hannah stated, "The sad truth is that most evil is done by people who never make up their minds to be good or evil."
2. Though her works cover a wide range of topics, she is most wildly known for dealing with the subjects of *power* and *evil.*

Born and raised in Iowa, Herma Geneva Albertson Baggley (1896-1981) became the first female naturalist when she worked for the National Park Service in Wyoming. A pioneering teacher and botanist, Herma was a lecturer, guide, writer and ranger at Yellowstone National Park. In 1936, she co-authored *Plants of Yellowstone National Park*, a rare field guide still currently in use. After her death in 1981, Herma left behind a legacy in Yellowstone of not only information but also the development of many nature trails.

Upon receiving her under-graduate degree, Herma began her summer by working at Yellowstone National Park as a naturalist. She helped lay out the first nature trail to *Old Faithful* and was the trail's only guide for three years. During that time, the crowd of hikers grew to three hundred, to hear her expertise of the flora and fauna. Herma also served as a relief lecturer at the open-air amphitheater on Firehole River's banks and Old Faithful Lodge.

A display of wildflowers in the lobbies of the lodge and at Old Faithful Inn (as well as supervising the gathering of wildflower centerpieces) was all Herma's doing. When summer was over, she accepted a permanent position. After being assigned to Mammoth Hot Springs, Herma was injured and began working in the Mammoth Museum and Information Office. Because the park was only open during the summers, she began teaching high school science.

Herma received her master's degree in botany (1929) and taught for a year before returning to Yellowstone. She continued to document the park's flora and fauna, writing over twenty-two articles for the NPS.

DID YOU KNOW?

1. Herma organized other women in the National Park Service Women's Union as they fought with male rangers for suitable housing for women inside the park.
2. She also endured tourists who quoted her own research back to her!

"We are guilty of many errors and many faults, but our worst crime is abandoning children, neglecting the fountain of life. Many of the things we need can wait. The child cannot."

Lucila Godoy Alcayaga (1889-1957) was known by her pseudonym, Gabriela Mistral. A Chilean poet-diplomat, educator and humanist, she became the first Latin American author to receive a Nobel Prize in Literature (1945). Her lyrical poetry, inspired by powerful emotions, "made her name a symbol of idealistic aspirations for the Latin American world". Mistral's central themes were nature, betrayal, love—including a mother's love, sorrow and resiliency. She also wrote about Latin American identity formed from a mixture of European and American influences. Gabriela advocated for women's rights, children, the poor and other disadvantaged groups in her community.

After she was refused admission to the Normal School in *La Serena* because of her writings, Gabriela groomed herself for a teaching career and for the life of a writer and intellectual. Studying on her own, she was able to receive a teaching certificate in 1910. She taught elementary and secondary school for many years before her poetry made her famous.

Gabriela began writing poetry while teaching. Her *Sonetos de la Muerte* published in 1914 made her famous throughout Latin America. But her greatest collection of poems, *Desolacion,* was not published until 1922. All of her lyrical voices represent differing aspects of Gabriela's personality. Her works have been interpreted by critics and readers as an autobiographical female voice that was marked by her intense awareness of the world.

Although Gabriela uses regular meter and rhyme in her verses, they are sometimes difficult to recite because of intentional breaks in prosodic (intonation, tone, rhythm) rules. It produces an intentional effect—making the reader uncomfortable with feelings of uncertainty and harshness. In her prose writing, she twisted and entangled language in unusual ways. Although she is mostly known for her poetry, Gabriela was an accomplished and prolific prose writer whose contributions to major Latin American newspapers had a large following.

DID YOU KNOW?

1. Gabriela was "the great singer of sorrow and motherhood for Latin America," according to Swedish writer Hjalmar Gullberg.
2. She was awarded Chile's National Literature Prize in 1951.

"I demanded more rights for women because I know what women had to put up with."

Political partner of the Argentine President, Eva Perón (1919-1952) was the second wife ofJuan Perón. A significant political figure in her own right, she was known for campaigning for female suffrage as she supported organized labor groups. Eva's enormous social welfare endeavors gained the support of the lower classes as they reaped its benefits.

Born María Eva Duarte (whose nickname was Evita), she grew to be a leading political figure in her native country as first lady. Growing up poor, Eva was greatly motivated to help the under-privileged. She was about twenty years old when she started her own entertainment business, the Company of the Theater of the Air, which produced radio programs. She attracted much attention as a celebrity.

Evita was twenty-six when she married Juan Perón, a colonel and government official. The following year he became Argentina's president. She proved to be a powerful political influence using her position as first lady to fight for causes she believed in—including women's suffrage and improving the lives of the poor.

Eva ran (in reality) the ministries of health and labor in her husband's government. She became a legendary figure in Argentinian politics; beloved by poor citizens, she worked hard to help. Establishing the María Eva Duarte Social Help Foundation in July 1948, Eva helped fight poverty in Argentina. Two years later it was renamed the Eva Perón Foundation.

DID YOU KNOW?

1. Eva She also founded and ran Argentine's first large-scale female political party.
2. She was only thirty-three when she died of cervical cancer.

An Italian composer, Francesca Caccini (1587-c.1640) also was a lutenist, music teacher, singer and mother during the Baroque era. She was one of the best-known female composers and performers of her lifetime. Caccini was also the highest paid musician in the Medici Court. How about that for an early 17th century female composer?

Born into a very musical family, Francesca Caccini's childhood home was filled with music, art and literature. Educated in the sciences and language, she also learned to read music and play keyboard, guitar, lute, harp, theorbo and viols. By age thirteen, she was performing in women's ensembles—very fashionable at the time. Offered a position by the French king after a performance, her father's fear of retribution from the Medici forced her to decline. In 1607, Frances became employed by the Medici court in Florence.

Working for the Medici proved fruitful and Frances became the highest paid musician at Court. By 1630, she was publishing music of varied styles. Frances used these compositions to teach her students. Her father boasted to all who heard him; she had produced over three hundred works. Her mastery of music, whether it be vocal or instrumental, was respected by patrons as well as fellow musicians. In 1642, she penned her first opera for a royal visit by Crown Prince *Wladislaw.*

After the opera's success, she was commissioned for two more staged works but suddenly found herself a widow. Relocating to Lucca, Frances met and married an aristocrat who died soon after she gave birth to their son. After years of urging by the Medici, she returned to Florence where she was sustained by their protection. Once there, Frances' daughter was able to enjoy a singer's life by entering a convent. Together, mother and daughter were lauded for their talented musicianship.

DID YOU KNOW?

1. Her surviving stage work, "La Liberazione di Ruggiero", is arguably considered the oldest opera by a woman.
2. Her nickname was "La Cecchina."

GAIA

Greek Goddess of Earth, Gaia (Gea, Gaea) is one of the primordial deities. She has complete control over the plants and rocks of the world. Gaia is the ancestral mother of all life and is called the "Mother Goddess". Her superhuman strength and durability comes from Her being a Titan. She, along with Ouranos, created the world and all life in it. With Ouranos, Gaia had twelve divine children called Titans. She is widely worshipped in Greece; She is the ancestor to most of the deities. Gaia is also the first Goddess associated with the vitally important Oracles (a priest or priestess speaking the will of the gods).

Gaia is Mother Earth. She is the reason the mountains, seas, plains and rivers, as well as the heavens, were formed. The chief antagonist of the heavenly gods, Gaia rebelled against Her husband, Ouranos, and also came into conflict with Zeus for the binding of Her Titan son Tartaros.

In ancient Greek cosmology, the Earth was a flat disc encircled by a river. Earth supported the seas and mountains upon her breast. Gaia is shown as an all-nourishing and all-producing mother. Because She had a mother-like presence, Gaia watched over oaths, marriages and was honored as a prophetess.

In Greek paintings, Gaia is depicted as a buxom, matronly woman rising up from the earth, inseparable from Her native element. Often clothed in green, She is sometimes accompanied by troops of Karpoi (fruits) and Hoair (seasons). Gaia first appeared as a divine being in Homer's poems, such as the *Iliad*. Stories are told of Ouranos hating the children He had with Gaia and thus imprisoned them in Her womb. This led to Gaia's allegiance with Her Titan son, Cronus, who wielded a sword and castrated Ouranos.

DID YOU KNOW?

1. Gaia was involved in overthrowing many other Greek Gods.
2. Her symbols include fruit, grain, and the planet Earth.

Also known as Umm al Banine, "Mother of the Children", *Fatima al-Fihri* (c. 800-880 CE) is recognized for creating the world's *first* academic degree-granting university still in existence. The University of *al-Qarawiyyin* is located in Fez, Morocco (859 CE), and is the oldest existing and continually operating educational institution in the world. Isn't that remarkable? She is regarded as the patron saint of higher learning and a visionary. Today, Fatima al-Fihri is highly respected and looked up to by Moroccan women for her kind-heartedness, wisdom, and perseverance, an inspiration to all.

An Arab Muslim woman from Tunisia, Fatima was from a well-educated family that emigrated to Morocco. She had a great passion for knowledge and was renowned for being a deep thinker. Upon her father's death, she invested his wealth in founding a mosque and an educational institution.

The establishment blossomed into the University of al-Qarawiyyin. Fatima personally supervised the construction of the university, purchasing the land around the mosque and mining it for resources needed. Situated in Fez, one of the most prominent cities in the Muslim world, the university played a leading role in academic relations between Europe and the Islamic world. Students and scientists from around the world travelled to study and lecture on subjects ranging from natural sciences to languages and astronomy. It was recognized as a major intellectual center during medieval times. Symposiums and debates were regularly held there.

While Europe was slogging through the Dark Ages with its lack of forward thinking, religious fighting, and cultural developments, the Islamic world was flourishing as it grew into the "Golden Age" of science, medicine, and beyond. Terms and concepts associated with higher education can be traced back to the practices found in al-Qarawiyyin. Fatima al-Fihri—another woman ahead of her time!

DID YOU KNOW?

1. Fatima studied at the University herself, and her degree is still on display there.
2. Still in operation, the university houses one of the world's oldest libraries, now open to the public. Can you imagine walking into a 1200-year-old library?

A Latina educator, Ines Maria Mendoza (1908-1990) was also a writer, mother, actress, ecologist and former first lady of Puerto Rico. Known affectionately as "Dona Ines", she is known for standing by the Spanish language, defying the new colonial authorities that wanted to replace it with English. As the longest serving first lady, she advised her husband regarding the public education system and championed Puerto Rico's ecology. She pioneered the conservation and protection of the country's flora and fauna and its ecological and scenic values. She was recognized as a civic, social and political leader in her own right.

An accomplished student, Ines' career began as a teacher, writer and newspaper columnist. Married to a painter, *Rafael Palacios*, for four years, they had two daughters together. A 1927 graduate of the school currently known as the University of Puerto Rico, and of Columbia University in 1931, Ines had a distinguished career as a schoolteacher. She met the future Puerto Rican governor in 1935, though they did not marry until 1946. This marriage produced two more daughters.

As a teacher, Ines defied the U.S. imposition of English and the ban on the Spanish language in Puerto Rico, continuing to teach in Spanish. Her defiance gained so much support that the imposition of English was abolished.

The *Ines Maria Mendoza Nature Reserve*, also known as *Punta Yeguas*, is located on the southern tip of Puerto Rico's eastern region in the coastal city of Yabucoa. The reserve features stunning landscapes of rolling pastures, treelined sandstone cliffs covered with forests rising up from narrow white-sand beaches. Endemic to Puerto Rico and restricted to the southeastern region of the island, the *Ortegon (Coccoloba rugosa)* is a very rare evergreen tree. There are eighty-five documented species of plants, birds, reptiles, amphibians and invertebrates in Punta Yeguas.

DID YOU KNOW?

1. Ines served as part of the Conservation Trust of Puerto Rico's (CTPR) first board of trustees.
2. Ines Mendoza high school is found in *Cabo Rojo*, Puerto Rico.

"Life is an unfoldment, and the further we travel the more truth we can comprehend..."

Born in Alexandria, Egypt, Hypatia (c. 370 CE-415 CE) was the most prominent mathematician and astronomer of her time. Known as the "mother of mathematics", she was the head of the Platonist school in Alexandria teaching philosophy and astronomy. She was renowned in her lifetime as an exceptional teacher and sage. Widely known for her unselfishness, desire to learn and mastery in teaching the sciences, Hypatia was extremely influential in her hometown. Tragically, she was brutally murdered by a Christian mob in Alexandria's streets.

Hypatia was the daughter of Greek scholar Theon Alexandricus, who educated her but refused to impose traditional roles on her. She soon established herself as a philosopher and mathematician in her own right. Her lectures were extremely popular; she soon had people traveling for many miles to listen and seek her counsel. Her philosophies and teaching abilities were greatly respected. Academics of the time led a quiet life, as did Hypatia.

Alexandria became increasingly divided as intolerant Christians gained power. The city that had once attracted the best minds of science, mathematics, philosophy and other disciplines soon found Jews, Pagans, and Christians fighting one another instead of living side-by-side in peace as they had done for centuries.

An extraordinary and influential woman, Hypatia found herself an easy target for the extremists led by Cyril, the head of the main religious body. He felt Hypatia's effect on Orestes (the head of the civil government) was too strong. Rumors spread which resulted in a mob gathering to kill Hypatia; her death on the streets at the hands of Christian monks who feared her and her influence was vicious. Once beaten, she was dragged through the streets and her mutilated body burned.

DID YOU KNOW?

1. Historian Stephen Greenblatt said her murder "effectively marked the downfall of Alexandrian intellectual life."
2. When Hypatia edited *On the Conics of Apollonius,* Hypatia made the concepts of hyperbolas, parabolas and ellipses easier for us to understand—thus changing the world!

"O love, what strange and wonderful fits: one sole thing, one beauty alone, can give me life and deprive me of wits."

> Gaspara Stampa (1523-1554) was a 16th century poet, musician and singer. She was highly admired for her lyrical verses, penning more than three hundred during her short lifetime. Most of her literary works were published posthumously. Gaspara Stampa is considered one of the greatest female poets of the renaissance; her life was tragically cut short by illness.

After Gaspara's father died, the family moved to Venice where the children were well educated in literature, music, history and art. Both she and her sister, Cassandra, were excellent singers. Their household became a magnet for leaders in Venetian literary and artistic circles. The traumatic loss of her brother when she was only twenty had a devastating effect on Gaspara. She briefly pondered the idea of retreating to a nunnery. After reconsideration, she resumed her life in Venice.

About this time, she met Count Collaltino and began writing poems in his honor almost immediately. Their relationship continued for almost seven years before beginning to cool. Gaspara took the break-up badly, entering a long period of melancholy which bordered on depression. Remarkably, the poetry she wrote at this time was reputedly some of her best. Using the emotional pain she felt, Gaspara wrote strong and intelligent poetry; her work at this time ensured she would be remembered as one of the most influential female poets of the 16th century.

Trying to bounce back by taking another lover and performing madrigals that she had written, Gaspara continued to work diligently under the name Anaxilla. Around that time, though, her health began to deteriorate. Moving to Florence hoping the better climate would help her regain good health, Gaspara's poetry began to reflect despair. Her many emotional traumas and health problems undoubtedly contributed to her despondency. Returning to Venice in 1554, Stampa contracted a high fever and died shortly thereafter. She was only thirty-one years old.

DID YOU KNOW?

1. Stampa's poetry was often compared to that of Sappho.
2. Most of her poems were published posthumously.

"Old age is like a plane flying through a storm. Once you're aboard, there's nothing you can do. You can't stop the plane, you can't stop the storm, you can't stop time. So one might as well accept it calmly, wisely."

An Israeli politician, Golda Meir (1898-1978) helped found the state of Israel in 1948. She was later elected its fourth prime minister. Golda was the first woman to hold that post. Known for her bluntness, strong will and determination, important historical events happened on her watch including the Munich Massacre and the Yom Kippur War. Golda Meir was a teacher, mother, kibbutznik, stateswoman and called "the Iron Lady" for demonstrating resolve and always following her convictions without compromise.

Born Goldie Mabovitch in Kiev, Ukraine, she emigrated to Milwaukee, Wisconsin with her family in 1905. She attended Milwaukee Normal School (now the University of Wisconsin-Milwaukee). In 1921, Golda and her husband, Morris Myerson, immigrated to Palestine and joined the *Mer\avya kibbutz*. During WWII, she emerged as a forceful spokesman for the Zionist cause, negotiating with the British mandatory authorities.

In 1946, British officials arrested and detained many Jewish activists including Moshe Sharett, leader of the Political Department of the Jewish Agency. Golda stepped in to replace him and worked for the release of her comrades. On May 14, 1948, she signed Israel's independence declaration. Also that year she was appointed Minister to Moscow. When hostilities broke out between Arab countries and Israel that same year, she returned home and was elected to the Israeli Parliament (1949) serving in that body until 1974.

Golda also served as Minister of Labor (1949–56), then was appointed Foreign Minister in 1956. At that point, she Hebraized her name to Golda Meir (meaning to illuminate or to burn brightly). In 1966, Golda became Secretary-General of her party, *Mapai*. With the sudden death of Prime Minister Levi Eshkol in early 1969, the seventy-one-year-old Golda assumed the post of premier, becoming the world's third female prime minister. She remained Prime Minister of Israel until retiring in 1974.

DID YOU KNOW?

1. Golda was often described as the "the strong-willed, straight-talking, grey-bunned grandmother of the Jewish people."
2. In Israel, Golda's image is imprinted on their ten-shekel bronze and silver coins.

"I hope the leaving is joyful; and I hope never to return."

Magdalena Carmen Frida Kahlo y Calderón (1907-1954) was a Mexican painter who is admired as a feminist icon, best known for her brightly colored and uncompromising portraits, self-portraits and works inspired by nature and Mexican artifacts. Frida is celebrated in Mexico for the attention she gave to the indigenous culture and by feminists for her portrayal of the female experience. She was also widely known for her Marxist leanings.

Frida's famous quote "My painting carries with it the message of pain" describes the tremendous amount of pain she went through during her life. Around the age of six she contracted polio, which caused her to be bedridden for nine months. On September 25, 1925, Frida was traveling on a bus when it collided with a streetcar. She was impaled by a steel handrail; it went into her hip and came out the other side. Frida nearly died suffering multiple fractures to her spine, a shattered pelvis, a broken foot and a dislocated shoulder.

After spending several weeks at the Red Cross Hospital in Mexico City, Frida returned home to recuperate further. She endured thirty operations during her lifetime. As she progressed during her recovery, she began painting. She finished her first self-portrait the following year. In 1929, Frida was married to Mexico's famous muralist, Diego Rivera. A tumultuous and non-traditional union, Frida and Rivera kept separate but adjoining homes and studios in the San Angel neighborhood of Mexico City.

In 1953, she had her first solo exhibition in Mexico City. Bedridden at the time, Frida did not miss out on the exhibition's opening, arriving by ambulance. She spent the evening talking and celebrating with the event's attendees from the comfort of a four-poster bed set up in the gallery just for her. Sadly, Frida Kahlo died the following year.

Did you know?

1. In 1984, Mexico declared Frida's artwork part of their natural cultural heritage, which prohibits the exportation of her art.
2. Frida is considered an icon by the LGBTQ community, Chicanos and feminists.

Ganga is a Hindu Goddess of the holy river, the Ganges. She is worshipped by both Hindus and Buddhists who believe bathing in the river purifies them and liberates them from the cycle of life and death (*Moksha*). Pilgrims immerse ashes of their family in the Ganges, which they believe brings their spirits closer. Ganga is known by many other names, *Bhagirathi, Jahnavi, Nikita* and many others. The Goddess lives in many sacred places along the river and brings good fortune through Her purifications. Candlelit floats are often released into the river to honor Her and the Gautama Buddha.

Ganga is described as the melodious, the fortunate, the eternally pure and the delightful. She is lovely in appearance and leaps over mountains in sport as well as provides bedding that bestows water and happiness. Ganga is considered a friend or benefactor to all.

In artwork, Ganga is depicted as a fair-complexioned woman sitting on a crocodile, wearing a white crown and white sari. A water lily is held in Her right hand and a lute in Her left. When shown with four hands, She carries a water-pot, a lily, a rosary and has Her last hand in a protective position.

Her divine vehicle (Vahana) is an animal with the head of a crocodile and the tail of a dolphin. The crocodile represents our reptilian-like brain that reminds us we use our intellect to outgrow fear when facing problems. The Goddess not only faces fear, but She uses it as a vehicle to move Her forward on a path to greater growth, strength and beauty. You and I can do exactly the same thing. Through Her Vahana, Ganga teaches us to take a problem by the horns, pull it deep into the flowing water of life and spin it until a solution appears.

DID YOU KNOW?

1. Ganga is revered in Nepal as a guardian water Goddess.
2. Unlike other Goddesses, Ganga has no destructive characteristics.

An extraordinary woman, Frances Dana Barker Gage (1808-1884) was an American women's rights activist, abolitionist, writer and lecturer, advice columnist, poet, teacher and mother of eight children. How did she have time for all of that? As a working mother, she was ahead of her time—a feminist before the word was acknowledged in the U.S. (1910). Known as "Fanny" to many, she influenced and mentored Clara Barton, a lifelong friend. Outspoken and cerebral, she educated herself and her family. Determined to overcome the limits set for women of her time, she lectured on abolition, temperance, moral integrity and human rights.

Her professional writing career, which helped support her family, began with weekly columns for the *State Journal* until she wrote about her opposition to the "Fugitive Slave Law," at which time she was fired. Persisting, Fanny wrote for *The Ohio Cultivator*. Gaining regional notoriety, she contributed to the *Western Literary Magazine*, New York's *Independent* and many others. Fanny extended her circle of friends by writing to like-minded women such as Amelia Bloomer and Harriet Martineau.

A talented public speaker, Fanny easily stepped into the role of orator and public organizer.When the family lived in St. Louis, she discovered her ideas unwelcome at the local newspaper. After threats of violence to her and her family, and an attempt to burn them out,they moved eastward, finally settling in Columbus, Ohio.

When the Civil War broke out, with four of her sons fighting for the Union, Fanny became a relief worker. Upon hearing about the Port Royal experiment, she headed to South Carolina to help *freedmen* adjust to life as well as teaching them to read.

DID YOU KNOW?

1. After the war, Fanny continued to support freedmen and help locate missing soldiers.
2. Fanny and James Gage were married for thirty-five years—during which time he totally supported Fanny's strong desire to help others

A Swiss science writer and educator, Jane Haldimand Marcet (1769-1858) was a mother of four. In fact, she was the very first science writer ever, publishing *Conversations on Chemistry* in 1806—published anonymously until 1837 when Jane's name appeared as the author. Her book(s) were noted for their precision, accuracy and thoroughness. She was a strong advocate for education, especially for women.

Jane had been educated at home, along with her brothers. She managed a household of twelve children at age of fifteen when her mother died. She married Alexander Marcet, a physician with strong curiosities in chemistry in 1899. The two began conducting experiments in their home laboratory. The Marcets were part of a literary and scientific social circle that included many leading writers and scientists of their time.

After attending the chemistry lectures of Humphrey Davy, Jane wrote her best-selling book, *Conversations on Chemistry*. It became very popular because she wrote in a way that anyone with little formal education could understand, especially women and the poor. Women and those of few means were not given many opportunities to study the sciences during the eighteenth century.

Her book was user-friendly and treated its subject thoroughly, comprised of two volumes, three hundred pages each. It featured conversations between an adult who understood chemistry and two children, both girls, who made comments and asked questions. Jane followed that up with two more books: *Conversations on Political Economy* (1816) and *Conversations on Vegetable Physiology* published in 1829. Jane was a true pioneer in science education.

DID YOU KNOW?

1. Other writings included a primer on political economy for working people and a number of stories and teaching books for young children.
2. Jane did not allow her name to appear on her books until her later years.

Irene Joliet-Curie

A French chemist, Irene Joliet-Curie (1897-1956) was battlefield radiologist, activist, physicist, mother and politician of Polish ancestry. She was awarded the 1935 Nobel Prize in Chemistry, along with her husband, in recognition of their synthesis of *designer* radioactive elements. These elements are now used in tens of millions of medical procedures every year, saving millions of lives. Mother of two and a passionate member of the feminist movement, Irene promoted women's education, speaking out for war refugees and also served on the World Peace Council.

Raised by her paternal grandfather, Irene was taught to love nature, poetry and radical politics. By age eighteen, she was running radiology units in mobile field hospitals, teaching nurses to run X-ray machines and operating them personally on the Belgian front. After WWI, Irene completed her degree in mathematics and physics at the *Sorbonne*. While working toward her doctorate, she became her mother's lab assistant at the Radium Institute.

By 1928, the newly married Joliet-Curies were experimenting with gamma rays to identify the make-up of atomic nuclei. Six years later, they discovered *beta decay* (positron emission). This discovery allowed radioactive materials to be created quickly, cheaply and plentifully—changing the face of medicine. The Nobel Prize for Chemistry brought fame and recognition with it.

Did you know?

1. Wanting to bring attention to their misogyny, Irene continually applied to the French Academy of Sciences, knowing she would be rejected because she was a female.
2. Irene's lifelong exposure to radiation took its toll. Her early death at age fifty-eight was most likely caused from X-ray work in WWI and repeated exposure in the lab.
3. Her husband, Frederic, and her mother Madame Curie also succumbed to radiation exposure.

"It is never too late to be what you might have been."

> Born Mary Ann Evans (1819-1880), she was a British novelist, journalist, poet and translator. Her books were known for their realism and psychological insight. Although some female authors published using their own names during her lifetime, Mary Ann wanted to escape the stereotype of women's writing always being limited to lighthearted romances. Thus, she used the pen name, George Eliot.

A voracious child reader and obviously intelligent, her father invested in an education not often afforded women. As Mary Ann lacked physical beauty, her father thought she had little chance of marriage. When her mother died in 1836, Mary Ann moved with her father to Coventry and lived with him until his death in 1849. The closeness to Coventry society brought new influences. Through them, Mary Ann was introduced to more liberal and agnostic theologies. When she began to question her religious faith, her father threatened to throw her out of the house—a threat he never carried out.

In 1850, she began furnishing writings to the *Westminster Review'* a leading journal for philosophical radicals, she later became its editor. Mary Ann now found herself at the center of a literary circle in which she met George Henry Lewes. She lived with him until his death in 1878, creating a scandal, he was still legally married.

Lewes encouraged Mary Ann to write. *Adam Bede*, her first novel, was published in 1859 to great acclaim. She used her male pen name to ensure her works were taken seriously. The popularity of George Eliot's novels eventually brought social acceptance. The home she shared with Lewes became a meeting place for writers and intellectuals.

DID YOU KNOW?

1. Queen Victoria was a great fan of George Eliot's novels.
2. Mary Ann was an abolitionist supporting *Irish Home Rule* as well.

The longest-reigning female pharaoh of Egypt, Hathshepsut (1507-1458 BCE) ruled for more than twenty years during the 18th Dynasty of Egypt. Her name means "Foremost of Noble Women". She is celebrated as a powerful female ruler whose reign was very successful, though her existence only came to light during the 19th century. All public recognition of her had been erased.

Hathshepsut had been elevated to the position of God's Wife of Amun sometime after she was married to Thutmose II. The highest honor an Egyptian woman could attain after the position of queen actually bestowed more power on her than most queens ever knew. When Thutmose II died, his son Thutmose III was still a child. Therefore, Hathshepsut became regent—controlling state affairs until he came of age. Seven years into that regency, Hathshepsut changed the rules and had herself crowned pharaoh of Egypt.

She began her reign by marrying her daughter to Thutmose III (who was her stepson) in order to secure her position. Hathshepsut also had reliefs placed on public buildings that showed Thutmose I making her his co-ruler. Hatshepsut began acting like a true pharaoh by immediately commissioning building projects and sending out military expeditions to Syria and Nubia. In all her projects, campaigns and policies, Hathshepsut relied heavily on one of her courtiers, Senenmut. Her most famous project is the Temple of Hathshepsut.

DID YOU KNOW?

1. Hathshepsut was forgotten after Thutmose III backdated his reign to the death of his father. Was this karma for her changing the rules while regent?
2. All her achievements as Pharaoh were then ascribed to him until the 19th century when *Champollian* (a French historian and linguist) discovered her name. It's marvelous that a gentleman gave credit back to Hathshepsut after it had been stolen from her by her stepson.

GEORGIA O'KEEFFE

"To create one's world in any of the arts takes courage."

An American Painter and teacher, Georgia Totto O'Keeffe (1887-1986) was best known for her canvasses depicting flowers, New York skyscrapers, animal skulls and southwestern landscapes. Georgia is known as the "Mother of American Modernism". She was the first female painter to gain respect in New York City's art world. She rarely signed her paintings, but sometimes wrote on the back. Georgia O'Keeffe was also the first woman to ever have a retrospective at the Museum of Modern Art in Manhattan (MOMA).

After regaining her health from typhoid fever, O'Keeffe traveled from Chicago to New York City in 1907 to continue her art studies. She later took courses at Columbia Teachers College for the academic year 1914–1915, then began teaching art at Columbia College in South Carolina. There, Georgia created a series of avant-garde abstract charcoal drawings attracting the attention of photographer and gallery director Alfred Stieglitz. Captivated by her work, he and Georgia began a correspondence and, unbeknownst to her, he exhibited ten of her drawings in 1916.

After confronting him about the exhibit, Georgia decided to let it continue. In 1917, he presented her first solo show. The pair fell in love and romance blossomed. Stieglitz and Georgia married in 1924. He championed her work and promoted her career. Inspired by the liveliness of the modern art movement, she began experimenting with perspective, painting larger-scale close-ups of flowers.

In the summer of 1929, Georgia found a new direction for her art when she made her first visit to northern New Mexico. The architecture, scenery and regional Navajo culture inspired her. She often returned to New Mexico, which she called "the faraway", in the summers to paint. Georgia permanently relocated to Ghost Ranch (north of Abiquiu) in 1940. She remains one of the most important and innovative artists of the 20th century.

DID YOU KNOW?

1. Georgia disliked being called a "woman artist", wanting simply to be recognized as an "artist".
2. She lost much of her eyesight in 1972 to macular degeneration.

Gula (also known as Ninkarrak) is a Babylonian Goddess of healing. A patroness of doctors, healing arts and medical practices, Her name means "Great" and is often interpreted as "Lady of the Wall"—a protective barrier. In Sumeria, "the great physician of black-headed ones" is often mentioned in medical papers and chants, and called "Great Healer". Her iconography shows Her always accompanied with a dog and surrounded by stars. Gula is also associated with the underworld and transformation.

Gula was frequently invoked in curses as She is the one doing the healing. It was thought She could bring earthquakes and storms when angered. People appeased Her through worship at temples where dogs roamed freely and took part in ritual sacrifice. As a greatly respected Goddess, She cares for and protects Her people. Originally a Sumerian deity known as Bau or "Goddess of dogs", Her worship spread throughout what is now southern Iraq.

Considered to be the "Supreme Healer", Her son, Damu, is thought to be Her intermediary through which Her powers are given to doctors. Ninazu, another of Her sons, is associated with serpents—symbols of transformation, the underworld (transition) and healing (transformation). He carried a staff with serpents intertwined on it, a *caduceus,* which the Greeks and Egyptians adopted. That staff with intertwined snakes can be seen in medical facilities worldwide as the symbol of *Hippocrates*—the "father of medicine".

Ancient Mesopotamia had two types of doctors, medical doctors that treated illness with medications, medicinal plants and charms were called Asu. Healers who relied on so-called 'magic' or rituals and incantations to drive away evil spirits were call Asipu.

DID YOU KNOW?

1. Illness and disease were thought to come from the gods as punishment, or from demons, evil spirits or the angry dead. Sadly, there are some in our society today who have not evolved from that ancient way of thinking.
2. Doctors in ancient Mesopotamia made house-calls, though sometimes they would treat patients in the temples.

Geertruida Wijsmuller-Meijer

> Geertruida Wijsmuller-Meijer (1896-1978) was a Dutch resistance fighter who brought thousands of Jewish children and adults to safety before and during WWII. Called "Auntie Truss", she preferred no attention be given her accomplishments. Geertruida risked her freedom and her life to arrange *kindertransports.* Our world needs more of this kind of compassion and courage.

Geertruida, who was childless, got involved in social work which is where she became familiar with the Jewish Refuge Committee and the Committee for Special Jewish Interests. As a woman of means and position, she was able to use a variety of connections in Europe and the UK to organize and carry out kindertransports. From late 1938-1940, she was getting Jewish children out of Nazi Germany and into the Netherlands, then they traveled on to Britain.

After the Netherlands surrendered, Geertruida continued her rescue and resistance efforts, helping Jews from Poland and the Baltics escape to Palestine via Marseilles. She always accompanied the transports, delivering food, medicine and forged documents to camps in unoccupied France. The Gestapo arrested and interrogated her in 1941 but ended up releasing her. Geertruida started keeping a lower profile, but continued to work, sending packaged food to Westerbork, Bergen-Belsen and Theresienstadt camps.

In 1944, she stepped up again to save a large group of child refugees, this time persuading the Germans that the Jewish children were actually Aryan. Instead of being sent to Auschwitz, they were sent to Bergen-Belsen and then Theresienstadt, where they received preferential treatment, surviving the war. After the war, Geertruida remained in the public arena serving on boards and fighting to advance the rights of the disabled. Sadly, she was forgotten shortly thereafter.

Did you know?

1. Geertruida located displaced children in Germany after WWII ended.
2. Upon her death, she was called the "Mother of 1001 children, who made it her job to save Jewish children ".

LUCY BAKEWELL AUDUBON TUESDAY, WEEK 23

Lucy Bakewell Audubon (1787-1874) was an educator, philanthropist and mother of four (losing two daughters in infancy). Spending many years as a single parent—because of husband John's travels—Lucy Audubon also dealt with great financial stress and ruin. She contributed to the family's income as a teacher during their forty years of marriage. Educated and physically strong, she held the family together during her husband's absence.

Born in England, the Bakewell family immigrated to the U.S. in 1801, settling near Philadelphia, Pennsylvania. Educated, Lucy taught the Frenchman (John James Audubon) English in exchange for painting. They married in 1808 and moved to Louisville, Kentucky, where Lucy birthed two sons. After investing in a steam-powered grist mill, the couple lost some of their investors causing it to close (1819). The loss of finances and prestige shattered Audubon emotionally, but his wife was his tower of strength.

While John left his family to embark on an expedition, Lucy Audubon remained at home raising their two sons. She became the breadwinner of the family. Arriving in Louisiana (1821), she began teaching in exchange for room and board. She was later hired as a local teacher, conducting classes for young ladies. Lucy founded a second school where she was not only given a nice home to live in, but she earned respect and social standing for her personal achievements—remarkable in an age when women were barely able to earn wages.

Frustrated with her husband, Lucy wrote letters expressing deep bitterness for putting his art and his books above family. He eventually returned to America and they reconciled. Purchasing a fourteen-acre triangle of land along the Hudson River and deeding it to his wife gave Lucy some compensation for decades of separation, hardship, having to support him financially.

DID YOU KNOW?

1. Lucy also taught music, sewing, social conduct, swimming and horsemanship.
2. She went back to work at age seventy (after her husband died) to support her two sons and their families who had great financial difficulties.

Janaki Ammal Edavalath Kakkat (1897-1984) was an eminent Indian plant scientist. A pioneering female botanist and cytogeneticist, she inspired her nation, India, to protect its rich plant diversity. She developed several hybrid crops still in existence. Her most notable research was with sugarcane and eggplant. Janaki also collected and researched medicinal plants. Known in her country as the "mother of botany", Janaki was bestowed the Padma Shri in 1977. An extraordinary Indian woman, she went against her country's hugely patriarchal and ultra-conservative culture to follow her academic dreams.

Janaki was teaching at Women's Christian College when the University of Michigan offered her a prestigious Barbour scholarship. She left immediately, usurping her family's plans, an arranged marriage. Receiving her doctorate in 1931, Janaki returned to India, she began developing a sweet hybrid of sugarcane to alleviate importing sugarcane from Java. During the process, she also developed several hybrids by crossing differing grasses.

Moving to Norfolk, England (1940), Janaki began working with geneticist Cyril Dean Darlington researching the way chromosomes influenced heredity. After working together five years, the pair coauthored the *Chromosome Atlas of Cultivated Plants* (1945) which is still used today.

The following year, the Royal Horticultural Society in Wisley offered her a position as a cytologist (the study of plant and animal cell structure). She became the society's first woman to hold a salaried position on their staff. One of the areas of her research was the botanical use of colchicine, a medication that affects a plant's chromosomes by creating larger and quicker growing plants.

Due to India's famines, Prime Minister Nehru requested her return to boost the country's agricultural production (early 1950s). Once there, Janaki became distressed at the country's deforestation. She then began her mission of preserving her native country's indigenous plants.

Did you know?

1. Janaki is credited with making India's sugarcane varieties sweeter.
2. There is a rose named after her.

American author and suffragist, Grace Gallatin Seton Thompson (1872-1959) was also a mother, adventurer, artist and geographer. She established *Biblioteca Femina*, a collection of over two thousand books written by women from around the world and housed at Northwestern University Library. Grace joined the campaign for women's suffrage when she was just seventeen.

Grace was writing for San Francisco newspapers by sixteen, using the pen name Dorothy Dodge. Her first book was published in 1900. *A Woman Tenderfoot* chronicled her trip through the Rockies on horseback. Her book connected the dots between literature and women's rights by encouraging women to expand their social and physical horizons by traveling. Grace even designed a riding costume that allowed women to ride astride to make travel easier.

A feminist who was "born believing in suffrage", Grace fought diligently against America's misogyny. She led the Connecticut Woman's Suffrage Association for a decade, despite not being able to vote because her husband was a British citizen. After women won the right to vote in 1920, they began lobbying lawmakers to recognize their citizenship be no longer tied to a man. Not until 1936 was the Cable Act (1922) repealed, allowing married women to retain their citizenship if marrying a foreigner.

Grace traveled substantially in the 1920s and 1930s, striking out for locations around the globe, including Egypt, Japan, Hawaii, China, India and South America. Whether riding by donkey in the Libyan desert or traveling by elephant in Vietnam, she continued to trek the world and write about her adventures. What fun!

DID YOU KNOW?

1. In France during the First World War, Grace put together a motor unit of women who provided food and aid to soldiers. She was later awarded medals by both France and Britain for her service.
2. She was one of the organizers of the "Camp Fire Girls" in 1912.

Helen of Anjou (1235-1314 CE) was Queen Consort of Serbia and mother of four children. She founded the first school for women in medieval Serbia and was the first Serbian queen to become a saint in the Serbian Orthodox Church. She was well known for her religious tolerance. Why can't we be the same?

Helen was said to have been of royal and French blood, though which royal line is still being debated. She ruled solely for thirty-seven years, though she was Serbian Queen for more than sixty years. She had no army because *she didn't need one.* Isn't that incredible?

Helen contributed significantly to the cultural rise of medieval Serbia. She encouraged transcription of books in monasteries, which she later gave out freely. Her library was the first found in a Serbian court. Helen founded the first girls' school in medieval Serbia. Her palace was in modern-day Kosovo. A successful administrator, she presided over regions with mixed Serbian Orthodox and Roman Catholic populations. Of high moral principles, she spoke several languages and was mild of character.

Helen had a diplomatic flair and knew exactly what and when to speak. Towns and villages destroyed by wars or weather were rebuilt. She established both Orthodox and Catholic hermitages and was revered by both churches. Her cooperation with neighboring countries was also well known and respected.

DID YOU KNOW?

1. Queen Helen was well educated, known for listening to the voice of the people and considered one of the leading women of her time.
2. Her girls' school was founded in the 13th century. Pretty amazing, yes?

"Perhaps women have always been in closer contact with reality than men: it would seem to be the just recompense for being deprived of idealism."

A French composer and writer, Marcelle Germain Tailleferre (1892-1983) was the only female member of the group of composers known as "Les Six". But because of circumstances in her life, Germaine never gained as much acclaim as the male members of 'Les Six'. She was a piano prodigy with a phenomenal memory for music. Her abilities at the harpsichord and affinity for the styles of music originally composed for it gave her excellent standing, her works retaining the influence of Faure and Ravel.

Germaine began her studies at the *Paris Conservatoire* (1904) despite her father's opposition and her equal talent in art. She displayed exceptional musical expertise and precociousness from a very early age and began composing at the age of five. Germaine wrote many short pieces during her student years, though she didn't formally begin to study composition until much later in her formal training. Her compositional training was first with Koechlin, and informally with Ravel.

Her commitment to progressive musical ideas during the early 1920s gave her a measure of notoriety throughout the musical scene in Paris. Nevertheless, her compositions never abandoned their allegiance to the traditional French "voice" that was passed down to her from Faure through Ravel, giving her music a seductive grace and charm. Her light-hearted, rather humorous use of modernist technique was captivating.

Germaine was married twice. Jealousy of her success and discouragement about her compositional work by both husbands took a heavy toll. She found her creative energies being drained, her lack of self-esteem and sense of modesty held her back from publicizing herself more. Germaine continued to compose music for children throughout her career which some writers have suggested helped to retain the spontaneity, freshness and charm that characterizes her finest works. She enjoyed composing various genres, preferring chamber works after 1945.

Did you know?

1. Germaine changed her last name from Taillefesse to Tailleferre to antagonize her father.
2. She continued composing until just a few weeks before her death at age ninety-one.

Hanwi (Han wi) is the moon spirit in Sioux mythology. Her names means "Night Sun". The Sioux tribe, being ancient and deeply spiritual, consists of three main groups, the Lakota, the Dakota and Nakota. Hanwi speaks the Sioux language, which is the fifth most spoken indigenous language in North America. As the moon Goddess, She guards Her people during the night protecting them from evil spirits. Her believers are always safe when the "Moon Goddess" is watching.

Legend tells us that because of her husband Wi's fickleness, Hanwi is the wandering moon. In the Sioux creation story, Hanwi's place beside her husband was taken by a mortal, at Wi's insistence, at the banquet of the gods. The Sky God, Skan, punished Wi by taking Hanwi from Him and allowing Wi to only rule during the day. Because Hanwi rules the night, She is often viewed with part of her face hidden from the shame of Wi's betrayal.

It is believed that the moon has much stronger light because it pierces through darkness. Hanwi can do this for Her followers, piercing dark or negative beings and protecting one from them. When the moon is out, Hanwi is watching over Her followers, and it becomes a time of cleansing. Her followers are always safe while She is watching.

A face can show inner shadows of guilt, negativity, stress, shame and fear. When facing our shadows, guilt and shame often appear. By letting go of toxic thoughts and emotions, essentially facing our dark side, people heal and grow stronger. Hanwi's power lies in Her light, cleansing believers of feelings that no longer serve them. That action of letting go (under Her light) allows self-empowerment and renewal of spirit. We all need to remember the importance of facing our dark side.

DID YOU KNOW?

1. In ancient times, people planted by the moon. Even my grandfather planted his garden by moon cycles, especially potatoes.
2. Some religions personify the Divine Feminine with the moon—as woman, we share the same twenty-eight-day cycle.

Born a free Black woman in Philadelphia, Harriet Forten Purvis (1810-1875) was an African American abolitionist, suffragist and mother of eight children. Known to family and friends as Hattie, she helped form a biracial women's abolitionist group, the "Philadelphia Female Anti-Slavery Society" with her mother and sisters. Along with her husband, Robert, Hattie hosted anti-slavery happenings at her home. The couple also ran an "Underground Railroad" station outside of Philadelphia, aiding around nine thousand escaped slaves heading to Canada! How brave she was, wouldn't you agree?

An educated refined woman, Hattie was raised by well-to-do parents. Her father, James Forten, set up a school so his Black children would learn a whites-only curriculum. Classes were amended with at-home tutoring of music and languages. The Forten household provided a meeting place for like-minded abolitionists from both races. Marrying Robert Purvis, the couple spread their anti-slavery message using their home on Lombard Street in Philadelphia as a base.

During her husband's absence, Hattie not only raised children but advanced the abolitionist cause. Working side-by side, she was not scared when a mob mistakenly believed Robert was a white man, becoming violent at a local convention. Inter-racial marriage was taboo and illegal in the United States until 1960. As their family grew so did their commitment. Since Philadelphia schools were still segregated, the older children attended integrated schools in New York and New Jersey. The Purvis household soon developed into an intellectual gathering place for abolitionists.

When sheltering runaways in their Philadelphia home became too dangerous, the family moved to the country. Their rural Byberry home was outfitted with a trapdoor where slaves were hidden. Hattie congregated like-minded people at her home as a leader of the "Female Vigilant Society." They collected monies and clothing for weary travelers on the underground railroad.

DID YOU KNOW?

1. She and her husband founded the Gilbert Lyceum (secondary school).
2. Hattie worked diligently to desegregate Philadelphia's streetcars and was involved with the Free Produce Society (boycotting produce grown and picked by slaves).

"The general plot of life is sometimes shaped by the different ways genuine intelligence combines with equally genuine ignorance."

Lucy Craft Laney (1854-1933) founded the first school for Black children in Augusta, Georgia (1883). An educator and civil rights activist, Lucy was one of the first African Americans to have her portrait displayed in Atlanta at the Georgia State Capitol. She helped found Augusta's branch of the NAACP and was active in the National Association of Colored Women. Lucy had the courage and ethical reputation to hold young students accountable to high levels of excellence, bringing out their best character.

Born during slavery to free parents, Lucy was taught to value education. Despite it being illegal in Georgia for Blacks to learn to read, Lucy learned by age four. By 1869, she entered the first class of Atlanta University. Lucy graduated three years later from their teaching program.She taught for ten years before deciding to establish her own school.

Settling in Augusta, Lucy founded the first school for Black children in the city. With just six initial students, the popularity of the school attracted enough attention to have 234 students enrolled by the end of the second year. (Talk about a hunger for knowledge.)

Lucy began asking for donations but was often turned down. Francine Haines stepped forward with a $10,000 donation which helped expand the curriculum. Lucy then changed the name of the school to "The Haines Normal and Industrial Institute." While in Augusta, Lucy became a member of the "Niagara Movement"—a Black civil rights movement whose members included cutting-edge African American attorneys.

DID YOU KNOW?

1. She was principal for fifty years at "The Haines Normal and industrial Institute."
2. An active member of the NAACP, Lucy also helped integrate the outreach of the YMCA and YWCA.

America's premier woman botanist, Jane Colden (1722-1766) fought an uphill battle. Her absence of formal schooling, being ignored by some leading botanists, and her female gender created roadblocks she had to overcome. Jane learned science from her father, a man who felt women were not capable of accurate and thorough scientific study. When he recognized her interest in natural history and natural philosophy, Cadwalleder Colden encouraged her. Jane's name was well known by some botanists of her day from her correspondence with them. She discovered two new American species, *Triadenum,* also known as St. John's Wort, and *Coptis groenlandica,* commonly called three-leafed golden thread.

Despite an 18th century attitude against women's education, her father's interest in science inspired Jane to start drawing and studying plants around her Hudson Valley home. If women were to become scientists in her day, they usually chose botany, most likely because of a plant's beauty and its healing properties—women were viewed as caretakers. Another obstacle was Latin, a language not taught in America but used for the scientific naming of plants.

As her father was aging and needing help categorizing plants, Jane stepped forward to assist. Around that time, she began communicating with other botanists—a common way to share drawings and descriptions of new discoveries. By the late 1730s, Jane was studying and drawing plants. Astonishingly, she wrote a manuscript with over 340 ink drawings giving detailed descriptions of her leaf drawings and medicinal applications.

During her studies of the surrounding hillsides, Jane discovered two new plant species. She immediately wrote to Carolus Linnaeus, the famous Scottish botanist who authored *Systema Naturae*—which Jane's father had translated from Latin for her studies. Jane suggested a name for the plants which Linnaeus ignored—he was uncertain of their origination. By the time he was proved wrong, Jane's part in their discovery had been forgotten. How sad is that?

Did you know?

1. Jane Colden has never been recognized or celebrated for her scientific work.
2. Americans learned of her unnamed manuscript seventy-five years after its publication. It was later given the title *Flora of New York.*

"Poetry is life distilled."

Gwendolyn Elizabeth Brooks (1917-2000) was one of the mostly highly respected, influential, and widely read poets of the 20th century. A much-honored poet, writer and teacher, she was the first African American author to win a Pulitzer Prize in 1950. Her poems condense the very best aspects of 'Modernist' style with the sounds and shapes of various African American forms and idioms. Gwendolyn was the Illinois' poet laureate, and the first Black woman to serve as poetry consultant to the Library of Congress.

Rejected by many of her own race because she lacked athletic skills, was light skinned and had a good quality of hair, Brooks was deeply hurt and spendt much of her childhood writing. She was thirteen when she published her first poem "Eventide". After attending junior college and working for the NAACP, Brooks developed her writing in poetry workshops. Focusing on the urban Black experience, she published her first collection, *A Street in Bronzeville* in 1945.Describing her style as "folksy narrative", Gwendolyn used free verse, sonnets and other forms to paint lyrical portraits of Black urban poor.

She published her first and only novel, *Maud Martha* in 1953. The book details its title character in short vignettes that talk of being rejected by prejudice from both whites and lighter-skinned African Americans, mirroring her own personal experience. In her novel, Gwendolyn's message is to "accept the challenge of being human and to assert humanness with urgency".

Her later works took on politics more overtly, bringing forward the "problems of color and justice". Gwendolyn's activism and interest in supporting Black literature led her to change publishers choosing a fledgling Black publishing company in the 1970s. Making global connections between what was happening beside her and what was going on in the world, she traveled to Kenya, Tanzania and Ghana. The enhanced consciousness was reflected in her poetry and her daily walk through life.

DID YOU KNOW?

1. Her book of poetry entitled *Annie Allen* won her the Pulitzer.
2. Her inability to find a babysitter limited her travel to award ceremonies. Ring any bells?
3. She held the position of Illinois' Poet Laureate from 1968 until her death in 2000.

"The power to question is the basis of all human progress."

> A central figure of the Indian National Congress (political party), Indira Priyadarshini Nehru Gandhi (1917-1984) was the first female Prime Minister of India. She served three consecutive terms and was reelected to a fourth term in 1980. Indira was very popular when first elected because of her farming policies. She was plagued with corruption accusations for which she spent time in jail but came back to lead her nation into the nuclear age. Assassinated by her two Sikh bodyguards in 1984, revenge for "Operation Bluestar", Indira is seen as a strong-willed leader who brought India to become the lone regional power of South Asia.

Growing up an only child to a father who was India's Prime Minister and a sickly mother led to much unhappiness. Ill health and WWII interrupted her studies in England. Indira married Feroze Gandhi in 1942 against her family's wishes. The couple had two sons. In the 1950s, Indira became unofficially her father's personal assistant. Toward the end of that decade, she served as president of the Congress. After the death of her father, she served in Prime Minister Shastri's cabinet.

Indira was elected Prime Minister in 1967. Because she was a woman, party officials thought she would merely be a puppet for their control. Her first eleven years as PM proved her strength of resolve, holding on to her policy positions and going to war with Pakistan over Bangladesh. Later on, high inflation, drought and 1973 oil crises made her popularity drop. She was found guilty of corruption.

Instead of stepping down, Indira called a state of emergency, giving herself dictatorial powers. During those two years, widespread atrocities were carried out. Indira was reelected in 1980. Her order for military action "Operation Bluestar" at the *Golden Temple* (1984) against Sikh militants led to her death by trusted bodyguards.

DID YOU KNOW?

1. A BBC poll named her "Woman of the Millennium" (1999).
2. In 2020, *Time* magazine named her one of the world's 100 powerful women who defined the 20th century.

Beginning her world-renowned painting career at the age of seventy-eight, Anna Mary Robertson Moses (1860-1961) was a true American gem. Known as "Grandma Moses", her artwork has been shown and distributed worldwide. Giving birth to ten children and losing five of them during infancy astounds me. I'm amazed she survived the emotional pain. Starting a new career at her late age proves just how gutsy she was. Classified as an American folk painter, Grandma Moses documented rural life after her hands became too arthritic to embroider. When painting with her right hand became too painful, she used her left.

At the age of twelve, Anna left her one-room school to begin working for a neighboring farmer. For the next fifteen years, she continued doing chores or housework, cooking or sewing for wealthy families. One of them noticed her admiration of Currier and Ives prints and purchased chalk and wax for her. The prints stirred her grade-school desire for painting landscapes.

When she was twenty-seven, she met and married a "hired man" –Thomas Moses. In 1905, they moved to a New York farm where they raised crops and their children. Anna helped support the family by selling different homemade foods. In 1927, Thomas died, leaving her to work the farm with their oldest son. When Anna was in her seventies, she began devoting most of her time to her childhood passion—painting. Self-taught, she had little regard for perspective and proportion, simply wanting to depict rural life.

A New York collector, Louis J Caldor, happened to spot her artwork hanging in a local store and purchased them all. Dubbed "Grandma Moses" by the New York Press, her paintings were on display at the Museum of Modern Art in New York City. From there, she went on to having a one-woman show in the city.

DID YOU KNOW?

1. Her award-winning autobiography, *My Life's History*, was published in 1952.
2. On her 100th birthday, Governor Nelson Rockefeller declared "Grandma Moses Day". This amazing woman lived to be 101!
3. She was honored with a U.S. commemorative stamp with her painting *Fourth of July* in 1969.
4. Anna was a good friend of Norman Rockwell; they lived across from one another on the New York-Vermont state border.

A Greek Goddess capable of both good and evil, Hecate's name means "worker from afar". She is especially associated with the moon, regeneration, doorways, magic and witchcraft, creatures of the night and necromancy (communicating with the dead). Hecate is a Titaness of magic, having absolute control and Divine authority over magic, witchcraft and sorcery. Known as "Queen of the Night" and "Queen of the Crossroads", She owns the ultimate skeleton key—the key that unlocks the door to all realms. Hecate serves as the intermediary between all realms. She rules wisdom, choices, atonement, victory, vengeance, travel and has the power to give or refuse any mortal's wish. She is a powerful Goddess indeed.

A shrine to Hecate is placed at the entrance of homes or even cities, hoping to ward off evil spirits that roam the world. At one time, Hecate was the chief deity of Caria, now in western Turkey. In art, She's depicted as a single figure, though in later periods, statues show Her having three faces and three bodies united. Sometimes Hecate is wearing a knee-length maiden's skirt and hunting boots.

Her name is invoked for justice, especially for sexual crimes against women and girls. Hecate is cited when justice is not forthcoming from other channels. She is also petitioned for fertility, especially in female children.

Her power to banish ghosts or bring victory in battle is well known. As Goddess of birth, death and purification, Hecate is an exceptionally powerful spirit. Renowned for Her expertise in plants and their healing powers, Hecate's magical garden at Colchis on the Black Sea sat next to Her temple.

DID YOU KNOW?

1. Her emblems are the star and crescent moon; Her sacred animals snakes, toads, dragons, cats and especially dogs.
2. Hecate's symbols are paired torches, dogs, red mullet, serpents, keys, polecats, daggers and Hecate's wheel.

Harriet Jacobs (1813-1897) was an African American writer, feminist, abolitionist and mother of eight. Born into slavery, she overcame trauma and shame to write her autobiography *Incidents in the Life of a Slave Girl* –now considered an American classic. Jacobs hid in her grandmother's attic for seven years, the roof so low she could not stand, after escaping her owner. (I can't even begin to imagine.) Upon arriving in New York, she worked as a nanny while she contacted abolitionist and feminist reformers. Throughout and after the Civil War, she went to the Union-occupied parts of the South and, along with her daughter, helped organize and establish two schools for fugitive and freed slaves.

Harriet Jacobs had been taught to read, write and sew at age six by the daughter of Dr. Norcom, her de-facto master. Continually harassed by him and wanting to avoid the sexual victimization he intended, Jacobs ran away and hid. Seven years later, in 1842, she escaped via boat to New York and was eventually reunited with her children.

In 1853, Jacobs took her first steps toward authorship, writing several anonymous letters to the *New York Tribune*. In the first letter, she broached the sexually sensitive subject of female slave's sexual abuse and their mothers' attempts to protect them from it. Jacobs primary motive in deciding to write her book *Incidents in the Life of a Slave Girl* was to address white women of the North on behalf of thousands of "slave mothers still in bondage" in the South.

In confessing her sorrow, shame and trauma of her willing participation in a liaison that produced two illegitimate children, Jacobs wanted to indict the southern patriarchy for its sexual brutality of black women like herself. By acknowledging her transgressions when she was a girl, Jacobs articulated a much bolder (and sadder) truth— that the morality of free white women had little to no ethical relevance or authority when applied to enslaved black women of the South. What courage she had!

DID YOU KNOW?

1. Harriet was a friend of both Lucretia Mott and Susan B Anthony.
2. She succumbed to tuberculosis at age eighty-four.

"Special children must have special schools with well-trained teachers who used materials adapted to those children's capabilities. They should not be abandoned to state institutions where conditions were appallingly inhumane."

A teaching pioneer in special education, Margaret Bancroft (1854-1912), at the age of twenty-nine, chartered the first private boarding school for children with disabilities in New Jersey. She believed children with special needs should have specialized programs adapted to their unique physical and mental needs. The "Haddonfield Bancroft Training School for the Mentally Deficient and Peculiarly Backward" (1883) strove to develop innovative teaching techniques for the disabled.

Margaret recognized that children with developmental disabilities had the ability to learn when given individualized attention, patience and love. She decided to devote her life to that purpose. Now known as the Bancroft Training School, Margaret created a specialized program valuing the importance of proper nutrition, personal hygiene, exercise, sensory and artistic development and lessons suited to her students. The pupils participated in different forms of recreation including trips to the circus, theater, museums and concerts.

Bancroft Training has grown significantly in order to meet the needs of children, adults and their families with their diverse challenges. Specialized programs were created for children with autism, as well as for those with severe behaviors associated with disabilities. As a result of huge advances in health care and technology, Bancroft Training responded to people with acquired brain injuries and neurological conditions by establishing Bancroft Neuro Rehab. It provides rehabilitation services, including residential rehab, structured day programs, even outpatient services.

Margaret championed the cause of developmentally disabled children and fought for their right to adequate health care and education until her death. The school has grown since its inception into a large institution with many facilities, not only in New Jersey, but Delaware as well. What a marvelous achievement, don't you agree?

Did you know?

1. Margaret also helped organize a women's club "Haddon Fortnightly" in 1894. The club is still active over one hundred years later.
2. The club promotes educational, literary, and social interests for its members.

Recognized as the world's first female explorer, Jeanne Baret (1740-1807) was a French botanist who was simply looking for plants when she stepped aboard the *Etoile* in 1766. Jeanne posed as an assistant to Philibert Commerson, another French botanist selected for Louis Antoine de Bougainville's round-the-world journey. She had to disguise herself as a boy in order to travel as Commerson's assistant—French Royal Ordinance forbade women on French Navy ships.

Growing up in rural France allowed Jeanne to become very familiar with gathering and learning different plant species. Without any formal education, she became known as an "herb woman" having a particular knowledge of medicinal plants. Jeanne became a housekeeper for Commerson after his wife died in childbirth.

Setting sail from Nantes, France, Jeanne collected her first plants in Uruguay, Commerson was ill. The pair worked together in Brazil gathering specimens and writing observations. There, she discovered a delightful flowering vine graced with pink and violet flowers. She named the plant Bougainvillea in honor of the ship's captain. Those of us living in the tropics are quite familiar with prolific bougainvillea.

After sailing to the Pacific Ocean, there are differing accounts of how Jeanne's gender was revealed. Whether by Tahitians or the ship's crew members, some accounts describe violence against her on board the *Etoile*. When the ship stopped off in Mauritius in the Indian Ocean, Commerson's old friend, Pierre Poivre, invited the pair to disembark and stay. With Bougainville wanting to be rid of the woman on board, Jeanne and Commerson agreed.When her partner became ill and died, Jeanne stayed on in Port Louis; land was granted to her there.

DID YOU KNOW?

1. The relationship between Jeanne and Commerson grew after a time. Eventually they had a child together.
2. When Jeanne returned to France in 1775, she was granted a pension for her hard work and courage on the voyage.
3. It wasn't until recent years that Jeanne's role as a botanist has been recognized.

"So you're the little woman who wrote the book that made this great war." Abraham Lincoln, 1862.

World-renowned American author, Harriet Elisabeth Beecher Stowe (1811-1896) was an abolitionist, social activist and mother of seven children. She and her husband sheltered runaway slaves for the Underground Railroad. Her book, *Uncle Tom's Cabin*, or *Life Among the Lowly*, shed light on the harsh conditions of African American slaves. After its publication and rampant success in 1852, Harriet became the best known American in the world! Her novel—the best-selling book of the 19th century—motivated the abolition movement which led to the Civil War's genesis.

In Cincinnati, Harriet began her career by teaching. Joining the "Semi-Colon Club," she made friends with local like-minded literary aficionados of the day. Living across the river from Kentucky, she was able to see first-hand the terror and beatings suffered by escaped slaves. There were also anti-slavery debates given at Lane Theological Seminary. Those debates resulted in a mass exodus of students from Lane to Oberlin Collegiate Institute, students of all races were accepted there.

Harriet, along with her husband and seven children, moved to Maine in 1836. Later she began publishing weekly installments of *Uncle Tom's Cabin* in serial form in a national newspaper. Her book of the same title was published in 1852. The goal of the book was to educate people to the horrors of Black slavery in the South. With her books flying off the shelf, Southerners became enraged.

Sales overseas also flourished, because there were no international copyright laws, Harriet earned nothing from them. She traveled to Britain where her popularity was unprecedented. When she arrived, there were ten versions of her book on theatre stages in London. Harriet went on to write dozens of books and articles.

DID YOU KNOW?

1. Harriet wrote thirty books that included novels and three travel memoirs plus many articles and letters.
2. You will find landmarks dedicated to her in Florida, Ohio, Connecticut and Maine.
3. Harriet lived next door to Mark Twain in Hartford, Connecticut.

An Indian politician and freedom fighter, philanthropist Sucheta Mazumdar Kripal-ani (1908-1974), was also India's first woman Chief Minister. She served as the head of the Uttar Pradesh government—India's largest province from 1963-1967.

When *Sucheta* received her master's degree in history from St. Stephen's College in Delhi, India was a country charged with nationalist sentiment, the freedom struggle was gaining momentum. She began work at Banaras Hindu University (BHU) as a lecturer. Once she joined the Indian National Congress, she quickly rose in rank during the *Quit India Movement* (1942). She is credited as being the first head in the Congress of the Women's department.

Because Gandhi was very impressed by Sucheta's dedication, he helped appoint her as Organizing Secretary of the *Kasturba Gandhi National Memorial Trust* (1946). When violent riots broke out in *Noakhali* (present day Bangladesh), Sucheta and Gandhi visited the riot-torn area giving hands-on service to victims. By the end of 1946, Sucheta was elected a member of the Constituent Assembly and because of her high regard, was included in the subcommittee to draft the charter for the Constitution of India. Sucheta was chosen in 1949 as a delegate to the UN General Assembly.

Her next accomplishment was being elected in India's first general election (1952). Sucheta served as Minister of State for small-scale industries. She was re-elected five years later, this time as a congressional party candidate. Because of her brilliant intellect and vibrant oratory skills, she quickly became an illustrious member of Parliament.

Thanks to Sucheta's hard work, intelligence, honor, and calm demeanor, she was able to overcome problems efficiently. Thus, she campaigned for the fourth *Lok Sabha* election and won (1967). Retiring from politics in 1971, Sucheta and her husband made a home in Delhi. As philanthropists, they generously supported the *Lok Kalyan Samiti,* an NGO established to aid low-income groups in India's capital city.

DID YOU KNOW?

1. As Chief Minister, she helped squash the state employees strike, vowing not to raise their wages. I have to disagree with her on that one.

"Every morning I am a beginner."

Born Joanna Eckhart (1893-1992), Hanya Holm was a German dancer, choreographer, lecturer, mentor, and most importantly, dance educator. One of the "Big Four" founders of American modern dance, Hanya was witty, disciplined and uncompromising as a legendary teacher. She successfully adapted German training with American rhythm. Hanya started a summer dance institute (1941) in Colorado Springs, Colorado, to complement her own touring company which she started in New York in 1936.

Hanya's parents were able to give her a progressive education at a convent in Mainz, Germany. She developed a strong sense of self-discipline there, gained respect for knowledge and discovered her passion for music. She also learned to appreciate spontaneity and improvisation through rhythmic movement while receiving further musical training in Frankfurt. After watching a dance performance by Mary Wigman, Hanya changed her focus from music to dance.

Spending a year at Wigman's school, Hanya began teaching dance. By 1929, she had become co-director of the Wigman Central Institute in Dresden. When she began touring the United States in 1930, a branch of the school was created in New York with Hanya as its lead instructor. Her method of teaching was to help students discover where movement came from within the body, liberating each student to develop his or her own style.

By 1936, Hanya had broken ties with Wigman and gave her own name to the school and company which had been touring. Greenwich Village was now her home and she became a U.S. citizen in 1939. Hanya began lecturing as well as teaching, touring and choreographing. Her dances were "lyrical celebrations of movement". She established her summer institute in Colorado Springs. In 1952, Hanya Holm was the first person to claim copyright on a choreographic work—the Broadway musical, *Kiss Me Kate*. It was the first of twelve musicals she would choreograph, including *My Fair Lady* and *Camelot*.

DID YOU KNOW?

1. Hanya told her students, "You have a perfect right to branch out, if you have the stuff in you, if you discover your own richness, if you have something to say."
2. Hanya taught dance until she was ninety-two-years-old! She lived ninety-nine years.

Greek virgin Goddess of the hearth, Hestia is one of the twelve Olympian deities. Her special powers and skills are keeping the hearth fires lit on Mount Olympus and in Greek homes. She also helps keep peace in the family and teaches people how to build their homes. Hestia is considered the Goddess of hearth, home, architecture, domesticity, family and the state. She is described as a kind, forgiving, discreet Goddess with a passive and non-confrontational nature.

Hestia is usually portrayed as a modest middle-aged veil-wearing woman. Sometimes She is standing by a large fire and carrying a staff or holding some flowers in her hands. Her symbols are the hearth, the fire and the kettle. And Her sacred animal is the pig. Hestia's sacred plant is the Chaste tree.

The hearth in Greek culture is very important, symbolizing the heart and soul of the household. Hestia is the personification of the hearth and She receives sacrifices at all the temples of the Gods as each one has its own hearth. It is tradition that She receives sacrifices before the other gods. Hestia also receives the first and last libation offering at any feast, She is mentioned first in any prayers and oaths. A town's hearth is maintained continuously by the community, usually by unmarried women specially selected for that purpose.

There is a custom to take the flame from Hestia's public hearth in the mother city and carry it to a newly founded city. Nowadays, that same flame is the Olympic torch which is to be held and carried at the Olympic Games ceremony. It is never allowed to die, just like in ancient times.

Did you know?

1. "Goddess of the sacrificial flame" is another of Hestia's titles.
2. The Goddess receives sacrifices at the communal hearth each time a new magistrate begins and ends a term of office and before council meetings.

HARRIET TUBMAN

"Slavery is the next thing to hell."

An American abolitionist icon, Harriet Tubman (c. 1820-1913) was a nurse, a mother, women's rights suffragist and civil rights activist. She acted as a cook, an armed scout and a spy for the Union Army during the Civil War. Harriet helped rescue hundreds of slaves.Born into slavery, Araminta (Harriet) Ross Tubman endured physical violence each day.

Her most severe injury happened when she refused to help restrain a runaway slave. The overseer threw a two-pound weight, striking her in the head, knocking her unconscious. She endured severe headaches, seizures and narcoleptic episodes the rest of her life.

In 1844, Araminta changed her first name to Harriet. In 1849, worried that she and the other slaves on the plantation where she lived were going to be sold, Harriet decided to run away, eventually arriving in Philadelphia. Having first encountered the Underground Railroad when she escaped in 1849, Harriet became very involved helping family and others still living in slavery. Between 1850 and 1860, Harriet made nineteen trips following the Underground Railroad from the South to the North. Guiding over three hundred people which included her parents and siblings, from slavery to freedom earned her the nickname "Moses" for her leadership.

When the Fugitive Slave Law was changed in 1850, Harriet rerouted the Underground Railroad to Canada. One of her best-known missions was the raid on Combahee Ferry in South Carolina in 1863. Harriet worked with Union Colonel James Montgomery during this raid to free over seven hundred slaves. In early 1859, abolitionist Senator William H. Seward sold a parcel of land on the outskirts of Auburn, New York to Harriet. The Auburn property became a refuge for her family and friends. She spent the years after the war living there, tending to her family and others who had taken up residence with her.

DID YOU KNOW?

1. President Biden's administration is currently making efforts to place Harriet's likeness on the front of the $20 bill—efforts to do so earlier had been stopped in 2017.
2. Since 1913, she has been an icon for courage and freedom.

"One test of the correctness of educational procedure is the happiness of the child."

An Italian physician and educator, Maria Tecla Artemisia Montessori (1870-1952) was an innovator, peace activist, and mother. An icon best known for the educational philosophy bearing her name, Maria looked at instruction from a scientific point of view. Believing that education should prepare a person for all aspects of life, she designed materials and techniques that promoted a natural growth of learning in students. Maria was among the first women in Italy to receive a medical degree, working in the fields of psychiatry, education and anthropology.

Always ahead of her time, thirteen-year-old Maria began attending a boys technical school. After seven years of engineering, she started pre-med, receiving her degree in 1896. In her work, Maria developed an interest in special needs children. Her success with developmentally disabled children spurred her desire to test her teaching methods on *normal* children, which she did.

In Rome, Dr. Montessori developed the "Montessori method" for children from six to twelve. She began with the required Italian curriculum of her time. Maria discovered that an elementary child could master academic subjects usually not taught until middle or high school when allowed to work independently instead of being taught in groups led by a teacher.

When in classes with six to twelve- year-old students, inspiring and teaching each other, elementary children thrived. Young students absorbed knowledge from their surroundings, essentially teaching themselves. This led to pupils working at a much higher level than was previously thought possible at that age.

Forced into exile from Italy in 1934, Maria moved to England, then to Amsterdam. "Education and Peace" was the theme of the Sixth International Montessori Congress (1937—Amsterdam) and the beginning of her peace activism. She and her son, Mario, spent 1939-1946 interred in India because of WWII. They continued to develop Montessori methods there, as well as speak out for world peace.

Did you know?

1. Maria Montessori was nominated twice for the Nobel Peace Prize.
2. In 2020, *Time* nominated her as one of the Top One Hundred Women of the Year.

An American inventor, Lillian Moller Gilbreth (1878-1972) was a teacher, author, industrial engineer, psychologist and a mother of twelve children. (You read that right, twelve!) As a pioneer in ergonomics, Lillian patented many kitchen appliances including the famous trash can with a foot-pedal lid-opener, electric food-mixer and shelves inside the refrigerator door. She is known as the "Mother of Modern Management." Lillian, one of the first female engineers to earn a Ph.D., is considered the be the first industrial/organizational psychologist.

For over forty years, Lillian's career combined psychology with the study of scientific management and engineering. Her perspective as a wife and mother was included in her research, writing, and consulting work. She became a pioneer in what is now known as industrial and organizational psychology. Lillian helped industrial engineers recognize psychological dimensions of the workplace.

She wrote numerous publications, as well as co-authoring with her husband, Frank, multiple books and more than fifty papers. However, in their joint publications, her name was not always given as co-author, possibly due to publishers' disdain of the female writer. She and her husband were equal partners in Gilbreth, Inc.—a management and consulting firm. Becoming adept at "time-and-motion" studies, they named their methodology the *Gilbreth System*. Their research on fatigue was a forerunner to ergonomics.

During WWI, the Gilbreths did pioneering work with the rehabilitation of amputee veterans. After her husband's death, Lillian continued to research, write and teach, in addition to consulting with manufacturers and businesses. She was also instrumental in developing the modern kitchen, making it more efficient. Lillian created the *work triangle* and linear-kitchen layouts still used today, including inventing items we now take for granted.

DID YOU KNOW?

1. As "America's first lady of engineering" she was in demand as a professor and lecturer even after retiring from Purdue University.
2. At the age of eighty-six, Lillian became a resident lecturer at MIT. She died at the age of ninety-three.

"No one knows the color of a flower 'till it is broken."

Best known for her association with the Imagist movement, Hilda Doolittle (1886-1961) was a prolific poet, novelist, translator, memoirist and self-proclaimed pagan mystic. The first woman awarded the American Academy of Arts and Letters medal, Hilda became an icon for both LGBTQ rights and feminist movements when her poems, plays, letters, and essays were rediscovered during the 1970's and 1980's.

Hilda travelled to Europe in 1911, intending to spend only summer vacation, but remained abroad for the rest of her life. Upon meeting Ezra Pound, H.D. (her pen name) grew interested in and quickly became a leader of the Imagist movement (favoring precise imagery and sharp language), though her works went far beyond Imagism. She helped define what came to be called 'free verse' and was among the early users of a stream-of-consciousness narrative.

H.D. found her *raison d'etre* from her early personal relationships that led to her artistic identity. Later, her friendship with Sigmund Freud helped her deal with WWI traumas—the death of her brother, her father, a stillborn child and the breakup of her marriage to Richard Aldington. Her earliest poems found recognition when they were published by Harriet Monroe in *Poetry* in 1913. H.D.'s first volume of verse, *Sea Garden*, published in 1916, established her as an important voice among radical young Imagist poets.

Her writing is distinguished by the intense strength of her images, economy of language and use of classical mythology. Birth and death along with love and war are the central concerns of Hilda's work.

DID YOU KNOW?

1. Sadly, Hilda's many works did not receive widespread appreciation or acclaim during her lifetime. Another woman ahead of her time!
2. Her rediscovery in the 1970's began when feminists identified with her questioning views of gender roles.

Kate Warne (1833-1868) was an American female law enforcement agent. She holds the honor of being the first female detective in the Pinkerton Detective Agency and the United States (1856). Kate is best known for thwarting the "Baltimore Plot", an attempted assassination of President Abraham Lincoln. Allen Pinkerton later declared the "pioneering female detective" one of the five best detectives he had ever worked with.

Kate first approached Allen Pinkerton, a Scottish immigrant, for a detective's position at age twenty-three. Though it took effort on her part to convince him she was equal to the task—Kate pointed out that she would be able to assume the role of woman's confidante, not something a male could do. She also pointed out that men liked to brag around women. For those two reasons, Pinkerton acknowledged the advantage of a female detective and Kate was hired.

Her first assignment was to get a lead on the theft of $10,000.00 from the Adams Express Company railroad. After ingratiating herself to the suspect's wife, Kate quickly learned the husband had stolen the money, as well as where it was hidden. The money was recovered and the bandit convicted. On another occasion, Kate thwarted a plot to poison the wealthy Captain Sumner. Posing as a fortune teller to Sumner's sister, Annie Thayer, Kate listened to the story of Annie and her lover's upcoming attempt to murder the captain for his fortunes. The lover was caught and convicted for his wife's murder.

Kate's success was due to her charm and gracious personality. Her career was filled with many triumphs, none as well regarded as thwarting the Baltimore Plot. Once she exposed the plot by going undercover at secessionist parties, Lincoln posed as an invalid traveling on a night train with his caregiving sister, Kate. They slipped through Baltimore undetected, evading the assassins.

DID YOU KNOW?

1. Kate was in charge of the Female Detective Bureau (established by Pinkerton) as Supervisor of Women Agents.
2. Pinkerton is still operating today as Pinkerton Consulting & Investigations, Inc d.b.a. Pinkerton Corporate Risk Management.

A Canadian ethnomusicologist, Ida Ruhdorfer Halpern (1910-1987) overcame rheumatic fever at age nineteen to earn distinctive honors from both Canada and Queen Elizabeth. Born in Vienna, Austria, she fled German occupation around 1940. As a musicologist, Ida recorded over four hundred ancestral First Nation songs, allowing their culture's music to be preserved. In doing so, Ida brought forth recognition and respect to that civilization's art—quite an achievement for someone walking around with a weak heart.

As a child, Ida loved the piano and began taking lessons at age six. Her study of classical languages and German literature fed her music interests. After being hospitalized for a year with rheumatic fever, she was forced to give up playing the piano. The disease was found to have damaged her heart permanently and playing it would cause too much strain. Ida turned to musicology, earning her Ph.D. from the University of Vienna.

Fleeing Austria when the Nazis invaded, Ida and her husband settled in Canada, via Shanghai. As the first woman in Canada to hold a Ph.D. in musicology, she set about building a career by opening her own music studio, she initially gave piano lesson. She also began teaching music appreciation at the University of British Columbia. Becoming involved in Vancouver's society, Ida was drawn to the "folk music" of the First Nations.

Interviewing Native Americans regarding their ancestral music, Ida tread carefully. Such music was sacred, taking her six years to win their confidence in order to record the songs. At the time, it was actually illegal to celebrate First Nation cultures. Nonetheless, she persisted. Working with the *Kwakwaka'wakw* and *Nuuchahnulth* tribes, she collected around three hundred songs initially. Assisted by Mungo Martin, a *Kwakwaka'wakw* artist and songwriter, she documented another 124 songs. Ida painstakingly studied and described the music, relying on the tribes' explanations and translations

Did you know?

1. Sadly, her contribution of First Nation's music has been overlooked for various reasons.
2. Queen Elizabeth awarded a medal, Commander of the Most Excellent Order of the British Empire (CBE) in 1957.

Known as the "Queen of the Heaven", Inanna is a Goddess from ancient Mesopotamia. She is connected to love and beauty, war and justice, sexuality and governmental power. Originally worshipped in Sumeria, neighboring areas of Assyria, Akkad and Babylonia soon claimed Her as their own, calling Her Ishtar. Inanna was seen as Venus, the brilliant star of the morning and evening, and identified with that Roman Goddess. She is named in many Mesopotamian myths in which She bestows knowledge and culture.

Because of Her strength and courage, Inanna is often accompanied by a lion. A symbol of Her supremacy over the "king of beasts", She is sometimes pictured riding him. Armed for battle, Inanna carries a quiver and bow. Independent and gutsy, She does as She pleases. Cunningly manipulative and threatening, Inanna is often trying to fix situations that Her impulsive behavior generates. Certainly, She is never depicted as a Mother Goddess. Listed among the seven initial celestial powers, Inanna formed the basis of other deities in different cultures.

Showing both kind and calculating traits speaks volumes about how the Sumerians understood femininity. Women held an equal place in their culture. Inanna has endured throughout history due to her accessibility and distinguished status.

Her symbols are roses, lions and jeweled encrusted wands, her themes are sky, Universal Consciousness and law, peace, unity, love and leadership. Animals associated with Her are sheep, lions, scorpions, owls and doves. Inanna's colors are silver, gold, red and green. Her downward climb to the Underworld was to gain knowledge of death and rebirth.

DID YOU KNOW?

1. More of Her symbols include a hook-shaped knot of reeds and an eight-pointed star.
2. Inanna has become important to feminists as She first appeared in the male-dominated Sumerian pantheon as equal or more powerful.

An Egyptian suffragette, Nour Al-Huda Mohamed Sultan Sha'arawi (1879-1947) was apioneering feminist, author, philanthropist, nationalist and mother. She influenced women throughout the Arabic world with her activism. Huda founded the first philanthropic society run by Egyptian women and was the first to establish a school for girls in 1910 that focused on academics instead of skills. She helped to organize the largest women's anti-British demonstration in 1919 and three years later founded the Egyptian Feminist Union. That same year, Huda became famous by simply stepping off a train in Cairo and removing her hijab (veil). She is considered the founder of Egypt's feminist movement.

Huda was born into a wealthy family and also into the harem system. The system kept women secluded in separate buildings, guarded by eunuchs, veiled and concealed from the outside world. All women, except for peasants working in the countryside, were veiled. The harem system and veiling were traditions followed by Christian, Jewish and Muslim women.Were you aware of that?

When Huda founded the philanthropic society in 1908, she believed having women run projects would challenge traditional thinking, a woman needing a man's protection. It also set aside the idea of women existing merely for men's pleasure. Founding the Egyptian Feminist Union allowed women to focus on issues of suffrage, increased education, women's dress and their freedom of movement. When Egypt was given independence from Britain in 1922, women were expected to go back to the harem system. (Oh no!)

Huda did not believe in the *old* ways, and so continued to advocate for women's rights. At the International Women's Suffrage Alliance in Rome (1923), Huda argued that women in ancient Egypt had equal rights to men. It was only under foreign domination that those rights were lost. Her second argument was Islam also granted equals rights to women and men, but current interpretations of the Koran were incorrect. Speaking out her beliefs took great courage, wouldn't you agree?

Did you know?

1. Huda was awarded Egypt's *Order of the Virtues* (a knighthood for females) in 1945.
2. She continued her philanthropic projects as well as fighting for women's rights her entire life.

"It is not the color of the skin that makes the man or the woman, but the principle formed in the soul."

A free-born African American educator, Maria W. Miller Stewart (1803-1879) was also a journalist, lecturer, abolitionist and women's rights activist. The first American woman of any race to address a crowd of mixed gender and race in the United States (1832), Maria was also the first African American woman to write and publish a political manifesto. Her calls for Black people to resist slavery, oppression and exploitation were considered very radical. Ahead of her time, she influenced Frederick Douglas, Sojourner Truth and Frances Harper.

Orphaned at the age of five, Maria was "bonded out" to work as a servant for a local minister in Hartford, Connecticut. Her education began at sixteen, and she eventually moved to Boston where she married a man whose prestigious career brought them some wealth and earned the Stewarts a place in Boston's Black middle class. Her husband's early death and the tragedy of being denied her inheritance because of dishonest white executors compelled Maria to begin speaking out against racial and gender discrimination.

Maria first wrote a collection of political tracts which she shared with William Lloyd Garrison; he published them in his newspaper, *The Liberator*. She then gave a total of four publicized speeches between 1831-1833. Criticized for her boldness and for violating the taboo prohibiting women from appearing on public platforms to address men, Maria joined the Female Literacy Society in New York City and began teaching Black children—though at a fraction of the salary paid to white teachers. She continued to speak out eloquently on behalf of education.

DID YOU KNOW?

1. Maria also established a school in Washington D.C. for the children of escaped slaves during the Civil War.
2. She believed Black children merely needed the proper tools to succeed. And so they did.

"I will have nothing to do with a bomb!"

Lise Meitner (1878-1968) was an Austrian-Swedish Physicist who was part of the team that led to the discovery of nuclear fission. She was the first woman from the University of Vienna to be awarded a doctorate in physics, only the second in the world to achieve that honor. Lise was also the first woman to become a full professor of physics in Germany. Fleeing the Nazis, she lived for many years in Sweden and ultimately became a citizen. Many consider her the "most significant woman scientist of the 20th century." How cool is that?

After earning her doctorate in 1906 summa cum laude, Lise attended Max Planck's lectures at Berlin in 1907 and joined Otto Hahn in research on radioactivity (she did the physics while he worked on the chemistry). But as an Austrian-Jewish woman, she was barred from the main labs and lectures, allowed to only work in the basement.

In 1912, Lise and Hahn moved to a new university with better lab facilities. Their partnership was dissolved when she had to flee the Nazis in 1938. She continued their work in Sweden, calculating the energy released when uranium atoms were split—which Hahn had been working on in Vienna. Hahn received the 1944 Nobel Prize in Chemistry for his research, while Lise was ignored despite her involvement in their joint research. The Nobel mistake, never acknowledged, was partially rectified in 1966 when Lise, Hahn and Strassman were awarded the Enrico Fermi Award.

Lise's male colleagues nominated her for the physics Nobel twenty-nine times, and for the chemistry Nobel nineteen times. Records do not entirely explain why none of these nominations were successful, though her Jewish ethnicity certainly played a factor during the war years. How sad and pathetic.

Did you know?

1. The scientists in the Nobel nomination pools (at the time) were all white males.
2. Chemical element 109 is called meitnerium in Lise's honor.

A 12th century German abbess, Hildegard of Bingen (1098-1179) was a writer, philosopher, theologian, visionary, polymath, composer and poetess. She wrote theological, botanical, and medicinal texts, composed liturgical songs and poems. A constructed language known as *Lingua Ignota* is credited to her as well. Some say Hildegard of Bingen was the pioneer of opera, sexology and scientific natural history. Known as 'Sibyl of the Rhine', she produced major works of theology and visionary writings.

Hildegard of Bingen was admitted into the Benedictine monastery in Mount St. Disibode to fulfill the educational requirements for a nun when she was only eight. At eighteen, Hildegard received her nun's status. Twenty years later, she succeeded *Jutta* as the Mother Superior.

Possessing remarkable healing abilities, Hildegard garnered immense respect as a doctor. People began flocking to her side to benefit from her healing prowess. She soon gained the title of *miracle woman*. (She used tinctures, herbs and precious stones.) Her two books on medicine, *Scivias* and *Causae et Curae*, covered a wide range of medicinal cures involving herbs. Works on botany, geology and saints' biographies were also penned by Hildegard.

Fond of drama, she wrote plays as well as poetry. She is credited with the invention of opera—she wrote and directed the first opera ever performed. Hildegard had an incredible passion for music which she entwined with her love for composing poetry. Seventy poems and a musical play, entitled *Ordo Virtutum*, were written by her. Her soaring melodies are still popular today. Her music is described as monophonic and consisted of one melodic line.

DID YOU KNOW?

1. Hildegard is most famous for her spiritual concept of *Viriditas* – "greenness" - the cosmic life force that infuses the natural world.
2. Scholars describe her music as highly melismatic (singing in a single syllable) often with recurrent melodic units.

Lakshmi Bai (1828-1858) the Rani of Jhansi was an Indian Queen in (present day) Uttar Pradesh, India. At her birth, her given name was Marnikarnika Tambe, her nickname Manu.A leading warrior of India's First War of Independence, she was venerated as an early symbol of resistance to British rule. The Rani (Hindu Queen) became a symbol of bravery, patriotism, and honor and her generosity was unbounded. Rani Lakshmi Bai is celebrated by her country's people as a woman who lived to go against perceived notions of 19th century Indian ladylike decorum. She is regarded as a national heroine.

The British government was intent on expanding and protecting its political and economic presence in India, forcefully taking over entire states. As the reigning queen of the Jhansi province, Lakshmi Bai tried to keep her state separate from British rule. The policy "British invocation of lapse" gave the British claim to the lands of Indian kings (Rajas) without male heirs. In the case of Jhansi, Governor-General Dalhousie chose not to accept the adoption of *Damodar Rao* (Bai's stepson) and proceeded to annex the kingdom. (Of course he did.)

Despite Lakshmi Bai's several letters to Dalhousie, the Governor-General refused her requests. She was forced to abdicate rule and abandon the fort in Jhansi. The next three years were filled with increased resentment and hostility toward the British, the Great Rebellion began in May 1857.

Bai enlisted and trained 14,000 troops, preparing for war by moving back into the fort at Jhansi.The British, led by Major-General Sir Hugh Rose, battled for more than two weeks before overtaking the fort. The Indian rebels retreated to Kalpi, and mounted an attack on Rose's troops. It was there that Bai was shot and killed during battle, the British claimed victory.

DID YOU KNOW?

1. Bai has been dubbed India's "Joan of Arc".
2. She was regarded as the "most dangerous of all Indian leaders."

Ina Boyle (1889-1967) was an Irish composer who never heard her compositions performed. Just now, nearly one hundred years later, the world is discovering her magical works. She was the most prolific female Irish composer before 1950. Her compositions include numerous genres—chamber, choral and orchestral works, as well as opera, vocal music and ballet. A handful of her works were performed during her lifetime, even winning awards. But the majority of Ina's compositions remain unpublished and were never performed.

As caregiver for her parents and a sister as well as keeper of their estate, Ina lived her whole life in Dublin, it may be part of the reason her music is not well known. She was home-schooled and her first music lessons were from her father. Her governess instructed her in violin and cello. By age 11, she was studying harmony and theory with Samuel Myerscough, the founder of Leinster School of Music in Dublin.

Ina received recognition in 1913, winning first and second prize for her *Elegy* and *The Last Invocation* in the composer's competition of *Sligo Feis Ceoi,* a renowned platform for artists, musicians and thespians. Studying harmony, composition and counterpoint, Ina published two anthems in 1915, though they were never performed. By 1923, she was sailing on a steamship to England to begin her studies with Ralph Vaughn Williams.

It was during her studies with Williams that Ina began composing larger works, including her ballet *Virgilian Suite.* Sadly, her beautiful compositions found no favor with Ireland. But she persisted with Williams' guidance despite the invalidation back home. Ina's studies with him continued until the outbreak of WWII when she could no longer travel to England. There was also great difficulty getting her works published because of the war.

DID YOU KNOW?

1. A high point for Ina during the war was a special concert by Radio Éireann Orchestra in 1944.
2. You can hear her music on YouTube.

Isis

Isis (meaning woman of the throne) is an Egyptian Goddess of love. She is known as the Goddess of the moon, life, death, healing and rebirth. The essence of femininity, She is exalted in Her role of motherhood and wife. Isis protects women and children, as well as heals the sick. Her extraordinary powers of healing bring other gods back to life. In Her traditional roles as wife, mother, healer and protector of the dead, She is worshipped as the Goddess of good fortune, the sea and travel.

It is said Isis gives much power and honor to women, reflecting the higher status women enjoyed in Egypt in ancient times. A "Goddess with Ten Thousand Names", Her strong character has been adopted by feminists worldwide. In the heavens, Her symbol is the star Sept (Sirius) and Her sacred animals include cows, snakes and scorpions. Isis is the patron of hawks, swallows, doves and vultures.

Pictures of Isis show Her a beautiful woman wearing a sheath dress with a solar disk or cow's horns on her head. Sometimes She is represented as a scorpion, a bird, a sow or a cow. Isis is often shone wearing an empty throne on Her headdress, symbolizing Her husband's absence following His death and Her role as the seat of the power of pharaoh.

In some forms, Isis is shown to be a woman with outstretched wings making Her the Goddess of the wind. She is often seen with Her child son, Horus, and with a crown and a vulture.Isis became the most powerful of all Gods and Goddesses in ancient Egypt—a position that was originally held by the Sun God, Ra.

DID YOU KNOW?

1. Because She was the "People's Goddess", Isis helped Her followers in many different ways.
2. Isis is a major Goddess. Her worship spreads throughout the world.

"The shorter Negro stood gazing at the horrible death of his brother without flinching. Five minutes later he was also hanged."

An African American journalist, Ida B. Wells Barnett (1862-1931) was an activist, educator,Feminist and mother of five. She led an anti-lynching crusade in the United States in the 1890s. Ida went on to found and become integral in groups striving for African American justice. She was awarded a Pulitzer Prize posthumously in 2020 "for her outstanding and courageous reporting on the horrific and vicious violence against African Americans during the era of lynching".

Born a slave in Mississippi, Ida and her family, along with the rest of the slaves of the Confederate states, were decreed free thanks to the Emancipation Proclamation about six months after her birth in 1863. She raised her five remaining siblings after her parents and a younger brother died of yellow fever. In May 1884, after having bought a first-class train ticket, Ida became outraged when the train crew ordered her to move to the car for African Americans. She refused on principle. As Ida was forcibly removed from the train, she bit one of the men on the hand. She then sued the railroad, winning a $500 settlement in a circuit court case. The decision was later overturned by the Tennessee Supreme Court. (Shit!)

This injustice led her to pick up a pen and write about issues of race and politics in the South.Ida's articles were published in black newspapers and periodicals. Later, she would become the owner of two different newspapers. Working as a teacher in Memphis, her outspoken criticisms of the condition of the segregated public city schools got her fired in 1891.

A lynching of three friends in Memphis incensed Ida and led her to begin an anti-lynching campaign in 1892. Three African Americans— Tom Moss, Calvin McDowell and Will Stewart —were arrested and brought to jail for defending their store. A mob grabbed them from their cells and lynched them.

DID YOU KNOW?

1. An investigative journalist, Ida was one of the founders of the NAACP.
2. She discovered that Southerners cried *rape* as an excuse to cover up the true reason for lynching—Black economic progress and its threat to whites.

An Argentine educator and medical doctor, Maria Teresa Ferrari Alvarado (1887-1956) was also a writer, mother and women's rights activist. The first female university professor in Latin America, she was one of the first women allowed to teach medicine. A pioneering researcher in women's health, Maria Ferrari studied the use of radiation therapy rather than surgery for uterine tumors. She also developed a vaginoscope that revolutionized women's health care in Brazil. An ardent feminist, Maria also established the first maternity ward and gynecological services at the *Hospital Militar Central of Buenos Aires* in 1925—which lead to the first incubation services in the country.

Maria enrolled in medical school in 1904 while she continued to teach. Her enrollment was frowned upon, but there was no legal precedent to bar her admission to the National University of Buenos Aires. She was awarded her medical degree in 1911. After completing her residency, Maria applied to teach at the university level. Instead, she was offered a teaching post at the School of Midwifery. Outraged, she fought against prejudice and misogyny for thirteen years which prevented her advancement.

Meanwhile, she undertook additional medical study in Europe and the United States, learning pioneering techniques that she brought back to Argentina. In 1925, Maria was appointed as the Argentine governmental delegate to the First Child Welfare Congress in Geneva, Switzerland.

Maria won her fight in 1927 and was granted a professorship. She was appointed head of gynecology and maternity at *Hospital Militar* in Buenos Aires, a post she held until 1939, when she was forced out by the new conservative government. (One step forward, two steps back.) A passionate feminist, Maria established the Argentina Federation of University Women in 1936, while she pushed for recognition of women's civil and political rights. She specifically wanted to improve women's legal status and open educational doors for all women.

DID YOU KNOW?

1. In 1939, Maria was ultimately made a *full* professor, receiving the title *Profesor Extraordinario* of Obstetrics.
2. She introduced radiation therapy and Cesarean Section innovations to Argentina.

"I want you to understand that your first duty is to humanity. I want others to look at us and see that we care not just about ourselves but about others."

> Born Sarah Breedlove (1867-1919), Madame C. J. Walker was a pioneering Black entrepreneur, activist, philanthropist, mother, and the first recorded female self-made millionairess in America (*Guinness Book of World Records*).

Born to Louisiana sharecroppers, Sarah was orphaned at age seven, married at fourteen and widowed at twenty. She and her two-year-old daughter moved to St. Louis where she began attending night school while working as a laundress. It was there that she met Charles J. Walker. He would become her second husband.

She was inspired to create hair products for Black women after a scalp disorder caused her to lose most of her hair. Mme. Walker came up with a treatment that would completely change the hair care industry for African Americans. The "Walker System" involved scalp preparation, lotions and iron combs. Even though there were other products on the market for Black hair, they were largely created and marketed by white businesses. Mme. Walker differentiated her products by emphasizing their attention to the health of the women who were using it.

Mme. Walker began by selling her homemade products directly to Black women, gaining their loyalty thanks to her personal approach. She went on the employ a whole fleet of saleswomen to sell her products, calling them "beauty culturalists. Mme. Walker then opened a beauty salon and factory in 1908 in Pittsburgh, Pennsylvania. Moving her business headquarters to Indianapolis in 1910 gave her more access to railroads for distribution and a larger population of African American customers. She left the management of the Pittsburgh branch to her daughter, A'Lelia. Mme. Walker traveled to Central America and the Caribbean to expand her business, then relocated to New York City in 1916.

Did you know?

1. At the height of production, the Madame C.J. Walker Company employed over three thousand people, largely Black women who sold Walker's products door-to-door.
2. Arriving in Harlem, she quickly became involved in the NAACP's anti-lynching movement and expanded her philanthropic activities nationwide.

"...we were raising our standard of living at the expense of our standard of character."

Pioneering the art of investigative journalism, Ida Minerva Tarbell (1857-1944) became known by some as "Madame Muckraker". An American writer, biographer, educator and lecturer, Ida penned the 1904 book *The History of the Standard Oil Company* bringing down the Standard Oil monopoly by exposing John D. Rockefeller's shady dealingswith major railroads. Ida's prolific writing took on the "big boys" of business in the early 20th century. Part owner of *The American Magazine,* she traveled throughout the U.S. lecturing on world peace, labor operations, tariffs and women's issues.

Born in a log cabin in Erie County, Pennsylvania, young Ida dreamed of becoming a scientist. Fascinated with the planets and stars, geology and botany, she discovered she hated teaching and began to write for a local magazine. When Ida began working with the powerful editor, Sam McClure, readers found her writing voice fresh and exciting. After penning a biography of Abraham Lincoln, she was recognized as his foremost biographer. Other biographies followed.

Wanting to "expose the ills of American society," McClure requested an article on American businessman, John D. Rockefeller. Because she grew up in oil-refining country, Ida reluctantly researched what she thought would be a boring story. Discovering Rockefeller's back-handed dealings that led to the "Cleveland Massacre", she began writing "a damning portrayal of big business" proving Rockefeller's pettiness and continued use of illegal practices. Her bestseller led to the Hepburn Act of 1906 and the creation of the Federal Trade Commission in 1914.

She and McClure raised enough money to open Phillips Publishing Company and purchase *The American Magazine.* Instead of exposing the ills of people and business, the magazine concentrated on what was "right" with the world.

DID YOU KNOW?

1. With her book generating much fame, Ida had unknowingly created a new form of journalism—muckraking. Though she hated the term, she embraced investigative journalism and saw herself as an historian instead.
2. Often called a feminist because of her actions, Ida did not support the women's suffrage movement.

Leizu, also known as Xi Ling-shi (c. 27th century BCE), was a legendary Chinese empress and wife of the Yellow Emperor. She is credited with the discovery of silk, the silk reel and she invented the silk loom. According to the Chinese, there are at least two different accounts of the origin of the silkworm. When Leizu shared her discovery, a new industry was born—sericulture (the raising of silkworms and the production of silk). Empress Leizu is called the Goddess of Silk because of her discovery, innovations and inventions.

Whether a silkworm cocoon fell into Leizu's tea while she sat under a mulberry tree or she dropped it into her teacup is inconsequential. She separated a fine thread from the cocoon and wound it round her finger. The fourteen-year-old convinced her husband to give her a grove of mulberry trees in order for her to domesticate the worms that made the cocoons. Sericulture was born and kept a state secret by the Chinese.

Eventually, the secret leaked out, reaching the Korean peninsula around 200 BCE. It took several more centuries for sericulture to travel to the west. Around 300 CE, India began establishing the industry.

Because of her discovery and the planting of more mulberry trees, Leizu was able to experiment with the thread, developing a way in which cloth could be made. She taught other women how to make silk and to embroider with the silk cloth. Today, China accounts for 74 percent of the global raw silk production and 90 percent of the world export market.

DID YOU KNOW?

1. Leizu is worshipped in China and is called "Silkworm Mother."
2. Ever since her discovery and innovations, only women are charged with making cloth from silk.

"I wasn't really naked. I simply didn't have any clothes on."

Freda Josephine McDonald Baker (1906-1975) was much more than a world renowned entertainer. Josephine was a WWII French resistance fighter, a civil rights activist, actress, singer and mother to twelve adopted children from different countries. One of the most successful African American entertainers in France, Josephine was the first African American to star in a motion picture. After serving with the French resistance, the *Black Pearl* was awarded the *Croix de Guerre* by the French military and named a *Chevalier of the Legion d' Honneur.* She was given a French military funeral and a twenty-one -gun salute, the only American ever to receive such an honor.

Growing up in poverty, Josephine became a live-in domestic for white families in St. Louis at age eight. Dropping out of school by thirteen, she worked as a waitress and lived on the streets. Married at thirteen and again at fifteen, she took up vaudeville dancing, traveling to New York City where she found some success.

Josephine was performing in Paris at the *Theatre des Champs-Elysees* when she was only nineteen! She became an instant success with her erotic dancing style and began touring Europe. She was the first African American star to visit Yugoslavia via the Orient Express. By 1936, Josephine was singing as well as acting in films.

When WWII broke out, she began working with the Red Cross in Africa and the Middle East entertaining troops. During Germany's occupation of France, Josephine gathered information and smuggled messages hidden in her underwear and written into her lyrics for the French Resistance. Josephine was indeed, another astonishing woman. I wish I could have known her.

DID YOU KNOW?

1. Calling her twelve children the *rainbow tribe,* the "Creole Goddess" wanted to prove that people from around the world could live and work together in harmony. If only we had learned.
2. Refused entrance at NYC's famous Stork Club in 1951 because of her skin color, the "Black Venus" began crusading for racial equality in the US until her death in 1975.

An ancient Roman Goddess, Juno (meaning youthfulness or rejuvenation) is a protector and special counselor of the state. She is the Roman equivalent to Hera, queen of the gods in Greek mythology. She held powers over marriage, pregnancy and childbirth. Juno's weaknesses were jealousy and vindictiveness. A daughter of Saturn, She is the wife of Jupiter and mother of Mars, Bellona, and Juventas. Juno protected the nation as a whole, but kept special watch over all women and aspects of their lives. Her symbols are the crown, the moon and the lily.

Among other identities, Juno is known as *Juno Sospita* (Juno the Savior), the chief deity of the city of *Lanuvium.* As a protector of one in confinement, Juno was often pictured wearing a goat skin, carrying a spear and shield. As *Juno Lucian* (Light bringer), She was the Goddess of childbirth. No offering can be made at Her temple unless all knots are undone because the presence of a belt could hinder the delivery of a woman's child at birth.

Juno Moneta, the Moon Goddess, is a deity unique to Rome. There, She is a protectress of funds, thus money in ancient Rome was coined in Her temple. She also is the Roman Goddess of Good Counsel (meaning Advisor), giving good advice to people in general, especially those about to be married. The Roman mint was housed in Her temple in Rome.

The fluid nature of Her identity makes Juno one of the most broadly worshipped Roman deities, evidenced by the large number of temples and festivals in Her name.

DID YOU KNOW?

1. One of the three original Roman gods (Jupiter, Juno, and Minerva), a great temple was built in their honor named Capitolium.
2. Her sacred animal is the peacock.

""You see a man drowning, you must try to save him even if you cannot swim."

A Polish humanitarian, Irena Stanislawa Sendler (1910-2008) was a nurse, activist, mother of three and a social worker serving in the Polish Underground Resistance in WWII. Irena and her helpers falsified over three thousand documents to aid Jewish families. While in charge of the children's division of Zegota, she helped rescue an additional 2,500 children from the Warsaw ghetto, placing them in convents or with non-Jewish families. Pretty gutsy, yes?

As a twenty-nine-year-old watching Germans invade her beloved Poland, Irena began offering Jewish refugees food and shelter. When the Warsaw ghetto was erected in 1940, she began saving the orphan children. Using her papers as a social worker (and papers from the Contagious Disease Department), Irena was able to gain entrance to the area. Using different methods of escape, she and her ten helpers smuggled children out of the ghetto. Sometimes a child would be hidden under a stretcher, other times taken out through sewer pipes. They even hid them in gunny sacks, suitcases, sometimes a toolbox occasionally functioned as a smuggling method. If a child could rattle off Christian prayers, they could be smuggled out through the church next door.

Irena (code name *Jolanta*) made sure wherever children were placed the families knew they were to be returned to Jewish relatives after the war. Each child was given a false identity. Sendler kept the only record of true identities in jars buried beneath an apple tree in a neighbor's backyard.

Arrested and tortured in 1943, Irena was sentenced to death for not revealing names or locations of Jewish families and children. She absolutely refused to betray her associates. *Zegota* (the Polish Underground group assisting Jews) bribed prison officials and Irena escaped from *Pawiak* prison. After the war, she dug up the jars and reunited children with surviving family members.

DID YOU KNOW?

1. Sadly, almost all the parents of children Irena saved died at *Treblinka, a* death camp.
2. She became world-famous thanks to Kansas students telling her story in their play, *Life in a Jar.*

> Marion Dickerman (1890-1983) was an American educator, suffragist, political organizer and close friend to Eleanor Roosevelt. Dedicated to improving education, progressive reform, and politics, Marion was also active in the Red Cross during WWI serving at the Endell Street Military Hospital in London, staffed by women only. An avid supporter of women's rights, Marion campaigned for the abolishment of child labor and protective labor legislation for women.

Marion received her Bachelor of Arts degree from Syracuse University (1911) and her graduate degree in education the following year. Briefly teaching in Canisteo, New York, she moved on to Fulton, New York where she taught American history. When WWI broke out, Marion jumped into war-related activities, working with the Red Cross as well as the Liberty Loan (war bonds) drive. Returning home from London, she discovered she had been elected to oppose Thaddeus Sweet, an anti-woman suffrage Republican speaker of the New York State Assembly.

Unable to win the election, she received enough votes to make sure Sweet would not become the Republican's nominee for governor. Marion then accepted a position as dean of New Jersey State College in Trenton. Unhappy, she moved to New York City in 1922 to join the faculty as vice-principal of Todhunter School (a private girls school).

When Marion met Eleanor Roosevelt in 1922, their like-mindedness developed into instant friendship. Nancy Cook, Marion's life partner, Eleanor and Marion became steadfast friends and worked together for the Women's Trade Union League, the Democratic National Committee and the League of Women Voters. President Roosevelt named Marion to the President's Commission to study industrial relations in Great Britain and Sweden (1938). Marion helped secure an isolationist platform in foreign policy that FDR badly wanted. After WWII, Marion actively directed educational programming for the Marine Historical Association.

DID YOU KNOW?

1. Marion, Nancy and Eleanor's friendship lasted fifteen years.
2. The three shared ownership of Val-Kil property and Val-Kil Industries (a factory providing additional income to local farm families by producing pewter, homespun cloth and furniture by traditional methods).

MAGGIE LENA WALKER

"No person is your friend who demands your silence or denies your right to grow."

Maggie Lena Draper Walker (1864-1934) was an African American businesswoman, teacher, mother and political activist working for women's suffrage. The first woman in the United States to charter a bank as well as serve as its president, Maggie also published a newspaper—*The St. Louis Herald*. She worked tirelessly to help African Americans achieve economic and social independence.

Maggie's mother was a former slave and assistant cook in the mansion of Elizabeth Van Lew, an abolitionist and philanthropist. While her mother also ran a small laundry service, Maggie worked by her side daily, learning organizational skills and gaining business experience. She taught grade school for three years until 1886. She married Armstead Walker Jr. that same year. Maggie left teaching to take care of her family and work with the Independent Order of St. Luke—a fraternal society that ministered to the sick and aged promoting humanitarian causes that Walker had founded in 1903.

On June 20, 1914, Maggie's son, Russell Walker, age twenty-five, shot and killed his father, having mistaken him for a burglar for whom both he and his father had been searching. Russell was arrested and charged, but later acquitted. The loss left Maggie to single-handedly supervise a large household.

Her investments and work kept the family comfortable. She published a newspaper in 1902, *The St. Luke Herald*. Shortly after, she chartered the "St. Luke Penny Savings Bank." Maggie was the bank's first president, earning recognition as the first woman to charter a bank in the United States. (The St. Luke Penny Savings Bank's leadership included many female board members.)

DID YOU KNOW?

1. Maggie agreed to serve as chairman of the board of directors when the bank merged with two other Richmond banks.
2. She never fully recovered from the tragic episode involving her son and her husband's death; Maggie died eight years later after battling with depression and alcoholism.
3. Her statue stands on Broad Street in Richmond, Virginia.

Isabelle de Charriere (1740-1805), also known as Belle van Zuylen in the Netherlands, was a Dutch Swiss writer and philosopher of the Enlightenment. She is best known for her letters and novels, though she also wrote pamphlets, music and plays. Isabelle took a keen interest in society and politics. Educated, outspoken and free-spirited, religion was a problem for her. She believed the privileges of the aristocracy, to which she belonged, frequently led to a vacuum filled with pride of ancestry and pleasures *of the chase*. Smart woman.

Isabelle soon realized she would not be able to air her true, independent opinions in public writings. And so she turned to letters and other writings that were circulated unobtrusively to express how she felt about society and politics. Most of these writings failed to survive—which added to Isabelle's awareness of the inferior and precarious situation of women. To achieve some measure of freedom during that time, and for centuries to come, it was essential for women to be married.

Marriage was not a free choice, which she felt was an unacceptable situation. Social class, wealth, hereditary considerations or business were, sadly, the guiding principles of marriage.Not until she was thirty-one did Isabelle embark on a marriage of convenience.

By 1783, she had withdrawn into herself because she was unhappy. From there forward, Isabelle used her freedom to write and publish. A stream of novels, short stories, plays, essays, pamphlets and poetry poured out of her focusing on these concerns: morality, culture, politics, social conditions, education, women's position in society, marriage, etc.

DID YOU KNOW?

1. Isabelle also produced various musical compositions and extensive letters, considered brilliant and captivating.
2. Her charming honesty and expressions of present-day femininity give her modern and universal appeal.
3. Her debut literary work at age twenty, published in 1763, caused a scandal and was taken off the market by her parents.

Madam Yoko or Mammy Yoko (c. 1849–1906) was a leader of the *Mende* people in Sierra Leone. Combining the power given her from the secret *Sande* society, her superior lineage and shrewd choice of husbands, Yoko became a leader of considerable influence. She enlarged the Mende Kingdom and at the time of her death, was the ruler of the vast Kpaa Mende Confederacy, originally fifteen separate kingdoms. She ruled as a Paramount Chief until her death in1906.

Originally called *Soma*, she changed her name to Yoko at her Sande initiation ceremony, during which time Yoko became known for her beauty and graceful dancing. The Sande society initiates girls into adulthood using rituals of body piercings, skin removal, a pledge of secrecy, and female circumcision.

Supposedly conferring fertility, instilling morality and proper sexual demeanor, the secret society also championed women's social and political interests. With the Sande, Yoko was able to display remarkable power, not only amongst women, but the Mende society as a whole. She was the lioness, the spiritual mother of all the young girls who fell into her hands.

Though they may have been warriors, men never ruled as masters in the Kpaa Mende nation. Oral tradition confirms that the chiefdoms were often ruled by women, the ultimate masters of life and death. In 1878, following her third husband's death, Yoko became the Chief of *Senehun*. By 1884 she was officially recognized as chief of Senehun, also known as "Queen of Senehun". This recognition came from the British as well as her own people. Yoko managed to reach that status despite her aversion to missionaries and her refusal to convert to Christianity.

DID YOU KNOW?

1. Yoko was awarded a silver medal by Queen Victoria for her loyalty to the British.
2. Reasons for her suicide at age fifty-six are disputed.

"I don't think Ed Sullivan had anything to do with Carib Song."

Katherine Dunham (1909-2006) revolutionized American dance by going to the roots of Black dance. She was an anthropologist, ethnologist, choreographer, dancer, author, scholar, mother and social activist. As a dancer-choreographer, Katherine was best known for assimilating African American, Caribbean, African and South American movement styles and themes into her ballets.

One of the first African American women to attend the University of Chicago, Katharine Dunham earned bachelor, masters and doctoral degrees in anthropology. A founder of the anthropological dance movement, Katherine created the *Dunham Technique*—a fusion of ballet with modern and Afro-Caribbean dance over drum rhythms.

In 1930, she formed a dance company, *Ballet Negre*—one of the first Negro ballet companies in America. And in 1933, Katherine opened her first dance school, the Negro Dance Group, in Chicago. Reviving Ballet Negre in 1934, the dance company appeared at the Chicago World's Fair. Using her talent and insight, Durham was able to re-direct the energy of violent street gangs through the performing arts.

Katherine was always a formidable advocate for racial equality. Because of this, she refused to perform at segregated venues in the U.S. Politically active, she fought for both domestic and international rights issues. In fact, at eighty-two, she went on a forty-seven-day hunger strike to protest the U.S. government's repatriation policy for Haitian immigrants. (Can you imagine going on a hunger strike when you're eighty-two? Amazing...)

In 1946, the Dunham School became the Katherine Dunham School of Arts and Research. It was composed of The Dunham School of Dance and Theatre, the Department of Cultural Studies and the Institute for Caribbean Research.

DID YOU KNOW?

1. Katherine is known as "the matriarch and queen mother of Black dance."
2. She died from natural causes just one month short of the ninety-seventh birthday.

Lilith is a Goddess in Mesopotamian mythology and Jewish folklore. She's best known as Adam's first wife who was rejected by God and Adam for having ideas of Her own. She is demonized by Judeo-Christianity. Lilith's powers ranged from having super-human strength to teleportation, telekinesis, owning energy rays and knowledge of the occult.

Her name means "the night" and She embodies emotional and spiritual aspects of darkness, sensuality, unbridled freedom and terror. She is now seen as a Goddess that represents the *put-upon wife* who flees to freedom, whose liberation becomes a celebrated paradigm. An elegant Goddess, She is also fearless and gifted with immortality. Her sacred animals are Anzu birds (night owls, eagles and vultures) and serpents.

Some scholars believe Lilith was inspired by Sumerian or Mesopotamian myths. Stories are told that Lilith, who was created by God (not from Adam's rib), and Adam didn't exactly see eye-to-eye on sexual positions. Arguing over "who was on top" became a constant fight that ended when Lilith fled. Uttering God's name, Lilith flew into the air never to return to the Garden of Eden.

Three angels were sent to locate and return Her to the garden. Discovering the runaway by the Red Sea, the angels commanded that She return to Her husband. Lilith refused even after they threatened to drown her.

Early accounts appear to combine different stories of female demons. The result is a story told of Lilith, an assertive wife who rebels against God and Her husband, being replaced by another woman. She was thus demonized by Jewish folklore as a dangerous baby killer. Later legends characterize Her as a beautiful woman who seduces men and gives birth to demon children. Dozens of stories abound regarding Lilith's demonic side, all written by men.(No surprise there.)

DID YOU KNOW?

1. Lilith is associated with sexual temptation, storms, illness and death. I wonder why.
2. Lilith is called the "Queen of Demons"—a title given by whom?

"True peace is not merely the absence of war, it is the presence of justice."

Laura Jane Addams (1860-1935) was an American activist, progressive social reformer, feminist, sociologist and author. The first American woman awarded the Nobel Peace Prize in 1931, she was as internationally respected for her peace activism. Jane co-founded and led Hull House, a settlement home that provided child-care, practical and cultural training plus education to largely immigrant neighborhoods in Chicago.

Jane Addams was an ardent feminist by philosophy. In the days before women's suffrage, she believed women should make their *own* voices be heard through law-making and therefore should have the right to vote. After graduating college, Jane began to study medicine but left because of poor health. She then spent almost two years reading, writing and considering what her future objectives should be.

Hoping to rid the world of war, Jane created opportunities or seized those offered her to advance the cause. In 1906 she gave a course of lectures at the summer session of the University of Wisconsin which she published the next year as a book, *Newer Ideals of Peace*. She spoke out for peace at a ceremony commemorating the building of the Peace Palace at The Hague in 1913. Following that speech, Jane lectured for two years against America's entry into the First World War.

In January of 1915, Jane accepted the chairmanship of the Women's Peace Party, an American organization, and the presidency of the International Congress of Women four months later; it convened at The Hague. She worked with labor as well as other reform groups toward goals including the first juvenile-court law, tenement-house regulations, an eight-hour working day for women, factory inspections and workers' compensation. Jane also strove to seek justice for immigrants and African Americans and advocated research aimed at determining the causes of poverty and crime, all the while supporting women's suffrage.

DID YOU KNOW?

1. Jane was the second woman to receive The Nobel Peace Prize—Bertha von Suttner was the first in 1905.
2. Her intelligence and open-mindedness helped to tear down societal barriers.

Born in Quebec, Mary Adelaide Nutting (1858-1948) was a nurse, educator, author, humanitarian and suffragette. A pioneer in American nursing and hospital administration, she was very influential in raising the standards of nursing education and conveying it to universities. An independent woman with a strong drive, Mary championed education and medical care for all. She established the *American Journal of Nursing* (1900) as well as founded the Maryland State Association of Graduate Nurses. Mary is the preeminent figure of modern nursing, publishing and contributing to writings that are pivotal in nursing academics even today.

Though not initially attracted to medicine, Mary was more interested in music and arts. In fact, she began her career teaching music at a girls school in Newfoundland. When John Hopkins University in Baltimore opened its first nursing program, Mary decided to enroll along with seventeen other students. She graduated two years later and was offered a position as head nurse. Mary quickly climbed the ranks with her exemplary nursing and administration abilities. She was appointed assistant superintendent of nurses, then superintendent, and finally principal of the training school.

As principal, Mary extended the program one year, reorganized the curriculum to incorporate field experience and influenced the school to begin offering scholarships. At the same time, she was making important contributions to the nursing profession nationally. After helping Columbia University (NYC) establish its nursing program, Mary was offered a professorship. When she accepted, she became the first woman in the nation to hold such a position.

While at Columbia, Mary helped establish a graduate program of extended nursing training (1910). She was later named the head of the department. One of Mary's most significant achievements was helping to establish professional standards in the nursing field, resulting in numerous awards. Her nursing doctrine professed a "humanistic approach"—nurses would serve as medical professionals and social workers.

DID YOU KNOW?

1. During WWI, Mary was appointed by President Wilson to chair the committee on nursing for the Council of National Defense.
2. The "Mary Adelaide Nutting Award" is granted once a year to someone who has continued the development of nursing education.

"Never doubt that a small group of thoughtful, committed citizens can change the world.."

A cultural anthropologist, Margaret Mead (1901-1978) was a writer, teacher, lecturer and mother. Best known for her studies of the Oceania peoples, she formulated ideas about the powerful effects of social convention especially on adolescent girls. Margaret is considered one of the most influential anthropologists in history, inspiring anthropological feminism, the sexual revolution and other countercultural trends. Her famous theory of *imprinting* was, simply put, that children learn by watching adult behavior. She was awarded the Presidential Medal of Freedom posthumously.

In her first study, *Coming of Age in Samoa* (1928), Margaret observed Samoan children moving easily into the adult world of sexuality and work. That contrasted with children in the United States whose lingering Victorian restraints on sexual behavior and increased separation of children from the productive world made youth a needlessly difficult time.

Margaret wrote in *Sex and Temperament* (1935) that Westerners' deep-seated belief in innate femininity and masculinity worked only to aggravate these troubles. She described the widely varying temperaments exhibited by men and women in different cultures, from the nurturing men of the Arapesh tribe (northernmost Papau New Guinea) to the violent women of the Mundugumor tribe, located further east on the island. She maintained that social convention, not biology, determines how people behave.

When WWII began, Margaret and her husband founded the Institute for Intercultural Studies. Her post-war field work took her back to Manus (New Guinea) in 1953 for more observation. She believed cultural patterns of racism, bloodshed and environmental exploitation were learned. Margaret wrote in *New Lives for Old* that the members of a society could work together to modify their traditions and to construct new institutions which led to her famous quote.

Did you know?

1. Margaret's pediatrician was Benjamin Spock, who incorporated some of her beliefs and practices int his own writings.
2. President Jimmy Carter awarded her the Presidential Medal of Freedom posthumously in January of 1979.

Jane Johnston Schoolcraft, aka Bamewawagezhikaquay (1800-1842) was one of the earliest Native American literary writers. Schoolcraft was of Ojibwa and Scottish-Irish heritage. Bamewawagezhikaquay means "Woman of the Sound the Stars Make Rushing Through the Sky". She was the first known Native American literary writer. As a poet, storyteller, translator and essayist, Schoolcraft was dedicated to preserving her people's cultural contributions by committing them to word.

For nearly two centuries, Native American poet Jane Schoolcraft's reputation and writings have been overshadowed by her husband, a celebrated Indian agent and ethnographer. But it is he who was responsible for the survival of Jane's writings, some of which he printed after her death. As a child, Jane's British fur-trading father encouraged her early interest in literature. He nurtured her interest with his large library and his own poetry.

The Schoolcrafts were married in 1823, and three children were born to that marriage. Henry Schoolcraft shared in his wife's literary interests but focused on the publishing of his studies of Indian culture using his wife's knowledge and family connections. Jane's writings, on occasion, appeared under Henry's name. At times, he even copied some of her manuscripts and had them published, with or without her permission. (Talk about controlling husbands!)

Jane's tales were rooted in Ojibwe storytelling. They were her versions of traditionalstories rendered in English. She used these stories to convey Ojibwe history, their everyday life and their appreciation of the world around them. Her poems, on the other hand, were personal and private, written about nature and expressing Jane's pride in her Ojibwe heritage.

DID YOU KNOW?

1. *The Sound the Stars Make Rushing Through the Sky: The Writings of Jane Johnston Schoolcraft* (2008) is a collection of Schoolcraft's lost poems, edited by Robert Dale Parker.
2. Jane's poetry reveals strong anticolonial sentiment as well as her physical and emotional pain experienced upon her young son's death.

Elizabeth Catherine Montour, better known as Mme. Montour (1667-c.1753) was not only a local leader of Algonquin and French-Canadian ancestry, but a diplomat, interpreter and a mother. Although well known, most people referred to her as Madame or Mrs. Montour. She is one of the few Shamokin females deemed to be significant. Creative and independent, Mme. Montour spoke English, German, Algonquin, Iroquois and French. Her eccentric character and her services as interpreter mark her as unique among females of her day.

One historian claims Mme. Montour was originally known as Isabelle Couc (Isabelle and Elizabeth were considered the same name). Regardless, she was born to a French father and an Algonquin mother. Born near Three Rivers in New France (present day Quebec), she married Joachim Germano at age seventeen. Historical records place her in Albany, New York in 1709. Separated from her husband, she was living among the English and working as an interpreter for the English governor.

After the murder of Mme.'s father or brother (sources vary), she became even more important as a cultural intermediary. Mme. married again, this time to an Oneida war captain, Carondawana. Around that time, she became an interpreter and diplomatic consultant for Robert Hunter, governor of New York. Her work behind the scenes as facilitator of cross-cultural cooperation was paramount for the region. She became one of Hunter's most trusted advisers.

When Mme. Montour and her husband moved to the Province of Pennsylvania (c.1727), she became an important adviser to Pennsylvanian officials. She also worked for private traders.Both Mme. and her husband worked closely with the Oneida diplomat, Shikellamy. However, after Mme.'s husband was killed in battle, Shikellamy began excluding her from Pennsylvania's diplomatic circles. He wanted to tighten his control over contracts between the Europeans and the Iroquois. Eventually, she simply withdrew from official life.

Did you know?

1. Though she could not read or write, Madame Montour signed all public documents with an *X*.
2. Confused historians still debate whether Mme. Montour was her niece or actually Isabelle Couc. Records are not clear.

"You have to be taught to be second class; you're not born that way."

A Grammy winning singer, Lena Mary Calhoun Horne (1917-2010) danced, sang and marched her way through life. A civil rights activist, she advocated for human rights and was blacklisted during the 1950s. Her road to Hollywood and stardom was not paved with gold, she was never featured in a leading role because of her race. But a star she did become—despite Hollywood prejudices. A talented icon, Lena's determination and refusal to compromise led the way for other African American performers.

At a very young age, Lena wanted to perform. Despite her family's disapproval, she began dancing at twenty-six in Harlem's Cotton Club. Voice lessons came next, followed by landing a role in an all-Black Broadway production of *Dance with Your Gods*. Lena then became a featured singer with the Noble Sissle Society Orchestra, she then moved on to perform as a solo act in different New York City clubs.

When Lena joined a white swing band, she was often humiliated by racial prejudice. In particular, hotels and restaurants that catered to white clientele saw her as less than equal, undeserving of respect. A conversation with her friend, Paul Robeson, spurred Lena to become a notable voice for the African American's struggle for equal rights and justice.

By 1943, Lena was receiving a number of movie roles and was the highest paid African American entertainer in the U.S. As a performer, whether singing or acting, Lena refused to accept any roles that were disparaging to a woman of color. As an activist, she attended the "March on Washington", performed at rallies in the South and worked for the National Council for Negro Women.

DID YOU KNOW?

1. As an activist, Lena worked alongside Eleanor Roosevelt in attempts to pass anti-lynching legislation.
2. After the deaths of her husband and son, Lena struggled out of depression to perform again, touring both England and the United States.

Ma'at (pronounced May-et) is both Goddess and the personification of truth and justice. Her name means "that which is straight" (implying order, justice and harmony). She represents righteousness, world order, stability, morality and continuity. Ma'at also represents balance and unending cycles, the flooding of the Nile and the king of Egypt—a cosmic outlook rejecting the idea that the universe could ever be destroyed. She brings an afterlife to peaceful law-abiding people, but death to those who were violent and cruel. Ma'at is pictured as a young woman, sometimes with wings on each arm, or with an ostrich feather on Her head.

Ma'at's feather is an integral part of the "weighing of the heart of the soul" ceremony in the afterlife. The heart of the soul of a dead person is weighed on the scales of justice against the feather. Ma'at, though often identified by the feather symbol, was also designated by a plinth (an architectural support or base). This symbol signifies Ma'at as the foundation upon which Egyptian society was built.

Ancient Egyptians invoke Her name in stories of a long-lost past on Earth when all peoplewere responsible for their own lives and that life should be lived with other people and the Earth in mind. Perhaps we could invoke Ma'at's name to help us live the same way.If lives are lived harmoniously in the will of the gods, that person is then living in harmony with the concept of Ma'at.

A person has the free will to live however they wish, but there is a price to pay—judgement in the Hall of Truth in the afterlife. In some images, the Goddess is seen sitting atop the scales at the moment of judgment. In other images, She is present near the God Osiris.

DID YOU KNOW?

1. Ma'at gave the gods their ability to breathe.
2. In Ancient Egypt, it was expected that priests, Pharaohs and their families embody Ma'at's ideals.

"You can no more win a war than you can win an earthquake."

Jeannette Pickering Rankin (1880-1973) was an American peace activist, suffragist, reformer and politician. She was the first woman to hold federal office in the United States, elected to the U.S. House of Representatives in 1916. Jeanette was a vigorous feminist and lifetime pacifist.

After graduating from high school, Jeannette attended the University of Montana, graduating in 1902 with a BS degree in biology. She found her calling in the women's suffrage movement. While living in Washington, Jeannette became active in the drive to amend that state's constitution to give women the right to vote. The measure passed in 1911, Jeannette later returned home to Montana to win the right to vote for the women of her home state—passed in 1914.

Two years later, she made a run for the U.S. House of Representatives, winning despite the fact that many women still did not have the right to vote. The day of her swearing in, Jeannette sponsored a bill to amend the U.S. Constitution for women's suffrage. During her two-year term, she also introduced the first bill that would have allowed women citizenship independent of their husbands and also supported government-sponsored hygiene instruction in maternity and infancy. Fancy that—in 1916, nonetheless.

Voting against WWI was very unpopular. Running for the Senate in 1918, Jeanette lost and became a lobbyist. Running on an antiwar platform in 1940, Jeannette once again won election to the House. She created a furor as the only legislator to vote against the declaration of war on Japan in 1941. (That was damned gutsy.) Jeanette's staunch opposition to war made her a spokesperson for veteran's rights since she recognized them as pawns in the games of politicians.

DID YOU KNOW?

1. Jeanette Rankin is the only woman ever to serve in Congress from Montana.
2. The year preceding her death, Jeanette (age 92) was considering another Congressional run because of her opposition to the Vietnam Conflict.

A pioneering British correctional/alternative educator and social reformer, Mary Carpenter (1807-1877) was also a philanthropist, abolitionist, writer, prison reformer, suffragist and founder of three schools. A true heroine of corrections education, Mary created "The Ragged School Movement" which taught literacy and provided food and clothing to the poor of all denominations. A non-conformist with a life-long passion for India, Mary's Unitarianism and friendships with people of every color made her stand out from the more provincial and narrow-minded of Bristol, England.

Born to a Unitarian minister, Mary was educated in her father's school for boys. By the age of twenty, she left home to work as a governess, but returned to assist her mother when she opened a school for girls. Mary's inherited interest in reform issues leaned toward juvenile delinquents. Opening her first "Ragged School" in 1846, she began publishing papers on delinquent children in 1850. While Parliament worked on its Reformatory Schools Act, Mary opened a reform school for boys in 1852 and followed up two years later with a reform school for girls. After publishing two books on education reform, Mary continued her pleas for annual financial aid for Ragged Schools.

Within months, Mary's interests focused on women in India. Traveling there in 1866, she spoke to government officials regarding education and prison reform. She then went on to North America and spoke on prison reform because she was highly regarded for her expertise. Returning to Bristol, Mary took up the cause of women's rights and campaigned for their access to higher education. Just before her death, she signed a petition to allow women into medical schools.

DID YOU KNOW?

1. Mary was one of the most prominent speakers of her day.
2. Remaining single, she adopted Rosanna, a five-year-old girl, in 1858.

MARGARET THOMAS MURIE WEDNESDAY, WEEK 31

A pioneering conservationist, Margaret Elizabeth Thomas Murie (1902-2003) was a naturalist, author and an adventurer. Dubbed the "Grandmother of the Conservation Movement" by both the Wilderness Society and the Sierra Club, she helped with the passage of the Wilderness Act, and was very influential in creating the Arctic National Wildlife Refuge. Known as "Mardy" to most everyone, she was one of the first women to take a leading role in America's conservation movement,

Graduating from the Alaska Agricultural College and School of Mines (the University of Alaska, Fairbanks), Mardy earned a degree in business administration. She married Olaus Murie, a biologist, that same year (1924). Three years later, the Muries worked side-by-side studying elk, sheep and numerous other animals after they became Wyoming residents. After WWII, they purchased a dude ranch that became a hub to stimulate conversations and problem solving methods to protect the wild. They also worked as director and secretary of the Wilderness Society, helping draft recommendations for policies and legislation.

In 1956, the Muries recruited U.S. Supreme Court Justice William Douglas to help persuade President Eisenhower to create the Arctic Range by setting aside eight million acres—which was expanded to nineteen million acres and renamed in 1980. As part of the 1980 legislation, the Arctic Range was expanded and renamed the Arctic National Wildlife Refuge.

The intellectual and scientific foundation for creating a new generation of larger natural parks was an ideal way of preserving an entire ecological system. Mardy traveled to many places after the death of her husband. She ventured to Alaska, Tanzania and New Zealand studying wild areas, assessing them for their qualities and working to protect nature from exploitation. Widely recognized for her efforts, Mardy received the J.N. Ding Darling Conservationist of the Year Award (National Wildlife Federation's highest honor) just prior to her one hundredth birthday.

DID YOU KNOW?

1. President Clinton awarded Mardy the Presidential Medal of Freedom in 1998.
2. She died at age 101.

"Aviation is poetry ... It's the finest kind of moving around, you know, just as poetry is the finest way of using words."

Jessie Redmon Fauset (1882-1961) was an African American editor, poet, essayist, novelist, literary critic and educator. Her literary works helped to sculpt African American literature in the 1920's as she portrayed a true image of African-American life and history. As literary editor for NAACP's magazine *The Crises,* she contributed to the "Harlem Renaissance" by promoting works that related to the social movements of that era. As a member of the NAACP, Fauset represented them in the Pan African Congress (1921). By the 1930s, people had stopped talking about her and her books. It wasn't until the 1970s and the feminist movement that Fauset gained praise and overdue recognition.

Graduating valedictorian of her high school class, Jessie automatically received a scholarship to Bryn Mawr. When she arrived, M. Carey Thomas, the president of the school, promptly shipped her off to Cornell University because that school, unlike Bryn Mawr, accepted African Americans. Graduating from Cornell with Phi Beta Kappa honors and going on to study at the *Sorbonne* in Paris was just the beginning for Jessie. She went on to earn her master's degree in French from the University of Pennsylvania.

Following college, she began teaching French and Latin in Baltimore and Washington D. C. In 1912, Jessie began writing articles for *The Crises.* She contributed for several years before becoming the journal's editor in 1919. As editor, Jessie introduced unknown writers like Langston Hughes and Gwendolyn Bennett, among others, giving them a national audience.

She published several novels during this time known for portraying middle-class African-American life. Her debut novel, *There is Confusion*, describes the struggle that a middle-class black family goes through to obtain social equality. Leaving *The Crises* in 1926, Jessie returned to teaching French at a Bronx high school.

DID YOU KNOW?

1. Jessie Redmon is recognized today as an important part of the "Harlem Renaissance".
2. She married Herbert Harris and they moved to New Jersey—where *she persisted* in promoting African American art.

MOLLY BRANT (KONWATSI'TSIAIENNI)

Also known as Mary Brant, Knowatsi'tsiaienni, and Degonwadonti, Molly Brant (c.1736-1796) was a Mohawk political trailblazer in New York and Canada during the American Revolution era. The consort of Sir William Johnson, a British Superintendent of Indian Affairs, Molly had eight children. An influential and effective Iroquois ally to the British Crown during the Revolution, she founded Kingston, Ontario. Long ignored and denigrated by U.S. historians, she is recognized as the most powerful Mohawk woman in the New World from 1759-1776.

Molly was educated in European fashion during her youth at Canajoharie, New York. When she was just eighteen she traveled to Philadelphia with a group of Mohawk chiefs to discuss fraudulent land transactions. This first introduction into the world of political responsibility would lead her to become a "Clan Mother." Initially Johnson's housekeeper, she became much more when they developed a romantic relationship in 1759. Even before their marriage, Molly assimilated both European and Indian culture into her life and felt equally at home in both worlds.

After Johnson's death (1774), she moved her family back to Canajoharie and established a trading post. She was able to influence the Iroquois toward an alliance with the British during the American Revolution. She sheltered and fed loyalists, supplying them with arms and munitions. It was Molly who sent word to English forces that the militia's General Herkimer was marching to rescue the besieged Fort Schuyler. Loyalists ambushed Herkimer's troops, resulting in heavy casualties to both sides.

Because of these actions, Molly was forced to flee her home in the Mohawk Valley and head to Fort Niagara. There, she directed her attention to keeping the Six Nations (especially the Mohawks) on the side of the British. After the war ended, Molly settled at Kingston, Canada, receiving a substantial military pension for her war efforts. As an Iroquois political instrument, Molly was unequaled.

DID YOU KNOW?

1. There is a statue of her likeness in Kingston, Ontario.
2. Since 1994, Molly has been honored in Canada as a "Person of National Historic Significance."

A French composer, Lili Boulanger (1893-1918) was the first female to win the Grand Prix de Rome for musical composition in 1913. Despite singing as well as playing piano, violin, cello and harp, her music has been over-shadowed by her untimely death at age twenty-four and the legacy of her older sister, Nadia.

A Parisian-born prodigy, Juliette Marie Olga Boulanger (pronounced Boo-lawn-jay) was found to have perfect pitch at two-years-old. Known to family and friends as Lili, she showed remarkable musical aptitude at an early age and began studying with *Gabriel Faure.* Lili suffered from poor health early in life, and so, whenever she felt up to it, by the age of five, she began sitting in on classes with her sister at the *Paris Conservatoire.*

At sixteen, Lili's mother encouraged her to pursue an occupation. Because of her poor health, her mother believed her prospects for marriage impossible. Lili began diligently studying harmony, counterpoint, fugue and composition. Her first attempt at the *Grand Prix de Rome* in 1912 had to be withdrawn because of illness. She returned the next year, winning in 1913 for her cantata, *Faust et Helene.* A contract with one of the most important music publishers at the time, *Ricordi,* was a result of her success. It provided a regular income, a place to publish her works and a platform for publicity.

In spite of WWI, Lili remarkably produced over fifty works in her ten years of composing. The inspiration or possibly the need to come to terms through her music with the prospect of an early death was unique to her. Lili Boulanger's last work was an efficient setting of the *Pie Jesu.* Dictated to her sister, Nadia, from her deathbed, it became a requiem for herself.

DID YOU KNOW?

1. Lili's early death was caused by intestinal tuberculosis. Her weakened immune system was the result of pneumonia at age two.
2. Her death left her *La Princesse Maleine* unfinished.

Maeve (meaning strong or intoxicating) is queen of Connaught in Irish mythology. An ancient earth Goddess, She was a decisive and forceful leader, assembling one of the mightiest fighting forces in Irish mythology when Her status was questioned. Her themes are fairies, magic, protection, leadership and justice (law). She also attends to human affairs by providing protection and wise leadership. Today, Maeve is often represented as a symbol of the power of women over men in terms of sexuality, cunning or courage.

Homage to Maeve goes back over five thousand years in Ireland, almost three thousand years before the arrival of the first Celts. Beltane is a time when tribes would gather at *Uisneach,* the sacred center, where they would feast together with great magic in the air. Maeve reigned over the annual festivities.

It is said She had animals lie about Her body, particularly birds on Her shoulders whispering their wisdom in Her ears. Maeve reminds us as women to hold on to what is ours and to awaken to life around us. Our fires are re-lit with beauty and vitality, laughter and delight by Her.

Queen Medb (an aspect of the Goddess Medb) reigned during a time when Celtic women maintained a status of freedom and equality that was not granted to women in other parts of the world. She opens the door to our acceptance of our own sovereignty, to claiming our truth.

DID YOU KNOW?

1. Maeve's beauty and sexual know-how were renowned, and no high king could be crowned without first having a consummation ceremony with her in the royal bed.
2. Her color is red; it is She who reminds us of our passion and power, love and desire, anger and war.

"I am not afraid... I was born to do this."

> Jeanne D'Arc, (c. 1412-1431 CE) was a medieval peasant girl who, claiming to receive visions from God, led the French army to a momentous victory in the Hundred Years' War. Convicted of heresy and burned at the stake by the English after her capture, "The Maid of Orleans" is considered a heroine of France and was canonized as a Catholic saint.

Joan cropped her hair and dressed in men's clothes to make the eleven-day journey across enemy territory to *Chinon*, the site of the crown prince's palace. Joan promised Charles she would see him crowned king at Reims, asking him to give her an army to lead to Orléans. Going against his counselor's and general's advice, Charles granted her request, and Joan set off to fend off the *Siege of Orléans* in March of 1429 dressed in white armor and riding a white horse. Joan led several assaults against the French enemy driving the Anglo-Burgundians from their bastion and forcing their retreat across the Loire River.

After that victory, Joan was ordered to lead a Burgundian assault on *Compiégne*. While defending the town and its residents, she was thrown from her horse. The Burgundians took her captive and sold her to the English. The English could not prosecute a woman who claimed she was serving God but could not allow even the suggestion that she was telling the truth because that would mean God was on the French side of the conflict. They finally convicted her of being a heretic and burned her at the stake in May 1431 CE.

The trial of Joan of Arc was reviewed as early as 1452 CE, found to be invalid, and Joan was exonerated and proclaimed a martyr in 1456 CE. She was later canonized and is one of the patron saints of France to this day.

DID YOU KNOW?

1. It took a little over twenty years for Joan to be exonerated by Charles VII.
2. The private words spoken between Joan and Charles remain unknown.

"A'ohe lokomaika'i i nele i ke pana'i." "No kind deed ever lacks its reward."

Mary Abigail Kawena'ulaokalaniahi'iakaikapoliolelen NaleilehuaapeleWiggin Pukui (1895-1986) was a Hawaiian educator, author, scholar, translator, anthropologist, composer, chanter, hula expert and mother to three daughters. Known as the "Noah Webster of Hawaii", Mary provided fundamental critical reference cultural guides. Recognizing Hawaii's language and culture were being lost, she spent at least fifty years at Bishop Museum working with anthropologists, ethnologists, biologists and others. She co-wrote the Hawaiian Dictionary to help them understand her islands. Her notes, oral histories and hundreds of audio tapes are preserved at the Bishop Museum in Honolulu, Hawaii.

Raised by her maternal grandmother, a sacred high priestess, Mary lived in a traditional hut with dirt floors. She was taught the Hawaiian religion, history, dance and language. Hawaiian traditions began to suffer with the influx of tourists from America after Hawaii was annexed in 1898. Upon the death of her grandmother, Mary returned to her parents' home. She was encouraged to embrace advantages that white people brought while still maintaining her heritage. She was soon bilingual and navigating both cultures.

When Mary was introduced to the staff at Bishop Museum in 1921, she began to work closely with anthropologists, translating her language for them and recording stories and chants of Hawaii. She was officially hired in 1937 as translator, researcher, consultant and teacher. Meanwhile, Mary continued to publish translations of Hawaiian stories. Learning how to conduct field research like a trained anthropologist, she and her mentors conducted personal interviews, collecting stories and objects.

By the 1940s, Mary Kawena was working with the Army Corps of Engineers as Hawaii's culture expert. After losing her husband in 1943, she helped publish *Introduction to the Hawaiian Language with the English-Hawaiian, Hawaiian-English Dictionary*. She went on to teach, demonstrating traditional practices and even taught the Hawaiian language.

DID YOU KNOW?

1. Mary Kawena co-authored more than fifty books as well as 150 songs.
2. Her translations and audio tapes gave her legendary status in Hawaiian culture and history.
3. Mary taught her three daughters the same traditions she learned, including hula dancing and the Hawaiian language.

"Study as if you were going to live forever; live as if you were going to die tomorrow."

An American astronomer, Maria (pronounced Ma-RYE-ah) Mitchell (1818-1889) was also a librarian, naturalist, abolitionist and educator. She discovered a comet in 1847 that was later called "Miss Mitchell's Comet." Maria was the first internationally known woman to work as both a professor of astronomy (Vassar) and a professional astronomer. She was also the first woman ever elected Fellow of the American Academy of Arts and Sciences and the American Association for the Advancement of Science. A feminist, she believed in equal rights for all irrespective of gender or race. As a personal protest against slavery, Maria refused to wear cotton clothing.

After Maria's father recognized her budding interest in astronomy, he began teaching astronomy to her using his home telescope. She completed her studies at Cyrus Peirce's "School for Young Ladies." Maria became Peirce's teaching assistant until 1835, when she opened a school of her own on Nantucket. She decided to allow all children regardless of race to attend—a very controversial move at a time when most schools were segregated.

The following year, Maria became the first librarian for Nantucket's *Athenaeum*. She held that position for twenty years while helping her father with astronomical observations and geographical calculations for the U.S. Coastal Survey at night. After discovering the new comet in 1847, she became a celebrity. Maria accepted a computing position for the U.S. Coastal Survey, tracking the movements of planets—particularly Venus—and compiling tables of their positions to assist sailors in navigation.

She was appointed professor of astronomy at Vassar in 1865—the first person appointed to the faculty. Maria was also named director of the Vassar Observatory. Despite having to fight for higher wages (and winning), she taught at the college until her retirement in 1888. She maintained an advocacy for science and math education for women throughout her life.

DID YOU KNOW?

1. Maria began following Unitarian principles, becoming involved in the anti-slavery movement.
2. She also helped found the Association for Advancement of Women (AAW).

"If laws are unjust, they must be continually broken until they are altered."

An African American publisher, Josephine St. Pierre Ruffin (1842-1924) was a journalist, civil rights leader, suffragist, editor, philanthropist and mother of five children. As editor and publisher for *Women's Era*, she pioneered the first national newspaper published and edited by and for African Americans. Josephine also founded, along with her daughter and Boston school principal Maria Baldwin, the "Women's Era Club" in 1894. Believing a national organization for black women was needed, she founded and named the National Federation of Afro-American Women, a year later, uniting with the Colored Women's League renamed the National Association of Colored Women.

During the Civil War, Josephine was involved in not only civil rights causes, but charity work and the woman's suffrage movement. In 1879, she established the Boston Kansas Relief Association. It was a charitable organization that provided food and clothing to black Bostonians who were migrating to Kansas. She also recruited African American men for the 54th and 55th regiments of the Union Army.

Josephine's philanthropic work brought her in close touch with Susan B. Antony, Elizabeth Cady Stanton and Booker T. Washington. Her particular interest was the development of the African American women in New England and also across the nation. She worked closely with many leaders, including Julia Ward Howe and Lucy Stone.

When the national Federation of Afro-American Women convened in Boston, its mission was to demonstrate the existence of a large number of educated, cultured African American women. They wanted to "come to the front, willing to join any others in the same work and welcoming any others to join". Continued resistance by all-white national women's clubs reinforced Josephine's commitment to the importance of the African American women's movement, she remained an active participant throughout her life.

DID YOU KNOW?

1. Josephine was one of the founding members of the Boston NAACP (1910).
2. A bust of her sits in the Massachusetts State house.

"I am not afraid of the pen, or the scaffold, or the sword. I will tell the truth wherever I please."

An Irish-born American educator and activist, Mary G. Harris Jones (1837-1930) was called "Mother Jones" from 1897 onward. She became a prominent union and community organizer who helped coordinate major strikes. Mary also helped co-found the Industrial Workers of the World. A mother and dressmaker before becoming an ardent activist, Mary helped organize "The March of the Mill Children" in 1903—a three-week trek from Philadelphia to New York that brought public attention to the evils of child labor, energizing efforts to end it by law.

Mary, a self-proclaimed "hell-raiser," was originally from County Cork, Ireland. The nineteenth century's most famous female labor activist, she was once labeled "the most dangerous woman in America" by a US attorney. Mary started working as a teacher in a Michigan Catholic school, then moved to Chicago and became a seamstress. After relocating to Memphis to take another teaching position, she married George Jones (1861). Tragedy struck during the yellow fever epidemic of 1867. She lost her entire family to the illness, dressing in black the rest of her life. (Can you imagine the grief she must have felt?)

Returning to Chicago, Mary built a successful dressmaking business only to lose everything in Chicago's Great Fire of 1871. Finding solace at Knights of Labor meetings, she took up the cause of working people six years later. She focused on industrialization's rising number of working poor, shrinking wages and long hours. The employees also had no health insurance. Her organizing abilities for Pittsburgh's Great Railroad Strike (1877) were brilliant.

Fearless, Mary led hundreds of strikes, pausing only to write and publish three books in 1899-1901. A beloved leader and electrifying speaker, she assisted in the struggle to unionize streetcar, garment and steel workers even into her eighties. How many of us could survive the trauma of losing a husband, four children and her business going up in flames to go on and become an icon?

DID YOU KNOW?

1. Mother Jones became a symbol of labor's fight for decent treatment and wages.
2. The 1903 march trekked from Philadelphia to President Teddy Roosevelt's home in New York.

Marie Louise Fuller, aka Louie Fuller/ Loie Fuller (1862-1928) was once the most famous dancer in the world. A pioneer in modern dance and theatrical lighting, "La Loie" was also an actress, choreographer, mentor, writer and innovator. An icon for Art Nouveau artists, she is internationally recognized as the inventor of the "Serpentine Dance" –an astounding variation on the *skirt dance* of the 1890s. Loie held the patents for stage lighting that included the first use of luminescent salts and chemical compounds for gels and slides. Such an innovator!

Loie began her career as a child actress at the feet of her vaudeville performing parents. By 1896, she had moved from the Midwest to New York to appear in assorted theatre productions. After seeing Kate Vaughan's version of skirt dances in London, Loie returned to the U.S. and eventually created her own version called the Serpentine Dance. She then began adding more and more cloth to her costume designs, at one point adding sewn-in wands to help her control the massive amounts of fabric.

Loie then began experimenting with stage floor lighting which soon became the focus of her performance. By this time, she was performing in Paris—since American audiences did not appreciate her new version of skirt dancing (1892).

In Europe, her pioneering work was not only appreciated and respected, but Loie made many friendships with French scientists and artists. Among them was Marie Curie, she had sought her out for advice on the use of radium in lighting techniques. Loie was a regular performer at *Folies Bergere* in Paris; she used many lighting techniques that are standard today: the color wheel, scenic projections, black curtained backdrop, glass flooring and specialized individual lighting on the performer.

DID YOU KNOW?

1. Loie helped found the Maryville Museum of Art in rural Washington.
2. The first expat American dancer, she also had a dance school and company in Paris.

"There is a world beyond ours, a world that is far away, nearby and invisible."

The first Mexican *curandero* (medicine woman), or *sabia* (one who knows), Maria Sabina Magdalena Garcia (1894-1985) was a shaman, poet and visionary. Known as the "priestess of mushrooms," her history and reputation led her to serve as a bridge between the ritual and mystical worlds of the *Mazatec* people and the mystical exploration of the Western World. Her words were always sung or spoken in poetry. *Homera Aridjis* called her "the greatest visionary poet in twentieth-century Latin America." Maria was the first Mazatec shaman to allow Westerners to participate in a psychedelic mushroom *velada* (healing ceremony).

Raised in *Huautla de Jimenez*, a town in the *Sierra Mazatec* area of the Mexican state of *Oaxaca*, Maria never learned to read or write. She expressed herself through the voice of "the sacred mushroom" in a language that could not be taught or acquired. Her chants were translated from the Mazatec tongue first into English, and later into Spanish. Maria's healing sacred mushroom ceremonies, velades, were based on the use of psilocybin mushrooms, and are known for introducing the western world to entheogenic mushrooms.

Maria Sabina is regarded as a sacred figure in *Huautla* and considered one of Mexico's greatest poets. She did not take credit for her poetry, believing mushrooms spoke through her. Psilocybin is the foremost mind-altering substance in "magic mushrooms." This substance can profoundly change moods, sensory and time perception and sense of self.

DID YOU KNOW?

1. Maria Sabina is most likely the most famous Mexican healer to have ever lived.
2. Mazatec sacred mushroom (veladas) have survived into the 21st century and are accepted now by the Catholic Church in Sierra Mazatec.

A pioneering Mexican American civil rights activist, Josefina Fierro de Bright (1914-1998) assisted in organizing resistance toward discrimination in America's Southwestern states. She co-founded "El Congreso de Pueblo de Habla" a group that fought for Mexican immigrants' civil rights as well as Mexican American workers' rights. She may be best known for spearheading the "Sleepy Lagoon Defense Committee" that raised funds for defense attorneys of young Mexican Americans being abused while jailed.

After graduating from high school, Josefina moved to Los Angeles to live with an aunt. She fell in love with and married John Bright, a Hollywood actor who encouraged her activism.

Her organizing abilities helped Josefina emerge as an important mover and shaker of the Los Angeles Mexican community. In 1938, she collaborated with Luisa Moreno to establish "El Congreso de Pueblo de Habla"—an organization working toward the advancement of Mexican civil rights. It was their goal to generate equality for Hispanics. An inspiring orator, Josefina traveled throughout California and the Southwest demonstrating and speaking out against Latinx discrimination in education, housing and the workplace.

One of Josefina's greatest accomplishments happened during the "Zoot Suit Riots" of 1943. American servicemen, off-duty policemen and civilians used billy clubs and other weapons to beat Latino, Black and Filipino youth, stripping them of their suits and leaving them lying bloodied in the streets. Local policemen stood on the sidewalks watching the violence and then arrested the victims! Can you imagine that horrific scene?

Josefina flew to Washington D. C. to plead for help. A military order was quickly issued to keep servicemen on base. As her advocacy efforts garnered more attention, Josefina was labeled a "communist subversive" and harassed by the FBI. (No surprise there.) By 1948, she feared arrest and deportation. Leaving the U.S., Josefina moved to Hermosillo, Mexico.

DID YOU KNOW?

1. Josefina was the daughter of immigrants who had fled Mexico's revolution.
2. She was an educator previous to becoming active in Mexican American civil rights.

An American pioneer in women's education, Mary Mason Lyon (1797-1849) founded Wheaton Female Seminary in Norton, Massachusetts (present day Wheaton College). She went on to establish Mount Holyoke Female Seminary (now Mount Holyoke College) located in South Hadley, Massachusetts, serving as its first principal for twelve years. Mary combined intellectual challenge with solid moral purpose as an educator, believing students from all financial backgrounds deserved equal opportunities for a quality education.

Growing up on a New England farm, Mary was taught the value of hard work. Though she left school at age fourteen, within three years Mary was teaching, earning $.75 a week. Men were paid $10 to $12 a month. Teaching was her raison d'etre for furthering her education. She began spending time at lectures when she was not in the classroom. For the next twenty years, Mary taught in eastern and western Massachusetts as well as southern New Hampshire.

Quickly becoming an authority on women's education, she developed her own philosophy of education during those years. A gifted teacher, Mary's reputation grew as she gained experience and blossomed into a first-rate administrator. Her desire to create an institution of higher learning for women burned brightly. For three years, Mary traveled the countryside seeking donations; she developed a curriculum as well as supervising and overseeing the construction of a building. She hired teachers, purchased equipment and selected students while some on-lookers ridiculed her efforts as "wasted on women."

Always believing women deserved the same educational opportunities as men, the Mount Holyoke Female Seminary opened to eighty students in 1837, despite America's ongoing depression. Each one had to pass a difficult oral exam of English grammar, US history, math, and geography. Quite the innovator, don't you agree?

Did you know?

1. Mount Holyoke required all students to work, regardless of family wealth.
2. Vassar and Wellesley Colleges were both patterned after Holyoke.

A German-born Swiss naturalist, Maria Sibylla Merian (1647-1717) was also a scientific illustrator and mother of two daughters. She discovered facts about plants and insects that were previously unknown. Maria was one of the first naturalists to study insects. She recorded and illustrated the life cycles of 186 insect species and is remembered as one of the most important woman scientists of the Enlightenment era. Maria had the courage to go on scientific expeditions at a time when they were normally only taken by men.

At the age of thirteen, Maria began to collect and study insects. She was fascinated by the metamorphosis that insects underwent over the course of their lives. Her first serious study was a collection of drawings and descriptions of the life cycle of silkworms. By thirty-two, she published her first scientific book, *The Wonderful Transformation and Singular Flower Food of Caterpillars … Painted from Life and Engraved in Copper.* This was not simply a book of illustrations, but a book intended to share what she had learned with others.

Maria's work impressed male scientists and established her as a significant new voice in the growing field of entomology, the study of insects. In 1699, she sold her entire portfolio of art and specimens using the funds to buy passage to the Dutch colony of *Suriname* on the northeast coast of South America. (That took guts.) While there, she discovered unknown animals and insects in its interior. Her classification of butterflies and moths is still used today. Remarkable, isn't it?

In 1705, Maria self-published her most important work, *The Metamorphosis of the Insects of Suriname.* Her book allowed European scientists to learn about an entirely different ecosystem without sailing across the Atlantic Ocean, solidifying Maria Sibylla Merian's status as one of the most important scientists in Amsterdam.

DID YOU KNOW?

1. Maria bred and studied the insects that she illustrated—other still-life artists merely painted them.
2. There has been renewed interest in her work and illustrations since 2005. Check it out on the internet—you'll be glad you did.

A Mexican American journalist, Jovita Idar Vivero (1885-1946) was an activist, teacher, nurse and suffragist. Often facing dangerous situations, she never backed down. Jovita single-handedly safeguarded her newspaper headquarters when the Texas Rangers came to shut it down. She also crossed the border to serve as a nurse during the Mexican Revolution.

From an early age, Jovita was exposed to journalism and political activism. She began teaching in 1903 but resigned due to segregation and poor conditions for Mexican American students. The Mexican American community in Texas frequently faced violence and lynching. Her father's newspaper, *La Cronica*, was a source of news and activism for Mexican American rights. Working for the paper, Jovita often wrote articles speaking out about racism and supporting the revolution in Mexico.

She and her family organized the *Congreso Mexicanista* (a political convention) to unify Mexicans across the border to fight injustice. Jovita and her brothers began to advocate for women's rights. She founded and was elected first president of *La Liga Feminil Mexicaista* (the League of Mexican Women) in 1911. They began by providing education for Mexican American students.

After returning from the Mexican Revolution, where she worked as a nurse, Jovita wrote for the *El Progreso,* a newspaper. One of the articles she wrote protested President Woodrow Wilson's decision to send U.S. troops to the border. The U.S. Army and the Texas Rangers did not appreciate it. (A woman speaking her mind, imagine that?) The Rangers went to the offices of *El Progreso* to shut it down. When they arrived, Jovita stood in front of the door and would not let them in! However, they did return later and forced the newspaper to close. Undaunted, Jovita continued to write and advocate for the fair treatment of Mexican Americans. She returned to her father's paper and began running it after his death in 1914.

DID YOU KNOW?

1. Jovita later moved to San Antonio, where she established a free kindergarten for children.
2. She single-handedly held off the Texas Rangers-would you have the courage to do that?

"You know that women are always looked upon as nothing, but we are your mothers, you are our sons, our cry is all for peace, let it continue."

> Nanyehi, (1738-1822) whose anglicized name is Nancy Ward, was a "Beloved Woman of the Cherokee Nation"— she was called "Ghigau." The only female on the Cherokee General Council allowed to vote, she was also leader of the Women's Council. Like *Beloved Women* of other tribes, Nanyehi was responsible for decisions about justice and vengeance. The name Nanyehi means "She who walks among the spirits."

Nanyehi came to power in the Cherokee Nation at seventeen. Already married and the mother of two, she joined her husband on a Cherokee campaign against the Creek Nation. Fighting alongside her husband when he was killed, she picked up his rifle and led the warriors to a victory that expanded their territory in northwest Georgia. Marrying an English trader in the late 1750s, she took the anglicized name Nancy Ward. They had a daughter together before he returned to his English wife and family in South Carolina.

Nanyehi counseled restraint and patience against the outbreak of the American Revolution in 1775. Many in the tribe wanted to seize the opportunity to drive out colonists who had been encroaching on Cherokee lands. An outspoken opponent, *Tsiyu Gansisi* led an attack on a white settlement anyway which sparked a full-scale war with the Americans. Soldiers invaded Cherokee territory from Georgia to North Carolina (1777), destroying all major Cherokee towns except Chota—spared because of Nanyehi.

She addressed the U.S. treaty commissioners in 1781 to negotiate an end to the fighting. Believing peace was only possible if both sides saw themselves as one people, she felt women might make this possible. Americans could not grasp the power of women in the Cherokee nation and so the fighting continued.

DID YOU KNOW?

1. Nanyehi's actions during the American Revolution have earned her an honored place in American history.
2. Because she tried to westernize the Cherokee, some see her as a traitor.
3. Nanyehi had a vision of the "Trail of Tears" before her death. More than four thousand Cherokee died on that journey.

Frances Lois Weber (1879-1939) was a Hollywood icon that has been forgotten. An actress, a screenwriter, a trail-blazing film director and producer, Lois is one of the "most important female directors the American film industry has known." She is also considered the most important film director of silent film. Lois Weber, America's first genuine "auteur"—a film maker involved in all areas of production utilizing motion pictures to put forth their own philosophies. Lois brought to the movies her concerns for social justice and humanity while acting in one hundred films, directing 135, and writing 114 more. She and her husband made the first sound films; she is also the first American woman director to own her own film studio.

Lois began her film career after acting in the theatre. Raise your glass to her, for she was not afraid to expose hypocrisy while building her business. Whether it be abortion, prostitution, birth control, nudity or social inequity, Lois Weber tackled all of them with her favorite art form—film. And in early 20th century Hollywood, the censors roared in protest.

She began making films alongside her husband. By 1916, Lois was at the pinnacle of fame when she produced her three most memorable films: *Shoes, Where Are My Children* and *The Dumb Girl of Portici*. Considered her masterpiece, *The Blot* (1921) focuses on teachers struggling due to inadequate salaries—an issue still rampant in the 21st century.

Lois was considered the "premier woman director of the screen and author and producer of the biggest money-making features in the history of the film business" by 1920. She pioneered the use of the *split-screen* and then jumped into experimenting with sound and filming on location.

DID YOU KNOW?

1. It has taken a full century for Lois Weber and her films to gain our respect.
2. Currently, many are being shown at film festivals around the world, and some are available on DVDs or streamed on-line.

"If you can just see beyond the veils; for it is 'all' an illusion and a test, and one of the greatest Divine Mysteries of this life cycle."

A Louisiana Creole practitioner of Voodoo, Marie Catherine Laveaux (1801-1881) was an herbalist, midwife, and mother of fifteen (that's right-fifteen) children. Renowned as the "Voodoo Queen of New Orleans", her powers included healing the sick, giving altruistic gifts to the poor and overseeing spiritual rites. Beloved by many, feared by others, Marie Laveaux was always respected. A lifelong Catholic, she was actively involved in charitable works for children and condemned prisoners. Revered even in death, some say Marie continues to work her magic from beyond the grave.

Born a free woman of color in the French Quarter of New Orleans, Marie Laveaux was a leader in the multiracial religious community giving consultations and holding ceremonies. During her lifetime, she was known as "The Priestess of the Voodoos". By the 1830's, Marie's combination of clairvoyance, healing abilities, charisma, beauty, intimidation, and good business sense enabled her to be in a leadership position of a multiracial religious community.

Holding weekly ceremonies at her home on St. Ann Street, Marie led St. John's Eve celebrations on Lake Pontchartrain's shores. The annual summer solstice celebration consisted of bonfires, drumming, singing, dancing, ritual bathing and a communal feast. Referred to in the newspapers as "Her majesty" sheds light on the reverence with which Marie was held.

Marie sold charms and pouches of gris-gris (a combination of herbs, oils, stones, bones, hair, nails and grave dirt). She also told fortunes and gave advice to residents of New Orleans from every social class. Nursing and some minor surgery were included in Marie's skills, as well as taking the sick into her home. Her brand of voodoo incorporated African, Native American and Catholic religious practices. Marie connected with spiritual forces through dance, music, singing and the use of snakes. (snakes? Yikes.)

DID YOU KNOW?

1. Marie stated out as a hairdresser. Her beauty salon's main clientele were New Orleans' high society.
2. She was New Orleans' third female voodoo queen.

"The Mulatto Solitude" (c.1772-1802) was an abolitionist and heroine in the fight against slavery on French Guadeloupe. A female figure of insurgents in Guadeloupe, Solitude symbolized Caribbean women and mothers who battled to protect the principles of equality and freedom.

Though little is known of her early life, Solitude is celebrated in Guadeloupe for her role in the struggle for lasting freedom since 1802. The French had abolished slavery in 1791, but Napoleon's forces sought to resurrect the sugar-based economies of Saint-Domingue (Haiti), Guadeloupe and other French Caribbean islands. In the mid 1790s, she joined the maroon settlement of *La Goyave*. During an attack by French General Desrouneaux, she became the leader of a small group that escaped to the hills of Guadeloupe.

In 1802, more French ships arrived carrying troops ready to enforce Napoleon's decree to reinstate slavery on the island. Battles broke out as Africans and their descendants fought to preserve their sacred freedom. Despite being pregnant, Solitude mobilized her followers to join Louis Delgres' forces against the French military. Struggling until surrounded and outnumbered, Delgres and his troops let the soldiers advance into their territory before igniting stores of gunpowder.

The strategic suicide plan killed approximately four hundred French soldiers and most of the maroons. Solitude survived the attack but was captured and detained in a Basse-Terre prison. A military tribunal was held in which she and the other survivors were sentenced to death. Because she was pregnant, Solitude was temporarily pardoned until she gave birth to her baby, the child would become the legal property of Solitude's owner.

The day following her baby's birth, Solitude was executed. (What a cruel act of hatred.) After her death, she disappeared from history until the 1960s. Today, her name adorns squares, avenues, a library and a museum room in Guadeloupe. Solitude's bravery and courage are remembered in songs, poems, music and books.

Did you know?

1. Solitude was only thirty years old when she was executed.
2. Her statue adorns *Héros aux Abymes Boulevard* on Guadeloupe.

MARY McCleod Bethune   TUESDAY, WEEK 34

"The true worth of a race must be measured by the character of its womanhood."

> The daughter of former slaves, Mary McCleod Bethune (1875-1955) was one of the most important Black educators of the twentieth century. She was also a political activist, philanthropist, humanitarian, mother and stateswoman. What an extraordinary life she lived.

Born on a rice and cotton farm in South Carolina, Mary attended school in a one-room "Black" schoolhouse. After receiving a scholarship and attending *Scotia Seminary* (now Barber-Scotia College) she went on to study at Dwight L Moody's Institute for Home and Foreign Missions in Chicago (now the Moody Bible Institute). Once she was told Black missionaries were not needed, Mary planned to teach other African Americans, realizing education was the key to racial advancement.

In Palatka, Florida, Mary ran a school and began an outreach to prisoners. After becoming estranged from her husband, Albertus Bethune, she founded the Daytona Normal and Industrial Institute for Negro Girls in Daytona Beach. The school merged with the Cookman Institute for Men and became Bethune-Cookman College in 1923, one of the few places African American students could pursue a college degree. Mary was president of Bethune-Cookman College from 1923-1942 and from 1946-1947.

Mary became involved in government service to both Calvin Coolidge and Herbert Hoover. In 1935, her most significant role came from President Franklin D. Roosevelt when she was appointed special advisor on minority affairs. Mary became a close personal friend to both Roosevelts during her time working for the president's administration. Much of Mary's life after 1942 was spent devoted to social causes.

DID YOU KNOW?

1. At least sixteen different schools across the U.S. have been named in Mary Bethune's honor.
2. Over the course of her life, she received eleven honorary degrees.

"No life is so charming as a country one in England."

> An English Victorian biologist, Marianne North (1830-1890) was a prolific botanical artist. She is best known for her plant and landscape paintings, her plant discoveries, writings, epic world journeys and the creation of the "North Gallery" at the Royal Botanic Gardens, Kew.

Marianne trained as a vocalist until her voice gave out. She then devoted herself to painting flowers. Upon the death of her mother (1855), she began traveling around Europe with her father, a member of Parliament. After a visit to Kew Gardens with her father, Marianne became fascinated with the natural world, the tropics and its plants.

Devastated by her father's death, she found comfort as she continued to paint. She also began traveling alone during a time when Victorian society dictated women only travel with a husband or male chaperone. During 1871-1885, Marianne traveled profusely visiting fifteen countries in fourteen years.

She painted people, places and plants from Brazil, to India, Japan, Jamaica and America. At the suggestion of Charles Darwin, Marianne even travelled to Australia and on to New Zealand. When she painted, Marianne broke the rules there as well. Using a limited palette and only certain colors, she painted with oils. The combination created vibrant colors. Her style was somewhat impressionistic; it allowed Marianne to finish most of her paintings in one day. While some critics viewed this as a weakness, others found her paintings vibrant, creating a joy they found palpable. She discovered the giant pitcher plant in Borneo—a rare Amaryllis—which was named *Crinum Northianum* in her honor.

Summer of 1879 found her writing Sir Joseph Hooker with an offer to donate her works with a gallery to house them. Opened in 1882, the gallery holds 838 of Marianne's paintings today. You can see them for yourself when you visit the Royal Botanic Gardens.

DID YOU KNOW?

1. *Northea Seychellanna* was named after her discovery and painting of the tree.
2. Her scientific accuracy before photography has given Marianne's paintings permanent value through generations.

"There is absolutely no cure for stupidity."

Bold, courageous, and beautiful, Kassia (also spelled Kassiane, Cassia, Elkasia, Kasia, Ikasia) was a Byzantine poet, scholar, composer and abbess. Born around 810 CE, her strong voice emerged from her birthplace of Constantinople. Kassia founded her own convent and is one of only two Byzantine women who wrote using her own name. She is one of the first medieval composers whose works still survive. Kassia penned 789 poems, some of which are *gnomic* verse (epigrams put to verse). The Orthodox Church celebrates her feast day as September 7th.

Coming from a wealthy family, Kassia was talented and well educated. As a teen, she corresponded with Theodore the Studite—one of the most significant 9th century theologians. He was astounded at her knowledge for one so young. One of the most famous legends of Kassia dealt with her appearance in the emperor's "Bride Show". Chosen as one of the semi-finalists, Emperor Theophilus picked her to receive the "golden apple" and become his wife.

When handing her the glass apple, Theophilus stated, "What a flood of base things come from a woman." (Not exactly the words to a woman's heart!) Kassia promptly replied "…but also from woman better things spring," as she rejected the apple. After refusing the emperor, she became a nun, eventually founding her own convent in western Constantinople. It was there that she became a composer and prolific verse writer. She is the only composer of her time whose music was put in official hymnbooks.

When fierce debate broke out over religious icons, brave Kassia stood up in the icons' veneration. For her actions, she was subjected to a scourging with a lash. Always outspoken, Kassia later said, "I hate silence when it is time to speak."—words we all need to live by.

DID YOU KNOW?

1. Fifty of her hymns exist today, some in the Byzantine liturgy.
2. The Orthodox Church celebrates her feast day on September 7th.

A *Xhosa* prophet(ess), Nongqawuse (c. 1841-1898) told of a visit by ancestors whose nstructions culminated in the Xhosa cattle killing movement and subsequent famine of 1856-1857 in what is now Eastern Cape, South Africa.

An orphan whose parents were killed in the Battles of Waterkloof, it is told Nongqawuse was quite conscious and aware of the tensions between the Xhosa and the colonial forces. The Xhosa were experiencing several attacks upon their community and institutions by British colonial authorities beginning as early as 1779.

Lung-sickness was widespread amongst the cattle of the people. Greatly influenced by her uncle, a deeply religious man, Nongqawuse and a friend were guarding the crops, chasing away birds when two strangers appeared, requesting she relay ancestral pronouncements. After reporting the instructions to her uncle, Mhlakaza, he reported the nine pronouncements to royal officials. Their initial reservation turned to acquiescence. The slaughter of cattle began, cultivation ceased; witchcraft, incest, and adultery abandoned.

The mass cattle killing went on for thirteen months. In compliance with Nongqawuse's prophesies the Xhosa men killed their cattle and destroyed their corn. Thousands of people died. From then on, Mhlakaza became interpreter and organizer of Nongqawuse's prophesies and visions. When the promises failed to materialize, her and Mhlakaza were pressured to account for unfulfilled prophesies. People began to lose faith and the British swooped in on the vulnerable Xhosa. Nongqawuse was turned over to the British by the chief of *Bomvana*. Later, she was taken to the Pauper's Lodge in Cape Town as a prisoner.

DID YOU KNOW?

1. The ancestors told of the British being swept into the sea if their instructions to kill all cattle were followed. The numbers ranged from 300,000-400,000 head of cattle slaughtered.
2. Nongqawuse predicted their ancestors' promises would be fulfilled and the sun would turn red on Feb 18th, 1867. (It didn't.)
3. There are some reports she lived on a farm in Cape Colony after her prison release.

A French composer, Jeanne Louise Dumont Farrenc (1804-1875) was a pianist, teacher and mother. Well known at the time for her chamber music, she also composed many orchestral works. Louise was the only woman appointed to be a professor at the famous *Conservatoire de Paris* during the 19th century. She was a virtuoso, performer and equality campaigner. Arguably, Louise is called "the greatest woman composer of the 19th century."

After completing her studies at the Paris Conservatory, Louise began her career as a concert pianist, becoming quite famous. She married a fellow student in 1821, Arisitide Farrenc, who was a great proponent of his wife's compositions. He supported her entirely by publishing her works and encouraging her to write more.

In 1842, she became the only woman to be appointed as a professor at the same conservatory during the 19th century. Louise continued to teach there for thirty years, becoming one of the greatest piano professors in Europe. While she was teaching and touring, Louise penned symphonies, overtures and chamber music. Although she was writing celebrated music, she was paid far less than male professors of the same caliber. After much protesting to the authorities, she let her music do the talking. Louise wrote her famous *Nonet in E flat* to great acclaim. Finally, her request for better pay was granted. (Better late than never—I'm not sure.)

Louise also edited a book about early musical performance styles that was very well received. Together with her husband, she penned an anthology of early music. *Le Tresor des Pianistes* was a twenty-three volume set of books about piano and harpsichord music. Most famous for her performances, her written music never received the attention it deserved. Nonetheless, Louise Farrenc kept composing until the premature death of her daughter in 1859.

DID YOU KNOW?

1. Her work fell into oblivion due to sexism, although music connoisseurs of the time appreciated it.
2. Thankfully, Louise's work is beginning to resurface in the 21st century.

Minerva is the virgin Roman Goddess of wisdom and learning, medicine, visual arts, meditation, inventiveness, commerce, poetry, spinning and weaving, the professions, and later on—war. (Quite the versatile Goddess, don't you think?) In ancient times, the sacred *Quinquatria* festival was held annually in her honor from March19-23rd. Minerva is a "Goddess of the people" and revered by both politicians and plebeians. A Goddess of victory and Goddess of warriors, She is shown wearing armor, a helmet and carrying a spear. Her themes are earth and home, and is often depicted with an owl, symbolizing Her ties to wisdom and knowledge. Minerva is also found holding an olive branch, embodying her association with peace.

Ovid, the Roman poet, in *Fasti III* called Minerva the "Goddess of a thousand works." As Minerva Medica, She was the "Goddess of medicine" and as Minerva Achaea, she was worshipped at Luceria. Her worship expanded throughout the Roman Empire, even into areas of Britain. She dwelt at the heart of any civilized society, with Apollo and Mercury being Her natural partners.

Minerva was sometimes depicted as being *swift* and "having eyes like a cat." These imply she had quick intelligence and skillfulness. Her sense of fairness and equity endears Minerva to those whose talents (instead of birth) set them apart from others. She is thought to have invented the flute by piercing holes in boxwood. Not liking how flute-playing made Her cheeks puff out, She threw the flute by the river where it was found by a satyr. (So that's where he got his flute!)

DID YOU KNOW?

1. Minerva's symbols are snakes and owls, geraniums and olive trees.
2. She is commonly identified with the Greek Athena.

LUCRETIA MOTT

"The world has never yet seen a truly great and virtuous nation because in the degradation of woman the very fountains of life are poisoned at their source."

A women's rights activist, Lucretia Coffin Mott (1793-1880) was a U.S. Quaker, abolitionist, pioneer social reformer and mother of six. She developed the idea of reforming the position of women in society when she was amongst the women excluded from the World Anti-Slavery Convention in 1840. Lucretia helped found the organized women's rights movement in the U.S. She dedicated her life to the goal of human equality despite infuriating ministers, politicians, journalists and even her fellow Quakers. (Good for her!)

At fifteen, when Lucretia began teaching, her interest in women's rights was ignited. Solely because of her sex she was paid half the salary male teachers were receiving at the same school. She married James Mott, an associate teacher from the school, in 1811 and the couple moved to Philadelphia. About 1818 Mott began to speak on religion, temperance, peace, the abolition of slavery, and questioning social reform.

In 1833 Mott attended the founding convention of the American Anti-Slavery Society. Immediately thereafter she organized its women's auxiliary, the Philadelphia Female Anti-Slavery Society, of which she was chosen president. Four years later, she helped organize the Anti-Slavery Convention of American Women.

In May of 1838 her home was nearly destroyed by a mob after the burning of Pennsylvania Hall. Rebuffed as a delegate to the World's Anti-Slavery Convention in London (1840) because of her sex, Lucretia still managed to make her views known. A fluent, charismatic speaker, she retained her poise before the most hostile of audiences. After the Civil War, she worked to secure the franchise and educational opportunities for freedmen. With the passage of the Fugitive Slave Law in 1850, she and her husband opened their home to runaway slaves escaping via the Underground Railroad.

DID YOU KNOW?

1. Lucretia continued to be active in the causes of women's rights, peace and liberal religion until her death in 1880.
2. She co-wrote the "Declaration of Sentiments" at the 1848 Seneca Falls Convention.

MARY-COOKE BRANCH MUNFORD

A Virginia social activist, Mary-Cooke Branch Munford (1865-1938) was an educator advocating for women's rights, civil rights, women's education and their suffrage, as well as health and labor reform. A mother of two, she dedicated her life to improving education in the South. Denied a college education, Mary-Cooke fought for the advancement of women's education while trying to improve race relations. She was the first woman to sit on Richmond's school board.

Focusing initially on education reform, Mary-Cooke helped establish the Richmond Education Association which promoted public education. Most areas of Virginia had underfunded schools. The REA was mainly concerned with increasing education in rural areas. At the turn of the twentieth century, only four men's colleges were located in the state. At the University of Virginia, she led a campaign to coordinate college for white women there. The Co-ordinate College League introduced legislation for the women's college, but their efforts were defeated. (The College of William and Mary did admit women in 1918.)

Mary-Cooke held office in many other Virginia organizations, including the Equal Suffrage League of Virginia, the National Child Labor Committee, the Virginia League of Women Voters and the Women's Committee of the Council for National Defense to name just a few. If there was an issue Mary-Cooke believed in, nothing stopped her from getting involved.

After the death of her husband in 1910, Mary-Cooke devoted more time to fighting against the discrimination of African Americans. She believed deeply that as a white noblewoman, her responsibility lay with helping to care for African Americans. Her nurturing attitude came from her own family's history, employing servants. Mary-Cooke worked to improve sanitation and maintenance in Black neighborhoods to make it equal to that of white neighborhoods. Alongside Janie Porter Barrett, she organized the Virginia Industrial School for Colored Girls in 1915. She also was a founder of the Virginia Inter-Racial League.

DID YOU KNOW?

1. Mary-Cooke founded a Saturday afternoon club to discuss civic issues but dropped out after discovering the discussions focused on Homer and Goethe instead of child labor and municipal sewage systems.
2. She became a trustee at historically Black Fisk University in Nashville.

"Nothing in life is to be feared, it is only to be understood. Now is the time to understand more, so that we may fear less."

Polish scientist Marie Sklodowska Curie (1867-1934) was an inventor, teacher, mother and naturalized French physicist who became the first woman to win a Nobel Prize in both Chemistry and Physics. She pioneered research in the field of radioactivity, enabling radioactive isotypes to be isolated. During the First World War, she designed a practical use of X-rays; Marie also discovered two new elements, polonium and radium. Her pioneering scientific work was more remarkable because of discrimination against women in science at the time. She broke down many barriers for women in science and became the first female professor at the University of Paris in 1906. Amazing, yes?

Opportunities in Poland for advanced study in physics and mathematics were limited. Marie moved to Paris (1891) where, after working as a governess, she was able to study at the *Sorbonne* while living with her sister. She went on to get a degree in physics and the mathematical sciences. In 1898, Marie discovered two new elements, radium and polonium. Continuing her studies, she was awarded her Doctor of Science degree in 1903.

Marie and her husband, Pierre, along with *Henri Becqueral,* shared the 1903 Nobel Prize in Physics for their pioneering work developing radioactivity. After her husband's death in 1906, Madame Curie became Professor of General Physics at *The Sorbonne*. In 1911, she was awarded a second Nobel Prize in Chemistry for the discovery of radium and polonium. She was the first woman to win the Nobel twice in two different fields of science.

Not long after, Marie built a radium institute with two laboratories. One lab studied radioactivity, the other did biological research for cancer treatment. Marie was also a WWI heroine. She developed mobile x-ray machines, known as *Petit Curies*, that could be used in field hospitals and vehicles during wartime. They enabled nearly a million soldiers to be diagnosed.

Did you know?

1. Marie died from aplastic anemia (a blood disease) from radiation exposure.
2. At the time, people used radium in toothpaste, drinking cups and bath salts.

"The bird that would soar above the level plain of tradition and prejudice must have strong wings."

Writing one of the earliest feminist novels, the influence of Katherine O'Flaherty Chopin (1850-1904) was not realized until seventy years after its publication. Typical of 19th century wives, Kate focused on raising six children and managing the household until her husband died of swamp fever. Published at the peak of her popularity in 1899, her scandalizing novel *The Awakening* drew condemnation for painting a true picture of women's sensuality. Scalded by critics, Kate returned to producing short stories until her sudden death from a brain hemorrhage at fifty-four. Her famous novel is now considered a classic. (So there ya' go.)

Growing up in the French community in St. Louis, Kate was exposed to Catholic teachings through her school. Her main interests, reading, writing and music, were the result of the French educational emphasis she absorbed at school and from her mentor, Mary O'Meara. In 1879, Kate married Oscar Chopin, the two settling in New Orleans. When Oscar's cotton brokerage went bust, the family of eight moved to Natchitoches Parish—which was to provide much substance for Kate's later novels and short stories.

In deep debt upon her husband's death, Kate moved her children back to St. Louis to her mother's house. The following year, her mother's death, shortly after her husband's, left her devastated and depressed. A family friend suggested she start writing in order to work through her grief.

By 1890, Kate was publishing short stories and articles in various literary magazines. Considered a "regional writer", her powerful literary qualities were ignored. Her second novel, *The Awakening,* brought her intense scrutiny and negative criticism. Discouraged but unstoppable, she turned back to the short story genre, portraying women with personal wants and needs.

DID YOU KNOW?

1. Kate is credited by some as pioneering the early feminist movement.
2. Sadly, she received no awards for her literary works.

Mughal Empress Nur Jahan (1577-1645 CE) was one of the most powerful women of seventeenth century India. Her name means "Light of the World." She played an unprecedented role in running the vast Mughal empire. Nur Jahan was strong-willed and known for her charity. She was also a poet, mother, an expert hunter, astute politician and an innovative architect as well as favorite wife of Emperor Jahangir (he loved his wine and opium to excess). Today's historians view her as a feminist hero.

Within nine years of her marriage to the emperor, Nur Jahan acquired all the rights of sovereignty and government normally due him. She was virtually in charge of the whole empire until the emperor died in 1627. Finding herself both powerful and uniquely positioned, Nur Jahan utilized her skills in administration, politics, economics and the arts.

Since women were not supposed to appear with men in court, Nur Jahan ruled through trusted males. She approved all orders and grants of appointment in the emperor's name and oversaw all promotions and demotions within the royal government. She took special interest in women's affairs and rights, giving them land and dowries for orphan girls. Since Nur came from a line of poets, she naturally wrote and encouraged this among the court women.

Fighting between Jahangir's sons for power, however, slowly nicked away at her reign. Upon Jahangir's death, Prince *Khurram* proclaimed himself *Shah Jahan*. He forced Nur Jahan into confinement. Her imprisonment ended her influence at court, she spent the last years of her life in exile in Lahore.

Did you know?

1. Nur Jahan was Emperor Jahangir's twentieth wife.
2. Legend tells of her contributions to a variety of fine arts, including gifts of opulent textiles.
3. Indu Sandaresan's *Taj Mahal Trilogy* published 2002-2010, revolves around her life.

"You don't sing to feel better. You sing cause that's a way of understanding life."

> Gertrude Pridgett Rainey (c. 1885-1939) was one of the first professional African American blues singer-songwriters. Called "The Mother of the Blues", Ma was a majestic singer on stage, draped in long gowns dripping in gold and diamonds. A shrewd business-woman, Ma wrote many of her own songs. Her deep contralto voice, raw and sometimes gravelly when she wished, lent itself to capturing Black southern rural life. Ma's strong, unapologetic voice and liberated bisexuality captured the hearts of the 1920s Jim Crow South.

She began performing at a talent show around age twelve, graduating to Black minstrel shows quickly. By 1904, she married William "Pa" Rainey, and the couple was soon billed together as "Ma and Pa Rainey" in Rabbit's Foot Company performing as "Black Face Song and Dance Comedians and Jubilee Singers." When the popularity of blues music increased, Ma became well known. It was about this time that Bessie Smith came under Ma's wing, the more experienced singer helped Bessie get her start.

In 1923, Ma was discovered by a Paramount Records producer. After signing a contract, she made her first eight recordings in Chicago. Ma recorded over one hundred records in the next five years with Paramount, dubbing her the "mother of the blues" and "Songbird of the South." When she began touring with the Theater Owners Booking Association, Ma was performing with Tommie Dorsey and the Wildcats Jazz Band to both white and Black audiences.

Although most of Ma's lyrics sing of sexual love between men and women, some of her lyrics reference bisexuality or lesbianism. The 1970s lesbian movement lays claim to her *Prove It On Me*. By 1930, Ma's style of "classic blues" was no longer fashionable.

DID YOU KNOW?

1. Her music inspired poets Langston Hughes and Sterling Brown.
2. The proprietor of three theatres in Columbus, Georgia, Ma performed until her death at age fifty-three.

Modjadji (meaning Ruler of the Day) is the "Rain Queen," a hereditary queen of the *Balobedu* people of Limpopo Province in the middle of South Africa. The succession to the position of Rain Queen is matrilineal, going to the eldest daughter. She is believed to have Goddess-like powers which include the ability to control the clouds and rainfall. The Rain Queen is viewed as a sacred figure, not allowed to be married—though the fourth Rain Queen broke with this custom and married. She bares children by her male relatives and has wives who serve as her maids.

It is told that the Balobedu settled in the area about four hundred years ago after migrating south from present-day Zimbabwe. Men ruled the tribe, until the Balobedu king (claiming prophetic guidance) started a line of female leaders by impregnated his daughter.

Modjadji VII, when she begins her reign at eighteen in 2023, will be a queen in the true sense. In 2016, President Jacob Zuma made the Balobedu one of the handful of tribal monarchies recognized by the African state. When coming of age, *Masalanabo Modjadji VII* will rule at the same level as the powerful *Xhosa* and *Zulu* kings. She will hold influence over more than one hundred villages and receive a government paycheck. The Rain Queen will live at the royal compound surrounded with lush gardens— home to the world's largest cycad trees, while the surrounding area remains parched.

Since the early death of *Modjadji VI* in 2005, the Balobedu tribe has been without a Rain Queen. When Modjadji VII is crowned, it will not only restore the Rain Queen, but it will also be a financial gain for the tribe.

Did you know?

1. The Rain Queen must shun public functions according to custom.
2. The only way she can communicate with her people is through male or female councilors.

"It is unthinkable that a national government which represents women should ignore the issue of the right of all women to political freedom."

An American suffragist and women's rights advocate, Lucy Burns (1879-1922) was a passionate rights advocate both in the U.S. and in Great Britain. She spent more time in prison than any other American suffragist. Lucy was absolutely fearless!

Lucy traveled to Europe to attend graduate school. She was studying linguistics at Oxford University when she encountered the militant "suffragettes" of the Women's Social and Political Union (WSPU) led by Emmeline Pankhurst and her daughters. After joining up, Lucy was arrested several times along with other protestors. She met Alice Paul, also an American who had joined the WSPU actions, in a London police station.

Returning to the US, Lucy moved to Washington D.C. to lead the Congressional Committee of the National American Woman Suffrage Association (NAWSA) with Alice. Their first undertaking was an enormous parade held on the day prior to Woodrow Wilson's inauguration. The event, attracting five thousand marchers, was an enormous success, though the marchers were confronted by a jeeringly hostile crowd. But Lucy and Alice broke away to form a new organization—The Congressional Union for Woman Suffrage (CUWS) in 1914 which became The National Woman's Party (NWP) in 1916. Radical and militant, they called for a constitutional amendment that would ensure women's right to vote across the U.S.

"The Night of Terror" happened in November of 1917, when Lucy and other NWP members were jailed in the Occoquan Workhouse in Virginia for their White House picketing. The suffragists were beaten, terrorized and force fed by guards. They handcuffed Lucy's arms over her head for the whole night, then placed her in solitary confinement. After her release, she commenced touring and giving speeches on behalf of women's right to vote. In other words, *she persisted*.

DID YOU KNOW?

1. The suffragettes were also called "silent sentinels" and the first group to protest by picketing in front of the White House.
2. The Lucy Burns Museum is in Lorton, Virginia on the site of the former Occoquan Workhouse.

An American educator, businesswoman and mother, Minnie M. Geddings Cox (1869-1933) was also one of the first African American women to serve as US Post-master (1891). After receiving lynching threats, she was forced to leave her position for lack of protection from either the sheriff or the mayor of Indianola, Mississippi. The situation became national news, creating a debate about race, states' rights and federal powers. Later, Minnie and her husband opened the Delta Penny Savings Bank, one of Mississippi's first Black-owned banks. Courageous innovators, don't you think?

Born in the Mississippi Delta to business owning parents, Minnie's early life had some privileges. Educated at Fisk University in Nashville, she recognized the leadership potential Black educated women held. After graduation (1888), Minnie began teaching in Indianola, Mississippi. She met and married Wayne W. Cox, the founder and principal of her school. The two had one daughter. Having more in common with white professional people, the family lived on the predominantly white side of the tracks.

In 1891, President Benjamin Harrison appointed Minnie as postmistress of Holmes County. When Grover Cleveland took office, she lost the position but was made post-mistress of Sunflower County when President William McKinley won in 1897. Minnie garnered a substantial raise, and along with their education and property holdings, gave the Coxes social and economic clout.

Competing for governor, James. K. Vardaman began agitating locals with fears of "negro domination." His venom reinforced political and economic trepidation. Finally, threats of lynching caused Minnie to tender her resignation, which President Teddy Roosevelt promptly refused. He closed the post office temporarily. Without local safety guarantees, Minnie and her family fled. Months later, the Coxes returned to Indianola and opened a bank. Her story mostly forgotten, "Minnie Cox and the Indianola Affair" remains an important chapter in American history.

DID YOU KNOW?

1. The Coxes also founded the Mississippi Life Insurance Company, one of the first Black-owned insurance companies offering whole life insurance.
2. A Post Office building in Indianola is named after her (2008) commemorating the barriers she overcame. (Nice tribute to a persevering woman.)

"Mary Anning is probably the most important unsung (or inadequately sung) collecting force in the history of paleontology." Stephen J Gould, 1992.

Considered to be the woman who discovered dinosaurs, Mary Anning (1799-1847) was a prolific British fossil collector, paleontologist, and amateur anatomist. She lived on the coast of the English Channel in the Jurassic fossil beds (Lyme Regis) and is named amongst one of the most important figures in the history of science; her discoveries bolstered the theory of extinction. Mary overcame chronic poverty, lack of formal education, dangerous excavations, cynicism and sexism to become the woman we now recognize as a pioneering paleontologist. (She was no shrinking violet!)

Mary taught herself anatomy, scientific illustration, geology and paleontology. Despite her lack of formal scientific training, her local area knowledge, discoveries, and skill at categorizing fossils secured her reputation among paleontology's male—and largely upper-class—ranks.

Mary's first major discovery was made with her brother when they found an ichthyosaur's remains Although it earned the family a mere twenty-three pounds at that time, it is considered a momentous find. In 1823, Anning discovered the first-ever Plesiosaurus and captured the complete fossil in a scientific drawing. Initially the fossil was considered fake. After close examination, *Georges Cuvier* (French anatomist) declared it to be authentic, making Mary famous. In 1828, she discovered the fossil of a *Pterosaur species Dimorphodon macronyx*. It was the first skeleton of this flying reptile that was found in the British Isles. (She later discovered a better skeleton in 1829 and a different type of *Plesiosaurus* fossil in 1830.)

It was Mary's 1829 discovery of an extinct fish species, *Squaloraja,* that is considered to be a major boost to the theory of evolution. The skeleton looked like it was an in-between species, part stingray and part shark.

DID YOU KNOW?

1. Mary was one of nine children, but only her brother Joseph and she survived into adulthood.
2. Struck by lightning when she was fifteen months old, Mary lived to age forty-seven when she died of breast cancer at the pinnacle of her career.
3. Charles Dickens wrote an article about her life in February of 1865.

Lorena Hickok (1893-1968) was a pioneering American journalist, author and biographer. Better known as Hick, she stormed into the male-dominated world of journalism working for papers in the Midwest and New York before becoming one of the first women to have a byline with the Associated Press. She was appointed chief investigator for the Federal Emergency Relief Administration (FERA). Hick also did promotional work for the 1939 World's Fair and the Democratic National Committee. Her twenty-year career as a nationally syndicated columnist was cut short and over-shadowed by her close friendship with Eleanor Roosevelt.

Violence and instability shaped her growing-up years. Hick was forced to move from school to school as her father sought work. His consistent beatings of her and her sisters forced Hick to leave home at fourteen and begin working as a maid. In 1912, she enrolled at a college in Appleton, Wisconsin. Ridiculed by classmates and unable to adjust, she flunked out and was hired by *the Battle Creek Evening News.*

She eventually transferred to the *Minneapolis Tribune* in 1917. Thomas J. Dillon, the *Tribune's* managing editor, recognized Hick's talents and taught her the newspaper business. By 1928, the Associated Press hired her to write feature stories. Quickly making a name for herself by covering politics and dramatic stories, she won the coveted right to have her name appear as a by-line atop the articles.

Meeting Eleanor Roosevelt in 1932, the two became quick and trusted friends. Their campaign experience led to a lifetime of devotion to one another. As the investigator for FERA, Hick visited thirty-two states and provided detailed reports of living conditions and politics to FDR, Eleanor and Harry Hopkins (the head of FERA). An acute observer, she was able to assess problems communities faced quickly that helped the Roosevelts and Hopkins see things clearly, resulting in positive actions to help the nation's poor.

DID YOU KNOW?

1. Hick was America's best-known female reporter by 1932.
2. She authored several books, and co-authored *Ladies of Courage* with Eleanor Roosevelt.

Queen of the *Ambundu* Kingdoms of *Ndongo* and *Matamba,* located in present day northern Angola, Nzinga Mbande (1583-1663) came into power after the death of her father and brother. A skilled political ambassador ruling during the rapid growth of African slave trade and the encroachment of the Portuguese Empire, Nzinga fought for independence and stature for her kingdom in a reign that lasted thirty-seven years. She is remembered for her intelligence, her political and diplomatic wisdom and brilliant military tactics.

Born into a royal family of *Ndongo*, Nzinga's father became king when she was ten. She received military training as a warrior to fight alongside him. She was able to participate in many official duties, including legal councils, war councils and important rituals. Nzinga was also taught Portuguese by visiting Portuguese missionaries.

Multiple crises befell the Ndongo. In 1571, Sebastian of Portugal ordered the Ndongo be conquered. By the time Nzinga's father became king (1593), their people had been at war with Portuguese troops for ten years. He tried various methods of handling the crises but was unable to change the situation. After her brother came to power, he appointed Nzinga ambassador to the Portuguese.

Fiercely negotiating with *Dom Joao Correia de Sousa,* Nzinga was able to reach an agreement with them which included the withdrawal of Portuguese troops from Ndongo lands and recognize its sovereignty. She also made sure the people weren't required to pay tributes. In return, Nzinga agreed to open trade routes to the Portuguese. The Ndongo would also agree to study Christianity and be baptized. After becoming queen (1624), Nzinga continued to fight Portuguese incursions. Because independence would not come for another 351 years, it proves Nzinga was very much ahead of her time.

DID YOU KNOW?

1. It was not until 1975 that armed resistance to the Portuguese resulted in an independent Angola.
2. A statue of Queen Nzinga stands today in Largo do Kinaxixi, Luanda, Angola.

Maddalena Casulana

"I want to show the world, as much as I can in this profession of music, the vain error of men that they alone possess the gifts of intellect and artistry, and that such gifts are never given to women."

> The first woman to ever print and publish her own musical compositions, Maddalena Mezari detta Casulana Vicentina (1544-1590) was also an accomplished professional singer, lutenist and teacher. A pioneering female Italian composer of the Renaissance, very little is known of her life. Publishing music during an era that revered only male composers, Maddalena led the way in the 16ᵗʰ century for woman composers of today. She is best remembered for her madrigals.

An independent woman from modest means, Maddalena chose to earn her own living during a time when women were the property of their father, brother or husband. Receiving her earliest musical education in Florence, her first madrigals were written in 1566 in a collection entitled *Il Desiderio*.

She published a full volume of her works a mere two years later. Entitled *First Book of Madrigals for Four Voices*, Maddalena dedicated her book of music to Isabella de' Medici, a close friend. Isabella, a notoriously free-spirited noble woman was the main subject of her works.

Not much is heard or written of Maddalena between 1570 and 1580. Perhaps she was married during this time, there is simply no record of her whereabouts or her actions. Reappearing in 1582, it is recorded she sung at a wedding in Perugia. Her final book of madrigals was printed in 1583. Her style was chromatic and contrapuntal—styles common during the Renaissance.

Did you know?

1. Other composers of that time, including *Phillipe de Monte* and *Orlande de Lassus,* thought highly of her works.
2. Sixty-six of her madrigals have survived.

MORANA

Slavic Goddess Morana (Marzanna in Polish, Marena in Russian) is associated with seasonal rites based on the ideas of birth, death and rebirth of nature. "The Mother of souls," this ancient Goddess is connected with the death of winter and rebirth in spring, She is in command of the natural world. An all-powerful Goddess of winter, Morana is also thought to be associated with agriculture. She is one of the most well-known deities in Slavic mythology.

Her celebrations are held around the spring equinox, March 21st, with processions of children and adults carrying handmade Morana dolls to the nearest river, lake or pond. Singing traditional songs, they throw the effigies into the water or set them on fire. The tradition of burning or drowning an effigy of Morana celebrating the end of winter is carried on today. This festival in Poland is called *Topienie Marzanny*.

She is perceived as the personification of winter and the symbolic drowning ends that season and affirms the re-awakening of nature. Different tribes practiced differently, but all with the same premise. Morana is often pictured as a pale, black-haired woman with claws; She had turned bitter and cold becoming winter-like when betrayed by Her husband. It is believed She lives in a mirrored palace where two rivers meet. The palace is guarded by serpents, the river around Her home is bottomless.

Morana is forever entwined with Vesna, the Goddess of spring and rebirth. They could not exist without each other. The ancient Slavs believed the sun descended into the underworld in the winter. Thus, Morana is associated with darkness and death. Despite being known initially as a Goddess of fertility and life, She soon withered into an evil, deadly force after betrayal.

DID YOU KNOW?

1. Morana's symbols are dolls (poppets) and water.
2. She has been compared to Hecate and sorcery.
3. Morana is also associated with dreams.

"I believe that the influence of woman will save the country before every other power."

A prominent U.S. suffragist and orator, Lucy Stone (1818-1893) was an abolitionist, mother, and organizer promoting rights for women. In 1847, she became the first woman from Massachusetts to earn a college degree, graduating with honors. Lucy began lecturing for the antislavery movement as a paid agent for the American Anti-Slavery Society right out of college. She is considered one of the most prominent leaders of the 19th century suffrage movement. Lucy co-edited the premier women's suffrage newspaper, the *Woman's Journal,* until her death.

Though she was almost thirty when she completed her education, Lucy's career prospects seemed dim since few professions were open to women. Renowned abolitionist William Lloyd Garrison hired her for his American Anti-Slavery Society. She began traveling extensively, lecturing tirelessly. Lucy wrote and delivered abolitionist speeches while also becoming active in women's rights. Like other female abolitionists, Lucy was often heckled and at least once physically attacked by a mob. Nevertheless, she proved so popular she was out-earning many male lecturers.

In 1850, two years after the Seneca Falls Women's Rights Convention, Lucy organized the first national Women's Rights Convention in Worcester, Massachusetts. She set another precedent in 1858 when she reminded Americans of the "no taxation without representation" principle. Refusing to pay property taxes, the impoundment and sale of the Stones' household goods was her punishment.

In 1869, Lucy broke with suffragists Elizabeth Cady Stanton, Susan B. Anthony and others over passage of the fourteenth and fifteenth amendments to the Constitution, which granted voting rights to Black men but not to women. Lucy willingly accepted this measure for her abolitionist goals while continuing to work for women's suffrage.

DID YOU KNOW?

1. Anthony, Stanton, and Lucy Stone have been called the 19th-century "triumvirate" of women's suffrage and feminism.
2. Lucy started a dress revolution when she began wearing long bloomers beneath a skirt shortened to mid-calf. (Omigod.)

Islamic scholar and Fula princess, Nana Asma'u bint Shehu Usman dan Fodiyo (1793-1864) was an educational leader, poet and mother who lived in what is now northern Nigeria. She transformed the tradition of women as the first teachers of Islamic religious knowledge. Nana Asma'u educated men, women and children, establishing the *yan-taru*—female teachers who traveled to rural areas to improve Hausa women's education in the 1830s. Her poems, written in three languages, continue to help educate even in the twenty-first century. Nana Asma'u is honored in northern Nigeria as a pioneer in the field of women's education and an early feminist icon.

Fluent in Arabic, *Fulfulde, Hausa and Tamacheq Tuareg,* and well versed in Arabic, Greek and Latin classics, Nana Asma'u was a product of the vibrant Muslim tradition of educating women. During the 1830's, she formed a group of female teachers who travelled throughout their caliphate educating women from all different backgrounds. Rich or poor, Muslim or non-Muslim, all were welcomed by the *"jajis"* who in turn taught their own groups of learned women, the yan taru.

In what was a predominantly an oral culture, learning was overwhelmingly given in the same manner. Repetition and memorization dominated, especially when it came to poetry. Nana Asma'u's poems were designed to be as accessible as possible to the widest range of women. She wrote in *Fulbe* for the aristocracy of the caliphate, and in *Hausa* for the population at large. Her extensive use of mnemonic devices made memorizing much easier for her students.

Nana Asma'u 's educational work served three purposes: intellectual, spiritual, and political growth. Her works include and expand upon the *dan Fodio's* (Islamic mystic) strong emphasis on women leaders and women's rights within the Sunni community and Islamic law. She also wrote instructions to governors and debated freely with scholars of foreign princes across all of North Africa.

DID YOU KNOW?

1. More than sixty of her written works survive today.
2. The government of Nigeria's Sokoto State is currently establishing the Nana Asma'u University of Medical Sciences.

An English paleontologist, Mary Morland Buckland (1797-1857) was also a marine biologist, scientific draftswoman, teacher and mother of nine children. Much of her fossil reconstructions can be seen today at the Oxford University Museum of Natural History.

Mary Morland Buckland was surrounded by geology from childhood. She became a talented illustrator for her husband, Rev. William Buckland, and many other paleontologists. Later on, she was curator for fossils at Oxford's museum. Mary started her career as a teenager drawing illustrations and providing specimens for George Cuvier, regarded as founder of paleontology, as well as for the British geologist William Conybeare. She created models of fossils, labeling them for the Oxford University Museum of Natural History, studied marine zoophytes and repaired broken fossils.

Mary's fossil passion was matched in the man she married, William Buckland, already one of the key figures in early geology and paleontology. They first met in a carriage, both reading copies of Cuvier's latest work. After their marriage in 1825 they honeymooned on an epic fossil-fest across Europe, visiting many of the famous sites and names in paleontology. On top of raising and teaching nine children, Mary was invaluable to her husband's work. She wrote as he dictated, edited, produced illustrations for his books, took notes of his observations and wrote much of it herself.

She also assisted her husband in his contribution to *The Bridgewater Treatise*, an eight-volume work. When *Geology and Mineralogy* came out in 1836, it was recognized by others that much of William Buckland's professional success was due to the collaboration of his wife. Mary then expanded her own scientific interests in marine biology and microscopy, discovering the perfect blend for her artistic and scientific abilities. She continued her scientific research until the day before she died.

DID YOU KNOW?

1. Despite her busy schedule, Mary promoted education in the villages wherever they lived.
2. Her teaching of geography to students in Islip was frowned upon as people thought it was giving the lower class "ideas above their station." Can you imagine?

"I'm not afraid of storms, for I'm learning how to sail my ship."

An American novelist and poet, Louisa May Alcott (1832-1888) was a Civil War nurse, teacher, abolitionist and lifetime supporter of women's right to vote. Her most famous work, *Little Women,* was followed by *Little Men.* Louisa's work introduced readers to educated, strong female heroines, a writing style that greatly impacted American literature.

Because Louisa's father was an educator, she took very early to reading and writing. Fortunate to study under Thoreau, Emerson and Hawthorne, she also had to turn to domestic work and teaching to alleviate her family's financial woes. Louisa turned to writing as emotional support as well as financial need. Her first book, a collection of short stories, was published in 1854. Her stories, signed "A.M. Barnard," were often lurid and violent tales with depictions of strong, self-reliant, imaginative women.

When the Civil War started in 1861, Louisa served as a nurse in a Union hospital. Unfortunately, halfway through her assignment she contracted typhoid fever. Her experience in the hospital as a patient and a nurse inspired the novel *Hospital Sketches,* bringing her the first taste of fame.

After the war, one of Louisa's publishers asked her to write a novel for young women. She published her famous work, *Little Women,* in 1868. It was first published in a series of short stories but was eventually compiled into one book. *Little Women* was an instant success. The book cemented Louisa Alcott as one of the foremost novelists of the 19th and early 20th centuries. After moving to Europe, she published another classic, *Little Men.*

DID YOU KNOW?

1. Louisa was one of the founders of Boston's "Women's Educational and Industrial Union."
2. She was treated for typhoid with a compound containing mercury, which biographers now believe brought on an auto-immune disease that eventually led to her death at age fifty-five.

QUEEN AMINA

The legendary Hausa Muslim warrior queen of Zaria in the savanna region of West Africa, Amina (1533-1610) was the earliest woman to reign as *Sarauniya* (queen) in a male-dominated society. Amina expanded the territory of the Hausa people of north Africa to its largest borders in history. Modern Nigeria has erected a statue of her, spear in hand and riding a horse at the National Arts Theater in Lagos State.

Born into a wealthy family, her father was a peaceful ruler over his caliphate and they prospered. The crown passed to Amina's brother upon her father's death. She chose to spend time honing military skills with the *Zazzau* (the city state) warriors. She emerged as a leader of the calvary. Upon her brother's death after a ten-year rule, Amina had become a fierce warrior and earned the respect of the military. She was able to assume the reign in 1576.

Queen Amina came to rule when Zazzau was situated at the crossroads of three major trade corridors. There was continual warring amongst the *Songhai* (ruling elite) people competing for control of the trade routes. Leading her first military charge only a few months after taking power, Amina continued to fight and expand her kingdom to its greatest in history. Leading an army of twenty thousand men, she tried to annex a huge territory that cost her thirty-four years of almost constant warring.

The expansion of Queen Amina's kingdom made it the center of all of *Hasauland*, which was the traditional east-to-west trans-Saharan axis. This guaranteed prosperity for her kingdom. Amina is credited as the architect of the strong earthen walls that surround the city of *Zaria*, and in all *Hasau* states. She built many of these walls, some of which remain standing today.

DID YOU KNOW?

1. Politically, walls were considered prestigious, their size a measure of a ruler's ability to command labor of his/her subjects.
2. Amina remains a controversial figure, her existence still questioned by some scholars.
3. Her success as sovereign did not have a trickle-down effect on subsequent female leaders.

"Fear is a disease that eats away at logic and makes man inhuman."

An American contralto, Marian Anderson (1897-1993) was the first African American to sing at the Metropolitan Opera in New York. For forty years she performed with renowned orchestras throughout the world and for world leaders. She was also the first African American to perform at the White House (for the Roosevelts). Marian worked as a delegate for the United Nations Human Rights Committee and sang at the "1963 March On Washington."

When Marion first began performing in the United States (1925), many concert opportunities were closed to her because of her race. Three years later, she left for Europe and made her debut in London. Marian was able to win a fellowship from the Julius Rosenwald Fund that helped pay for her move to Berlin in 1930 where she studied German and lieder music. "Marian Mania" soon broke out across Europe, particularly in Scandinavia. Her repertoire covered everything from German lieder (German songs from the 19th century), Italian opera, Russian folk songs and traditional African American spirituals.

The rise of Nazism casted its dark shadow over Marian's European booking, so she headed back to the U.S. Despite being the first African American to perform at the White House, she was forced to ride in segregated train cars and perform for whites-only audiences. (How ridiculous is that?) Finding no hotel to house her after her Princeton University performance, Albert Einstein invited her to stay at his home.

Marian preferred to focus on her music, not on politics. By 1940, she had performed all over the globe, including Cuba, France, Brazil and Russia. In addition, she went on to sing at Eisenhower and Kennedy's inaugurations—another first for an African American.

DID YOU KNOW?

1. In 1963, Marian was given the Presidential Medal of Freedom.
2. She also was awarded the Congressional Gold Medal in 1977.

MORGAN LE FAY

Morgan le Fay (meaning Morgan the Fairy) is a powerful Sorceress who lived at the time of King Arthur and Camelot. She changes shapes at will, and has the power to heal. According to some sources, Morgan Le Fay is King Arthur's sister (or half-sister). Other stories identify Her as an enchantress known as Nimue or the "Lady of the Lake." A protector of those She loves, Morgan le Fey is a benefactor of various medieval heroes.Renowned for Her beauty, magical skills and knowledge of herb lore, She is a semi-Divine healer trusted to care for King Arthur. Other folk stories tell of Morgan le Fay as a seducer of men and someone to be feared for Her trickery.

In *Camelot*, Morgan le Fay opposes Arthur and schemes to destroy his court by exposing the affair between Guinevere, his wife and Sir Lancelot. As the enchantress *Nimue,* She tricks Arthur's magician, Merlin, into falling in love with Her. After learning Merlin's secrets, Nimue imprisons Merlin behind invisible walls.

In other stories, a very different side of Morgan le Fay is shown. As the leader of the nine women who guard the island of Avalon, She lives in a castle beneath a lake surrounding the magical island. Appearing as a very benevolent figure, She gives Arthur Excalibur and takes him to Avalon when he is fatally wounded.

Morgan le Fay seems to have been derived from the Celtic deities *Morrigan, Macha and Modron* (a Divine mother). As queen of the land of Fairy, She appears in both French and Italian romances. Emerging first in the Arthurian legends of *Geoffrey of Manmouth's* twelfth volume, *Vita Merlini,* it was Morgan le Fay who first threw Excalibur into a lake.

DID YOU KNOW?

1. Morgan usually presented Her favorites with a ring keeping them close by Her side.
2. Her character has once again begun appearing in a variety of roles in fantasy, historical fiction and other genres. Check it out.

"Today a reader, tomorrow a leader."

> Sarah Margaret Fuller (1810-1850) was an author, editor, teacher, journalist, women's rights activist and political activist. She is best known for her feminist writing and literary criticisms in 19th century America. She was the first woman allowed to use the library at Harvard College, and was also the first full-time American female book reviewer in journalism. Her seminal book *Woman in the Nineteenth Century* is considered a major feminist work in the United States. Fuller's death at sea was a tragic loss for her family, colleagues and womankind.

Margaret Fuller, considered America's first true feminist, received a rigorous classical education. Her father, a senator, disappointed that his child was not a boy, gave her intense lessons. She became entwined with Massachusetts intellectuals, Ralph Waldo Emerson among them. Margaret conducted "Conversations" with prominent intellectuals of the day pioneering the idea that women could argue philosophy on a par with men.

Her intellectual precociousness gained her the acquaintance of various Cambridge intellectuals, but her intense forthright manner put many people off. By the time she was in her thirties, Margaret had gained the reputation as the best-read person in New England. In 1840, she co-founded the transcendentalist journal *The Dial*, which she edited before joining the staff of the *New York Tribune*. Margaret then published *Woman in the Nineteenth Century* (1845) which became a feminist classic.

Traveling to Rome as a war correspondent (1847) she met Giovanni Angelo, the *Marchese d'Ossoli,* a liberal thinker ten years younger than she. They became lovers, had a son in 1848, and married the next year. She, her husband and son sailed for the United States in 1850. The ship ran aground in a storm off Fire Island, New York. Their bodies were never recovered.

DID YOU KNOW?

1. Margaret's early writings had a profound impact on women suffrage campaigners such as Susan B. Anthony.
2. She had a premonition of her death, saying just days before leaving for the U.S., "It seems to me that my future upon Earth will soon close ... I have a vague expectation of some crisis—I know not what."

"Anything that is as old as racism is in the blood line of the nation. It's not any superficial thing-that attitude is in the blood and we have to educate about it."

An African American educator and orator, Nannie Helen Burroughs (1879-1961) was also a civil rights activist, feminist, businesswoman and religious leader. Her speech "How the Sisters Are Hindered from Helping" at the 1900 National Baptist Convention won her instant fame. Nannie founded the National Training School for Women and Girls and was appointed by President Hoover to chair a special committee on African American housing in 1931.

After excelling in school, Nannie graduated with honors from M Street High (now Paul Laurence Dunbar High School). Despite her academic achievements, she was turned down for a Washington D.C. public school teaching position. Some historians speculate the elite Black community discriminated against Nannie because of her darker skin. Nonetheless, she decided to start her own school to educate and train poor working Black women in 1909. Pretty determined, wouldn't you agree?

Once established, she served as president of that institution until her death in 1961. The school was very popular in the first half of the twentieth century. At the time, there were very few career choices for Black women, other than domestic opportunities. In 1964, the school's name was changed to Nannie Helen Burroughs School.

Nannie also wrote about the need for Black and white women to work together to achieve the right to vote, believing suffrage for African American women crucial to protect their interests in a discriminating society.

While devoting her life to the education of Black women, Nannie also defied cultural constraints of gender and race. Her work foreshadowed the main principles of the Civil Rights Movement of the 1960s and 1970s.

DID YOU KNOW?

1. Nannie organized the Harriet Beecher Stowe Literary Society in Washington D.C.
2. She was a published playwright. Her play *The Slabtown District Convention* needed several reprintings and wording updates throughout the twentieth century.

MARY CARSON BRECKENRIDGE

Mary Carson Breckenridge (1881-1965) was an American nurse, mother, midwife and founder of the Frontier Nursing Service. This service provided comprehensive family medical care to the Appalachian Hill people. She is known as "The Mother of Midwifery." Her establishment of U. S. childhood and neonatal medical care systems dramatically reduced mortality rates of mothers and infants.

After her husband's death in 1906, Mary (an aristocratic woman) decided to begin a career in nursing. Her first nursing endeavor was focused on providing victim care during the 1918 influenza epidemic in the slums of Washington, D.C. She joined the American Committee for Devastated France in 1923, organizing a visiting nurse program. It was so successful that two years later her nurses and midwives were caring for children and pregnant women throughout France.

In 1921, Mary returned to the United States and tried to establish schools of midwifery. She vowed to start one. Following her studies at Columbia, Mary returned to Europe to study midwifery at the British Hospital for Mothers and Babies in London, then traveled to Scotland for further study. Traveling back to Kentucky in 1925, Mary established the Kentucky Committee for Mothers and Babies—later named *Frontier Nursing Service* (FNS). She personally funded six nurse-midwives trained in England and Scotland to service over one thousand rural families by the early 30's, riding horses and mules because there were no reliable roads.

As the program grew, it received large donations from her influential family's political and social connections. Six healthcare clinics as well as *Mary Breckinridge Hospital* and *Mary Breckinridge Home Health Agency* are active today. People travel from around the world to study the rural healthcare system that Breckinridge founded. She remained director of FNS until her death in 1965.

DID YOU KNOW?

1. During her time at FNS, over 250,000 vaccines were given to rural Kentuckians.
2. You can find her autobiography *Wide Neighborhoods: A Story of the Frontier Nursing Service* on Amazon.
3. Sadly, midwifery has never become popular as a vocation in the U.S.

"Perhaps this very instant is your time."

> The first woman to be named Poet Laureate to the Library of Congress, Louise Bogan (1897-1970) also wrote fiction and was a literary critic. She is considered one of the major American poets of her time, overcoming much to gain that accolade.

Her parents' troubled marriage and an emotionally unstable mother caused the family to move often. Her restless childhood and her mother's frequent and lengthy disappearances baffled the family, haunting Louise most of her life and influencing her poetry to speak of love, grief, mistrust and betrayal. By 1923, Louise had published her first collection, *Body of This Death*. She was also a widow struggling to raise a daughter, Maidie Alexander, on a low income. Around that time, Louise recognized and had begun to seek help for depression; she'd battle it for the rest of her life. A recluse, she disliked talking about herself. Therefore, little is known about her life.

The majority of Louise's poetry was written in the earlier half of her life. Through her poetry, she addressed raw and difficult personal feelings. Not only was it difficult being a female poet in the 1930s and 1940s, but her lower-middle-class Irish background and limited education also brought on much ambivalence and contradiction for Louise. She even refused to review female poets in her early career.

As a critic, Louise was known for her fairness and generosity, focusing on the strengths of authors she admired, especially Theodore Roethke's—who became a good friend. However, she saw the confessional poetry of Robert Lowell and John Berryman as distasteful and self-indulgent. Louise authored six poetry collections as well as several books of prose and translations.

DID YOU KNOW?

1. She reviewed poetry for *The New Yorker* for over thirty-eight years.
2. She was described by Brett C. Miller as "one of the finest lyric poets America has produced."

A Taino Indian *cacique* (chief), Queen Anacaona (1474-1503) was a Caribbean musician, composer, poet and mother. She was one of the most respected people in their culture. Her name means "golden flower." Executed at the age of twenty-nine by Spaniards, Anacaona is memorialized in contemporary art and literature not just in Haiti, but across the Caribbean. She is known for her bravery opposing Spanish invaders acquiring the status of one of the founders of Haiti.

Anacaona was raised to rule, she was the sister of a chief. It is said she was one of the people who welcomed Christopher Columbus to the Haitian island. After her brother's death, she became a powerful ruler. Anacaona had great responsibility, determined to do the best for her people.

The Spaniards returned to the island, pillaging it through massacre and slavery. Knowing the troops had much better weaponry and that rebellion would get them nowhere, Anacaona decided diplomatic techniques were best used. She started building relationships with the invaders by encouraging intermarriage between Taino royalty and high-ranking soldiers. The peace did not last long.

In 1502, Spain's new governor, Ovando, held very different views on how to exploit Haiti. He felt the most dangerous local was Anacaona, thinking her charms had seduced Spaniards and made them submit to her. His suggestion of a peace treaty in which she had to gather eighty of the most influential Taino was embraced. A Spanish army attended the conference, burned down the building and tortured the most prominent Taino into declaring against Anacaona.

After her trial, legend claims, she was offered clemency if she became a concubine to a high-ranking Spanish official. She refused and was quickly hanged. When Queen Isabella of Castille was informed of the governor's cruelty and bloodthirsty methods, Ovando was quickly dismissed. (Too little, too late.)

DID YOU KNOW?

1. The "golden flower" queen is also known as Haiti's "poet queen."
2. A statue commemorating her life and legacy is located in Leogane, Haiti.

A gifted Viennese singer and pianist, Anna Katharina Martinez (1744-1812) composed music during the Classical Era (c. 1750-1820). Also known as Marianne von Martinez, she was the author of the only symphony composed by a woman during that era. Marianna was considered a keyboard virtuoso and wrote extensively for the instrument. Enjoying much fame throughout Europe in her lifetime, she has since been nearly forgotten.

Studying under her tutor, Metastasio, Marianna became fluent in four languages as well as received keyboard lessons and was encouraged to develop her singing voice—all by the age of ten. Demonstrating potential as a gifted composer, she was encouraged to develop that medium. A virtuosic player, even as child Marianna regularly performed before the Imperial court. Her compositions, particularly for voice, possessed coloratura (elaborate ornamentation of melody) proving she was an excellent singer. She was composing masses by age sixteen.

Because she never married, Marianna was able to devote many hours to her music, necessary because of the many barriers to women when it came to compositional employment. The list of her works that survive includes: two oratorios, four masses, six motets, psalm cantatas, secular cantatas, three keyboard sonatas, one keyboard concerto and one symphony.

She and her sister, Antonia, held regular weekly *salons* (soirees devoted to music and art) in their home. Meanwhile, Marianna wrote music for associates, the court and religious events. She also established a singing school for young women successfully training them as excellent musicians.

DID YOU KNOW?

1. Of over 150 compositions, only sixty-five of hers survive today.
2. Though she was highly accomplished and sought after, Marianna never sought an appointed position—it was unacceptable for a woman of her class at the time.

Nana Buluku

Nana Buluku (or Nana Buku) is the female Supreme Being in the West African traditional religion of the *Fon* people (Dahomey) and the *Ewe* people (Togo) and grandmother of all Goddesses. She is believed to be the most honored deity and the origin of any form of worship and religion in West Africa. It is said that Nana Buluku created the universe and gave birth to the moon and the sun. Her areas of influence involve women and children's issues, life and death, healing, rape, ecology and swamps.

Nana Buluku named the moon *Divine Spirit Mawu*, and the sun *Divine Spirit Lisa*. In many folk songs and tales, Nana retired after Her hard work and left the world in the hands of Her twin children. To this day, many traditional societies fear and respect twins, especially those that appear as girl and boy.

Millions of West Africans were captured, enslaved and shipped across the Atlantic during the colonial era. They were forced to work on sugarcane, cotton and tobacco plantations. These people brought their religious ideas with them, including their belief in Nana Buluku. She is usually pictured as an old woman, older than creation itself. Nana is found in French, Dutch and British West Indies, as well as among the African communities of French Guiana, Suriname, Guyana, Brazil, Trinidad, Martinique, Haiti and other Caribbean islands.

Nana Buluku embodies the archetype of the *wise woman*. She likes being alone or with Her grandchildren. Because of Her strong connection with nature, environmental issues are very important to Her. She hates the way we are destroying our planet. Nana absolutely will not tolerate spousal or child abuse.

DID YOU KNOW?

1. Nana's colors are black, white, purple, green and red.
2. Her symbols are the Moon, Baobab tree, leaves and angelfish.

MARIE POPELIN

"To create, not a free woman…but a liberated woman, honorably liberated, by work, by talent and by science."

Marie Popelin (1846-1913) was a Belgian lawyer, educator and pioneering feminist icon. She was the first woman ever admitted to study law in Belgium, graduating from the Free University of Brussels (1888) summa cum laude. Outraged at being rejected from the bar, Marie dedicated herself to equal rights between men and women, founding the *Ligue du Droit des Femmes* (League for Women's Rights). Marie Popelin became known as the "founding mother" of Belgian feminism.

Well educated for her time, Marie and her sister Louise taught at an institution run by the leading feminist teacher *Isabelle Gatti de Gamond* from 1864-1875. At age thirty-seven, Marie decided to change careers and began studying law. In Belgium, the law did not technically forbid women from practicing as a lawyer, but in practice, life was quite different. After her application to the bar was rejected, the judge argued that "the nature and social role of women made it impossible for Marie to practice her profession".

She appealed to a higher court with the same discouraging results. The legal case became known as "the Popelin Case." It had an enormous impact on the feminist movement in Belgium. (Women were not admitted to the legal profession—able to practice law—until 1922.)Dedicating herself to equal rights between men and women, Marie was fully supported by other noted feminists. Founding the *Ligue Du du Droit des Femmes* was just the first step. She began traveling around the world to form partnerships with other feminist organizations. These travels culminated in the *Conseil National des Femmes Belges* (National Council of Belgian Women) which brought together all the feminist movements in Belgium.

DID YOU KNOW?

1. One of their accomplishments gave women the ability to have savings accounts separate from that of their husbands (1900).
2. Marie was the first woman in Belgium to receive a doctorate in law.

"...When shall they (parents from my country) come out of the wrong and false notions of supposed superiority of boys over girls, of men over women?"

An educator and women's rights activist, Pandita Ramabai Sarasvati (1858-1922) was a social reformer, writer, mother and pioneer for the education and emancipation of women in India. A scholar and feminist, she broke nearly every rule and tradition that confined an upper-caste Hindu woman's life in nineteenth century India. Despite her increasing deafness, Pandita lectured in England, Japan and Australia, and taught Sanskrit as well as her mother tongue, *Marathi*. Her critique of Hindu patriarchy led her to be marginalized in India and ultimately omitted from mainstream history books.

Born *Rama Dongre*, a high-caste Brahmin whose father was a Sanskrit scholar, she was taught Sanskrit at home. Orphaned at sixteen by the Great Famine (1876-1878), Pandita traveled across India reciting Sanskrit scripture with her brother. By twenty, she was given the title Pandita (Scholar) and Sarasvati (Goddess of learning), acknowledging her advanced learning. Though very unusual for a woman to have learned Sanskrit—an ancient Hindu liturgical language reserved for Brahmin men—respect was given her by adding *Bai* to her first name.

Finding herself a widow after two years of marriage, Pandita traveled to England in 1883 in to pursue a medical degree. Sadly, her increasing deafness made that impossible, so she enrolled in a teaching program. She began to lecture as she studied social reform and education. Pandita published her first book in English, *The High-Caste Hindu Woman* (1887), which was a merciless indictment of the way Hindu women were treated—very persuasive since it was written by an insider.

Two years later, Pandita opened an institute for the education of young Hindu widows. *Sharna Sadan* (Abode of Wisdom) opened in Bombay with American support. It sheltered widowed girls, giving them a place to be educated and learn skills. Another orphanage, the *Mukti* (1898) drew great criticism from the Hindu patriarchy. (Of course it did.)

Did you know?

1. When Pandita traveled to America in 1886, her subsequent writings reveal her interest in economics.
2. She also wrote of Native American and African American impoverishment as well as gender inequality. Pandita definitely did not mince words, seeing and saying clearly while others stuck their heads in the sand.

Mary Eliza Mahoney (1845-1926) became the first African American professionally trained and licensed nurse in the United States in 1879. One of the co-founders of the National Association of Colored Graduate Nurses (NACGN), Mary was also one of the first African American members of the American Nurses Association.

After working at the New England Hospital for Women and Children as a teen, she continued there for fifteen years in a variety of roles including a nurse's aide. In 1878, at the age of thirty-three, Mary was admitted to their professional graduate school of nursing. After sixteen months, Mary completed the program. Forty-two women had begun the nursing program, only four were able to finish it. Upon graduation, Mary pursued her career as a private nurse to focus on the care and needs of individual clients, stepping away from overwhelming discrimination in the public nursing sector.

Her patients were mostly from wealthy white families that lived up and down the east coast. Mary was well known for her patience, efficiency and caring bedside manner. In time, she felt a group was needed which advocated for African American nurses. She co-founded the National Association of Colored Graduate Nurses (NACGN) in 1908. The association awarded her a lifetime membership in 1911 and elected her its national chaplain.

After decades as a private nurse, Mary became the director of Howard Orphanage Asylum, A respite for Black children in Kings Park, Long Island She served as director from 1911-1912 and finally retiring from nursing after forty years. However, she continued to champion women's rights, becoming one of the first women to register to vote in Boston after the ratification of the nineteenth Amendment.

DID YOU KNOW?

1. The Mary Mahoney Award is bestowed twice annually by the American Nurses Association.
2. The Mary Mahoney Memorial Health Center is located in Oklahoma City.

Lucy Maud Montgomery OBE

"I'm so glad I live in a world where there are Octobers."

A Canadian author, Lucy Maud Montgomery OBE (1874-1942) was best known for her series of novels beginning in 1908 with *Anne of Green Gables.* The book was an immediate success and made Lucy Montgomery famous, giving her an international following. She went on to publish twenty novels, 530 short stories, and thirty essays. Mother of three, Lucy was made an "Officer of the Order of the British Empire" in 1935, and was the first Canadian woman to be made a member of the British Royal Society of Arts.

Lucy began writing as a child when she found companionship through her imagination, nature and books. She had a brief teaching career (1898) before returning to Cavendish to care for her grandmother. During her years in Cavendish, Lucy wrote and submitted poems, stories and serials to Canadian, British and American magazines. She eventually made a comfortable income from her writing.

In 1905, she wrote her first and most famous novel, *Anne of Green Gables.* Unable to find a publisher, Lucy put the manuscript in a hatbox. Two years later, she submitted it again and it was accepted by Page Publishing of Boston. After her marriage to Rev. Macdonald, she not only assisted him in his pastoral duties but also ran their home while continuing to write best-selling novels, short stories and poems.

In her journals, she expressed her deep pain at the death of her infant son, the horrors of WWI and other overwhelming losses. Despite her problems, she continued to write, expressing her love of nature and beauty in her fiction, journals and letters. She was arguably Canada's most widely read author.

Did you know?

1. *Anne of Green Gables* has remained in print for more than a century. Incredible!
2. It was translated into at least thirty-six languages as well as braille.

"I shall call upon my fellow women. We will fight the whyte men. We will fight till the last of us falls in the battlefields."

An influential Queen Mother of the *Ashanti* empire (part of present-day Ghana), Yaa Asantewaa (1840-1921) was a successful farmer, mother, intellectual, politician, human rights activist and leader. She became renowned for leading the Ashanti revolution against British colonialism to defend the Golden Stool (a sacred symbol of the Ashanti kingdom, cultural system and power). Asantewaa means "Leader of warriors, brave and bold." She promoted emancipation as well as gender equality. Today, Asantewaa is honored in Africa as one of the greatest African women ever for her ability to empower her people.

As the Queen Mother, Asantewaa took on many responsibilities, especially being the Gatekeeper of the Golden Stool. Since she is the main advisor to the king, the Queen Mother must guard the Golden Stool and keep it safe. In 1896, the Ashanti began to rebel against British presence in their lands. The British promptly exiled Prempeh I, King of the Ashanti, along with his grandson, a powerful leader. They were shipped to the Seychelles.

To further establish authority, British Governor-General of Ghana (the Gold Coast) Frederick Hodgson demanded he be given the Golden Stool. This prompted a conference of Ashanti elders, who debated their next move. Highly disgusted at the behavior of her male counterparts, Yaa Asantewaa said if the men would not fight, she would gather the women to fight for the land. Her zeal and initiative led to her role as Commander in Chief of the army. How gutsy was that?

The final war began in March (1900) with Asantewaa leading the rebellion. Unfortunately, she was captured and sent to the Seychelles, where she died on the 17th of October, 1921. Yaa Asantewaa's War, known as the War of The Golden Stool, was the last major war led by an African woman.

DID YOU KNOW?

1. To this day, Africa has not been able to regain its stolen treasure from the British.
2. Wilhelmina J. Donkoh wrote, *"Nana Yaa Asantewaa was the most prominent of ....Africa's greatest leaders."*

"Never think of revising as fixing something that is wrong...think of it as an opportunity to improve something you already love."

A dynamic champion of modern music, Marion Eugenie Bauer (1882-1955) was an American composer, teacher, writer and music critic. She played an important role in forming the character of American music in the first half of the twentieth century. Similar to other female composers, Marion focused on composing song and piano solos before moving on to larger compositions. In total, she penned five music books as well as 160 compositions. But it was her impact on budding American composers that may have overshadowed her compositional works.

Born to a musically gifted father and highly educated mother, Marion began taking piano lessons from her older sister, Emilie. The family were French-Jewish immigrants who valued education and the arts. After completing high school, Marion moved to New York City to begin focusing on composition. Because she was fluent in both English and French, she was invited by pianist *Raoul Pugno* to study in Paris. She became the first American to study with Nadia Boulanger.

The years between 1906 and 1914 were filled with composing, studying and teaching piano. Although Marion never earned a college degree, despite her many years of study, she was hired as an instructor at New York University's music department. She earned the distinction of associate professor (1930) while also lecturing at Julliard and Columbia University. She even lectured at the Chautauqua Summer Music Institute annually while still composing. Marion taught many of the up-and-coming composers of the time, including Amy Beach and Ruth Crawford Seeger.

Aside from editing the Chicago-based *Musical Leader,* Marion also helped found the American Music Guild, the American Music Center and the American Composer's Alliance. Very often, she was the only woman in a leadership position for these organizations. Though she enjoyed many performances of her music, Marion endured age-old petty criticism. Dividing music into "masculine" and "feminine" categories continued to overshadow the value of her compositions and books.

DID YOU KNOW?

1. Though Marion retired from her position at NYU in 1951, she continued to lecture at Julliard.
2. Her compositions were conservative in nature and generally melodically driven.

A Goddess from ancient Sumeria, Nisaba holds power over writing, learning and all harvests. A scribe for all Sumerian gods, She originally was the Goddess of grain. Powerful and respected, Nisaba was a writer, transcriber, archivist and architect. She gave the gifts of reading and writing to her people and is available to help us with those as well. Sometimes written as "Nidaba" She is often depicted in written works as "a woman holding a gold stylus studying a clay tablet."

We can thank the Sumerians for inventing writing. Between 3500-3000 BCE, they began writing symbols on clay tablets in order to record figures while buying and selling grain. Writing developed from basic accounting to documenting laws, contracts, literature and history. Nisaba's worship grew to include communication, creativity, Universal Law, inspiration and dreams. Many Sumerian clay tablets end with the phrase "Nisaba be praised."

As written communication spread throughout Mesopotamia, so did Nisaba's power and prestige. She became known as the "scribe of the gods and keeper of both divine and mortal accounts." Some early seals from that era associate Nisaba with the construction of monuments, temples and other buildings.

Nisaba's symbols are pens, pencils, computers and books. Her animal symbol is the snake. As the Goddess who brought literacy and astrology to a Sumerian king, Nisaba is revered as "She who teaches the decrees." As an architect, She drew temple plans for her people, sometimes delivering them through dreams. An oracle and dream interpreter, Nisaba is the most learned of all deities.

DID YOU KNOW?

1. Another depiction of Her shows a woman with long-flowing hair crowned with a tiara that supports ears of corn and a crescent moon.
2. Her rule over grain and harvests reminds us of her role as an Earth Goddess Mother.

"It is better to wear out than to rust out."

An American Canadian abolitionist, Mary Ann Shadd Cary (1823-1893) wore many hats. A journalist, editor, publisher, educator, mother, women's rights activist and lawyer, Mary Ann was recognized as the first Black woman publisher in North America and the first woman publisher in Canada. While living in the U.S., her family was involved in the Underground Railroad. She opened a school for Black children in 1940. Fearless and outspoken, she played an important role in giving Black people a voice and advocating for women's rights.

When the Fugitive Slave Law of 1850 was enacted in the United States, it threatened to return free northern Blacks and escaped salves into bondage. Mary Ann and her brother moved to Windsor, Canada, across the border from Detroit, where she could create free Black settlements.

In 1853, she founded an anti-slavery paper, *The Provincial Freeman,* which was "devoted to antislavery, temperance, and general literature." Published weekly in Toronto, it ran for four years before financial challenges caused it to fold.

Because she was female, Mary Ann enlisted the help of male abolitionists to smooth her publishing efforts. Their names were placed on the masthead, but she was involved with every aspect of the paper. She traveled widely in Canada and the U.S. to increase subscriptions and publicly solicit funds for runaway slaves—doing so at great risk to her own safety because of the Fugitive Slave Law. In 1854, Shadd changed the masthead to feature her name, rather than McArthur and Ward. Her progressive thinking and unorthodox attitude alienated some people.

After the Civil War, Mary Ann moved to Washington D.C. where she started a school for children of freed slaves. She believed that education offered Blacks more opportunity. In 1879, Shadd graduated from Howard University with a law degree and thrusted herself into the women's suffrage movement.

DID YOU KNOW?

1. Mary Ann had to sue Howard University for entrance (females weren't allowed).
2. After winning that suit, she graduated from Howard with a law degree at age sixty. (!)
3. Mary Ann practiced law for the last ten years of her life.

A Puerto Rican educator, Dr. Pilar Barbosa de Rosario (1898-1997) was an historian, author, mentor and political activist. Charismatic, influential, and intelligent, Dr. Barbosa was revered on Puerto Rico. As a political activist, she insisted the New Progressive Party embrace social justice. Pilar was primarily a teacher, the first woman to join the faculty of the University of Puerto Rico. She was responsible for establishing the departments of history and social studies. Pilar also became a noted authority on the island's history—in 1933 she was named the nation's official historian. She was widely regarded as "the conscience of the ruling New Progressive party."

Pilar's father was the founder of the Puerto Rican statehood movement—which was a precursor of the New Progressive Party. His ideals were embraced by his daughter and became a tribute to his legacy. After Pilar received her doctorate in history from Clark University in Worcester, Massachusetts, she returned to the island and was offered a professorship of history at the College of Liberal Arts of the University of Puerto Rico, becoming the first woman to teach there.

In 1920, Pilar established the Department of History and Social Sciences and was its director until 1943. Active in her father's causes, she served as a political advisor and mentor to many politicians who shared the same views. When she died at ninety-nine, Pilar Barbosa was known as "the mother confessor to generations of Puerto Rican politicians, scholars and intellectuals."

DID YOU KNOW?

1. Pilar's father, Jose, a Black man, enraged at being denied higher education by the Spanish, graduated with honors from the University of Michigan Medical School (1882). He had to ask the American counsel to intervene so he could practice medicine in Puerto Rico. (No wonder he was pissed.)

2. Pilar served as Puerto Rico's historian until her death at age 98.

3. Charismatic, intelligent and influential, Puerto Rico honored her with a three-day mourning period.

"Unless I am allowed to tell the story of my life in my own way, I cannot tell it at all."

Mary Jane Grant Seacole (1805-1881) was a Jamaican-born British healer, adventurer, nurse, businesswoman and author of the first autobiography of a Black woman in Britain. As she tended to the injured and dying during the Crimean war, Mary was dubbed "The Creole with the Tea Mug." Largely forgotten from history—except in Jamaica where her recognition began in the 1950s—England honored Mary Seacole's contributions and achievements a century after her death. There are some who still try to discredit Mary's pioneering contributions to nursing.

Born to a Jamaican woman and a Scottish soldier, Mary learned her nursing skills from her "Doctress" mother, Mrs. Grant. A Caribbean Doctress used not only folk medicine but herbal remedies as well as traditional techniques to treat ailments and injuries. A Doctress was a combination of nurse, herbalist, midwife and masseuse that practiced good hygiene one hundred years before Florence Nightingale. (!)

Mary and her mother ran Blundell Hall which served as a convalescent home for military men recovering from illnesses like typhoid fever and cholera. In 1851, Mary traveled to Panama treating cholera victims, never charging the poor for her services. While there, she contracted the disease requiring a rest of several weeks.

With a strong desire to help the sick and wounded in Europe, Mary went to London. Rejected for a nursing post by authorities, she promptly traveled to Turkey to set up a "British Hotel" within a mile of British headquarters (during the Crimean War). The first floor of the hotel contained a restaurant and a store offering food, medicine and alcohol. The second floor served as a hospital and treatment center. "Mother Seacole" (as she was known by the troops) would head to the front lines afterhours to treat wounded and dying soldiers.

DID YOU KNOW?

1. A statue of her was unveiled at the entrance to St. Thomas Hospital in London (2016).
2. In 2004, Mary Seacole was voted the greatest Black Briton.
3. Her autobiography, *Wonderful Adventures of Mrs. Seacole in Many Lands* was published in 1857.

Marjorie Stoneman Douglas

"The Everglades is a test. If we pass it, we may get to keep the planet."

An American journalist, author, women's suffrage advocate and conservationist, Marjorie Stoneman-Douglas (1890-1998) was known for her staunch defense of the Florida Everglades. Also known as "The Lady of the Everglades," she was a pioneer advocate of that unique eco-system, involved in race relations, women's rights and urban development.

Marjorie enrolled at Wellesley College in Wellesley, Massachusetts majoring in English and contributed to and edited the college literary magazine. She graduated in 1912 with a BA in English and began working for the *Miami Herald* as a society editor. Later on, she had her own column, *The Gallery*, in which she included her own poetry.

During WWI, Marjorie became the first Floridian woman to enlist in the Navy. Discharged after a year, she joined the American Red Cross and went to Paris. Afterward, she returned home to Florida to edit her father's paper. Many of her articles focused on the problem of Florida's rapid commercial development. In 1920, Marjorie left the paper to write. She began publishing many books and short stories focusing on women, environmental issues and the history and life of Southern Florida.

Most importantly, Marjorie dedicated her life to preserving and restoring the Everglades. It took her five years to research and write *The Everglades: River of Grass*, published in 1947, the same year Everglades National Park was dedicated. It sold out of its first printing in thirty days. The book galvanized people to protect the region. Early on, Marjorie recognized that the Everglades is an ecosystem which depends not only on the flow of water from Lake Okeechobee into the park, but also on the Kissimmee River. "Friends of the Everglades" was started by Marjorie in 1969 to create awareness of the potential destruction of the Park by over-development.

Did you know?

1. At the age of 103, Marjorie was awarded the Presidential Medal of Freedom by President Clinton.
2. When she died at 108, John Rothchild said, "Her death was the only thing that could shut her up," and then added, "The silence is terrible."

One of the most influential figures in Hawaiian history, Emma Kalanikaymaka'ama-no Kaleleonalani Na'ea Rooke (1836-1885) was known and loved throughout the islands for her humanitarian efforts. Married to King Kamehameha IV until his death in 1856, she was involved in the expansion of the library (now part of the Library of Hawaii), helped establish a public hospital (Queen's Hospital) and formed an organization to promote hospital services.

Adopted at birth by her aunt and uncle, she grew to be an educated and dignified woman. Her adoptive father, Thomas Rooke, was an English physician who owned one of the finest collections of books on the island. It is no surprise that as queen, Emma was dedicated to education and health care.

Sailing to England to solicit funds for an Anglican cathedral and girl's school in Hawaii, Emma met with Queen Victoria and managed to raise $16,000 for both projects. She founded St. Andrew's Priory, an all-girls school K-12 with a college prep program. The Queen's Hospital (now known as The Queen's Medical Center) was founded in 1859 by Emma and the king. It was established in response to the diseases that were decimating the Hawaiian population.

When the king died only two years after their only son's death, Emma wanted to take his place leading the Islands. Unfortunately, her husband had not made the necessary arrangements for her to do so before his death. In 1874, an election was held and Emma lost. Her supporters rioted and attacked the courthouse. She acknowledged her defeat publicly, calming her followers—which is what a good leader would do, right?

DID YOU KNOW?

1. Queen Emma was renowned for her horsemanship.
2. She and Queen Victoria became life-long friends, both had lost sons and husbands.
3. Queen Emma was awarded the Dame Grand Cross of the Most Noble Order of Kamehameha I for promoting and defending the sovereignty of the Hawaiian Kingdom.

An American, Mary Stevenson Cassatt (1844-1926) was one of the leading artists in the Impressionist movement of the latter part of the 1800s. She was both a painter and a prolific printmaker. Exhibiting with the Impressionists in Paris, Mary specialized in portraiture and is best known for her expressive paintings of women and children. A feminist and suffragist, Mary spent her life working to change traditional attitudes about art, artists and a woman's professional role in society.

Mary, at the age of sixteen, enrolled in Philadelphia's Pennsylvania Academy of the Fine Arts in 1860. Not surprisingly, she discovered the male faculty and fellow students patronizing and resentful of her attendance. Mary also became frustrated by the curriculum's slow pace and inadequate course offerings. Leaving her frustrations behind, she decided to move to Europe where she could study the works of the old masters firsthand.

When the Paris Salon accepted her paintings for exhibitions in 1872, 1873 and 1874, shesecured her status as an established artist. Continuing to study and paint in Spain, Belgium and Rome, Mary eventually settled in Paris permanently. Invited in 1877 by her friend and mentor, Edgar Degas, Mary was one of three women—and the only American—to join a new group of artists, the Impressionists. She exhibited eleven of her paintings with them in 1879. The show was a smashing success commercially and critically, similar exhibits were staged in 1880 and 1881.

Mary's portraits were unconventional in their direct and honest nature. She was influenced by Japanese prints to develop a drawing style that blended European and Asian effects. Mary used her success to help others, mentoring young artists. She also helped American art collectors choose fine Impressionist works. Sadly, in 1915, Cassatt was forced to give up painting altogether as diabetes slowly stole her vision.

DID YOU KNOW?

1. Mary had numerous operations for cataract removal but was virtually blind the last ten years of her life.
2. Her favorite medium was oil on canvas, though she did use other mediums at times.

Mother Goddess of Chinese mythology, Nuwa (also Nugua) is best known for creating human beings out of yellow clay. Some scholars suggest She was the first creative Chinese deity, ancient China was a fiercely matriarchal society—childbirth seen as a miraculous occurrence not requiring male participation. In ancient artwork, Nuwa is shown with a snake body and a human head. She is also the traditional Divine Goddess of the *Miao* (Vietnamese, Thai, and Burmese people living in southern China). Her name is sometimes written as Nu Gua or Nu Kua and she is respectfully referred to as WaHuang (literally Empress Huang).

Nuwa is told of in many ancient Chinese myths performing various roles as wife, sister, man, tribal leader (even a great emperor at times) and creator. Most often, She is represented in a creative role, reproducing people after great calamities. Earliest literature talks of Nuwa repairing the heavens after a great flood. Early scholars also suggest She created the first Chinese deity. She is sometimes pictured as a gorgeous woman when not shown as a serpent with a human head.

The creation story implies that on each day of the week, Nuwa created a different animal. The seventh day She formed humans out of clay, flicking them throughout the world. (Sound familiar?) Known as Empress *Wa*, She is still a popular deity today and women usually pray to Her asking for divine assistance with marital affairs or fertility issues. Nuwa is regarded as something of an historical figure, with many temples dedicated to Her throughout the Chinese-speaking world.

Her most important temple is found in Hebei Province and is regarded as the ancestral shrine of all human beings. There are minorities in Southwestern China that celebrate Her as their Goddess. Their "Water-Splashing Festival" is one of the festivals that give tribute to Her sacrifices.

DID YOU KNOW?

1. Nuwa's courage and wisdom are favorite themes of Chinese poetry and paintings.
2. Her statue, "Sky Patching", was exhibited in New York City's Times Square on Earth Day 2012, symbolizing the urgency to protect Earth's ozone layer.
3. That statue now stands in Vienna's International Center.

MARY BOWSER

Mary Jane Richards Denman, aka Mary Bowser (c. 1839 -?) was an educated African American espionage agent, activist and teacher of *freedmen*. She had returned to her American home after being shipped off to Liberia by people believing Blacks would be happier with their own nation in Africa. Mary was inducted into the Military Intelligence Hall of Fame in Huachuca, Arizona in 1995 for her Civil War contributions.

Born into slavery on the Van Lew plantation in Richmond, Mary's intelligence was noted. Even after Mary was freed, Elizabeth Van Lew sent her to Philadelphia to a Quaker school to be educated. In 1861, Mary returned to Richmond to assist with Elizabeth's "war efforts" for the Union. Her espionage work began when Van Lew set up a network of twelve people to help the Union's cause. They would bring food and comfort to the Libby Prison where Union soldiers were held. What the prison officials didn't realize is that Mary and Elizabeth were also passing messages to and from Union soldiers imprisoned there.

Mary was skilled as an actress. She became an eccentric but highly capable servant, reassuming the position of a slave to help the Jefferson Davis family. Introduced into the Jefferson household by one of Van Lew's friends, Mary gained Varina Davis' confidence and was hired at the Confederate White House for domestic duties because of her capabilities.

Growing up in Richmond, it was easy for Mary to behave unobtrusively. She listened in on conversations to gain information without being noticed and because she was educated, Mary took advantage of reading military reports left lying around. She easily relayed information to Van Lew via bakery wagon deliveries or messages in baskets of food. After the war, Mary opened a school for freed men in St. Mary's, Georgia. She also lectured against racism and advocated for African American rights.

DID YOU KNOW?

1. Mary used the name Mary J. Richards to found the Georgia school.
2. She also signed her name Mary J. R. Gavin at times, leading to much confusion for historians. (Then again, historians are often confused about women...)

An American educator, Sarah Jane Woodson Early (1825-1907) was also an author, abolitionist and temperance activist. She was one of the first African American women on a college faculty—Wilberforce University—1858. Sarah was also the first Black American to teach at an historically Black college or university. She became the national superintendent of the Colored Division of the Women's Temperance Union, giving over one hundred lectures throughout a five-state region.

Her parents emphasized education for all their children. By the age of three, Sarah was memorizing songs and lengthy passages. After graduation from Oberlin College where she majored in the classics, Sarah was hired at Wilberforce University. She taught English and Latin. She also served as "Lady Principal and Matron." She taught in Black community schools in Ohio for several years and was the first principal at a public school in Xenia, Ohio. Sarah urged African American youth to follow careers in education and the sciences in order to enhance their race.

After the Civil War, Sarah taught in a new school for Black girls established by the Freedmen's Bureau in North Carolina. Though millions of Black Southerners began moving north after the war ended to escape violence, Sarah was determined to educate the children of the *freedmen*. Sarah continued to teach school for nearly four decades; she believed education was critical for the advancement of African Americans. In 1893, Sarah was named "Representative Woman of the Year" at the Chicago World's Fair (World's Columbian Exposition).

She broke barriers for women academics in a time when there wasn't much expected from women, much less a Black woman. Sarah was a woman who did not stop with her own education, but continued to educate others.

DID YOU KNOW?

1. Sarah wrote a biography of her husband centering on his rise out of slavery and is classified "a slave narrative."
2. By the time she retired, she had taught more than six thousand students. What influence she had on young lives.

A Scottish mathematician, Mary Fairfax Somerville (1780-1872) was an astronomer, geographer, science writer and mother of six. A member of the Royal Astronomical Society, she and Caroline Herschel were its first female members simultaneously (1833). Mary's influential writings integrated many different scientific disciplines. She was an enormous advocate of women's rights, both in women's suffrage and equality in education. Oxford University's Sommerville College—its first college for women—is named in her honor.

Throughout her life, Mary challenged assumptions of what women could achieve, especially in the sciences. Despite having little formal education, she combined a deep curiosity and keen observations of nature with an elementary education as a starting point to her career in the sciences. She taught herself higher mathematics and astronomy while maintaining a household.

She was the first woman to publish experimental results in the Philosophical Transactions of the Royal Society, and the only woman to have a sculptured bust placed in their great hall. In her book *Mechanism of the Heavens* (1831), she demonstrated her ability to communicate the intricacies of science and complex mathematics to large audiences. Taking on a number of different roles in her book, Mary became a guide, teacher, science historian and revisionist who added mathematical explanations as well as diagrams to make the workings of the solar system more comprehensible to English readers.

With its publication, Mary Sommerville became famous overnight. (Applause please.) Her third book, *Physical Geography* (1848) was the first English textbook on that subject. She wrote a total of four books.

DID YOU KNOW?

1. Mary Sommerville's signature was the first on John Mill's petition to Parliament seeking women's right to vote in 1868.
2. Her face appears on the Royal Bank of Scotland's ten-pound note.

"I do not wish them [women] to have power over men; but over themselves."

An English writer and feminist, Mary Wollstonecraft (1759-1797) was also a philosopher and advocate of educational and social equality *for* women. She authored a trailblazing feminist work that argued the educational system deliberately trained women to be frivolous and incapable. Mary, a mother of two girls, argued that women are not naturally inferior to men but are simply not educated in the same manner. She is recognized today as the "Mother of Feminism." Her ideas have changed the world.

After educating herself, Mary decided to support her family by writing. She also worked as a governess and taught school, experiences that inspired her views in *Thoughts on the Education of Daughters* (1787). The following year, she began working as a translator for a London publisher, Joseph Johnson. Her work, *A Vindication of the Rights of Woman* was published in 1792 and focused on a woman's place in society, calling for women and men to be educated equally.

Mary was an ethics and political philosopher whose examination of the condition of women in modern society retains much of its original radicalism. One of the reasons her pronouncements on the subject remain challenging is that her reflections on the status of the female sex were part of an attempt to understand human relationships within a culture increasingly governed by greed and consumption, which is (sadly) still true two hundred years later.

Her first published work was *Thoughts on the Education of Daughters*. Mary went on to write about politics, history and various aspects of philosophy in a number of different genres that included critical reviews, translations, pamphlets and novels. She also presented abortion and infanticide as negative consequences of moral double standards and women's submission to sexual objectification and exploitation by men. She was, indeed, ahead of her time. (Or are we just slow to grasp these concepts?)

DID YOU KNOW?

1. Mary died at age thirty-eight from septicemia just days after giving birth to her daughter, Mary (Shelley).
2. Mary Shelley, of course, was an accomplished writer and the author of *Frankenstein.*

Also known as Pimiko or Pimiku, Queen Himiko (c. 183- 248 CE) was a third century ruler of an ancient Japanese territory known as Hsieh-ma-t'ai or Yamatai (now Yamato). She was recognized by the Chinese as ruler of all Japan because of her state's power. Himiko is curiously absent from Japanese historical records but does appear in Korean and Chinese historical accounts. (Hmmm, I wonder why.) She was noted for being a *shamaness*, unmarried, and lived in a fortress served by a thousand women. Queen Himiko is representative of matriarchal prestige and independence in Japan two thousand years ago. Once again, patriarchal religions arrived to the detriment of the female gender.

Her role as shamaness or high priestess was not uncommon in East Asian cultures. Japanese history books do not call her by her name, simply "the Queen." Scholars do not agree on the location of Queen Himiko's state, but the majority consider the Nara region (thirty km. south of current day Kyoto) most likely. At the time of her reign, there were over one hundred kingdoms throughout the islands.

Himiko's state was the most powerful on the islands. Considered by the Chinese as ruler of all Japan (Wa), she exchanged diplomatic envoys with the ruling Wei dynasty. Exchanging gifts with the Chinese, they gave Himiko the honor of the title "Queen of Wa." Gifts were given to her in return for her tribute of fine cloth and slaves to them. Those beads, mirrors, and swords became part of the Japanese imperial regalia. In total, there were three diplomatic missions sent to China from Japan between 243 and 247 CE.

According to Chinese historians, the queen had been chosen by her people following nearly eight decades of uprising and war. She enjoyed a peaceful reign, living like a recluse in a towered fortress where she shared affairs of state with her younger brother.

DID YOU KNOW?

1. The most important Shinto sanctuary (the Grand Shrine of Ise) originated with Himiko.
2. Her rule was not totally erased, as scholars continued searching for her lost kingdom after WWI—digging for ancient texts and archeological sites raising her popularity to great heights.
3. Evidence reveals women's prestige and power in Japan two thousand years before Chinese, Buddhist and Confucian ideologies were imported.

"Art is communication spoken by man for humanity in a language raised above the everyday happening."

> A pioneer of European Expressionist dance, Karoline Sofie Marie Wigmann (1886-1973) was a German dancer and choreographer. She also pioneered dance therapy and movement training without pointe shoes. Her pupils numbered in the thousands. Mary was also a major influence on American modern dance. Her technique often consisted of "sliding, bouncing, vibrating, falling and dropping."

Rebelling against convention, Mary chose art for a career. Over her parents' objections, she enrolled in *Jacques-Dalcorze's* school *in Dresden-Hellerau* in 1911. When she found the school's rhythmical gymnastics too rigid, she enrolled in a summer course given by Rudolf von Laban's *School of Art* in Switzerland. Laban's school served as an arena for innovative, exciting artistic activity that created a radical and *avant-garde* community. Artistic and sexual freedom is what the school aspired to achieve. Mary, feeling free and at home, began formulating her own theories of movement.

Although she made her debut as a dancer in 1914, her triumphant career as dancer-innovator-choreographer began after WWI. Her impact on dance throughout Europe changed the course of dance history. In 1920, Mary opened a school in Dresden, which soon became a focal point of German modern dance. Her dance troupe first appeared in public around 1923; she toured Europe extensively, sometimes as a solo performer and sometimes with the troupe.

Offshoots of the Dresden school were set up all over Germany, Mary was officially honored by the government. But the Nazi authorities considered her to be a leftist and her dances too decadent. They decommissioned her school but allowed her to continue to teach in Leipzig during WWII. After the war, Mary continued to create and teach in Leipzig under Soviet occupation.

DID YOU KNOW?

1. Mary did not use typical ballet costumes and often incorporated masks into her dances.
2. Her dances were accompanied by *world music* incorporating fifes, gongs and drums from India and Thailand.

A benevolent deity, Oshun (or Osun) is commonly called the River Orisha (Goddess). She is a West African (*Yoruba*) Goddess typically associated with water, purity, fertility, love and sensuality. Considered one of the most powerful of all Goddesses, possessing human attributes such as vanity, jealousy and spite, She can heal and create life but also take it away. Oshun represents everything that is lush, fertile and juicy in our world and is connected to destiny and divination. Associated with white, yellow, gold, and sometimes coral, She is revered by many for Her abilities to heal the sick, foster prosperity and bring fertility. (Sounds like a wonderful Goddess to have on your side.)

The patron saint of the Osun River in Nigeria, Her devotees leave Her offerings and perform ceremonies at bodies of fresh water. Her ceremonies are held by rivers, streams and canals.

In Brazil, Oshun (Osun) has been adopted and worshiped in all Afro-Brazilian religions. She is the Goddess of freshwater rivers and waterfalls, wealth and prosperity, of love and beauty. Followers seek Her out for help with romantic relationships. She is known as the "Lady of Gold" in financial dealings, refering to copper—it was the most valuable metal in Brazil. The plants in Brazil associated with Her are aromatic, sweet, often yellow. They include mint and pennywort, as well as Kalanchoe pinnata.

Oshun, in Her form as the "Mother of Salt Waters" is known as *Yemaya*. Like the Egyptian Isis and later the Greek Diana, Oshun is the Goddess of love and is widely beloved. A protector of the poor, mother of all orphans, She is the one who brings them what they need in this life throughout periods of weakness.

DID YOU KNOW?

1. The peacock and vulture are both sacred to Oshun.
2. She is honored at the Oshun-Osogbo Festival, a two-week long festival on the river's bank at Oshun-Osogbo Sacred Grove, Nigeria.

Born a slave in Bermuda, Mary Prince (1788-1833) was the first Black woman to present an anti-slavery petition to Parliament. A storyteller, abolitionist and rebel, Mary was also the first African American to narrate and publish her autobiography.

During her lifetime, five different people claimed her as property. At the age of twelve, Mary was put to work in a different household from where her mother worked. Because of her rebellious nature, she was sent to Grand Turk Island. Eventually, Mary was sold to John Adams Wood, Jr. She worked for him for thirteen years, learning how to read and write. In 1826, Mary married a free Black man, Daniel James, which angered the Woods. They took her to London where she walked out the door a free woman—Britain did not support slavey except in British colonies. Good for her!

Mary was introduced to abolitionists who tried to help her find work as well as help her gain freedom from the Woods. She wanted to return to her husband in Antigua but could not if she were still owned by the Woods. In 1829, Mary began working for the Thomas Pringle household. He was especially interested in helping her write and publish her life story.

After *The History of Mary Prince, a West Indian Slave* was published (1831), there was an immediate reaction. The book exposed the full horrors of slavery in the British colonies.Two court cases ensued, with Mary as a witness in both. Her book influenced Parliament as well as the public and The Slavery Abolition Act of 1833 was finally passed. The 1833 act freed all Black slaves in the British Colonial Empire except those held by the East India Company, Sri Lanka and St. Helena. Mary Prince spent the rest of her life as a freed Black woman.

DID YOU KNOW?

1. Though she was illiterate, Mary Prince changed the world! That is so cool.
2. Very little is known of her life after the 1833 act freeing Blacks in the British Colonial Empire.

"The year 1876 has gone, but the famine has not – it stays in most horrendous forms here. The people are dying. The animals are dying…"

> Savitribai Phule (1831-1897) was an Indian educator, philanthropist, prolific writer, social reformer, feminist and poet. She is regarded as the first female teacher of India in 1847. Savitribai and her husband, Jyotirao Phule, opened a school for girls in 1848. She went on to establish a shelter for destitute women in 1864. Her life is heralded as a *beacon of light* for women's rights in India, she is often called the "mother of Indian feminism."

An illiterate child bride at age nine, her educated husband (age thirteen) taught her at home. They belonged to the Mali caste—a vocational Hindu caste found among those who traditionally worked as gardeners and florists. When Savitribai completed her teaching education, she taught local girls. She and her husband established India's first school for girls, many were lower caste. Only nine girls enrolled. Savitribai became headmistress and taught alongside trainee Fatima Sheikh and her husband's emancipated aunt.

Many people were shocked and outraged at the audacity of the couple to educate women. Unwilling to stop teaching, Savitribai endured innumerable abuses (tomatoes, cow dung, eggs and stones were thrown at her) and obscenities were shouted daily from orthodox men on her way to teach. (Can you imagine enduring that daily?)

Her husband gave her two sarees each course; one to wear on the way to work, which would be soiled by garbage thrown at her, and a fresh saree to change into before she started teaching. Returning home, Savitribai would change out of the filth covered saree.

Finally, the abuse ended after Savitribai slapped one of the ruffians in the face. Empowered, she established herself and started more schools, eventually being honored by the British government for her exemplary work. Between 1848 and 1852, Savitribai and her husband established eighteen women's schools. Savitribai Phule went on to question and eradicate many of India's social evils toward women.

Did you know?

1. The couple established fifty-two boarding schools for orphaned children and fed thousands daily. Amazing!
2. A prolific author and poet, she worked to abolish the discrimination and injustice in India based on caste and gender.

"Let the generations know that women in uniform also guaranteed their freedom."

A famed physician and women's rights activist, Mary Walker (1832-1919) was also a teacher, abolitionist and Civil War veteran. Perhaps she is most famous for becoming the first woman to receive the Congressional Medal of Honor in 1865—rescinded in 1917 but restored in 1977 by President Jimmy Carter. And justifiably so! A feminist seeking to change the restrictive styles of women's fashions of her day, she refused to wear traditional women's clothing. Mary was the second woman ever to graduate from Syracuse Medical College.

Mary's parents taught her to be a "free thinker." Pursuing a career in a traditionally male field, she enrolled in Syracuse Medical College, graduating with a Doctor of Medicine degree in 1855, the only woman in her class. Relocating to Columbus, Ohio, she opened a private practice. Returning to her home state not long after, she married fellow physician Albert Miller, retaining her last name and refusing to include *obey* in her wedding vows. Together they set up a joint medical practice.

Soon after the Civil War began in 1861, Mary began volunteering after she was rejected from becoming an Army surgeon (serving as assistant surgeon without pay). Mary (Dr. Walker) faced considerable verbal abuse over her tenacious demands to be appointed Army surgeon. Nonetheless, she earned a great deal of respect for her work. In September 1863, Mary became the first female U.S. Army surgeon following her commission by the Army in Ohio as a "Contract Acting Assistant Surgeon (civilian)."

While serving with the 52nd Ohio Infantry as assistant surgeon, Mary routinely crossed the lines to treat civilians. On one such journey in 1864, she was arrested by Confederate soldiers for spying. She spent four months in various prisons, subject to much abuse for her unladylike occupation and attire. Mary was released that August, after being imprisoned for several months.

DID YOU KNOW?

1. Mary was one of the first women to hem her skirt just below the knee and add a pair of trousers (called bloomers) to replace petticoats. What an uproar that caused!
2. Mary is the *only* woman in history to be awarded the Congressional Medal of Honor. Would you believe Congress tried to rescind her award? How pathetic!

"We have to break the mirror to be ourselves..."

A Belgian-American poet, novelist and memoirist, May Sarton (1912-1995) was a prolific author who resisted the label "lesbian writer." May Sarton (her pen name) wrote a total of fifty-three books. Her style was easily understood and called refined, calm and cultured by critics. May's books examine the themes of love, feminism, sexuality, friendship, relationships, the search for self-knowledge and inner peace.

Eleanore Marie Sarton fled Belgium in 1914 with her family, moving to Boston one year later. After a short stint in theatre, Sarton began to teach writing in 1936. Seven years later, she began writing full-time. Her writing earned more accolades from the public than her critics—saying May's writing was dull and her language common. She thought her poetry was more significant than her prose.

Traveling back to Europe, May met many extraordinary authors. By 1947, she had written five books. In the fifties she published her third and fourth novels, as well as a volume of poetry in 1953. Her novels told of concerns she had in real life. The following year, her first memoir came out. This genre brought May a tremendous audience of readers and correspondents.

In 1965, *Mrs. Stevens Hears the Mermaids Singing* was published. Considered May's "coming out", it was embraced by both feminist scholars and lesbians. This proved to be a turning point for Sarton, as her work began to be studied in colleges and universities, and written about in feminist journals and books. *Journal of a Solitude (1973)* has become a key text in women's studies courses, influencing generations of feminists. The book has never gone out of print since its publication. I so enjoyed reading it.

Did you know?

1. May wrote a total of fifty-three books; nineteen novels, seventeen books of poetry, two children's books and fifteen non-fiction.
2. She is a personal favorite of mine, a couple of her books rest on my shelves.

The first sovereign queen and last monarch of Hawaii, Lydia *Liliuokalani Paki* (1838-1917) was a talented songwriter and musician. She composed over 150 songs, including the Hawaiian national anthem "Aloha 'Oe." Queen Lili'uokalani gained the throne upon her brother's death. Her reign was short-lived, a group of American plantation and business owners—backed by the U.S. government—staged a coup in 1893. She dedicated much of her reign to restoring native Hawaiian rights and traditions, continuing that fight after the coup. Liliuokalani also helped raise funds for the Queen's Hospital, established a bank for women and set up a fund for the education of native Hawaiian girls. The Queen Lili'uokalani Trust to support Hawaiian orphans was also established by her.

During her brother's reign, European and American landowners began to plot against the Hawaiian monarchy. When he died and Lili'uokalani became queen, she was determined to restore the weakened Hawaiian monarchy. Indigenous Hawaiians supported her overwhelmingly. U.S. politicians felt goods would be imported more easily if an American government was installed in Hawaii. (More easily or more cheaply?)

In 1893, a group of foreign landowners conspired with the United States Marines to stage a coup against the Hawaiian monarchy. *The Hawaiian League* (a committee of thirteen led by Lorrin A. Thurston (a businessman in favor of annexation) removed all the queen's powers and installed a government made up of white Americans.

Lili'uokalani continued to advocate for the Indigenous Hawaiian government, arguing that she was the legitimate leader of Hawaii. A group of her supporters led an armed revolt (1895) to restore the monarchy. Though not involved with the plan, the colonial government blamed her for the uprising and she was tried on charges of treason. Convicted and imprisoned, she surrendered her claim to the throne in exchange for a pardon. The U.S. annexed Hawaii in 1898, becoming a state in 1959. Once again, I am very disappointed in the U.S. government's actions.

DID YOU KNOW?

1. Lili'uokalani and her husband adopted several children.
2. When she ascended the throne, Queen Lili' attempted to restore the monarchy and give voting rights to disenfranchised people through *constitutional* changes.

A renowned Canadian folk artist, Maud Kathleen Lewis (1903-1970) was best known for her colorful paintings of Digby, Nova Scotia's life and landscape. Born with birth defects and suffering from severe juvenile arthritis, she lived most her life in poverty. Her folk-art painting gained national recognition in 1964 and 1965. Those of us who live with Rheumatoid Disease can gain inspiration from this little woman's perseverance.

Nova Scotia born, Maud suffered numerous birth defects leaving her fingers painfully deformed, her shoulders hunched, her chin pressed into her chest and a painful gait. Rheumatoid Arthritis made it difficult for her to work, even as a young woman. Her mother gave her art lessons as a child, teaching her to hand paint Christmas cards with watercolors. They sold the cards to neighbors.

Her physical deformities brought her much grief and teasing from classmates. Dropping out of school at fourteen, she became a recluse. Marrying Everett Lewis, a fish peddler, in 1938 did not bring better circumstances. Living in a tiny cottage, Maud proceeded to paint every available surface; her stove, washbasin, walls, and window-panes were covered with brightly colored flowers, birds and butterflies. Using leftover house and boat paints that her husband scrounged for her, she created happy pieces of artwork that were sold to passers-by for never more than $10 during her lifetime.

Maud lived in relative obscurity until 1965, when a CBC documentary in which she was the subject, was broadcast. The publicity brought a flood of requests for her work, even a request from the Nixon White House. She was unable to fill some of the requests because of the increased crippling of her hands. Recently, the price of her paintings has gone up from $5 she collected from tourists; in 2017, one piece sold for $45,000 at auction!

Did you know?

1. Maud never blended or mixed colors.
2. Most of Maud's paintings are small due to the ever-advancing Rheumatoid Disease that limited her arm movement. What a trooper she was.

A Hindu Goddess married to Shiva, Parvati (meaning mountain) is a benevolent Goddess. She is seen as the civilizing, domesticating force who complements Him. Parvati is a maternal figure, raising Divine children, Ganesha and Kumara, with Her husband. She is considered a representation of Shakti (the female energy personified) and is linked to other forms of the Goddess. Some believe Her to be the ultimate manifestation of the Divine Herself. She is usually depicted as a beautiful dark-skinned woman seated on a large cat symbolizing Her ability to harness and control the wild aspect of nature.

Parvati symbolizes many honorable virtues, including domesticity, asceticism, fertility and devotion. She is one of the most important Hindu Goddesses honored as the "Mother Goddess," a universal source of energy and power. The lion acts as Her *vehana* (vehicle). When pictured with weapons, She is out to destroy ignorance, evil and ego. Regularly pictured alongside Her husband, they are considered intimately linked (the Lord who is half woman). This type of depiction confirms the fact that female and male are inseparable in the process of creating the universe and life.

Parvati is known by many other names, each representing attributes and aspects of Her. She is found extensively in ancient Indian literature, statues and iconography adorning Hindu temples in South Asia and Southeast Asia.

She is the focal point of the *Teej* festival held during the Hindu month of *Shravan* to welcome monsoon season. For the festival, women are dressed in colorful robes as unmarried women seek out suitable husbands. The festival is most famous among the *Rajasthan*. Other festivals where Parvati is celebrated and worshipped are the *Gauri*, *Navrati*, *Gauri Tritiya* and *Thiruvathira* festivals.

DID YOU KNOW?

1. It is believed Parvati lives on Mount Kailash in Tibet.
2. Recent scholars have Her related to the Goddesses Aphrodite, Isis, Mary and Artemis.

"... But I beg you to believe me; I have never done an act of espionage against France. Never. Never."

> A Dutch exotic dancer, Margaretha Geertuida Zelle MacLeod (1867-1917) was a courtesan, wife and mother. A victim of domestic abuse and historical circumstances, she was charged with treason while acting as a German spy and executed before a firing squad in Paris, October of 1917. She is now recognized as a scapegoat; France was trying to distract prying eyes from heavy casualties on the frontlines and fearing what she could reveal about dalliances French officers had with her. (Another cover-up. And they shot her!)

Margaretha reincarnated herself in Paris as Mata Hari after her husband abandoned and divorced her. A high-class exotic dancer, she dressed in ornately jeweled tunics and signature midriff-baring bustiers. She had many wealthy socially prominent lovers.

At the start of WWI, Mata Hari joined the German Secret Service after being recruited by one of her lovers, Berlin's Chief of Police. She continued to dance on stages in London, Paris, Antwerp and Brussels while the war raged. At the same time, she was secretly transmitting intelligence reports to Germany through various diplomats.

French authorizes learned of her activities, but having no evidence to convict her of espionage, they wanted her deported. But Mata Hari convinced them she was not a German agent, that she actually wanted to spy for the Allies. The French sent her on a secret mission to occupied Brussels while she continued taking orders from Germany. She eventually made her way to Spain where she met with German attaches, agreeing to transmit a series of cables back to Berlin. Using a code the French had already cracked, her actions suggest a deliberate attempt to remove herself from German service, which they promptly did.

Returning to France, she was arrested with Germany's final payment in hand. Her trial lasted only two days, focusing on her character, not her actions. It has since been found that she did not divulge any information of consequence to the Germans. (Figures.)

DID YOU KNOW?

1. Mata Hari's execution was reminiscent of Joan D' Arc in that she was exonerated *after* being put to death.
2. Today's historians believe her to be a *victim* of men instead of a *victimizer*.

"The greatest evil in our country today is not racism, but ignorance". Septima Clark (1965)

A pioneer of grassroots citizenship education, Septima Poinsette Clark (1898-1987) was called the "Mother of the Movement." As an African American educator, author and civil rights activist, Septima initiated literacy and citizenship workshops that played an important role in the drive to enhance voting rights and the civil rights of African Americans during the Civil Rights Movement. She was the personification of a "community teacher, intuitive fighter for human rights and leader of her unlettered and disillusioned people."

Septima was the daughter of a former slave. After graduating from secondary school in Charleston, she passed her teacher's exam and began her career. Charleston did not allow African Americans to teach in public schools in 1916, so the school where she began teaching was located on Johns Island. Septima taught throughout South Carolina for thirty years.

She branched out into social activism with the NAACP (1919) while teaching, joining their initiative to get Charleston to hire Black teachers. The effort succeeded, Clark began teaching at the Avery Institute (1919). In 1945, Septima worked with Thurgood Marshall and the NAACP on a case that sought equal pay for Black and white teachers. Her salary was tripled after the case was won.

Septima was particularly upset by the South's voting system. Blacks had the right to vote but were kept from voting by literacy tests. Many adult African Americans couldn't read—it was illegal for their enslaved parents and grandparents to be taught to read and write. Under her leadership as director of education and teaching, the Southern Christian Leadership Conference set up more than eight hundred citizenship schools. How cool was that?

DID YOU KNOW?

1. Septima received South Carolina's highest civilian honor, the "Order of the Palmetto."
2. President Carter honored Septima with a Living Legacy Award in 1979.

"Everything that I achieved in my life, I must thank Mileva. She is my genius inspirer, my protector against the hardships of life and science. Without her, my work would never have been started nor finished." Albert Einstein, 1905.

A Serbian physicist, Mileva Maric Einstein (1875-1948) was a mathematician, mother and first wife of Albert Einstein (from 1903 to 1919). There is much evidence she contributed significantly to his groundbreaking science. Given the prevalent bias against women at the time, her co-signature carried little weight.

Both Mileva and Albert were admitted to *Polytechnic Institute* in *Zurich* (1896). Inseparable after meeting, they had comparable grades except in applied physics where Mileva got the top grade of 5. She excelled at experimental work. On the oral exam, Professor Minkowski gave nearly perfect scores to the four male students but not to Mileva—only Albert got his degree.

Without a job, he refused to marry her. When Mileva became pregnant, Albert's mind remained unchanged. With an uncertain future, Mileva took the oral exam again in July 1901. Once more she was given failing marks. Forced to walk away from her studies, she returned to Serbia giving birth to a girl, *Liserl,* in January 1902.

Early in December 1901, Albert Einstein secured a post at the Patent Office in Bern. Mileva and he were married in 1903 after his father's death. The two scientists were publishing papers together with *both* signatures even before their marriage. The decision to publish *under Albert's name only* seems to have been taken jointly, despite working side-by-side. The Tesla Society (among others) has been gathering evidence proving the newest findings gathered on the *Theory of Relativity,* specifically Mileva Einstein's contribution, was significant. Evidence from a 1901 letter confirms this. Let's applaud the efforts being made to give Maria credit for her scientific contributions.

DID YOU KNOW?

1. Maria gave birth to two more children while they worked together.
2. After their divorce in 1919, Albert was awarded the Nobel Prize in Physics. Per the divorce agreement, the winnings were awarded to Maria as continuing child support.

"The rights of the individual should be the primary object of all governments."

A political playwright and satirist, Mercy Otis Warren (1728-1814) was an American poet and historian during the age of the American Revolution—a time when women were encouraged and expected to keep quiet on political matters. (Ugh, and it's still happening 250 years later.)

Through her writings, she gave voice to patriot complaints, detailed British atrocities and fiercely advocated for independence. A mother of five children and passionate feminist, Mercy became one of the most influential advocates of her time.

Mercy wed the politically active James Warren in 1754. After his election to the Massachusetts Legislature in 1766, they began hosting prominent citizens in their Plymouth, Massachusetts home, particularly those opposed to British policies.

Combining her unique vantage point and fervent beliefs with a talent for writing, Mercy began expressing her opinions. Writing poems, prose and plays, her early offerings were a trio of scathingly hostile plays in verse published serially in a Boston newspaper. *The Adulator* (1772) foretold of the Revolution; *The Defeat* followed a year later; in 1775 she published *The Group*, a satire. Published anonymously, the prose dramas, *The Blockheads* (1776) and *The Motley Assembly* (1779), no less acerbic, are also attributed to her. (Perhaps Dorothy Parker was a distant relative? They both had a gift for satire and sarcasm.)

Mercy published *Observations on the New Constitution* in 1788 detailing her opposition to the constitution's wording due to its emphasis on a strong central government. She maintained social and political correspondences with her friends John and Abigail Adams, writing of her belief that regulating women to minor concerns reflected not their inferior intellect but *subservient opportunities* offered to women to develop their talents.

DID YOU KNOW?

1. In 1805, Mercy finished a three-volume history, *A History of the Rise, Progress, and Termination of the American Revolution*.
2. She was considered the leading female intellectual of the Revolutionary era.

Queen Nanny of the Maroons

An eighteenth-century Maroon leader, Queen Nanny (c.1686-c.1755) successfully freed more than a thousand slaves during a period of thirty years. Helping them to resettle in the Maroon communities of Jamaica, she symbolized hope, strength and unity in times of crisis. Queen Nanny, born to the *Ashanti* tribe of Ghana, West Africa, is recognized as a female leader and warrior who promoted guerrilla warfare tactics against her British foes. (Way to go, sistah!)

Maroons were slaves in the Americas who had escaped and formed independent settlements. Nanny Town was one such settlement on the windward (eastern) side of Jamaica in the Blue Mountains. Queen Nanny was a Maroon woman who (along with one of her brothers) founded the village and named it. She held the position of the windward Maroons spiritual, cultural and military leader.

Of the utmost importance to the Maroons, spiritual life was incorporated into every facet of life, from raising children to forming military strategies. Spiritual practices such as Obeah (and voodoo in Haiti) evolved from Africa. As western culture was imposed on the colonial-ruled Caribbean, these African practices became outlawed and took on negative connotations which is pretty sad.

Nanny Town, because of its location tucked away in the mountains, thrived on agriculture, trading peacefully with her neighbors. The British colonials became embarrassed and threatened by the success of the Maroons and sent out hunting parties to scour Jamaican jungles. Nanny Town was overtaken and destroyed by the British in 1734. The war against the Maroons lasted from 1720-1739, at which time a truce was declared.

DID YOU KNOW?

1. After her death, many of the Maroons moved across the island to the leeward (western) side of Jamaica, it was less populated.
2. A modern portrait of her is on the Jamaican $500 banknote.
3. In 1974, Jamaica declared Nanny their only female national hero. Yay!
4. Many in Nanny's community attribute her leadership skills to Obeah (African mystical religion) powers.

NADIA BOULANGER

"The essential conditions of everything you do must be choice, love, passion."

French composer Juliette Nadia Boulanger (1887-1979) was a conductor, organist, educator, riter and scholar. She was the first woman to conduct major orchestras in Europe and the US. Nadia was a major influence on modern classical music, teaching Aaron Copland, Marion Bauer and Quincy Jones among others. Shaping the sound of the modern world, one composer called Nadia "the most influential teacher since Socrates." Nadia was considered a "one-woman graduate school." How's that for an accolade?

Growing up surrounded by music, Nadia began studying composition at the *Paris Conservatoire.* She wrote orchestral works as well as several chamber and choral pieces. When her younger sister, Lili, died at the age of twenty-four, Nadia stopped composing. She felt her works were now useless. From then on, Nadia did everything in her power to promote performances of Lili's works. She embarked on an extraordinary teaching career that would span her lifetime. Nadia began dedicating herself to developing a generation of talent, becoming one of the greatest music instructors of the twentieth century. Studying under her became almost "a rite of passage for American composers."

Whether it was conducting or performing, Nadia taught at the *Paris Conservatoire, Ecole Normale de Musique* and the American Conservatory at the *Chateau Fontainebleau.* She became a lifelong friend of Igor Stravinsky, conducting his premiers. She was the first woman ever to conduct the Royal Philharmonic Orchestra in London, the New York Philharmonic, the Washington National Symphony and others.

The broad range of her students musical styles and expressions indicate her open reception to an individual's creative expression. "Preconceiving the kinds of works her pupils were to write was never the Boulanger method" –Virgil Thomson

.

DID YOU KNOW?

1. Aaron Copland said, "Nadia Boulanger knew everything there was to know about music; she knew the oldest and the latest, pre-Bach and post Stravinsky, and knew it cold. All technical know-how was at her fingertips."
2. Nadia worked almost to the day of her death at age ninety-two.

Pele (or Pelehonuamea) is the ancient Hawaiian Goddess of volcanoes and fire and creator of the Hawaiian Islands. She is often called "Madame Pele" or "Tutu Pele." It is foretold Pele was forced to flee Tahiti in a great canoe. On different islands, She dug out fire pits, forging Hawaii's magnificent volcanic craters. Pele is a Triple Goddess of life and death, controlling the lava that gives Hawaii its rich fertile soil but also destroys everything in its path. She resides in one of the most active volcanoes in the world located at the summit of Kilauea, within Halema'uma'u crater at Hawaii Volcanoes National Park on the Big Island. Pele is best known for Her passion, volatility and capriciousness, and is the most visible of all the old Gods and Goddesses.

In folklore, Pele travels throughout the islands appearing to mankind as a young beautiful woman (or sometimes an old woman) often accompanied by a white dog. If you refuse Her requests, you will suffer Her wrath. Lava is a sacred piece of the Fire Goddess, tourists must never take a lava rock from the islands. Bad luck comes to anyone who dares remove a piece of her home.

Legend claims Pele fought with Her elder sister *Namakaokaha'i*, the Water Goddess. Pele, the Fire Goddess, initially landed on Kaua'i. Each time She thrust Her digging stick into the earth to dig a pit for Her home, Namakaokaha'i flooded the pits. Pele moved down the chain of islands in geological formation, eventually landing on the Big Island. She continues to make Her majesty known from the mountains to the seas. Hawaii's sometimes stark landscape is a reminder of Her powers to create and destroy.

DID YOU KNOW?

1. Ancient Hawaiians personified all natural forces as Gods and Goddesses.
2. Pele's name means "She who shapes the sacred land".

MumBett (1742-1829) was the first enslaved African American in Massachusetts to successfully sue her master for her freedom. Her courageous act encouraged the state to abolish slavery in 1788. After she won her lawsuit in 1771, MumBett adopted the name Elizabeth Freeman.

MumBett and her sister "Lizzie" were given by their owner Pieter Hogeboom into the possession of John Ashley of Massachusetts. MumBett served the family for nearly forty years. It is reported that Mrs. Ashley was cruel to her slaves. One day she attempted to strike Lizzie with a heated kitchen shovel. MumBett protected her sister by blocking Mrs. Ashley's strike but received a serious wound on her arm that never healed, leaving a permanent scar.

MumBett was clever and strategic. Though she never learned to read or write, she heard discussions of the Bill of Rights and the Massachusetts State Constitution in her master's house. She thought the language about *all people being created free and equal* might somehow apply to her. MumBett found a young lawyer who agreed to take her case. Theodore Sedgwick lived in a nearby Stockbridge and was known to support the anti-slavery cause.

A jury decided in MumBett's favor in 1771. After losing the case, her former master filed an appeal to the Supreme Judicial Court of Massachusetts but dropped the case a few months later. After winning her freedom, MumBett adopted the name Elizabeth Freeman. She was employed in the Sedgwick household, declining several offers by John Ashley to return to his home as a paid employee. She remained a beloved paid servant of the Sedgwick family for the rest of her life

Did you know?

1. In twenty years, MumBett saved enough money to purchase a plot of land. She lived there with her daughter, grandchildren, and great-grandchildren.
2. MumBett was also a midwife, herbalist and nurse.

"I tore myself away from the safe comfort of certainties through my love for truth - and truth rewarded me."

A French writer, Simone Lucie Ernestine Marie Bertrand de Beauvoir (1908-1986) was afeminist, political activist, social theorist and intellectual existentialist philosopher. A feminist icon, she wrote what is considered the "feminist's bible"—*The Second Sex*. Simonewas a remarkable philosopher of existentialism and a pioneering figure of philosophical feminism. She was known as an engaged intellectual who combined philosophical and literary productivity with real-world political action, leading to legislative changes.

A belatedly acknowledged philosopher, Simone de Beauvoir called herself the "midwife of Sartre's existential ethics" instead of a thinker in her own right. Her enduring contributions to the fields of ethics, politics, feminist theory, phenomenology (science of phenomena) and existentialism plus her activism and public intellectualism is now an established part of history.

Her book, *The Second Sex,* published in 1949, was controversial from the beginning. It was a critique of patriarchy that still confronts social, political and religious thought to justify women's inferior status. The book inspired a second wave of feminism that led to no-fault divorce, academic gender studies, greater access to education and contraception. It granted women other rights that helped them to overcome the "prey of the sexes" taking control of their own destinies. Her book also led to making sexual discrimination at work and marital rape illegal. The woman started a revolution!

An author of novels, essays, biographies and an autobiography, Simone's most enduring contribution to literature are her memoirs. She also gave us many monographs on philosophy, politics and social issues, publishing her first novel *She Came to Stay* in 1943.

DID YOU KNOW?

1. A previously unpublished Simone de Beauvoir novel will be released and translated in 2021—deemed too intimate to be published during her lifetime.

2. Her philosophy is *"To be free is not to have the power to do anything you like; it is to be able to surpass the given towards an open future; the existence of others as a freedom defines my situation and is even the condition of my own freedom."* Think about that for a few minutes. We owe much to Simone.

"The more clearly we can focus our attention on the wonders and realities of the universe about us, the less taste we shall have for destruction."

> World-renowned marine biologist and writer, Rachel Louise Carson (1907-1964) is recognized as one of the most important conservationists in history. She is also known as "the Mother of Modern Environmentalism." She challenged the use of manmade pesticides angering chemical companies, but her efforts led to the ban on DDT and other pesticides.

Rachel began writing stories (often involving animals) at the age of eight, she had her first story published when she was only ten. At Pennsylvania College for Women (known today as Chatham University), she graduated magna cum laude in 1929. She intended to pursue her doctorate in 1932 but was forced to take a full-time teaching position to help support her family during the Depression. After her father's unexpected death in 1935, she accepted a part-time position with the U.S. Bureau of Fisheries, submitting articles on marine life in the Chesapeake Bay to local newspapers and magazines. The following year, Rachel became the second woman hired by the Bureau of Fisheries for a full-time professional position as a junior aquatic biologist.

Her second book, *The Sea Around Us*, gave the world a new perspective on environmentalism coining the term *ecology*. But it was her last book, *Silent Spring*, published in 1962, that created a storm awakening society's responsibility to other forms of life. She minutely detailed a true hazard to our ecosystem, dangerous pesticides.

Silent Spring, the first book of its kind, drew fierce opposition from chemical companies. The subsequent firestorm resulted in Congress investigating its pesticide policy. Attacked by government officials and the chemical industry as an alarmist, she courageously spoke out. Called before a congressional committee in 1963, her expert testimony (along with others) culminated in the ban of DDT for crop use in 1972. DDT has been linked to breast cancer, liver cancer, lymphoma, leukemia and pancreatic cancer.

DID YOU KNOW?

1. DDT is still used in some areas of the world to kill malaria-carrying mosquitoes.
2. Because of the U.S. ban of DDT, bald eagles and peregrine falcons have survived extinction.
3. Rachel's influence led to a grassroots movement culminating with the Environmental Protection Agency (EPA) in 1970.
4. *Silent Spring* topped the NYT's Bestseller List for thirty-one weeks.

"Gods always behave like the people who make them."

An American author, Nora Zeale Hurston (1891-1960) was an anthropologist and film maker. Associated with the Harlem Renaissance, she was considered a pre-eminent writer of twentieth century African American literature. Her fiery intellect, infectious sense of humor and folksy writing style led her to become world-renowned as she told of life in the South. During her lifetime, Nora worked as a maid, childcare provider, substitute teacher and librarian as well as researcher, writer and filmmaker.

Graduating from Barnard College with a degree in anthropology, Nora began publishing short stories in 1920. Unfortunately, her work was often ignored by mainstream literary audiences though she did gain the attention of African Americans. Publishing three books between 1934 and 1939, the most popular was *Their Eyes were Watching God.* Nora shattered literary norms by writing about the experiences of a Black woman. These books established her as a major author.

Dedicating her life to educating others about the arts, Nora established a school of dramatic arts at Bethune-Cookman College in 1934. Five years later, she worked as a drama teacher at the North Carolina College for Negroes in Durham. Nora was also on the staff of the Library of Congress. Although she eventually received praise for her works, she was often underpaid, always in debt and poverty-stricken. As a result, Nora eventually entered the St. Lucie County Welfare Home when she could no longer care for herself.

DID YOU KNOW?

1. At the time of her death in 1960, Nora Hurston had published more books than any other Black writer in American history.
2. There has been a resurgence of interest in her publications since the late twentieth century.
3. Her work, almost forgotten, was revived by feminists and Black study scholars.

Ndate Yalla Mbodji (1810-1869) became the last great queen of the *Waalo* Kingdom in 1846 after the death of her elder sister. Waalo, one of the oldest and strongest kingdoms of Senegal since the eleventh century practiced the matrilineal system—giving the same privileges and rights to women as men. An educator and mother, Queen Ndate was a heroine of resistance against invading Moors and conquering French—who were stunned by her beauty and power.

Queen Ndate's ascension may have been easy but her rule quickly became a tireless effort to preserve what was left of Waalo after Arabs, French and Moors tried to take away their lands and colonize the kingdom. The Moors began encroaching in the mid 1850s, deeply angering the queen. At the same time, the French were taking control of their trade systems causing sub-chiefs and locals to lose power.

In 1855, Queen Ndate fought the French and the Moors, leading her troops successfully. Her army, made up of both men and women, was small but ferocious. After losing initial battles, they were able to surprise and defeat the French. This actually began the Senegal War of Resistance, which continued into the twentieth century.

The queen and her troops were able to fight off Moors and Arabs, leading to the creation of Senegambia. Captured by the French, she was exiled to northern Senegal where she remained until her death. By the time she was exiled, the Waalo was in ruins. Her son took over as leader until he was captured and exiled as well.

DID YOU KNOW?

1. Queen Ndate Yalla Mbodji continues to inspire as she remains a symbol of resistance in Senegal.
2. A golden statue of her can be found in Dagana, in northern Senegal, a tribute to her bravery and resistance.

"I love color. It must submit to me. And I love art. I kneel before it, and it must become mine."

A German painter, Paula Modersohn-Becker (1876-1907) helped introduce the styles of late 19th-century Post-Impressionists to German art. She was one of the most important representatives of early expressionism. Paula is recognized as the first female artist to paint a nude self-portrait. A mother, her brief life and career were cut short when she died from a postpartum embolism at thirty-one.

As a pupil of Fritz Mackenson in 1898, Paula joined the *Worpswede* , a group of regional artists who lived at an artist colony near Bremen, Germany. In 1901 she married Otto Modersohn. Spending two periods of study in Paris in 1903 and 1905, Paula discovered she was increasingly dissatisfied with the aims of the Worpswede artists. She pushed her depictions of women and her self-portraits in new directions in these years; by 1906 she had begun painting life-sized nudes. She tried to recreate how women were represented in Western art history.

Paula Modersohn-Becker's style continued to evolve, she combined a lyrical naturalism with broad areas of simplified color reminiscent of *Gauguin, Cézanne* and *Van Gogh* as her technique matured. More interested in expressing her inner feelings than in an accurate visual portrayal of reality, she is most often associated with the Expressionist style.

During the fifteen years she pursued art, Paula completed more than seven hundred paintings and one thousand drawings and prints. ((Amazing.) Despite selling only a few paintings during her lifetime, Paula's distinct style, daring subject matter and perseverance to overcome considerable barriers to women artists made her a leading painter for her generation. Undeterred by the meager recognition she received, she felt she had made a major leap forward with her large-scale nudes and self-portraits.

DID YOU KNOW?

1. When Paula painted, she used a limited palette of tempura and oils.
2. Her embolism was most likely caused by DVT (deep vein thrombosis), a pregnancy complication from lengthy bed confinement—customary of that era.

A favorite Goddess of Buddhists and Taoists, Quan Yin's (also spelled Kuan Yin) graceful statue is often seen in Chinese temples. Her name means "One Who Sees and Hears the Cry of the Human World." Sometimes seen as having eleven heads, She is a Goddess of fertility, compassion and mercy. Worshipped especially by women, Quan Yin comforts the sick, the lost, the troubled and the unfortunate. With Her growing popularity through the centuries, She is considered a protectress of farmers, voyagers, merchants and tourists. Her temple on the island of Putuoshan is a foremost pilgrimage place for Chinese Buddhists.

Quan Yin is usually depicted in a graceful stance, barefoot, wearing all white garments and holding a small vase or willow branch. She conveys a majestic selflessness and compassion making Her the best-loved of all Chinese deities. Having the greatest variety of presentations, Quan Yin is sometimes sitting on an elephant, upright on a fish, nursing a child or having anywhere from four to forty hands—with which She strives to ease suffering.

Occasionally, Quan Yin is shown riding a Buddhist lion. Courageous and strong, She can even tame fierce dragons. Regardless of the pose, She is always barefoot. Quan Yin is blessed with three birthdays, always the nineteenth day of the second, sixth and ninth months. A model of Chinese loveliness, one legend tells of Her self-sacrifice and dignity choosing to remain on Earth to assist mankind.

Many of Her statues can be found carved in jade. Representing the Maternal Goddess, the beholder of all sounds, the bestower of children, Quan Yin can be found on most home altars in Asia.

DID YOU KNOW?

1. In east Asia Quan Yin is associated with vegetarianism.
2. Quan Yin is the Chinese translation for the *bodhisattva* Avalokitesvara, known as Goddess of Mercy by Jesuit missionaries.
3. Each country has their own location for her home—Mount Potalaka in India, Mount Putuoshan—China, Naksansa in Korea and so on.

"Love all, trust few, and do right."

Known as one of the last survivors of the 1921 "Tulsa Race Massacre", Olivia Juliette Hooker (1915-2018) was an American educator, mentor, activist and pioneering psychologist. The first African American woman to enlist and serve in the US Coast Guard, Olivia did so after the Navy refused to allow an African American to enlist. She spent her life trying to gain restitution for people whose loved ones were killed in the massacre (approx. three hundred) and for nearly one thousand people who lost their homes and livelihoods during that twenty-four-hour raid. President Obama called her "A tireless voice for justice and equality." A traumatized six-year-old girl grew to be an advocate for civil rights as well as for people with intellectual and developmental disabilities. Amazing!

The Tulsa Race Massacre of 1921 was one of the United States most violent and deadly race riots. Spurred by *rumors* of a white woman being assaulted by a Black man, members of the KKK and white supremacist groups brought guns, axes, torches, and oil to the area destroying homes and businesses, leaving nearly ten thousand people homeless in what was then called Tulsa's "Black Wall Street."

After the riots, Olivia's family ended up in Columbus, Ohio where she earned her B.A. degree from Ohio State University (1937) and began teaching. Enlisting in the US Coast Guard in 1945, she earned the rank of Yeoman, Second Class during WWII. After the war, Oliva earned her master's degree from Columbia University. Working with women in the Albion County Correctional Facility, she found those deemed to have severe learning disabilities were treated unfairly.

"Approach them with an open mind", Olivia's motto continues today as the correctional facility helps women earn degrees and get job experience upon release. Earning her PhD. in clinical psychology in 1961, Olivia helped found the American Psychological Association (APA).

DID YOU KNOW?

1. Olivia joined the Coast Guard Auxiliary at age ninety-five.
2. In 2019, the US Coast guard commissioned their new fast-response cutter the USCGC Olivia Hooker.
3. She lived to be 103 years old.

Born Margaret Elizabeth Noble (1867-1911), Sister Nivedita was an Irish teacher, author, social activist, school founder, social worker and disciple of Swami Vivekananda. She opened a girls' school in 1898 in the Bagbazar area of Calcutta (Kolkata). Sister Nivedita was one of the most influential female figures in Indian history, working tirelessly for education reform.

Educated at Halifax College in York, Margaret began her teaching career in 1884 when she was just seventeen. Upon her return to England, she became a favorite writer and speaker of the "New Education" (preschool education) practices being advocated at that time. In 1895, she met Vivekananda in London and was captivated by his message of religious universalism and philanthropy. She helped him organize the Vedanta movement there and persuaded him to let her come to India.

After her initiation as a female disciple and changing her name, Sister Nivedita opened a girls' school and assisted in relief work organized by the Ramakrishna movement during the bubonic plague epidemic in 1899. A dedicated caregiver, she was driven by the desire to help and serve the poor. At that same time, she began to lecture on Hindu culture. Nivedita lectured on the plague, stressing the need for cleanliness and taking precautions to prevent spreading the disease.

In 1902, after Vivekananda's death, Nivedita turned her efforts to help promote the Indian independence movement. She also re-launched her school, which was expanded to include classes for married women. Nivedita promoted traditional Indian art and architecture while collaborating with Ernest Havell who had developed a style of art and art education based on Indian rather than western models. She also worked with Ananda Coomarasamy who was introducing ancient Indian art to the west. Nivedita also collected Indian myths and stories.

DID YOU KNOW?

1. Sister Nivedita was one of the first to propose a design for a national flag which was presented at the Indian National Congress in 1906.
2. In her search for truth, Nivedita left Christianity behind and began to follow the teachings of Gautama Buddha.

"I early conceived a liking for, and sought every opportunity to relieve the sufferings of others."

The first African American woman to become a physician, Rebecca Davis Lee Crumpler (1831-1895) was also a nurse, writer and mother. Her race and gender against her, Rebecca was one of the first female physicians to publish a book, *A Book of Medical Discourses*. The Rebecca Lee Society—one of the first medical groups for African American women—was named in her honor. Buried in an unmarked grave for one hundred-twenty years, donations enabled a granite gravestone to finally be erected in 2020.

Born in Delaware, she was raised by her aunt in Pennsylvania. Inspired by her aunt's selfless medical care of the locals, Rebecca traveled to Massachusetts to work as a nurse before applying to the New England Female Medical College in 1860. This occurred during a time when men thought women had brains 10 % smaller than themselves and lacked the physical fortitude to practice medicine. The school was often derided for attempting to teach topics inappropriate for "female sensitivities." Hopefully, we've come a long way from that kind of thinking!

Graduating in 1864, Rebecca became the only African American to receive a degree from the institution. The same year, the pioneering doctor opened a medical practice in Boston. After the Civil War ended, Rebecca collaborated with the "Freedmen's Bureau" to care for African Americans in Richmond, Virginia. While there, she was exposed to fierce racism from other doctors and administrative workers. Ignored by male physicians, Rebecca even had difficulty getting prescriptions filled! Despite the harassment, *she persisted.*

Upon returning to Boston in the late 1860s, Rebecca treated patients around her Beacon Hill home on Joy Street. Her pioneering accomplishments and courageous efforts forged a path for women bearing witness to her talent and resolve to help others. I feel she deserves much more recognition having to overcome two huge barriers—race and gender.

DID YOU KNOW?

1. Her Joy Street home is a stop on "Boston Women's Heritage Trail."
2. At the time of her schooling, most women were trained only in midwifery, but not Rebecca; she received an extensive medical education.

"Let no-one say the past is dead, the past is all about us and within."

An Aboriginal Australian writer and indigenous rights activist, Kathleen Jean Mary Ruska (1920-1993) was a poet, artist, mother and educator. Known as "Kath Walker" until 1988, she is recognized as the first modern-day Aboriginal protest writers. Changing her name to "Oodgeroo" was away of stripping the label given her by Australia's invaders. Her initial volume of poetry, *We Are Going*, is the first book published by an Aboriginal woman. Direct, charismatic, and dignified, Oodgeroo taught others about the spirituality of her ancestors, responsibility for the earth and the connection to all people. Our world needs more Oodgeroos.

A member of the *Stolen Generation,* Oodgeroo spoke out as a poet of Indigenous rights. The Stolen Generation (aka Stolen Children) were children of Australian aboriginal and Torres Strait Islander descendants who were removed from their families by Australian federal and state government agencies and church missions under their respective parliaments.

Referred to as half-caste or mixed-race, these children were still being forcibly taken in the 1970s. (Can you imagine?) The *Victorian Aboriginal Protection Act of 1869* was the earliest authorization to remove children from their homes. Approximately 100,000 children were taken. By 1969, all Australian states had repealed the Victorian legislation.

During the fifties, Oodgeroo had become interested in writing poetry. By the mid-sixties, her published work *We are Going* was a huge success. Overnight she became a bestselling poet with her plain-spoken technique and strong protest elements. Her poetry is full of slogans and inclusive language with easily understood rhyme schemes and allusions.

Oodgeroo became a prominent figure in the campaign for reforms to the Australian Constitution regarding the Stolen Generation. Oodgeroo spoke out through her writing of the loss of the Indigenous culture and how much suffering accompanied it.

DID YOU KNOW?

1. Oodgeroo joined the Australian Women's Army in 1942 after two of her brothers were captured by Japanese troops.
2. She received the award, Member of the Order of the British Empire (Civil), in 1970 for her contributions to her community.
3. Seventeen years later, Oodgeroo announced she was returning her MBE in protest of "two-hundred years of sheer unadulterated humiliation" of Aboriginal people.

QUEEN SEON-DEOK OF SILLA FRIDAY, WEEK 45

Queen Seon-deok (c.600-647) was the first female sovereign in ancient Korea. She ruled from 632-647 CE. Seon-deok's reign was renowned by the increased integration of Buddhism, already the official state religion. The construction of the *Cheomseongdae*, the oldest observatory in East Asia, took place under her. Seon-deok oversaw an extensive rebuilding program, especially of Buddhist temples. She helped unify Korea, the state became more centralized and the country saw a flourishing of arts, literature and sciences under her guidance. Generous, benevolent, wise and smart is how she was revered.

Seon-deok gained the throne because her father had no male heir. Interestingly, the queen ruling alone is testimony to the royal lineage's high status of women. It also illustrates the rigidity of the Silla social class system where privileges and obligations were based on one's birth and bloodline. The kingdom of Silla had authority over south-eastern Korea from the 1st century BCE to 7th century CE. Seon-deok's close neighbors were powerful and continued to harass them. Finally, the queen sent a diplomatic embassy to China to persuade them to help. It was not until 660s CE that the *Baekje* and *Gogureyo* (Korean neighbors) were crushed.

Seon-deok's domestic policies were more successful than her foreign policies. As the state became centralized and Buddhism encouraged, it enhanced the monarch's status. Seon-deok was able to create an extensive rebuilding program. The *Cheomseeongdae* observatory at *Gyeongju*, Silla's capital, still stands today, the oldest surviving observatory in East Asia and probably part of a larger complex dedicated to science and astronomy. Acting like a sundial, it is nine meters tall and has a south-facing window to capture the sun's rays.

Another important building project completed during her reign was the Buddhist temple at *Hwangnyongsa* (Temple of the illustrious Dragon). The temple housed a massive bell that weighed three hundred tons and was three meters high. Sadly, the temple was destroyed by Mongols in 1238 CE, leaving only the foundation.

DID YOU KNOW?

1. Seon-deok was the twenty-seventh ruler of the Korean Peninsula's three kingdoms.
2. She was only the second female ruler in East Asian history.

313

"There is nothing more interesting, nothing more moving than to feel that you have an entire audience in the hollow of your hand, laughing when you laugh, weeping when you sob, and shaking with anger."

A prominent nineteenth century French mezzo-soprano, Michelle Ferdinande Pauline Garcia Viardot (1821-1910), was also a composer, educator and mother of Spanish heritage. Though she began her professional career as a pianist, Pauline began her singing career after the death of her older sister, Maria Malibran. Her dramatic abilities while performing and wide vocal range inspired many composers including Camille Saint-Saens and Frederic Chopin to write music for her. Fluent in French, English, Italian, German, Spanish and Russian, she was considered one of Europe's most influential cultural icons of the century.

Born into the family of Manuel Garcia Sr.—a European premier tenor—she was raised by parents who surrounded her with professional musicians and artists. Pauline and her siblings were accustomed to having distinguished guests from around the world grace their home. Hearing their enlightened conversation made transitioning into their own musical careers much easier.

Speaking four languages by the age of four, Pauline had a deep desire to learn and was more disciplined than her older siblings. Nicknamed "the ant" by her family, she showed much musical talent early on. By the age of eight, Pauline was accomplished enough to accompany singers in her father's voice studio.

After her father's death, her mother, Maria Joaquina, insisted she set aside piano and concentrate on voice. Pauline's acquiescence was something she always regretted. After the sudden death of her sister, she was expected to carry on the family's tradition, being a great singer. Touring Europe, her first operatic role was in London at the Queen's Theatre in 1839. Her performance of *Desdemona* was quickly followed by a contract with the *Theatre Italien* in Paris. The night of her *Desdemona* performance, one critic wrote that "another great career has begun."

DID YOU KNOW?

1. Despite being a talented composer and performer, Pauline Viardot has somehow been forgotten.
2. She wrote a total of five operas and fifty Lieder.

The Celtic Moon Goddess Rhiannon is known as the Divine Queen of Faeries. She is the Goddess of fertility, rebirth, wisdom magic, transformation, beauty, artistic inspiration and poetry. Rhiannon manifests as a beautiful young woman dressed in gold, riding a pale horse with singing birds flying around Her head. The singing birds wake spirits or grant sleep to mortals. In the Celtic religion, She is the Welsh embodiment of the horse Goddess Epona and the Irish Goddess Macha. Rhiannon means "White Witch" or Great Queen. Poets, artists, and singers invoke Her name for inspiration. She is a good witch, a healer and extremely courageous.

Rhiannon's symbols are the color white, horses and the moon. Her themes—movement, communication, rest, ghosts, fertility and leadership. Ideally, she is worshipped at night with the Moon high in the sky, within a grove of trees. An altar of forest materials nestles within the forest. Her devotees call upon Her to reveal the truths in dreams and to remove the role of victim from our lives. Rhiannon teaches us patience, forgiveness and guides us to overcome injustice. She will aid us in magic concerning Moon rituals, fertility, prosperity and self-confidence. Sounds like we could all benefit from Her blessings.

On September 18th in Britain, people gather on the Berkshire hillside to scour the chalk of the Uffington White Horse (a prehistoric hill figure formed in trenches filled with white chalk). The ancient ritual has kept the image of the horse and the legend of Rhiannon alive and relevant.

DID YOU KNOW?

1. According to academic Miranda Green, "Rhiannon conforms to two archetypes of myth ... a gracious, bountiful queen-Goddess; and ... the 'wronged wife', falsely accused of killing her son."
2. Rhiannon is connected with three mystical birds. Read more about them in *The Birds of Rhiannon*.

A Lithuanian librarian at *Vilnius* University, Ona Simaite (1894-1970) used her position to aid and rescue Jews in the *Vilna Ghetto* during WWII. She was not only gutsy but brave under torture and gracious as well.

Born in Lithuania but educated in Moscow, Ona became a librarian at the University in 1940. Vilnius, Lithuania, was occupied by Germans at that point. Using the ruse of reclaiming over-due library books, she was able to slip in and out of the Jewish ghetto to provide prisoners with food, medicine and clothes. She also assisted the ghetto resistance by providing weapons, food, documents and medicine. Ona smuggled sleeping children out of the ghetto in potato sacs and hid adults in her apartment and in the university library.

She smuggled out important literary and historical documents for the *Paper Brigade* (a group of *Vilnius* residents who hid a large cache of Jewish cultural items from YIVO (the Yiddish Scientific Institute), saving them from destruction or theft by the Nazis.

In 1944, the Gestapo became aware of her activities, Ona was arrested. They interrogated and tortured her for twelve days, hanging her upside down and burning the soles of her feet.

Sentenced to death for not revealing any information, friends and colleagues from the university community protested on her behalf. They were able to get her sentence commuted, after paying a bribe, to internment—first in Lithuania, then to *Dachau*, and on to *Ludelange* camp in France. She managed to survive.

fter the war, Ona's main concern was to secure locations for texts about the destruction of the *Litvaks* and their culture. She worked tirelessly sending copies of novels to the *Centre de Documentation Juive Contemporaine* in Paris, to the *Ghetto Fighter House* and the *Jewish National and University Library* in Israel. Ona was equally determined to ensure that Israeli and American publications and other books she personally favored found their way into libraries in Soviet Lithuania.

DID YOU KNOW?

1. Ona adopted a Jewish girl in 1944.
2. She refused any and all honors after the war for her actions.
3. In 2015, a street in Vilnius was named *Simaites Street* honoring Ona.

An American academic, Sophinisba Preston Breckinridge (1866-1948) was an activist, social reformer, social scientist, political scientist, lawyer, author, diplomat and innovator in higher education. She was the first woman to pass the bar in Kentucky, the first woman to earn a Ph.D. in political science and economics, and then her J.D. from the University of Chicago. Sophinisba focused her energies as an academic on the education of social workers, instituting standards that were adopted throughout the U.S. She was also active in several reform movements including the NAACP and women's suffrage.

The first woman to be admitted to the Kentucky bar in 1894, Sophinisba then moved to Illinois and enrolled in the doctoral program at the University of Chicago, gaining her Ph.D. in political science in 1901 and her J.D. in 1904. She began working on issues of women's unemployment and juvenile delinquency. At the same time, she was writing for the *American Journal of Sociology* and teaching in the Chicago Social Center for Training and Practical Training in Philanthropic and Social Work (later renamed the School of Civics and Philanthropy).

While residing at *Hull House* (1907-1920), Sophinisba founded the Immigrant's Protective League. Then she negotiated the merger of the School of Civics and Philanthropy with the University of Chicago, making the university the center of social work in America. While focusing on housing, immigration, minorities and better working conditions for women, Sophinisba also worked as Chicago's health inspector and campaigned for federal child labor laws. She became a full-time professor at the Graduate School of Social Service Administration, instituting new methods in training social workers.

Sophinisba's passionate belief that social research could be used to create a better society made her a trailblazer in her field. In 1933, President Roosevelt named her a delegate to the Pan-American Congress in Montevideo, the first woman ever to be awarded that honor.

DID YOU KNOW?

1. She was a lifelong advocate of legislation for maximum hour and minimum wage control.
2. Sophinisba was an American delegate to the Women's Peace Congress at the Hague in 1915.

"the only honest, unselfish, indomitable hellcat in the history of conservation" (The New Yorker, April 17, 1948)

> An avid birdwatcher, Mabel Rosalie Barrow (1877-1962) was a pioneering conservationist, suffragette, New York socialite and mother. She established the Emergency Conservation Committee (ECC) in 1929 in order to expose the ineffectiveness of the conservation effort. Known as the "Hawk of Mercy," Rosalie was the most militant of conservationists. Founding the world's first birds of prey preserve, "Hawk Mountain Sanctuary," she singlehandedly ended decades of hawk and eagle slaughter in the Appalachian Mountains of Pennsylvania. Rosalie also led grass-roots campaigns for both Olympic National Park (1938) and Kings National Park (1940).

Born in New York City to a prominent family, Rosalie received a private education. She married a British engineer at age thirty-two, the couple eventually settled in the city. After hearing Sybil Margaret Thomas speak out against England's male dominated political system, Rosalie became a social activist back home. She joined the "Equal Franchise Society" in 1915 giving speeches, writing pamphlets, later serving as secretary-treasurer of the New York Woman Suffrage Party.

In 1921, Rosalie found solace from a broken marriage by walking through Central Park. There she found comfort watching birds, befriending other Central Park birders who took her under their *wing*. (No pun intended.) She quickly became immersed in the politics of the National Association of Audubon Societies (NAAS)—a precursor to the National Audubon Society. Rosalie learned that the NAAS was involved in activities that harmed birds instead of helping them.

The ECC was born of the effort to stop the killing of birds and the trapping and selling of animal furs to pay for Audubon employees' wages. The group also strongly championed the preservation of different species. Though many things were accomplished in the thirties and forties, the struggle persists today to expose National Audubon Society's continued activities that harm birds.

DID YOU KNOW?

1. Rosalie's education in natural sciences came from the likes of Aldo Leopold, J. "Ding" Darling and others.
2. The ECC (still active today) also spoke out against DDT and other toxins while championing virgin forests.
3. Rosalie has been dubbed "Conservation's First Lady."

PEARL S. BUCK (AKA SAI ZHENZHU)

"If you want to understand today, you have to search yesterday."

An American writer and novelist, Pearl Sydenstricker Buck (1892-1973) spent most of her early life in China. Best known for her novels of life in China, she was awarded a Pulitzer in 1932 and was the first American woman to win the Nobel Prize for Literature. A strong advocate of women's rights and civil rights, this mother of two also founded Welcome House, an adoption agency specializing in finding homes for Asian-American children.

Pearl was born in the U.S. but her parents went back to China when she was five months old. In 1909, upon completing her course work at boarding school in Shanghai, she moved back to the U.S. to study philosophy. Upon receiving her bachelor's degree, Pearl was offered and accepted a position as a psychology professor in Lynchburg, Virginia. Publishing her first novel, *East Wind, West Wind* in 1930, she quickly followed it with her next, *The Good Earth* highlighting the life of Chinese peasants and winning the Pulitzer.

After receiving the award in 1932, she relocated to the U.S. permanently, returning to academia at Yale earning an additional master's degree. Pearl and her husband, Walsh, adopted six children through the years. Alongside her writing career, she was active in humanitarian efforts to protect Asian Americans against racial intolerance by increasing awareness. She also ventured to improve living conditions of disadvantaged Asian Americans (particularly children). Consequently, Pearl founded the East and West Association in 1941.

In 1949, she started Welcome House, which specialized in the adoption of Asian-American children. In 1964, she established the Pearl S. Buck Foundation to further address issues of poverty and discrimination faced by countless children in Asian countries.

DID YOU KNOW?

1. Her statue stands in front of her former residence in Nanjing University (China).
2. She wrote over forty novels, twenty non-fiction, three autobiographies, three biographies and an incredible number of short stories.

An ancient Egyptian, Queen Tiye (1398-1338 BCE) was mother of at least seven children. She held a great deal of power in her husband's and son's reign. A trusted adviser and confidant to the king, the queen was known to be wise, strong, fierce, intelligent and able to gain the respect of foreign dignitaries, dealing with them directly at their request. She is recognized as the first Egyptian queen to have her name recorded on official acts. Tiye was also the beloved grandmother of King Tut.

Though history has forgotten her, Queen Tiye was one of the most educated and influential women of Ancient Egypt. The "Great Royal Wife" Tiye was not only beautiful but powerful. She was, indeed, the power behind the throne. Historians attribute her unconventional religious views (and strong political views) to her father's foreign origin. Tiye was married to Amenhotep III when she was about eleven or twelve. She regularly appears beside him in statuary, tomb and temple reliefs. Her name follows his on large commemorative scarabs.

The king adored Tiye and devoted numerous shrines across Egypt to her, besides dedicating a temple to her. The temple was constructed in Nubia (current-day Sudan) in the *Sedeinga* Pyramids where she was venerated as Goddess Hathor-Tefnut. He also had an artificial lake built for her.

When Amenhotep III died after reigning thirty-nine years, she arranged his burial in the Valley of the Kings. It is believed the queen died about twelve years later during an epidemic. Her remains, discovered in 1898, were unwrapped and severely damaged. DNA confirmed her identification, Egyptologists named her "The Elder Lady." Her mummy is in the Egyptian Museum in Cairo.

DID YOU KNOW?

1. You can find a photo of Queen Tiye's mummy on the internet.
2. Royal lineage was carried by the women of Ancient Egypt.
3. Her power was considered equal to her husband's.

"There's nothing in the world more thrilling [than composing], or practically nothing."

Rebecca Helferich Clarke (1886-1979) was a British-American classical composer and professional violist. An internationally renowned viola virtuoso, she became one of the first female professional orchestral players. Rebecca is best known for her chamber music featuring the viola, writing for herself and all-female chamber ensembles she played in. Described as the most distinguished British female composer of her generation, most of Rebecca's works have yet to be published; they were largely forgotten after she stopped composing.

Rebecca's gender strongly affected her life and career. While attending the Royal Academy of Music, her father pulled her out of classes after she was proposed to by a teacher. She attended the Royal College of Music, becoming one of the first female composition students. While there, she shifted her focus from violin to viola, the viola was just being recognized as a legitimate instrument. Selected to play in the Queen's Hall Orchestra made Rebecca one of the first female professional musicians.

She supported herself by playing viola, her father had kicked her out of the house for criticizing his extramarital affairs. Moving to the U.S. in 1916, Clarke began performing while her compositional career was peaking. With her viola sonata (1919), she entered a contest and tied for first prize, submitting under a male pseudonym.

Her compositions were often inspired by the strife in her personal life. Abused emotionally and physically by her father, with her mother ignoring it, led Clarke to doubt her creativity and her talent, while feeling she had to constantly prove herself as a female composer. (Abuse and neglect have a way of destroying our inner selves. Has this happened to you?)

DID YOU KNOW?

1. Since the late 1970s, interest and awareness in Rebecca's work has been revived.
2. Her musical output, showing great artistic fortitude, was brilliant despite only composing about one hundred works.

Goddess of the sea and marine animals in Inuit mythology, Sedna (Sanna or Sidne; Nuliayuk or Taluliyuk) is also known as the "Mother of the Sea" and "Mistress of the Sea." Her name in Greenland is *Arnakuagsak*, and is sometimes referred to as *Arnapkapfaaluk* ("Big Bad Woman") by the Copper Inuit. Sedna's story describes how She came to rule over *Adlivun*, the Inuit underworld. Because She provides the animals used for food in the harsh Arctic lands, Sedna is the most important Inuit deity. Her themes are thankfulness, providence, nature and abundance. She is highly respected and feared by the Inuit.

Sedna's story of how she became a Sea Goddess is told throughout the Arctic, varying from region to region. Beginning as a young mother, She becomes the Mother of sea creatures. As such She controls the availability of seals, walrus, fish, whales and other animals favored by Inuit hunters.

Most versions of the Inuit legend tell of a beautiful mortal woman who became ruler of Adlivun when her father threw her into the ocean from his kayak. He proceeded to cut off her fingers as she tried to climb back into the kayak. Those same fingers turned into the first sea mammals. Sedna lives as queen of the deep and "mistress of death and life" at the bottom of the sea. She decides how many animals can be slaughtered for food. Sedna is willing to provide for the people if they accept Her rules, for three days after the death of an animal their souls would remain with their bodies, keeping watch for violation of Her demands.

At that point, the animals' souls would return to the Goddess bearing information. If Sedna becomes unhappy with the information, She would punish the people with sickness, starvation and storms.

DID YOU KNOW?

1. At Killiniq, Labrador, Sedna is known as "Old-woman-who-lived-in-the-sea" and people throw offerings to Her.
2. Morsels of meat and bone, broken knives and worn-out harpoon heads are some of the Inuit offerings.

"It is terrible to see so much evil and to be powerless to fight against it."

> A Javanese princess who wanted to change the world, Raden Adjen Kartini (1879-1904) became a feminist advocating education for girls and womens' rights. A pre-eminent Indonesian hero, Kartini's activism centered on the forced marriage of female children denying them the right to seek an education. She helped establish a women's school just before her death at age twenty-five. Because of her example, the R.A. Kartini Foundation was established and began building schools for women in 1912, changing the world for Javanese women.

Kartini was born into a wealthy Dutch East Indies family. Their traditional Muslim family practiced Islamic rules of strict etiquette that you and I might question. She learned Dutch and read Europe's finest literature until age twelve, when Islamic law required she be secluded in preparation for marriage at age fifteen. But Kartini had other plans and she continued to read behind locked doors.

Her regent father was more liberal than most, allowing Kartini to read while learning the practicalities of being a wife. Because she was fluent in Dutch, she began corresponding with people in Java and the Netherlands. Kartini also read books by Dutch feminists which made a huge impact on her. European feminist thinking was stirring in her brain at a time when native Indonesian women's status was very low. Through her letters, she spoke of her unhappiness in isolation and her disappointment at not being allowed to continue her education while her brothers could do so. She wrote about her dislike of polygamy, laws that withheld equal rights for women and the brutality of the colonial caste system.

Kartini was able to open up a school for girls with the local government's help. Her dream of studying abroad to become a teacher ended with her arranged marriage at age twenty-four. Just as we try to balance work, marriage and family, so did Kartini.

DID YOU KNOW?

1. The title Raden Adjen is used by unmarried female nobility in Java.
2. Tragically, she died shortly after giving birth to her first child.

"Most new discoveries are suddenly seen things that were always there."

An eminent American philosopher, Susanne Katherina Knauth Langer (1895-1985) was an educator, mother and author. Best known for writing *A Philosophy in a New Key* (1924), she conceived a method to analyze origins, forms and reactions to art. Susanne rejected the notion that art was unexplainable, believing instead that art presents the essence of human feeling. One of the first American women to achieve a scholastic profession in philosophy, she had a strong influence in many fields, including psychology and anthropology. Since WWII, her theory is mostly abandoned, despite Susanne's mid-twentieth century significance. Or has her theory found its way into our "collective unconsciousness" in the music and art world?

Raised in Manhattan's West Side, Susanne's parents emigrated from Germany. As a child, her primary language was German, she carried a German accent throughout her lifetime. Susanne was exposed to much innovation and art, primarily music. Her strong love for nature was accompanied by her passion for reading and writing. She married a fellow Harvard student in 1921 and gave birth to two sons. After obtaining her Ph.D from Harvard, Susanne began teaching and lecturing, spending five years at Columbia University. She also taught at nine other prestigious colleges and universities between 1954-1962.

She believed symbolism to be the main concern of philosophy because it underlies all that humans know and understand. Susanne also felt that's what makes humans different from animals—our ability to use symbols. Believing all animals have feelings, humanities' capacity to feel is moderated by concepts, vocabulary and symbols.

One of the initial philosophers to recognize the concept of "the virtual," Susanne believed art connected to that same concept. She saw virtuality as "the quality of all things that are created to be preserved." Susanne later believed her main task was to assemble a science and psychology theory of the "life of the mind" using *process philosophy* traditions.

Did you know?

1. Her two main influences were philosophers Ernst Cassirer and Alfred North Whitehead.
2. Suzanne believed by going beyond scientific research that a rebirth of philosophical creativity would rise.

An Islamic medical and social worker, Rufaida al-Aslamia (c. 620 CE- ?) was a Saudi Arabian nurse and surgeon living at the time of the Prophet Muhammad. She is recognized as the first female Muslim nurse and first Islamic female surgeon. With her clinical skills, she trained other women to be nurses and to work in the health care field. Rufaida helped to solve social problems associated with disease while she helped children in need. She also cared for orphans, the handicapped and the poor.

Women in the early days of Islam had great influence in all spheres of life and they contributed to various fields such as business, charity, Hadith narration, nursing, education and social work.Rufaida al-Aslamia's father was a physician and her mentor. She initially obtained clinicalexperience from him.

Devoting herself to nursing and caring for the sick, Rufaida became an expert healer. She brought the advent of nursing 1,200 years before Florence Nightingale! A companion and follower of Mohammed, she gave first aid and water to wounded soldiers during holy wars.

She developed mobile nursing units that helped to better serve local communities that would be more effective on the battlefield. Proper hygiene and stabilizing the wounded for further surgeries were her imperatives. It is reported that after the conflicts were over Rufaida requested to have a tent inside *Masjid an-Nabawi* in Medina where nursing care would be offered, as well as training for future nurses.

During peacetime, Rufaida continued her humanitarian efforts by providing assistance and care to Muslim children in need. She garnered much praise for spending her life caring for the sick and dying and providing health education to the people of her city.

DID YOU KNOW?

1. Rufaida practiced medicine during a time of many holy wars.
2. The Rufaida Al-Aslamia Prize in Nursing is awarded annually at the University of Bahrain to a student excelling in remarkable patient care.

A lyric poet, Sappho of Lesbos *(c. 620-570 BCE) was so popular in ancient* Greece she was glorified in statuary and praised by figures such as Solon *and* Plato. Her poetry is written to be sung while accompanied by a lyre (known as lyric poetry). She was known as "The Poetess" and "Tenth Muse" and is classified as one of the greatest lyric poets of any age.

Widely read in antiquity, only fragments of her nine volumes survive. Contrary to popular thinking, her works were not destroyed by closed-minded Christians seeking to suppress lesbian love poetry but were lost simply through time and circumstance. Sappho wrote in the Aeolic Greek dialect (one of five Greek dialects) which was difficult for Latin writers to translate. They preserved poems which others had copied but did not copy others simply because they did not know her dialect.

Her name has leant itself to *lesbian* and *Sapphic*, both relating to homosexual women because her surviving poetry concerns itself with romantic love between women. Rather than speaking to gods or describing epic narratives such as those of *Homer*, Sappho's verses speak from one individual to another. Her poems speak simply and directly to the bittersweet difficulties of love.

Many critics and readers alike have responded to the personal tone and urgency of her verses, an abundance of translations of her fragments are available today. Frequent images in Sappho's poetry include flowers, bright garlands, naturalistic outdoor scenes, altars smoking with incense, perfumed ointments to sprinkle on the body and bathe the hair. In Sappho's poetry, love is an inescapable power that moves at the will of the Goddess.

DID YOU KNOW?

1. Sappho was most highly appreciated by Hellenistic (323 BCE-31 BCE) Alexandria.
2. It is estimated she composed around 10,000 lines of poetry, probably written on papyrus. Incredible.

"Nothing will turn a man's home into a castle more quickly and effectively than a dachshund."

The last ruler of the house of Hanover, Queen Victoria (1819-1901) gave her name to an era—the Victorian Age. She reigned as monarch of Great Britain and Ireland becoming Empress of India in 1877. While on the throne, the British monarchy took on its modern ceremonial character. She and Prince Albert had nine children, from whose marriages came many of the royal families of Europe. Victoria is the second-longest reigning British monarch, ruling for sixty-four years. An intelligent brave leader, she established Britain as the world's most powerful nation. She was known as "the grandmother of Europe."

Alexandrina Victoria led a sheltered life in Kensington Palace during her childhood. She was not allowed to see anyone besides her mother, half-sister and brother, and the comptroller of the household and reputed lover of the Duchess of Kent, Sir John Conroy. At age eighteen Victoria became Queen of Great Britain. One of her first decisions was to free herself from her mother and gain independence from the controlling atmosphere she had been brought up in.

Queen Victoria met many potential mates from royal houses across Europe after her coronation. Falling in love with Prince Albert of Saxe-Coburg and Gotha in Germany, their marriage took place in 1840. Victoria and Albert had a very close intimate relationship.

The Victorian Age came to epitomize an era of social conservatism and economic expansion. The nineteenth century was a time of unprecedented expansion for Britain in terms of both industry and empire. Although the queen's popularity ebbed and flowed during her years on the throne, towards the end of her reign she had become a symbol of British imperialism and pride. The Victorian period also saw huge advances in technology and science.

DID YOU KNOW?

1. The Victorian period became known as the Steam Age because it enabled people to travel easily throughout the UK and the world.
2. Queen Victoria also said, *"The important thing is not what they think of me, but what I think of them."* Good advice for all of us to follow.
3. After Albert's death at age forty-two, Victoria dressed in black for the rest of her life.

"That big, pure colorful golden voice would rise effortlessly, hitting the stunned listener in the face, rolling over the body, sliding down the shoulder-blades, making one wiggle with sheer physiological pleasure." Harold C. Schonberg, 1972.

> Daughter of Italian immigrants, Rosa Melba Ponzillo (1897-1981) was known as one of the two greatest voices of the twentieth century—Enrico Caruso being the other. An American-born trained operatic soprano, her voice was dramatic, known for its dark velvety quality. Rosa received almost no formal training before debuting at the Metropolitan Opera in 1918. She was a coloratura soprano who performed at the Met for nineteen seasons.

Rosa Ponselle began singing at popular restaurants in New Haven, Connecticut when she was only eleven years old. By 1915, she joined her sister, Carmela, in New York to create a popular vaudeville act, *Those Tailored Italian Girls*. It was during one of those performances that Caruso heard Rosa sing and was impressed with her. Rosa's voice emitted golden qualities, brilliance and had a flexible upper register that complimented the darkness and richness of her lower range.

Her initial contract with the Metropolitan Opera was for the 1917-1918 season. Rosa spent most of her twenty-year career there; she also performed at Covent Garden in London and at the *Maggio Musicale* in Florence, Italy. Famous for her extensive range, clarity of tone and emotional expressiveness, Rosa worked continually during her performing career to sustain and develop her voice.

Suffering from terrifying stage fright, she nonetheless persisted in her operatic roles, hiding her discomfort from the audience. After twenty years, Rosa Ponselle retired from the Met, becoming artistic director of the Baltimore Civic Opera Company in the late 1940s where she taught and encouraged young aspiring singers.

DID YOU KNOW?

1. Rosa kept recording into the seventies.
2. During her years at the Met, she sang twenty-two different roles, giving 266 performances.
3. She retired at the peak of her career.
4. Her singing voice was considered one of the most beautiful of the twentieth century.

An Egyptian Goddess of the sun, Sekhmet (meaning "the one who is powerful") also oversees war, destruction, plagues and healing. She is one of the oldest deities and one of the most powerful. Associated with disease, healing and medicine, Sekhmet is a solar deity, protector and warrior Goddess. She is often depicted as a lioness. Upon their death, she carries people to the afterlife. Sekhmet is called the "One Before Whom Evil Trembles" and "Mistress of the Dead." Said to breathe fire like the hot winds of the desert, She is the mother of a lion god, *Maahes*. Sekhmet is best known as the protector of Ma'at (balance or justice) and is often associated with the Goddesses Hathor and Bastet.

Envisioned in art as a fierce lioness, Sekhmet was sometimes shown as a woman with the head of a lioness, dressed in red. On her head she wears a sun disc encircled by a cobra and often holds the *ankh*, the symbol of life.

As Sun Goddess, She is connected with the scorching, searing, burning heat of the sun. Also known as *Nesert,* meaning flame, her fate is sealed as a terrifying Goddess. Her title of "Red Lady" connects her to the desert heat. Sekhmet was closely associated with the pharaoh, protecting him during war. Celebrations and sacrifices are often made to her for appeasement after war.

DID YOU KNOW?

1. Patron Goddess of all healers and physicians, Her priests were known to be very skilled physicians.
2. Her healing and protective aspects provide cures to various ailments she may have brought to mankind, such as disease and plague—this happens when humans go against her.
3. It is estimated over seven hundred statues of Sekhmet stood in one funerary temple, signifying her power, strength and readiness to carry the dead to the afterlife.

Recha Rottenburg Sternbuch (1905-1971) was a Swiss woman of Jewish descent who helped save *thousands* of Jews from the Nazis. A businesswoman, activist and mother, she and her husband, Yitzchak, were the Swiss representatives of "Va'ad ha-Hatsala"—a rescue committee of the "American Union of Orthodox Rabbis." Thousands of Jews being held in Austria's concentration camps were released because of Recha's negotiations. Isn't that incredible?

While pregnant, Recha would spend nights near the Austrian border, waiting for refugees to be smuggled into neutral Switzerland, as the Swiss border guards were turning them back. With the help of a Swiss police captain, Paul Grunzinger, the two smuggled over eight hundred refugees out of Nazi-controlled Austria. Once discovered, Recha was arrested and then jailed, causing her to miscarry. She persisted in her activism after being released, forging visas for hundreds of German and Austrian Jews and helping them to gain entrance to Switzerland. Recha also helped smuggle refugees to Palestine via China. Her commitment to aid Jewish refugees forced her to leave her own son's bar mitzvah, rushing to France in order to distribute visas and money to help French Jews escape deportation.

Recha also sent coded cables to contacts in the United States and Turkey, making them aware of the European genocide. Developing a friendship with Monsignor Phillippe Bernadini (from the Vatican), Recha was given access to Vatican couriers who would send resources to Jewish resistance organizations. Astonishingly, in 1944, Recha was able to contact Jean Marie Musy (former Swiss president and close friend of Heinrich Himmler—a leading Nazi party member). Charming Musy, she convinced him to negotiate with Himmler to release Jews from concentration camps for $1,000,000.00. About 1200 Jews were released before Nazi-Swiss collaborators shut down the exchange.

DID YOU KNOW?

1. After the war, Recha worked tirelessly locating surviving Jewish children and connecting them with Jewish people willing to foster or adopt them.
2. At the same time, she and her husband negotiated an agreement with Musy for the turnover of four concentration camps—with the guards standing trial, not being shot on site.
3. In addition, they negotiated the release of thousands of women from Ravensbruck and 15,000 Jews from Austria.

PAULINA LUISI TUESDAY, WEEK 48

"We women are familiar with the ulcers of our societies, because it is almost always our hands which apply the balm."

> Uruguay's first female physician and surgeon, Dr. Paulina Luisi Janicki (1875-1950) was a teacher, writer, editor, diplomat, social reformer and leader of her country's feminist movement. Highly respected, she founded the Consejo Nacional de Mujeres (National Women Council) as well as the Uruguayan and Argentine branches of the International Abolitionist Federation. Paulina also founded the Alianza de Mujeres para los Derechos Femeninos (Women Alliance for Women's Rights) and Uruguay's first feminine trade unions.

Born in Argentina to a Polish mother and a father of Italian descent, Paulina attended college in Uruguay. As the daughter of an educator and a socialist, she grew up with the desire to champion liberty and justice. She became an activist during her student years, later pioneering in science and feminism.

A story is told of the day she discovered a severed penis in her lab coat. At the end of class, Paulina held up the offending appendage and asked her all-male classmates, "Did one of you lose this?" (Don't you love it?) She paid dearly for that comment.

After graduation, Paulina began meeting influential women from South America and Europe. She worked tirelessly, teaching, writing and speaking for women's rights.

Paulina became the female voice of the Socialist Party using the name abuela (grandmother) while on-air in the early 1940s. Her strong female voice in a patriarchal soundscape of radio, politics and medicine garnered a huge following.

DID YOU KNOW?

1. As founder and editor of "Accion Feminina", Paulina's inspiring writings focused on feminine topics.
2. The Pan-American Conference of Women named her an honorary vice-president in 1922.
3. She remained an activist for women's rights until Uruguay gave the vote to women in 1932.
4. The Medical School of Montevideo named one of its faculty library pavilions after her.

> Born into slavery, pioneering inventor and entrepreneur Sarah Elisabeth Jacob Goode (1850–1905) became the first African American woman to be granted a patent by the U.S. Patent and Trademark Office. A Chicago furniture store owner, she invented a folding cabinet bed in 1885.

Sarah did not have a formal education. Like most children of her era, finding a school for Black children was unlikely, they learned a trade from their family members. Sarah learned carpentry and furniture-making from her father.

After receiving her freedom at the end of the Civil War, Sarah moved to Chicago and eventually became an entrepreneur. Along with her husband, Archibald, a carpenter, she owned a furniture store. Many of her customers, mostly working-class, lived in small apartments and didn't have much space for furniture, including beds. To solve the problem, Sarah invented a "cabinet bed", which she described as a "folding bed," similar to a Murphy bed.

When not in use, it could also serve as a roll-top desk, complete with compartments for stationery and other writing supplies. Sarah was perhaps inspired by folding trunk beds used for camping and travel which she owned.

The debate over who is the first Black recipient of a patent number rages on. Some assert Sarah was third, possibly the fourth African American woman to patent her creation. There are those who claim the first was Judy Reed in 1880. She patented a dough kneading machine. Other critics claim Martha Jones of Virginia as the first in 1868. Regardless, Sarah's innovation filled a desperate need, a form of which is still used today.

DID YOU KNOW?

1. In 2012, a science and math focused high school (the Sarah E. Goode STEM Academy) opened on the south side of Chicago.
2. She gave birth to six children, only three survived infancy.

Sor (Sister) Juana Ines de la Cruz (1648-1695) was a Mexican writer, philosopher, composer, dramatist, scholar, poet and Hieronymite nun. A staunch advocate for women's rights, she was the first published feminist of the New World (the Americas). Sor Juana was best known for her outstanding writing and influential perspectives on women and academics, portraying women as the seat of reason and knowledge despite misogynistic, patriarchal colonialism.

As a female, Juana Ines de Asbaje y Ramirez de Santillana had little access to formal education and was almost entirely self-taught. By the age of three, she had learned to read and write Latin. She composed her first poem when she was eight years old. The gifted child was sent to Mexico City to live with relatives. Tested by the Marquis de Mancera and his invited scholars, all were astounded at the seventeen-year-old's intellect. Her literary accomplishments garnered much fame across "New Spain".

Because of her "total disinclination to marriage" and her wish to "have no fixed occupation which might curtail my freedom to study," Sor Juana began her life as a nun, taking vows at the Convent of Santa Paula of the Hieronymite order in Mexico City in 1669. In her convent cell, Juana amassed one of the largest private libraries in the New World, together with a collection of musical and scientific instruments. Amazing.

The patronage of the viceroy and vicereine of New Spain (Mexico) helped her maintain her exceptional freedom. They favored her and had her works published in Spain. The prodigiously accomplished Sor Juana achieved considerable renown in Mexico and in Spain. Unfortunately, with fame came disapproval from church officials, the Archbishop of Mexico stripped her of any prestige she had earned during her lifetime. (What a jerk.)

DID YOU KNOW?

1. Sor Juana turned her nun's quarters into a salon visited by Mexico City's intellectually elite.
2. Today's scholars call her a "proto-feminist."

Queen of the Netherlands for fifty-eight years, Wilhelmina Helena Pauline Marie of Orange-Nassau (1880-1962) ruled longer than any other Dutch monarch. Outside the Netherlands, she is best known for her role in WWII; she proved to be a great inspiration to the Dutch resistance. A celebrated leader of the Dutch government in exile, Wilhelmina proved she was as capable as men by leading her nation through a major crises. She was popular for maintaining Dutch neutrality during WWII and solving many of the country's industrial problems.

Intelligent and strong-willed, Wilhelmina ruled within the limitations of what Dutch people expected from their elected representatives. At age twenty, she ordered a Dutch warship to South Africa to rescue Paul Kruger, the embattled president of the Transvaal. She gained international stature, respect and admiration of everyone worldwide.

Wilhelmina was a "soldier's queen." Being a woman, she could not be supreme commander, but she used every opportunity to inspect her forces, sometimes appearing without prior notice. Though she loved her soldiers, Wilhelmina was very unhappy with most of her governments' consistent military funding.

During the twenties and thirties, the Netherlands began to emerge as an industrial power. The queen's power reached its zenith during the economic rise in the thirties. When Nazi Germany invaded the Netherlands in 1940, Wilhelmina and her family were evacuated to the United Kingdom, despite her resistance. In Britain, Queen Wilhelmina took charge of the Dutch government in exile, setting up a chain of command and immediately communicating with her people. After the war, Wilhelmina abdicated power to her daughter, believing she had "finished her walk." Holland is the only nation to have female heads of state throughout the whole of the twentieth century. How cool is that?

DID YOU KNOW?

1. Wilhelmina ascended the throne at age ten (her mother Emma named regent).
2. She was the world's first female billionaire.
3. Her daughter, Princess Juliana, ascended the throne on her abdication.
4. A state park in Arkansas and Wilhelmina Bay in Antarctica are named in her honor.

"The greatest gift is not being afraid to question."

An American activist, Ruby Ann Wallace Dee (1922-2014) was a playwright, actress, screenwriter, poet, journalist, humanitarian and mother of three. She is best known for her civic work as well as her stage and film character Ruth Younger in *A Raisin in the Sun* (1961). Nominated for eight Emmy Awards, Ruby was the first Black woman to appear in major roles at Stratford, Connecticut's American Shakespeare Theatre. The National Medal of Arts was awarded to both she and her husband, Ossie Davis. They were also recipients of the Kennedy Center Honors (2004). Together, they won a Grammy for Best Spoken Word Album.

Growing up in Harlem, Ruby joined the American Negro Theatre as a teenager. She also attended Hunter College. In 1941, Ruby began using her first husband's middle name (Dee) as her stage name. Three years after their divorce, she married Ossie Davis with whom she would share not her personal life and career as well.

Ruby's first career breakthrough came in 1946 when she appeared on Broadway in *Anna Lucasta*. Her performing career lasted well into the twenty-first century. *A Raisin in the Sun,* Ruby payed Ruth Younger alongside Sidney Poitier's Waler Lee Younger, was her most memorable role. The play was written by a Black woman, Lorraine Hansberry. It focused on a Black Chicago family at the dawn of the Civil Rights Movement. The play premiered in 1959 and ran for 530 performances before it was turned into a film (1961).

Ruby and her husband were well known in the Civil Rights Movement. Both were arrested in 1999 for protesting the police shooting of Amadou Diallo. (Twenty years later, it's still happening!) Ruby was an active member of the Congress of Racial Equality, the NAACP and many others. For her activism, the Lifetime Achievement Freedom Award from the National Civil Rights Museum was given to her.

DID YOU KNOW?

1. Ruby was a breast-cancer survivor of more than three decades.
2. She was a Grammy, Emmy, Obie (Distinguished Performance by an Actress) and Drama Desk (recognizing Excellence in theater productions) winner.

Greek Goddess of the moon, Selene (or Luna Selene) is known simply as Luna in Roman mythology and in Chinese mythology as Chang'e. All of the world's early cultures had a Moon Goddess associated with the moon's power and energy. Selene has a number of different aspects and traditions depending on the culture celebrating her, but is worshiped at the new and full moons. She is usually depicted with a crescent moon on Her head, driving a chariot drawn by two snow-white horses through the skies. The air around Her glows from Her great shining light. The patron of femininity, Selene is known to have the power to ease childbirth, inspire love, mask reality and pierce illusion as well as powers surrounding dreams and intuition.

Selene's colors are silver and greyish white; her flowers are myrtle, willow, white poppy and the white rose. She has the power to lighten the night and to give us sleep. Having control over time, like the moon, She is constantly changing. She has no temple sites, Selene can be seen from everywhere. A number of other Goddesses are associated with the moon, but only Selene is represented by the Greek poets as *moon incarnate*. The moon features prominently in art and literature. Its influence on human affairs is a consistent feature of astrology though classified as a pseudoscience. (Pseudoscience? Tell that to anyone working in the emergency room on the night of a full moon—eyes will roll.)

The monthly cycle of the moon, contrasting from the sun's path, has been intrinsically linked to menstrual cycles by many cultures. Many religions and societies are oriented chronologically by the moon, such as the Hindu, and have religious significance during festivals and eclipses.

Even the ancient Germanic tribes were known to have a lunar calendar. The position of the moon in the skies is a harbinger of seasonal changes—which is often the way we are familiar with its influence in today's world.

DID YOU KNOW?

1. Selene's sacred animal is the horse.
2. In post-Renaissance Art, she is usually shown as a beautiful pale-faced woman with flowing black hair and driving Her silver chariot.

SOJOURNER TRUTH

> Born Isabella Van Wagener (1797-1883), Sojourner Truth was the first Black woman to successfully sue for her son's freedom from slavery after escaping to freedom with her daughter. She also spoke out against abolition and was a lifelong advocate for equality and justice, sponsoring a variety of social reforms, including women's property rights, universal suffrage and prison reform. During her lifetime, Sojourner Truth won three lawsuits—very unusual—especially for an illiterate ex-slave. She must have had courage and fortitude in buckets.

Born the daughter of slaves in New York, she spent her childhood as the abused chattel of several masters. She was known as "Belle" and her first language was Dutch. Between 1810 and 1827 Belle bore at least five children to a fellow slave named Thomas. Shortly before New York eliminated slavery in 1827, she found refuge with Isaac Van Wagener, who bought her freedom.

With her Quaker friends' help, she executed a court battle in which she recovered her small son, he'd been illegally sold into slavery in the South. Around 1829, she traveled to New York City with her two youngest children, supporting herself through domestic employment. In 1843, she took the name "Sojourner Truth." Once she was introduced to abolitionism, Sojourner began speaking out against slavery and in favor of women's right to vote.

In 1850, she traveled throughout the Midwest, where her reputation for personal magnetism preceded her and drew heavy crowds. Though she never learned to read or write, she dictated what would become her autobiography—*The Narrative of Sojourner Truth*—to Olive Gilbert, who assisted in its publication. She supported herself with proceeds from her book sales.

DID YOU KNOW?

1. Her famous "Ain't I a Woman" speech was delivered in 1851 at an Ohio Women's Rights Convention.
2. In 2009, Sojourner became the first Black woman to be immortalized with a bust placed in the halls of the U. S. Capitol.

At fourteen years old, Susannah "Susie" Baker King Taylor (1848-1912) was the first Black teacher of hundreds of runaway slaves. Susie also became a Civil War nurse, writer, activist and mother. She is recognized as one of Georgia's most significant women. Traveling with the Union's 33rd Infantry Regiment (1862-1866), Susie cooked and cleaned muskets as well as clothing, and nursed the wounded without ever being paid. After the war, she opened a private school for freed Black children. Her memoir *Reminiscences of My Life in Camp with the 33rd US Colored Troops* (1902) was the only account giving an *inside perspective* of the Civil War written by a woman.

Born into slavery, Susie was secretly taught to read and write. When she escaped to St. Simon's Island with other African Americans, she found safety with Union troops. Her education quickly caught the attention of officers who enlisted her to teach a *freedmen's* school on the island. Susie taught forty children in the day school and a large number of adults at night, all of them anxious to learn how to read. While there, Susie married a non-commissioned officer. When the island was evacuated, she traveled with her husband's unit, serving as a nurse and laundress while teaching Black soldiers the rudiments of literacy during their downtime.

Returning to Savannah, Susie opened a private school for freed children (1866). After her husband died, she returned to her native county (Liberty) and established another school. By 1868, she found herself once again in Savannah teaching freedmen, supporting herself and her small son by collecting tuition.

By 1880, Susie settled in Boston where she began working for the Woman's Relief Corps. She had become an outspoken racial justice activist by this time, and an acquaintance of Harriet Tubman and Ida B. Wells Barnett. Susie firmly advocated against discrimination and racial prejudice of any kind.

DID YOU KNOW?

1. Susie was the military's first Black nurse.
2. You can find an historical marker dedicated to Susie King Taylor in Midway, Georgia.

"Algebra is nothing more than geometry in words; geometry nothing more than algebra in pictures."

A French mathematician, physicist and philosopher, Marie Sophie Germain (1776-1831) was a revolutionary battling against the social prejudices of the era and a lack of formal training in order to become a celebrated mathematician. Sophie is best known for her work in number theory as well as her work in the theory of elasticity. She was the first woman to attend the French Academy of Sciences sessions.

Sophie began teaching herself mathematics when she was thirteen using the books in her father's library. Her parents tried to discourage her by taking away her clothes and depriving her of heat and light at night to make her stay in bed and prevent her nighttime studies. They failed.

In 1794, the *Ecole Polytechnique* was founded in Paris, and of course it did not let women enroll. Sophie was able to obtain lecture notes and study from them. Using a pseudonym, she submitted a paper on analysis to J. L. Lagrange at the end of the term. Amazed the paper's author was a woman, he became Sophie's mentor, introducing her to scientists and mathematicians. Sophie was also mentored for a time by Carl Frederich Gauss.

After Gauss became a professor of astronomy and quit corresponding with her, the French Academy of Sciences announced a contest to explain the "underlying mathematical law" of a German physicist's study on the vibration of elastic surfaces. Sophie submitted the only entry in 1811 but was not awarded a prize. The second time she entered, she received *honorable mention*. On her third attempt, in 1816, she won with her paper, *Memoir on the Vibrations of Elastic Plates*. The prize from the Academy introduced Sophie Germaine into the ranks of prominent mathematicians. She was praised by the *Institut de France* and invited to attend their sessions—the "highest honor that famous body ever conferred on a woman."

Did you know?

1. Because of her gender, Sophie was unable to make a career out of mathematics but worked independently throughout her life. Just another woman ahead of her time.
2. The Academy of Sciences in Paris annually awards *Prix Sophie Germain* to a French mathematician for research in mathematical foundations.
3. Sophie died from breast cancer at age fifty-five.

Sarah Winnemucca (c.1844-1891) was a Northern Paiute author, activist, peacemaker and educator. She devoted her life to protecting Native Americans in the face of an expanding United States. A nineteenth century visionary, she found herself quite often stuck between two cultures. Winnemucca's biography, *Life Among the Paiutes*, is the first English narrative written by a Native American woman.

For this young Paiute woman, being an American was a complicated process of adopting the behaviors and language of a people she distrusted. Translating between the two cultures became her life's work. As Sarah grew up, she recognized "whites" were not going away, and so she acquired the English name Sarah and began to master the English language. For the rest of her life, Sarah would straddle two worlds.

In 1878, Sarah worked as a messenger, scout and interpreter for General O.O. Howard during the Bannock War. She managed to save her father and his people. Her brave actions landed her on *The New York Times* front page in June 1878, but sowed mistrust between her and the tribes. Next, Sarah escalated her fight for reform. Many Paiutes died of starvation at Pyramid Lake (where land had been set aside for their reservation). Her face-to-face petitions and letters failed in improve living conditions for her people, so she began lecturing in San Francisco. She described abuses of reservation agents, particularly those of William Rinehart. He promptly called Sarah a drunk, a gambler and a whore. (Another jerk threatened by a woman speaking the truth.)

She became famous in 1883 when Elizabeth Peabody and Mary Peabody Mann invited her to lecture in New England. They also arranged for the publication of her book, *Life Among the Piutes: Their Wrongs and Claims*. But her criticism of American hypocrisy wasn't always well received. (No surprise there.) By the mid 1880's, she abandoned lecturing, exhausted and disillusioned. She turned her energies toward a school for Paiute children, teaching them to read and write English and training them in marketable skills.

DID YOU KNOW?

1. Her book is "the first known autobiography written by a Native American Woman."
2. The press often reported on her hundreds of lectures and called her the "Pauite Princess."

An Assyrian, Queen Sammu-ramut (c. 9th century-8th century BCE), better known as Semiramis by Greek writers, commanded an entire ancient Mesopotamian empire that stretched from Asia Minor to what is known today as western Iran. Her name means "high heaven." Despite Semiramis' reign only lasting five years, the Greeks cast her as a commander of armies and a builder of Babylonian walls along with other monuments throughout her empire. To some, she was seen as a beautiful femme fatale in a tragic love story. Nonetheless, she exercised a degree of political power unlike any other woman in the history of Mesopotamia, ruling with much wisdom and adoration.

A young widow of the governor of Syria, Semiramis married King Ninus after he fell in love with her. Within just a few years, King Ninus died. Semiramis assumed the role of regent for her son King *Adadnirai* III who was too young to rule upon his father's death. As Regent, she stabilized the nation.

Historians believe Semiramis initiated a number of building projects which earned her great admiration. She also led military campaigns. Setting out to emulate her late husband's agenda, it appears she ordered a new city to be built on the banks of the Euphrates River which became known as Babylon. Semiramis also built a royal palace and the temple of *Marduk*.

Other Greco-Roman authors claim Semiramis was behind the construction of Babylon's famous hanging gardens—one of the seven wonders of the ancient world. Historical evidence disputes this claim. After Babylon's construction, She launched military campaigns in Persia and Libya, quashing uprisings. Semiramis also organized the invasion of India, which, unfortunately, was a disaster.

DID YOU KNOW?

1. Semiramis was associated with "the Whore of Babylon" in a book, *The Two Babylons (1853)* by Christian minister Alexander Hislop. No evidence supports this claim about Semiramis.
2. His further negative claims are also unsubstantiated. He was one mixed-up dude. (And that's putting it mildly.)

Ruth St. Denis

"But in reality we are accompanied by the whole dancing universe."

An American modern dance pioneer, Ruth St. Denis (1879-1968) introduced eastern ideas to the art. She was also co-founder of the American Denishawn School of Dancing and Related Arts. Ruth St. Denis founded Adelphi University's dance program as well as the School of Nataya—which focuses on oriental dance. She believed the "art of dance" shouldn't be restricted to entertainment and technicality (like classical Ballet) but should exude spirituality and emotion.

Ruth Denis began her professional career in New York City in 1892 as a *skirt dancer* in a vaudeville house. She was given the stage name Ruth St. Denis by David Belasco, under his influence she toured the US and Europe. A cigarette poster changed Ruth's life in 1906 which eventually altered the course of modern dance in America. She spotted an advertisement that used an Egyptian image of the Goddess *Isis*, telling the story of civilization through movement.

Through her touring, Ruth was exposed to the work of several European and Japanese dancers, and her artistic imagination soared. She also studied dance techniques from India and Egypt. By 1914, Ruth had met and married Ted Shawn, her dance partner. The pair founded the Denishawn School and Company in Los Angeles. Her choreographic style broadened. *Music visualization* called for movement equivalents to the timbre, dynamic and structural shape of music. Another technique, *synchronic orchestra*, assigned one dancer to interpret the rhythms of each instrument in the orchestra.

The Denishawn had great success, but Ruth and Shawn struggled on both artistic and personal levels. By 1930, the company had crumbled, but Ruth continued to dance, teach and choreograph independently as well as collaborate with other artists.

Did you know?

1. Ruth St. Denis was raised on a small New Jersey farm. (We farm girls are amazing.)
2. Notable students of the Denishawn were Martha Graham, Doris Humphrey, Charles Weidman and Lillian Powell.

The much-revered Scandinavian Goddess of Sun and Healing, Sol (also known as Sunna-the Mistress of the Sun) is worshiped widely throughout Germany and Scandinavia. After She and Her brother created daytime and night time, they were assigned their destinies. Her brother Mani became the God of the Moon. Sol was to ride in the sky on a chariot drawn by Her horses, *Arvak* and *Allsvinn*. It is said in Norway, the Land of the Midnight Sun—where the sun hangs high in the sky for ten weeks—Sol is emphasizing Her power. Her themes are the sun, blessings, cycles, healing, movement and travel. Her colors are gold, yellow or red; Her symbols chariots, horses, the sun wheel and bonfires.

The Goddess of the Sun is not a major focus of the Norse people, unlike mythologies of other cultures. But Sol is honored as a deity of protection and victory in addition to being the Goddess of the sun. She was also a healer. Sunday originated as the specific day in Her honor.

Interestingly, in Norse mythology, the Sun is female, and the Moon, male. The sun, moon and stars were made from the gathered sparks that shot forth from *Muspelheim*, the Land of Fire. Solar eclipses represent times when *Skoll* (the wolf) is gaining on Her chariot in the sky, nipping at her. The speed of the sun's movement through the sky is attributed to Her outrunning the wolf, and at darker times, the wolf is closer.

Sol was also known as the "bright bride of heaven" and in addition to Her familiar powers, She is the "elf beam of deceiver of dwarves"—for those creatures were petrified by Her glance. Stone was important to her, as Her worshipers carved deep stone circles across the Scandinavian landscape as part of Her sacred rites. (So *that's* how they got there.)

DID YOU KNOW?

1. Nordic Bronze Age archeological findings indicate Scandinavians viewed the Sun as a life-giving heavenly body.
2. Sol gave birth to her daughter Sunna just before she was eaten by the wolf Skoll.

"There never will be complete equality until women themselves help to make laws and elect lawmakers.

A pioneer in the women's suffrage movement in the United States, Susan Bromwell Anthony (1820-1906) was president of the National American Woman Suffrage Association from (1892-1900) which she had founded with Elizabeth Cady Stanton. Susan's work helped pave the way for the Nineteenth Amendment (1920) to the Constitution, giving women the right to vote. Susan was also an abolitionist, teacher, writer and lecturer. She overcame oppression, discrimination, and objectification to emerge triumphant.

Raised a Quaker, Susan grew up in a politically active family who worked to end slavery as part of the abolitionist movement. When the family moved to Rochester, New York in 1845, their social circle included anti-slavery activist and escaped slave Frederick Douglass, who would later join her in the fight for women's rights.

Tireless in her efforts, Susan gave speeches around the country to convince others to support a woman's right to vote. She gave seventy-five to one hundred speeches a year for forty-five years, travelling throughout the United States by stagecoach, wagon, carriage and train. (Extraordinary!) Susan even took matters into her own hands in 1872 when she voted in the presidential election illegally. Arrested, she tried unsuccessfully to fight the charges. The judge fined her $100—she never paid it. (Good for her.)

The Nineteenth Amendment, ratified in 1920, was named the Susan B. Anthony Amendment as a final tribute to her. "Where, under our Declaration of Independence, does the Saxon man get his power to deprive all women and Negroes of their inalienable rights?" That about sums it up, yes?

DID YOU KNOW?

1. Her motto: *"Men, their rights, and nothing more; women, their rights, and nothing less."*
2. Susan died in 1906, fourteen years before women were given the right to vote.

"Convert your huge sadness to a huge work."

> An Iranian educator, Touran Mirhadi (1927-2016) was also an author, researcher and mother. As founder of the Farhad School in Tehran, Touran developed a progressive kindergarten and elementary school that became the source of many teaching innovations. An expert in children's books, Touran was co-founder of the Children's Book Council.

Touran first attended the *Tehran* University where she eventually majored in education and psychology. In 1946, she traveled to Paris and attended the *Sorbonne* getting a degree in educational psychology and an additional degree in kindergarten education (1951). She began teaching in Iran, first—kindergarten, then high school where she taught the French language. Touran's academic activities continued when she established Farhad kindergarten in 1955.

Her kindergarten work was embraced and welcomed by the parents. She was motivated to establish Farhad Elementary School next to the kindergarten. In 1971, she and her second husband established the Farhad High School. Together with two of her friends, Touran organized the first "Children's Book" exhibition at *Tehran* University in 1956. That exhibition led to additional crusades for children's books, thus the Children's Book Council was established in 1962. The Council's efforts made significant impact on children's literature both in Iran and elsewhere.

Her knowledge of German, French, Parsi and English helped get Touran recognition outside of Iran, resulting in invitations to international conferences on children's literature.She also worked to develop a collection of encyclopedias for young children and adolescents. After their initial publication in 1979, Touran continued her effort to enhance the twenty-five volume collection until her death. In addition to developing the encyclopedias, she wrote and published several texts and books.

DID YOU KNOW?

1. Touran is considered the founder of Iran's modern education system.
2. It was Touran's German mother, Greta, who taught her several languages.
3. Seeing the WWII devastation in Europe as a student, Touran solidified her belief that education, arts, literature and knowledge were the keys to preventing human misery and war.

Susie Walking Bear Yellowtail

One of the first Native Americans to graduate as a registered nurse in the United States, Susie Walking Bear Yellowtail (1903-1981) was known as the "Grandmother of American Indian Nurses." Serving on many national health organizations, Susie received many honors for her work. She worked for the Indian Health Service, brought modern health care to her people, as well as traveled throughout the U.S. to assess care given to indigenous people for the Public Health Service. She became the first Native American inductee of the American Nurses Association Hall of Fame. She and her husband served as goodwill ambassadors to several foreign nations in the 1950's.

Among the first *Apsaalooke* (Crow) people to achieve a higher education, Susie Yellowtailmaintained her Apsaalooke identity despite attending mission boarding schools where students were expected to give up their cultural languages, beliefs and cultural ways. Guided by her cultural heritage, she used her education to improve the lives of American Indian people.

Susie enrolled at Boston City Hospital's School of Nursing, graduating with honors (1923). She finished her training at Franklin County Public Hospital in Greenfield, Massachusetts, becoming the first registered nurse of Crow descent. After working with other tribes, Susie returned to the Crow Reservation and began working at the government-run Indian Health Services Hospital at Crow Agency (in Bighorn County, Montana). She then began traveling to other reservations as a consultant for the Public Health Service.

Wherever she went, Susie observed appalling living conditions and unmet healthcare needs on the reservations. She also saw the need for cultural competency among medical professionals working with indigenous people—immediate reforms needed in the Indian Health Service. Documenting her observations, Susie pushed for effective improvements. Speaking with experience, knowledge, and conviction to many people, both Indian and Non-Indian, they listened. She created the Community Health Representatives outreach program on reservations, becoming a "watchdog on health care for Indians."

Did you know?

1. Susie worked as a nanny and maid while attending school in order to pay for her room and board.
2. President John F. Kennedy awarded her the "President's Award for Outstanding Nursing" in 1962.

«A woman must have money and a room of her own if she is to write fiction.»

Virginia Woolf (1882-1941) was an English author and novelist who wrote modernist classics. A pioneer of modernism, she is also recognized as the greatest modernist literary personality of the twentieth century. She is most famous for her novels and her feminist writings. Her books are unique, they delve into a character's psychology, portraying what the character is thinking.

The early deaths of her mother, half-sister, and father, plus sexual abuse by siblings traumatized Adeline Virginia (Stephan) Woolf's childhood. She suffered from mental illness for most of her life. Despite that, she became a herculean influence in the field of literature. In 1912, eight years after her father's death, she married Leonard Woolf, a brilliant young writer and critic from Cambridge, England. For amusement, the couple founded Hogarth Press in 1917 by setting and hand-printing, on an old press, *Two Stories* by "L. and V. Woolf." A successful debut, they published many important books over the years.

Writing essays for the London's *Times Literary Supplement* when she was young and continuing over the years allowed Virginia to publish a two-volume series, *The Common Reader* (1925, 1933). Wolf's lectures, writings and public speaking forums influenced society's shift towards inclusion, diversity and equality.

In 1928, she began taking a grassroots approach to advocate feminism. Virginia started addressing undergraduate women in various colleges. Two of her nonfiction works that discuss the hardships faced by women writers and intellectuals were *A Room of One's Own* (1929) and *Three Guineas* (1938). She wanted to acknowledge the effects of industrialization as well as create awareness about birth control. (Almost one hundred years later, we need to do this!)

DID YOU KNOW?

1. Virginia was bisexual and believed in exploring her sexuality.
2. She was part of the nucleus that formed the Bloomsbury Group.
3. Her final London residence was destroyed by *the Blitz*.
4. Tragically, Virginia drowned herself in the River Ouse in March of 1941.

A prominent Chieftess of the Miami tribe, Tecumwah, aka Marie-Louise Pacanne Richerville (c. 1720- c. 1790), was a businesswoman and mother. Her name means "Parakeet" in the Miami language. She ran a successful trading post west of *Kekionga* (in present day Indiana), in which she did business selling supplies, horses and carts to those who were crossing the portage.

In Miami tribal society, women's leadership was respected, as it was in many native tribes until colonial settlers imposed male-dominated practices on Native American societies. Tacumwah married Antoine Richerville, a lesser French nobleman. Her brother, Pacanne, and she owned a stretch of valuable land between the Maumee and Wabash rivers. Travelers from the Great Lakes to the Mississippi River and Gulf of Mexico had to portage across their land. Tacumwah's trading post was strategically located to supply workers and goods over the eight-mile stretch from the eastern rivers to the western rivers.

Tacumwah was also village chief of her Miami tribe. Her marriage to the Frenchman produced four children. Richerville shared her portion of the trading post and portage business. However, when Richerville teamed up with the Maisonville brothers, they began charging Tacumwah and her brother, Pacanne, to use their own property. When Tacumwah sided with her brother, she was beaten.

After Tacumwah left the house, Richerville claimed they weren't married, that her properties and wealth belonged to him (as was the British and French custom). Tacumwah enlisted a rival, Charles Beaubien, to go to court and help her regain her lands and properties. The two were successful in their court battle and later married and had a daughter. The wealth that was passed down from Tacumwah and her brother enabled their descendants to purchase property, build houses, and avoid removal to a reservation in Kansas when many Miami were forcefully deported from Indiana.

Did you know?

1. Tacumwah was awarded her property in the court settlement, her brother the portage.
2. As political advisor to her son, Peshewa, she once placed a knife in his hand and ordered him to free a white prisoner who was about to be executed.

"It matters not to them what is the color of an artist's skin. If a man or a woman is a great actor, or a great musician, or a great singer, they will extend a warm welcome. ... It is the soul they see, not the color of the skin." (referring to European audiences.)

A trailblazing African American soprano, Matilda Sissieretta Joyner Jones (1868-1933) was often called "The Black Patti" in reference to Italian opera singer Adelina Patti. Considered among the greatest sopranos in the late nineteenth and early twentieth century, her repertoire included grand opera, light opera and popular music. The first Black woman to headline a concert at Carnegie Hall in 1892, Madame Jones (as she preferred to be called) sang for kings, presidents and world audiences. She became the highest paid African American entertainer of her time.

After receiving vocal training at the New England Conservatory, Madame Jones found little opportunity for her classically trained voice because of her race. She had "a big voice that spanned nearly two and a half octaves, from a low C to a high E. Her upper notes were described as clear and bell-like, and her lower register was said to have the depth of a contralto."

In 1888, an agent heard her sing and contracted her with the Tennessee Jubilee Singers for a two- year stint traveling the West Indies and South America. Madame Jones was the prima donna of the company and received rave reviews. Returning to the U.S., she was asked to perform at the White House, the first of four presidential invitations to come her way.

The same year, Madame Jones headlined at Madison Square Garden. The next two years found her traveling around Europe. By 1896, she abandoned her career as a soloist and became the lead singer for *Black Patti Troubadours*.

DID YOU KNOW?

1. Despite being held in high esteem, she never performed on the operatic stage.
2. Sadly, the vaudeville stage was the only forum that allowed Madame Jones to
3. work as a professional opera singer, which she did until retiring in 1916.

Greek Goddess of Wisdom, Sophia (meaning wisdom, or divine wisdom) is the center point of creation and represents the feminine aspect in all things, the keeper of the knowledge of all that is righteous and just. Wisdom Incarnate, Sophia is the Goddess of all those who are wise. Her faces are many: Divine Feminine, Mother of God to Gnostic Christians, Black Goddess, Mother of Creation and God's Bride. Her consort and assistant is Jehovah. Her sacred shrine, Hagia Sophia in Istanbul, Turkey, is one of the seven wonders of the world. Sophia's symbol, the dove, represents spirit. She is crowned with stars, a Middle Eastern icon, to indicate her absolute divinity.

Sophia is found throughout the books of the Bible, like Proverbs, and the apocryphal books of Sirach and the Wisdom of Solomon. She is usually associated with King Solomon, and it tells us in Wisdom 8:2,16,18, Solomon was married to Sophia. The Jews revered Sophia, Solomon put her in the temple in the form of the Goddess *Asherah*. When the patriarchal Christianity took over the world, it was feared Sophia would disappear.

With her continuing presence in the world and the Bible, venerations continue in the Eastern traditions and in the Russian Catholic liturgical service. Sophia's veneration survives in the west today in the form of Gnosticism, worshiping her as both divine female creator and counterpart(twin) to Jesus Christ. (Gnostics focus on the eradication of ignorance whereas Christians focus on the eradication of sin. That's quite a difference.)

Sophia's characteristics include righteousness, wisdom, love, communication, knowledge, creativity, protection, generosity and truthfulness. A *sophia woman* sees reality and tells it as it is; She has no fear of the truth. Sophia brings meaning to human experience with Her gift of understanding, knowing that only when one stands back, gaining emotional distance, one can see more clearly gaining strengths and appreciation. You and I need to remember that.

Did you know?
1. Mary Magdalene is identified as Sophia in the Bible.
2. Michelangelo's famous painting on the ceiling of the Sistine chapel shows God's arm wrapped around the beautiful Goddess Sophia.

Sybil Ludington

"Let me! I can ride as well as any man." "The British are coming! Fight, fight!"

A Revolutionary War heroine at age sixteen, Sybil Ludington Ogden (1761-1839) is best known for her all-night horseback ride to neighboring militia forces in Putnam County, New York and Danbury, Connecticut. The daughter of New York militia colonel, Henry Ludington, she either volunteered to rally the troops or was told to do so by her father. Since 1900, Ludington has received more acknowledgement with statues erected in her honor and a US Bicentennial postage stamp released depicting her on a horse. As usual, contemporary sources often try to disclaim her heroic efforts for lack of published accounts.

Colonel Ludington, having switched allegiance from the Crown to join the Patriots in 1773, was focused on preparing for battle when a rider arrived warning of a British invasion. His militia had disbanded in preparation for the upcoming planting season. Young Sybil rose to the occasion, riding forty miles through dark woods in pounding rain to alert the colonel's men of the danger on April 26, 1777. Rallying to her nighttime cries, hundreds of soldiers began gathering to fight the British. Ludington's troops arrived too late to save Danbury, though they were able to skirmish with departing soldiers.

After the war, Sybil married Edward Ogden when she was twenty-three years old. They had a son, Henry, and lived in Catskill, New York. Sybil's husband died of yellow fever in 1799. Four years after his death, she purchased a tavern and helped her son become a lawyer. Selling the tavern for a tidy profit, Sybil was able to purchase a home for her son and his family, she also resided there.

After her son's death, Sybil applied for a Revolutionary War pension, since her husband had served as a soldier. Her pension was denied, claiming she had insufficient proof of her marriage. (Makes you wonder, doesn't it?) Sybil Ludington, a Revolutionary War heroine, died in poverty at the age of seventy-seven.

Did you know?

1. Sybil was able to alert about four hundred militiamen riding her horse, Star.
2. Previously, Sybil saved her father from capture by placing lit candles in windows and marching her siblings (in military fashion) in front of them.

A pioneer of Japanese women's education, Tsuda Umeko (1864-1929) was one of five female students sent overseas as part of the *Iwakura* Mission in 1871. The Japanese government funded her education in the United States. After her return, Tsuda founded the "Women's Institute for English Studies" located in the *Kojimachi* district of Tokyo (1900). It is currently known as Tsuda College—one of the most distinguished women's institutes in Japan.

Tsuda believed education was the key to strengthening women's social status and devoted her life to helping Japanese women receive a higher education. Known as an exceptional educator, she set up a scholarship fund for Japanese women.

At the young age of seven, Tsuda's father volunteered her for the *Iwakura* Mission. One of the mission's purposes was to prepare girls to become *ideal* women to help westernize Japan. Tsuda began her U.S. education in Washington D.C. with Charles Landman (secretary of the Japanese delegation) and his wife, Adeline. The young girl spent ten years with the Landman's before returning to Japan.

Arriving back home, educated and thinking progressively, Tsuda had nearly forgotten the Japanese language. She was also very uncomfortable, tormented with the social status of Japanese women and its dominant patriarchal culture. Tsuda found women's curriculum lacking, focusing merely on training to be obedient wives and adequate mothers. Returning to the U.S., Tsuda furthered her studies in biology (disregarding Japan's ban on teaching sciences to women) at Bryn Mawr College. After three years of scientific study and research, Tsuda went home to Japan determined to help raise women's social and education standards.

Devoting her life to the higher education of women, she set up a scholarship for Japanese women. Public speaking and raising money became a priority. While teaching and publishing, Tsuda introduced western-style education to young women. With help from American women, the Institute gained recognition, generating innumerable opportunities for Japanese women.

DID YOU KNOW?

1. She was the first president of Tokyo's YWCA.
2. Tsuda will be featured on Japan's new banknotes to be issued in 2024.

A renowned midwife and medical practitioner, Trota of Salerno (c. 11th-12th century CE) was medieval Europe's leading authority on obstetrics. A renowned midwife, educator and writer, her works are appreciated for their practical information on gynecology and obstetrics. Trota promoted exercise, cleanliness, a balanced diet and avoidance of stress. She is alleged to have been the first female professor in the famous school of medicine in Salerno, Italy—a town famous for its wise female healers.

Salerno's position on the Italian coast gave it access not only to culture but to scientific and medical knowledge from Europe and Arabia. Patients from as far as England traveled there to be treated. Its "school of medicine" was equally famous, attracting students from all over the continent.

Trota contributed to at least three medical texts. Before she began treatments and writing her texts, women were entirely at the mercy of theological and philosophical ideas, most often bled, prodded and pulled. (Ugh.) In the eleventh century, the human body was thought to be dominated by four elements—hot, cold, wet, dry—and the four humors—blood, red bile, yellow or black bile and phlegm. Any systemic imbalances or *predominances* were detrimental and leading to disease. The progression or cure of the disease was based on the imbalance.

Some of Trota's texts gave detailed instructions about how to handle difficult births. Breech, posterior and other abnormalities at birthing were dealt with by turning the infant while still in utero. She mentioned using opiates to help dull labor pain—definitely at odds with the Church's teaching of that era. (What exactly did the Church know about giving birth??) Trota gave attention to more universal concerns such as bladder stones, hemorrhoids and abdominal pain. Treatment depended on the sex of the patient, using different remedies for men than for women. She even devised a treatment for male infertility.

DID YOU KNOW?

1. It was not until 1985 that historian John F. Benton realized history's error of misspelling her name from Trota (feminine) to Trottus (masculine). This brought credit back to her after her teachings had been historically credited to a man.
2. Her authentic work, *Practical Medicine According to Trota,* was forgotten until its rediscovery in the twentieth century.

"There is no great; there is no small; in the mind that causeth all."

> Zitkala-Sa, meaning Red Bird (1876-1938), was also known as Gertrude Simmons Bonnin. A Yankton Dakota writer, she was also an editor, translator, musician, educator and political activist. Fighting tirelessly for Native American rights and citizenship, Zitkala-Sa wrote several works documenting her conflicts with cultural identity and the pull she felt between her education and the Dakota culture. She played piano and violin and collaboratively wrote *The Sun Dance Opera*—the first ever American Indian opera. Zitkala-Sa founded the National Council of American Indians in 1926 and is recognized as one of the most influential Native American activists of the twentieth century.

Zitkala-Sa lived on the Yankton Indian Reservation in South Dakota until she was eight. Missionaries showed up on the reservation, taking her and several others to a Quaker school in Wabash, Indiana where they were taught English—speaking, reading and writing it. As an adult, she wrote of her terror and shame at school, having her braids "chopped off"; in her culture, that was a symbol of cowardice. But she also expressed her joy learning to read, write and play the violin. Zitkala-Sa attended the school for three years and while there, her name was changed to Gertrude Bonnin.

When Zitkala-Sa returned to the Yankton in 1900, she was greatly dismayed to find white settlers starting to occupy lands allotted to the Yankton Dakota under the Dawes Act of 1887. She began publishing articles describing the loss of identity felt by Native Americans. In the early 1900s, Zitkala-Sa published legends collected from Native American cultures, as well as autobiographical narratives. *Atlantic Monthly* and *Harper's Monthly* regularly ran her articles. This was just the beginning of her writing career.

Vocal activism for Native rights brought Zitkala-Sa and her family to Washington D.C. Instrumental in the passage of the Indian Citizenship Bill in1924, she continued to pursue more reforms for Native Americans.

DID YOU KNOW?

1. Published posthumously in 2001, *Dreams and Thunder: Stories, Poems, and the Sun Dance Opera* features her writings after 1904.
2. Much of her writing is liminal in nature showing tensions between assimilation and native traditions, between literature and politics—characterizing her dynamic work.

Vigdis Finnbogadottir GCMG

"If anything can save the world, women can."

> An Icelandic cultural figure and politician, Vigdis Finnbogadottir GCMG (b. 1930) is a teacher, translator, environmental activist, actress and mother. She became the world's first democratically elected female president in 1980, subsequently reelected three times, retiring from office in 1996. Vigdis was also the world's first single person allowed to adopt a child in 1972 after a hard-fought battle. Upon retiring, she was president of UNESCO (1999-2004). Vigdis co-founded the Council of Women World Leaders in 1997—it has current membership of nearly eighty former prime ministers and presidents. She is a pioneering leader, role model and symbol of unity around the world, continuing to fight for equality, human rights and democracy.

Born in Reykjavik, Vigdis Finnbogadottir studied in Paris, Sweden and Denmark before returning to Iceland to teach at the University. Drama, French and literature are her areas of expertise. She began serving as Artistic Director of the Reykjavik Theatre Company in 1972, the same year she became the first single person to adopt a child. Vigdis became a member of the Advisory Committee on Cultural Affairs in the Nordic countries (1980).

Running against three male candidates for the presidency of Iceland in 1980, Vigdis, a divorced single mother, made world history becoming the first democratically elected female president. Icelandic women attracted world attention in 1975 (International Women's Year) when they organized a general strike to show their importance—with 90% of Iceland's women participating.

A popular president, Vigdis became a prominent cultural ambassador for Iceland. She emphasized reforestation and land reclamation in Iceland's eroded areas and promoted education and care of youth, as well as the preservation of Iceland's heritage and language. Vigdis has been given the highest merit award from Denmark, France, Finland, Germany, Italy, Luxembourg, Norway, the Netherlands, Spain and Sweden. Wow. Sixteen universities and colleges have given her honorary degrees.

Did you know?

1. Since 1998, Vigdis has been Goodwill Ambassador of Languages for UNESCO.
2. She was awarded the Order of St. Michael and St. George (GCMG) in 1982 by Queen Elizabeth II.

"The grey hair.….means to a painter not just grey hair, but a certain grey – perhaps a grey with silver lights and warm shadows, perhaps an opaque cold grey, but a grey as different from other greys as one chord in music is different from others."

> British painter Vanessa Bell (1879-1961) was an interior designer and founding member of the Bloomsbury Group. She was best known for her colorful portraits, still-lifes and cover designs. A significant artist, her paintings have a powerful voice. Vanessa's artistic creations are complex, ranging from fabrics and furniture to wood-cuts, book covers and canvas paintings. A feminist, Vanessa was Virginia Woolf's sister and mother to three children.

When her father died in 1904, Vanessa and her siblings moved to 46 Gordon Square, Bloomsbury (regarded as the intellectual and literary capital of London). Vanessa organized the Friday Club in 1905, a painting and social club which met and exhibited until about 1920. In 1907, she married Clive Bell, soon to be a noted English art critic. The two formed the *Bloomsbury Group*, it gathered artists, intellectuals, and authors together to meet weekly for intellectual and political discussions.

Vanessa, Roger Fry and Duncan Grant founded an artists' cooperative for the decorative arts, the *Omega Workshops*, in 1913. The workshop, led by them, emphasized bold colors and simple designs for their textiles, pottery, clothing, furniture and interior schemes. Vanessa, trying her hand at different workshop trades, discovered she was particularly gifted in textile design. She soon became known for her interior designs.

Though her artwork was somewhat forgotten (even during her lifetime) and was sometimes thought to have been overshadowed by that of Grant, interest in her work resurfaced with Richard Shone's 1976 publication of *Bloomsbury Portraits*. Since then her textiles and paintings have been featured in solo exhibitions and included in others related to the Bloomsbury circle.

DID YOU KNOW?

1. Vanessa remains one of the most celebrated painters of the Bloomsbury Group.
2. As a feminist, she rejected debates on the ideal and deviant woman.
3. Later in life, she revealed her two half-brothers had sexually abused her.

Goddess of the Teotihuacan civilization of southern Mexico and northern Central America (Maya), Spider Woman, (Grandmother Spider) is often referred to as the "Great Goddess" wearing a frame headdress that often includes the face of a jaguar with a medallion in the center. On the medallion, an owl is usually depicted. The Goddess is shown to be among several spiders which usually have yellow bodies. Spider Woman is believed to have been a Goddess of the underworld, darkness, the earth, water and war. To the ancient Mesoamericans, the jaguar, owl and spiders were considered creatures of darkness.

Jaguars, the largest species of cat in the Americas, is the most important animal in mythology to the Mesoamericans. The fact that *Spider Woman* is associated with the jaguar lends itself to Her greatness. They are surprisingly good swimmers, often found near ponds and small lakes. This implies that the "Great Goddess" is connected to water. Because of their predatory nature, strong jaws, huge claws, and powerful musculature, jaguars are also associated with warfare—again lending these attributes to the Great Goddess.

Spider Woman's owl medallion provides additional proof She is thought to be a Goddess of darkness. The owl is one of the most recognizable night creatures, believed to be a messenger for lords of the underworld. In other cultures around the world, the owl is a symbol of darkness, evil, sorcery, death sometimes cherished as magical and wise.

Spider Woman is also revered by American Indians in the United States. The Pueblo and Navajo have a similar deity. Referring to Her as Spider Grandmother, She shares many traits with the Teotihuacan's Spider Woman. The Great Goddess spins her web, forever creating and connecting everything (String Theory?). Vibrating, pulsating, Her web connects every particle, every force in the universe.

DID YOU KNOW?

1. Murals found in a *Tepantitla* compound of Teotihuacan display a feminine deity that represents a Goddess of vegetation and fertility.
2. Her pictures and statues have been found in other Teotihuacan locations as well.
3. Very little of Her has been found in the Toltec culture.
4. Her colors are red and yellow, she is always shown wearing jewelry.

A Native American heroine and *Tonga/Kizh* medicine woman, Toypurina (1760-1799) was from the *Jachivit* village in Southern California. A resistance fighter, communicator and spiritual leader, she is best known for her direct involvement in the 1785 rebellion against the Mission San Gabriel, run by Spanish missionaries. She rallied several villages to fight against genocide, colonization and cultural oppression.

Born into the *Kumivit* tribe, from the area around Mission San Gabriel, Toypurina was just nine years-old when Spanish colonizers invaded the Los Angeles Basin. Over the next fifty years, more than twenty missions were established on her people's tribal lands while contagious diseases brought in by the Spanish killed thousands of *Tongva* people. The established missions were not only religious outposts, but strong military fortifications where the padres lived side-by-side with armed soldiers.

The Native Americans were punished by violent means if they practiced their spiritual beliefs and sacred customs, going so far as to abuse and rape the women, whipping and caning the men. Toypurina, by the age of twenty-four, was a respected religious leader and medicine woman. Learning to speak many of the Tongva languages made Toypurina a persuasive communicator. The impetus for the revolt seems to have been a banning of tribal dance within mission grounds. The uprising began on the night of October 25, 1785, and was quickly over as the rebels were ambushed by Spanish soldiers. Most of the warriors were captured, including Toypurina.

A trial sentenced seventeen of the warriors to public lashings, reserving the worst punishment for the leaders. Nicolas Jose and Toypurina were found guilty of leading the attack. After eighteen months of brutal imprisonment, Toypurina was *baptized* and exiled to the *San Carlos Borromeo de Carmelo* Mission (Carmel, California).

DID YOU KNOW?

1. According to trial records, Toypurina was forcibly baptized in 1787 at the San Gabriel Mission.
2. Scholars debate whether her marriage to a Spaniard, Manuel Montero, was a marriage of convenience (and one to protect herself from the harsh conditions of Spanish Missions) or acceptance of the Spanish religion.

An Iranian educator and activist, Tuba Azmudeh (1878-1936) established the first girls' school, *Namus* (Honor), in Iran in 1907. She overcame death threats and ignorance in order to educate Iranian females.

Before the 1905 Constitutional Revolution, women had no rights in Iran, child marriages were common and female education was against the Islam code. Tuba wanted to help educate women by starting a school and activists became interested in making changes. The first problem she ran into was the unwillingness of landlords to lease a house for a school, neighbors imagined it would be a center of corruption.

Outraged, the neighbors removed the school signboard or threw stones at it. They recruited loiterers (often psychopaths prowling the streets because there were no asylums) to walk onto school grounds and grin at the terrified girls—they would gather outside the gate to enjoy the frightening display and jeer. In reply to complaints from the school's governors, neighbors stated the best way to avoid further trouble would be to close this "den of iniquity and let no more girls through its gate."

Women's education became a symbol of sexual corruption and the clergy accused schools of being centers of prostitution. The school's founders, all of whom were women, made anxious efforts to justify educating girls by naming the schools in such a way as to encourage acceptance by the clergy. The choice of school names made this evident: *Namus* (Honor), *Effatiyeh* (House of Chastity), *Esmatiyeh* (House of Purity) and *Nasrotiyeh* (School for Veiled Girls).

Tuba Azmudeh continuously received death threats and was denigrated as immoral, the same abuse received by other female activists. Eventually, Namus expanded in size and curriculum and achieved prestige as progressive Iranians sent their daughters there to study. Tuba also began offering courses to illiterate adult women.

DID YOU KNOW?

1. She's credited with inspiring other female educators in Iran.
2. At the time of her death in 1936, Tehran newspapers were generous in their praise of Tuba, *"a devoted woman with strong determination who laid the foundations of Iran's first girls' high school."*

Victoria Claflin Woodhull

"It makes no difference who or what you are, old or young, black or white, pagan, Jew, or Christian, I want to love you all and be loved by you all, and I mean to have your love."

> The first woman to own a brokerage firm on Wall Street, Victoria Woodhull (1838-1927) was an author, activist and mother. She was also the first woman to start a weekly newspaper and the first woman to run for U. S. President. Victoria accomplished everything without any formal education and bundles of courage.

At fifteen, in order to escape her father's brutality, she eloped with Canning Woodhull, a patent medicine salesman claiming to be a physician. Victoria soon learned her husband was an alcoholic and a womanizer causing her to work outside the home to support the family. Returning to New York City, Victoria opened a salon; articulate radicals could spar intellectually while she gained fame as a gifted conversationalist. She acquired many close friends, becoming more interested in women's rights and women's suffrage.

Victoria and Tennie, her sister, were bankrolled by Cornelius Vanderbilt for financial ventures on Wall Street. Soon they opened their own brokerage house in 1879, making a fortune on the exchange. They used their earnings to start a newspaper, it was published for the next six years focusing on women's issues—advancing the editors belief that women could live as equals in the workplace, political arena and family circle. They promoted women's suffrage, labor reform and announced Victoria's candidacy for the presidency.

The paper became notorious for publishing controversial opinions on sex education, free love, short skirts, vegetarianism and licensed prostitution. It also exposed stock swindles, insurance frauds and corrupt congressional land deals. Victoria and Tennie were jailed in 1872, over a published story revealing an affair between the Reverend Henry Beecher and Elizabeth Tilton. They were later acquitted on a technicality but had to pay nearly $500,000 in bail and fines—an outrageous amount for the times.

Did you know?

1. There is an historical marker in Licking County, Ohio, to claim her as the "First Woman Candidate for President of the United States."
2. Victoria's running mate in 1872 was Frederick Douglass.

"Those who refrain from condemning—give their consent".

A celebrated Polish author of historical novels, Zofia Kossak Sczucka (1889-1968) was an improbable objector to Nazi persecution. Her novels were in demand in Poland and with English speakers worldwide, winning many awards. An anti-semitist, she helped save *thousands* of Jews during WWII by co-founding the "Front for the Rebirth of Poland" and "The Provisional Committee to Aid Jews" known as Zegota.

Coming from a prestigious family of writers and artists, it's no surprise Zofia became a famous author. Linked with the Czartak literary group, she wrote primarily for the Catholic press. Even though critics claimed her novels were two dimensional and too sensational, the Polish people cherished her books. Zofia was crowned with the Polish Academy of Literature's "golden laurel" in 1936.

With the German invasion of Poland, she began editing *Polish Lives,* an underground newspaper. Following this, in 1941, Zofia co-founded a clandestine anti-fascist organization, "Front for the Rebirth of Poland." In the underground, she used the name "Weronika." Shocked at the squalid and overflowing Warsaw ghettos, Zofia wrote her infamous pamphlet, "Protest," describing her own anti-Semitic feelings and the horrific conditions found in the ghettoes. Zofia also wrote about the deportation to death camps, calling for people to recognize their Christian conscience and stop the killing.

The following year, Zofia helped found Zegota—an organization of one hundred secret cells that provided money, medicine and food to Jewish people. It's estimated the members forged fifty-thousand documents (!) which included birth, death and marriage certificates. Even baptismal records were forged to "prove" ethnicity. Volunteers, including Zofia, also cared for over three thousand Jews hiding in Warsaw. She appealed numerous times to Poland's exiled government and people for help assisting refugees and she received it.

In 1943, the Gestapo arrested Zofia and transported her to Auschwitz. She survived. Another strong, courageous, gutsy woman!

DID YOU KNOW?

1. There is a memorial tablet commemorating Zofia on the outside of All Saints Parish Church in Gorki Wielkie.
2. In 2018, Zofia was awarded Poland's highest honor, the "Order of the White Eagle." It is one of the oldest distinctions in the world still given today.

"Education….It is an initiation into life of spirit, a training of the human soul in the pursuit of truth and the practice of virtue."

> Vijaya Lakshmi Pandit (1900-1990) was an Indian politician, writer and diplomat elected as the first female president of the United Nations General Assembly. A mother of three, she came from a prominent political family. Vijaya served as India's diplomat to the Soviet Union, the United States and the United Nations. She was president of the All-India Women's Conference (1941-1943) and founder and president of the All-India Save the Children.

Educated by governesses and tutors, Vijaya became the first woman to hold a cabinet post in pre-independent India. She took a leading role in India's politics, even being imprisoned three times in connection with movements of civil disobedience. Elected as a member of the Legislative Assembly of United Provinces in 1937, she became the Minister of Local Self-Government and Public Health until 1939. Vijaya resigned this post to protest the British government's declaration that India participate in WWII.

After her husband's death, she began traveling and lecturing in the US. Returning to India two years later, Vijaya was re-elected. She again began assuming the role of Minister of Local Self-Government and Public Health. That fall, she accepted the diplomatic mission as leader of India's delegation to the UN General Assembly (leading the delegation as well in 1947, 1948, 1952 and 1963).

Shortly after India's independence from Britain was declared in 1947, Vijaya joined the foreign service as a diplomat to the Soviet Union and then as diplomat to the United States in 1949. By September of 1953, Vijaya was the first woman and first Asian ever to be elected president of the U.N. General Assembly. Starting in 1954, she served as Indian ambassador to the United Kingdom. This included a tense period between the two countries at the time of the Suez and Hungarian crises of 1956.

Did you know?

1. Vijaya was described as "a luminous strand in the tapestry of India's freedom struggle."

1. She never received any formal education, yet she was president of the United Nations. The woman had brains galore.

Undeservedly forgotten, Ukrainian master artist Zinaida Yevgenyevna Serebriakova (1884-1967) was one of the first Russian female painters. Overcoming the death of her husband, she cared for her mother and four children after the "October Revolution of 1917." Struggling against poverty after earlier recognition for her works, Zina traveled to Paris. Stopped from returning to her family by Russian authorities, she spent years away from her children and her mother, funneling money back to them for sustenance and shelter. I cannot begin to imagine what life was like under Stalin. Can you?

Born to a renowned artistic family, Zina began drawing at an early age. After the death of her father when she was two, her family was forced to move to her grandfather Benois' apartment in St. Petersburg. Surrounded by artists of every kind, Zina learned music, painting and dance. By the age of twenty-one, Zina had married her cousin Boris. With political unrest mounting, the young couple traveled to Paris for a year. They returned to St. Peterburg and moved to the family estate in the Ukraine with two young sons.

Recognition for Zina's painting began in 1909 with the popularity of her self-portrait *At the Dressing Table*. Creating an immediate sensation with St. Petersburg critics, Zina began to dazzle with her brush. The birth of her two daughters led her to focus on painting females at work. Some of her painting style was classified as Neoclassical Revival—which was a return to classical painting with a contemporary flourish.

At the highpoint of her career, the October Revolution broke out. Tragedy struck and she was forced to take a commission in Paris. With the Russian authorities preventing her return, Zina traveled, painting beauty whether of people or nature. Finally, one year before her death, Zina's paintings were placed on display in Kiev, Leningrad and Moscow earning great acclaim.

DID YOU KNOW?

1. Zinaida finally became a French citizen in 1947.
2. She waited thirty-six years before being allowed to contact her family in Russia underneath "Khruschev's Thaw".

White Buffalo Calf Woman or White Buffalo Maiden (Pte Ska Win) is a sacred woman central to the Lakota tribes as their primary cultural prophet and healer. She gave the Lakota (also known as the Teton Sioux) the "Seven Sacred Rites"—sacred ceremonies to protect Mother Earth. White Buffalo Calf Woman brings inspiration, strength and the power of creation as well as daily protection. She is dressed in white buckskin, symbolizing prayers heard and promise of the prophecy (peace and unity to mankind) being fulfilled.

One of the most important tools in Lakota rituals is a *chanunpa* (sacred pipe). The story told how White Buffalo Calf Woman took the pipe and filled it with local tobaccos, then walked around a lodge four times. With this action She taught the Lakota people about the endless circle—a sacred road of life.

The bowl of the pipe is stone red, representing earth. A buffalo calf is carved in the stone facing the center, symbolizing the four-legged creatures who live as brothers among us. The stem is wood representing all things. Twelve feathers from the Spotted Eagle hang where the stem fits the bowl, representing our winged brothers. The seven circles on the stone bowl represent the seven rites in which the pipe is used.

When people smoke the sacred pipe, they send voices to *Wakan Tanka*, praying for and with everything. The sacred pipe binds the Lakota to all relatives and ancestors. White Buffalo Calf Woman told them the smoke rising from the bowl while She danced was the living breath of the "Great Grandfather of Mystery." She also taught them how to pray and dance. White Buffalo Calf Woman still inspires Native American rituals today, remaining an icon of the Lakota people.

DID YOU KNOW?

1. To Native Americans, the white buffalo calf is the most sacred living thing on Earth.
2. White buffalo births happen rarely, only once in ten million.

"I plead with this audience and the rest of America to give the Negro race proper recognition. Please forget the differences between white and colored. Respect the Negro's good qualities."

Historian Vernie Merze Tate (1905-1996) was a political scientist, philanthropist, author and world traveler. As the first African American to graduate from Oxford, she also was the first black woman to earn a Ph.D. in government and international relations from Radcliffe (the prestigious all-female school that later merged with Harvard) in 1941. Fluent in five languages, Vernie was also a Fulbright Scholar and lecturer (a very prestigious achievement indeed).

Dr. Vernie Tate accomplished many firsts as a Black American woman. Despite *Jim Crow* being alive and well in her home state of Michigan, she found teaching positions in other states. Furthering her education in England, Vernie took advantage of all the social, intellectual and cultural opportunities Oxford offered. With Hitler rising to power, she came back to the U.S. and volunteered to help prepare military officers for duty by training them in the languages and cultures of France and Germany.

Upon receiving her doctorate in government and international relations, Vernie arrived at Howard University where she was contracted as the first Black female historian in its history department in 1942. She spent the next thirty-five years there. Authoring many books, she wrote about European diplomacy, the history of Hawaii, the power struggles in the Pacific and nuclear weapons and their disarmament.

Chosen to represent the U.S. at UNESCO, Vernie counseled Dwight D. Eisenhower about disarmament. In 1950-51, she was awarded a Fulbright Scholarship to teach geopolitics in India. Not only did she teach there, she also taught and lectured in Thailand, Singapore, Hong Kong and the Philippines. Dr. Tate was also commissioned by the U.S. State Department as a photographer, researcher, and filmmaker producing travelogues of the places she'd visited.

DID YOU KNOW?

1. Vernie was valedictorian of her high school class.
2. She won many awards for her academic achievements as she traveled six continents, which speaks loudly for the power of education.

ACKNOWLEDGMENTS

This book would never have been born if not for Lenore Gaudin, who flew to the stars in September of 2020. Heartfelt thanks to Linda Kennard, a fabulous writer who believed my dream and cheered me on from the sidelines. Thanks to Dennis DeRose, my faithful editor—you made my writing better and I am grateful. Much gratitude goes to Michelle Goodhew for her marvelous ideas and creativity providing this book with an unforgettable cover. And for Joris and his staff at CuttingEdge Studio—formatters extraordinare. I raise my glass to friends Carol Clark, Charlotte Carl-Mitchell, Anna Coor and Ginny DeMarco for their marvelous research assistance from the Valley of the Sun—Phoenix, Arizona. To all of you—thanks from the bottom of my heart.

Author's Note

Dear Reader,

You may wonder why I have written this book. Simply put—because it's time; time for me to speak out, for us to celebrate (our) strength, brilliance, compassion, courage, creativity and persistence. You and I can identify with these women—their wisdom, compassion, ability to overcome obstacles like misogyny and racism, their courage to keep going despite the patriarchal culture we still endure in the 21st century.

Limited by word count (120,000) and page number (365), I have tried to give you a glimpse of women with whom we share our humanity, our struggle, our persistence. Any errors you may find—please forgive me. (And let me know by sending a letter or email.) Oftentimes, fact-finding was very challenging simply because women were left out of history books and papers, their accomplishments often ignored. I sincerely hope *365 Days of Gutsy Women* encourages you to do a little research on your own, discovering more about fearless females.

Wishing you all the best reading -

Rosemary Roenfanz

About the Author

With a passion for reading and writing, Rosemary Roenfanz pens this, her debut non-fiction. After a lifetime of motherhood, decorating and financial sales, she took on the challenge, writing *365 Days of Gutsy Women*. Living in the Sonoran Desert of Arizona with her cat Truman, Rosemary loves hiking, bird-watching, caring for her plants, singing in choirs, and talking with friends. She is mother to Eric, Jen, and Charlie; grandmother of Zane, Connor, Brady and Weatherby Rose. If you want to get in touch, please write her at *rosemary.roenfanz@gmail.com*

SOURCES

Abigail Scott Duniway

"She Flies with Her Own Wings"
http://asduniway.org/home/?__cf_chl_jschl_tk__=81977c82281fd74673b4756773e
86af6230d4f13-1611074961-0-ASFBumvEZWTeuNmdAmKJz_lAADtFvcYpg3g-
sMpDgBr86roZ54tKx0384qAdNoq9Bxrljo6LTUcOuYBqTzS3MmqJ8Rzh6Zm-Da-
FoGBSBhvzsAfJJUtyQExGqHf6LA4KOqI-GQpafnEh6DqDdPYCAs0ZJYuDg34e3k-
KvLAroYF3vT3jVTTNMA2jIr_xKpcnX5qZCe-6982lk_x6JQIfcao2Sy_Dk6wU96Ao_
iksBwBM_ixjJhYNf_0882fIBecn7NjjI_66rGM7QLVkM5lGv8ieJHef54L-8DQGwIMIO-
jqan57KY7Qg

https://www.oregonencyclopedia.org/articles/abigail_scott_duniway/#.YAcEZm-
RKiSI

https://en.wikipedia.org/wiki/Abigail_Scott_Duniway

Ada Lovelace

Wolfram, Stephen, Untangling the Tale of Ada Lovelace https://writings.stephenwol-
fram.com/2015/12/untangling-the-tale-of-ada-lovelace/

Ada Lovelace; Analyst, Metaphysician, and Founder of Scientific Computing
https://sdsc.edu/ScienceWomen/lovelace.html https://www.biography.com/scholar/
ada-lovelace

Adelina Otero-Warren

https://www.nps.gov/people/nina-otero-warren.htm

https://americacomesalive.com/adelina-otero-warren-1881-1965-suffragist/

https://en.wikipedia.org/wiki/Adelina_Otero-Warren

Adrestia

https://www.greekmythology.com/Other_Gods/Minor_Gods/Adrestia/adrestia.html

https://en.wikipedia.org/wiki/Adrasteia

Ahmose Nefertari

https://www.historyofroyalwomen.com/ahmose-nefertari/queen-ahmose-nefertari-
first-gods-wife-amun/

https://ancientegyptonline.co.uk/ahmose-nefertari/

https://www.encyclopedia.com/women/dictionaries-thesauruses-pic-
tures-and-press-releases/ahmose-nefertari-c-1570-1535-bce

Aine

https://thecelticjourney.wordpress.com/2013/04/17/aine/

https://www.ireland-information.com/irish-mythology/aine-irish-legend.html
Airmid

https://talesfromthewood.ie/airmid-the-irish-goddess-of-healing/

https://orderwhitemoon.org/goddess/Airmid/airmid.html

https://www.ancientpages.com/2018/02/02/airmid-irish-goddess-of-healing-and-herbs-and-one-of-the-tuatha-de-danann/

Akhilandeshwari

http://www.sutrajournal.com/akhilandeshwari-the-power-of-brokenness-by-laura-amazzone

https://www.hinduismtoday.com/modules/smartsection/item.php?itemid=5880

Ala

https://journeyingtothegoddess.wordpress.com/2012/03/14/goddess-ala/

https://www.africaresource.com/rasta/sesostris-the-great-the-egyptian-hercules/ani-the-mother-of-the-igbos-the-many-manifestations-of-ishtar/

https://en.wikipedia.org/wiki/Ala_(odinani)

Albertine Necker de Saussure

https://www.encyclopedia.com/women/dictionaries-thesauruses-pictures-and-press-releases/necker-de-saussure-albertine-1766-1841

https://en.wikipedia.org/wiki/Albertine_Necker_de_Saussure

Alexandra Kollontai

https://www.encyclopedia.com/history/encyclopedias-almanacs-transcripts-and-maps/kollontai-alexandra-mikhailovna

https://biography.yourdictionary.com/aleksandra-mikhailovna-kollontai

Alexandra van Gripenberg

https://www.brooklynmuseum.org/eascfa/dinner_party/heritage_floor/alexandra_van_grippenberg

https://www.encyclopedia.com/women/encyclopedias-almanacs-transcripts-and-maps/van-grippenberg-alexandra-1859-1913

https://prabook.com/web/aleksandra.gripenberg/727641

Alice Ball

https://www.thehindu.com/children/know-the-scientist-alice-augusta-ball/article33746836.ece

https://www.rejectedprincesses.com/blog/modern-worthies/alice-ball

Alice Freeman Palmer

https://education.stateuniversity.com/pages/2308/Palmer-Alice-Freeman-1855-1902.html

https://amazingwomeninhistory.com/alice-freeman-palmer-womens-education-pioneer/

Althea Sherman

http://uipress.lib.uiowa.edu/bdi/DetailsPage.aspx?id=340

https://shermanswifttower.org/althea-sherman/

https://en.wikipedia.org/wiki/Althea_Sherman

Amaterasu

https://www.ancient.eu/Amaterasu/

https://www.newworldencyclopedia.org/entry/amaterasu

Amy Lowell

https://www.poetryfoundation.org/poets/amy-lowell

https://poets.org/poet/amy-lowell

Amy Marcy Cheney Beach

https://www.thoughtco.com/amy-beach-composer-3529813

https://www.amybeach.org/about/biography/

https://www.britannica.com/biography/Amy-Marcy-Beach

Angelica Kauffman

https://nmwa.org/art/artists/angelica-kauffman/

https://www.britannica.com/biography/Angelica-Kauffmann

https://www.theartstory.org/artist/kauffman-angelica/life-and-legacy/

Anna Akhmatova

https://www.poetryfoundation.org/poets/anna-akhmatova

https://www.britannica.com/biography/Anna-Akhmatova

http://www.saint-petersburg.com/famous-people/anna-akhmatova/

Anna Julia Cooper

https://blackhistory.news.columbia.edu/people/anna-julia-cooper

https://douglassday.org/cooper/

https://en.wikipedia.org/wiki/Anna_J._Cooper

Anna Leonowens

https://www.thecanadianencyclopedia.ca/en/article/anna-harriette-leonowens
http://www.biographi.ca/en/bio/edwards_anna_harriette_14E.html
https://www.thoughtco.com/anna-leonowens-about-3529497

Anna Pavlova

https://www.imdb.com/namm0667816/bio
https://en.wikipedia.org/wiki/Anna_Pavlova

Anne Carroll Moore

https://www.encyclopedia.com/women/encyclopedias-almanacs-transcripts-and-maps/moore-anne-carroll-1871-1961
https://www.nypl.org/sites/default/files/archivalcollections/pdf/mooreac.pdf

Anne Clough

https://spartacus-educational.com/Wclough.htm
https://www.brooklynmuseum.org/eascfa/dinner_party/heritage_floor/anne_clough

Anne Morrow Lindbergh

https://www.nytimes.com/2001/02/08/books/anne-morrow-lindbergh-94-dies-champion-of-flight-and-women-s-concerns.html
https://en.wikipedia.org/wiki/Anne_Morrow_Lindbergh
https://www.nationalgeographic.com/history/article/she-was-a-record-breaking-aviator-but-her-husband-overshadowed-her-feats

Antonia Maury

http://vcencyclopedia.vassar.edu/alumni/antonia-maury.html
https://www.encyclopedia.com/people/history/historians-miscellaneous-biographies/antonia-maury

Aphra Behn

https://www.poetryfoundation.org/poets/aphra-behn
https://writersinspire.org/content/who-aphra-behn

Aphrodite

https://www.ancient.eu/Aphrodite/
https://www.britannica.com/topic/Aphrodite-Greek-mythology
https://www.thoughtco.com/facts-about-greek-goddess-aphrodite-1524419

Aqualtune

https://face2faceafrica.com/article/the-story-of-the-kongo-princess-who-led-10000-men-into-battle-and-was-later-enslaved-by-the-portuguese

https://kathmanduk2.wordpress.com/2009/02/06/black-history-month-black-hero-ines-part-2-aqualtune-an-enslaved-congo-princess/

Arabella Mansfield

http://uipress.lib.uiowa.edu/bdi/DetailsPage.aspx?id=249

https://law.jrank.org/pages/12257/Mansfield-Arabella.html

https://iowaculture.gov/history/education/educator-resources/primary-source-sets/government-democracy-and-laws/arabella

Artemis

https://www.britannica.com/topic/Artemis-Greek-goddess

https://www.ancient.eu/artemis/

Artemisia I, Queen of Halicarnassus

https://www.thoughtco.com/artemisia-warrior-queen-of-halicarnassus-3528382

https://peoplepill.com/people/artemisia-i-of-caria

https://www.ancient.eu/Artemisia_I_of_Caria/

Athena

https://www.greekmythology.com/Olympians/Athena/athena.html

https://www.ancient.eu/athena/

Audre Lorde

https://www.poetryfoundation.org/poets/audre-lorde

https://en.wikipedia.org/wiki/Audre_Lorde

https://www.theparisreview.org/blog/2020/09/17/the-legacy-of-audre-lorde/

Augusta Holmes

https://www.encyclopedia.com/women/encyclopedias-almanacs-tran-scripts-and-maps/holmes-augusta-1847-1903

https://www.allmusic.com/artist/augusta-holmès-mn0002286863/biography

https://www.rcm.ac.uk/research/archivedprojects/augustaholmes/

https://www.wqxr.org/story/celebrating-music-augusta-holmes/

Augusta Savage

https://americanart.si.edu/artist/augusta-savage-4269

https://dos.myflorida.com/cultural/programs/florida-artists-hall-of-fame/augus-ta-savage/

Ban Zhao

https://www.encyclopedia.com/women/encyclopedias-almanacs-transcripts-and-maps/ban-zhao-c-45-c-120-ce

https://www.newworldencyclopedia.org/entry/Ban_Zhao

Barbara McClintock

https://www.nobelprize.org/prizes/medicine/1983/mcclintock/facts/

https://www.pnas.org/content/109/50/20198

https://profiles.nlm.nih.gov/spotlight/ll/feature/biographical-overview

Barbara

https://www.classicfm.com/discover-music/barbara-strozzi/

https://www.amodernreveal.com/barbara-strozzi

https://www.allmusic.com/artist/barbara-strozzi-mn0000365512/biography

Beatrix Potter

https://www.peterrabbit.com/about-beatrix-potter/

https://www.biography.com/writer/beatrix-potter

https://beatrixpottersociety.org.uk/?doing_wp_cron=1612553599.8117630481719970703125

Belva Lockwood

https://blogs.loc.gov/headlinesandheroes/2020/09/belva-lockwood-suffragist-lawyer-and-presidential-candidate/

https://en.wikipedia.org/wiki/Belva_Ann_Lockwood

https://www.womenofthehall.org/inductee/belva-lockwood/

Bertha Bracey OBE

https://www.quakersintheworld.org/quakers-in-action/118/Kindertransport

https://en.wikipedia.org/wiki/Bertha_Bracey

http://jackwhite.net/quakers/bracey.html

Berthe Morisot

https://www.biography.com/artist/berthe-morisot

https://daily.jstor.org/how-impressionist-berthe-morisot-painted-womens-lives/

https://biography.yourdictionary.com/berthe-morisot

Bessie Smith

https://www.npr.org/2018/01/05/575422226/forebears-bessie-smith-the-empress-of-the-blues

https://www.biography.com/musician/bessie-smith

Betsey Guppy Chamberlain

https://www.newenglandhistoricalsociety.com/betsey-guppy-chamberlain-promotes-radical-notion-indians-people/

https://www.womenhistoryblog.com/2015/10/betsey-guppy-chamberlain.html

https://en.wikipedia.org/wiki/Betsey_Guppy_Chamberlain

Billie Holliday

https://www.biography.com/news/billie-holiday-strange-fruit?cmpid=email-bio-biography-2021-0303-03032021&om_rid=

https://billieholiday.com/bio/

https://en.wikipedia.org/wiki/List_of_awards_and_nominations_received_by_Billie_Holiday

Blodeuwedd

https://www.sunsigns.org/celtic-symbols-of-blodeuwedd/ https://en.wikipedia.org/wiki/Blodeuwedd

Boann

https://feminismandreligion.com/2016/07/27/boann-celtic-goddess-of-inspiration-and-creativity-by-judith-shaw/

http://www.thewhitegoddess.co.uk/divinity_of_the_day/irish/boann.asp

Borte Ujin

https://culturacolectiva.com/history/borte-ujin-mongol-empress

https://en.wikipedia.org/wiki/Börte

Boudicca

https://www.ancient.eu/Boudicca/

https://biographics.org/boudicca-biography-the-celtic-warrior-queen/

https://www.historyofroyalwomen.com/boudicca/boudicca-celtic-queen-defied-rome/

Bridget "Biddy" Mason

https://www.blackpast.org/african-american-history/mason-bridget-biddy-1818-1891/

https://www.nps.gov/people/biddymason.htm

Brigid (Brigantes)

https://mythopedia.com/celtic-mythology/gods/brigid/

https://en.wikipedia.org/wiki/Brigid
https://www.brighid.org.uk/goddess.html

Cai Yan

https://www.encyclopedia.com/women/encyclopedias-almanacs-transcripts-and-maps/cai-yan-c-162-239
https://peoplepill.com/people/cai-wenji
https://www.followcn.com/women/2018/06/15/cai-yan/

Caroline Herschel

https://mathshistory.st-andrews.ac.uk/Biographies/Herschel_Caroline/
https://royalsocietypublishing.org/doi/10.1098/rsta.2014.0210
https://www.sheisanastronomer.org/history/carolineherschel

Carrie Chapman Catt

https://www.catt.org/biography.html
https://www.womenshistory.org/education-resources/biographies/carrie-chapman-catt
https://en.wikipedia.org/wiki/Carrie_Chapman_Catt

Cartimandua Queen of Brigantes

https://www.ancient-origins.net/history-famous-people/mighty-cartimandua-queen-brigantes-tribe-and-friend-rome-002805
https://www.historic-uk.com/HistoryUK/HistoryofEngland/Cartimandua-Cartismandua/

Catharine Beecher

https://biography.yourdictionary.com/catharine-beecher
https://www.thoughtco.com/catharine-beecher-4691465

Catherine the Great

https://www.history.com/news/8-things-you-didnt-know-about-catherine-the-great
https://www.biography.com/news/catherine-the-great-peter-iii-marriage

Cecile Chaminade

http://www.listenmusicculture.com/mastery/cecile-chaminade
https://www.encyclopedia.com/people/literature-and-arts/music-history-composers-and-performers-biographies/cecile-chaminade

Changing Woman (Asdzaa Nadleehe)

https://www.encyclopedia.com/history/encyclopedias-almanacs-transcripts-and-maps/changing-woman

https://www.firstpeople.us/FP-Html-Legends/Changing_Woman-Navajo.html

Charlotte Mason

https://charlottemason.com

https://en.wikipedia.org/wiki/Charlotte_Mason

Chinquinha Gonzago

https://www.classicfm.com/discover-music/chiquinha-gonzaga-brazil-first-woman-conductor-choro-composer/

https://www.classicalmpr.org/story/2018/03/30/women-in-music-weekly-highlight-chiquinha-gonzaga

https://en.wikipedia.org/wiki/Chiquinha_Gonzaga

Christina Rossetti

https://www.poetryfoundation.org/poets/christina-rossetti

https://poets.org/poet/christina-rossetti

https://www.bl.uk/people/christina-rossetti#

Christine de Pizan

https://www.ancient.eu/Christine_de_Pizan/

https://www.brooklynmuseum.org/eascfa/dinner_party/place_settings/christine_de_pisan

https://www.britannica.com/biography/Christine-de-Pisan

Circe

https://www.greekmythology.com/Other_Gods/Circe/circe.html

https://www.ancient.eu/article/1372/interview-circe-by-madeline-miller/

https://www.britannica.com/topic/Circe-Greek-mythology

Clara Barton

https://www.nps.gov/clba/learn/historyculture/cbpaving.htm

https://www.womenshistory.org/education-resources/biographies/clara-barton

Clara Foltz

http://wlh.law.stanford.edu/wp-content/uploads/2010/10/AmNatBiogentry.pdf

http://www.laalmanac.com/crime/cr62.php

Clara Schumann

https://www.dw.com/en/the-power-woman-of-classical-music-clara-schumann/a-50415324

https://www.laphil.com/about/watch-and-listen/get-to-know-clara-schumann

https://www.classicfm.com/composers/schumann-c/

Cleopatra VII

https://www.ancient.eu/Cleopatra_VII/

https://www.biography.com/royalty/cleopatra-vii

Constance Markievicz

https://www.newworldencyclopedia.org/entry/Constance_Georgine,_Countess_Markiewicz

https://www.irishtimes.com/culture/heritage/constance-markievicz-an-infamous-advocate-for-women-and-workers-1.3718245

Daisy Bates

https://www.nps.gov/people/dbates.htm

https://www.womenshistory.org/education-resources/biographies/daisy-bates

https://ualrexhibits.org/legacy/bates/

https://www.thoughtco.com/daisy-bates-biography-3528278

Dame Ethyl Mary Smyth DBE

https://www.ethelsmyth.org

https://www.exploringsurreyspast.org.uk/themes/people/musicians/dame_ethel_smyth/

Devi

https://www.smithsonianmag.com/history/the-great-goddess-devi-68120189/

https://www.ancient.eu/Devi/

https://en.wikipedia.org/wiki/Devi

Doris Humphrey

https://www.britannica.com/biography/Doris-Humphrey

https://biography.yourdictionary.com/doris-humphrey

https://en.wikipedia.org/wiki/Doris_Humphrey

Dorothea Dix

https://www.ncbi.nlm.nih.gov/pmc/articles/PMC1470530/

https://www.womenshistory.org/education-resources/biographies/dorothea-dix

https://en.wikipedia.org/wiki/Dorothea_Dix

Dorothea Lange

https://www.biography.com/artist/dorothea-lange

https://www.npr.org/templates/story/story.php?storyId=126289455

https://en.wikipedia.org/wiki/Dorothea_Lange

Dorothy Bonarjee

https://www.bbc.com/news/stories-55430717

https://www.andrewwhitehead.net/blog/dorothy-bonarjee-bachelor-of-law

https://biography.wales/article/s12-BONA-NOE-1894

Dorothy Crowfoot Hodgkin

https://www.famousscientists.org/dorothy-hodgkin/

https://www.encyclopedia.com/people/medicine/biochemistry-biographies/dorothy-mary-crowfoot-hodgkin

https://www.sciencehistory.org/historical-profile/dorothy-crowfoot-hodgkin

Dorothy Parker

https://www.biography.com/writer/dorothy-parker

https://www.newworldencyclopedia.org/entry/Dorothy_Parker

Dr. Elizabeth Gould Bell

https://www.ncbi.nlm.nih.gov/pmc/articles/PMC5849977/

https://en.wikipedia.org/wiki/Elizabeth_Gould_Bell

Durga

https://indiacurrents.com/what-does-goddess-durga-symbolize/

https://www.scienceandnonduality.com/article/the-divine-mother-durga

Eagle Woman

https://www.britannica.com/biography/Eagle-Woman

https://peoplepill.com/people/eagle-woman

Edith Abbott

https://miamisclc.org/edith-abbot-the-first-woman-in-u-s-history-to-become-dean/

https://en.wikipedia.org/wiki/Edith_Abbott

https://www.ssa.uchicago.edu/edith-abbott

Edith Cavell

https://edithcavell.org.uk/

https://en.wikipedia.org/wiki/Edith_Cavell

Edith Cowan OBE

https://adb.anu.edu.au/biography/cowan-edith-dircksey-5791

https://www.womenaustralia.info/leaders/biogs/WLE0162b.htm

https://www.thefamouspeople.com/profiles/edith-cowan-7227.php

Edith Windsor

https://www.npr.org/sections/thetwo-way/2017/09/12/550502373/edith-windsor-lgbtq-advocate- who-fought-the-defense-of-marriage-act-dies-at-88

https://www.newyorker.com/tag/edith-windsor

Edmonia Lewis

https://americanart.si.edu/artist/edmonia-lewis-2914

https://www.smithsonianmag.com/smithsonian-institution/sculptor-edmonia-lewis-shattered-gender-race-expectations-19th-century-america-180972934/

https://www.biography.com/artist/edmonia-lewis

Edna St. Vincent Millay

https://poets.org/poet/edna-st-vincent-millay

http://www.millay.org/aboutmillay.php

https://www.biography.com/writer/edna-st-vincent-millay

Elizabeth Blackwell

https://www.womenshistory.org/education-resources/biographies/elizabeth-blackwell

https://cfmedicine.nlm.nih.gov/physicians/biography_35.html

https://www.biography.com/scientist/elizabeth-blackwell

Eleanor of Aquitaine

https://www.history.com/topics/british-history/eleanor-of-aquitaine

http://www.bbc.co.uk/history/historic_figures/eleanor_of_aquitaine.shtml

Eleanor Roosevelt

https://www.whitehouse.gov/about-the-white-house/first-families/anna-eleanor-roosevelt/

https://www.womenshistory.org/education-resources/biographies/eleanor-roosevelt

Elisabeth Abegg

https://www.yadvashem.org/yv/en/exhibitions/righteous-teachers/abegg.asp

https://www.encyclopedia.com/women/encyclopedias-almanacs-transcripts-and-maps/abegg-elisabeth-1882-1974

https://www.churchtimes.co.uk/articles/2020/24-january/faith/faith-features/a-stand-against-cruelty

Elizabeth Barrett Browning
https://poets.org/poet/elizabeth-barrett-browning
https://www.biography.com/writer/elizabeth-barrett-browning
https://www.notablebiographies.com/Br-Ca/Browning-Elizabeth-Barrett.html

Elizabeth Cabot Cary Agassiz
https://www.womenhistoryblog.com/2014/02/elizabeth-cary-agassiz.html
https://www.encyclopedia.com/women/encyclopedias-almanacs-transcripts-and-maps/agassiz-elizabeth-cary-1822-1907
https://peoplepill.com/people/elizabeth-cabot-agassiz/

Elizabeth Cady Stanton
https://www.womenshistory.org/education-resources/biographies/elizabeth-cady-stanton
https://www.history.com/topics/womens-history/elizabeth-cady-stanton
https://www.biography.com/activist/elizabeth-cady-stanton

Elizabeth Hobbs Keckley
https://www.whitehousehistory.org/from-slavery-to-the-white-house-the-extraordinary-life-of-elizabeth-keckly
https://www.virginiahistory.org/collections-and-resources/virginia-history-explorer/elizabeth-keckley
https://docsouth.unc.edu/neh/keckley/summary.html

Elizabeth I
https://www.biography.com/royalty/queen-elizabeth-i
https://www.history.com/this-day-in-history/elizabeth-crowned-queen-of-england
https://www.historic-uk.com/HistoryUK/HistoryofEngland/Queen-Elizabeth-I/

Elizabeth Key Grinstead
https://www.zinnedproject.org/news/tdih/elizabeth-key-wins-freedom/
https://www.lva.virginia.gov/public/dvb/bio.php?b=Key_Elizabeth_fl_1655-1660
https://www.womenhistoryblog.com/2008/01/elizabeth-key.html
https://www.thoughtco.com/elizabeth-key-history-of-american-slavery-3530408

Elizabeth Peabody
https://www.newworldencyclopedia.org/entry/Elizabeth_Peabody

https://www.thoughtco.com/elizabeth-palmer-peabody-biography-3530587
https://www.historynet.com/elizabeth-peabody-an-old-soul.htm

Elizabeth Philpot
https://trowelblazers.com/elizabeth-philpot/
https://www.tchevalier.com/remarkablecreatures/background/historicalfigures/index.html

Elizabeth Van Lew
https://www.nps.gov/people/elizabeth-van-lew.htm
https://www.battlefields.org/learn/biographies/elizabeth-van-lew
https://www.lva.virginia.gov/public/dvb/bio.php?b=Van_Lew_Elizabeth

Elizebeth Friedman
https://www.nsa.gov/About-Us/Current-Leadership/Article-View/Article/1623028/elizebeth-s-friedman/
https://time.com/5928583/elizebeth-friedman-codebreaker/

Ella J. Baker
https://ellabakercenter.org/who-was-ella-baker/
https://www.womenofthehall.org/inductee/ella-baker/
https://en.wikipedia.org/wiki/Ella_Baker

Ella Fitzgerald
https://www.npr.org/2019/09/05/749021799/the-joy-of-ella-fitzgeralds-accessible-elegance
https://en.wikipedia.org/wiki/Ella_Fitzgerald
http://www.ellafitzgerald.com/about/biography

Elvia Carrillo Puerto
Elvia Carrillo Puerto
https://womensactivism.nyc/stories/6525

Empodera/Elvia Carillo Puerto
https://www.lafronterasupply.com/our-dna-facts-about-mexico/elvia-carrillo-puerto-history

Emily Carr
https://www.thecanadianencyclopedia.ca/en/article/emily-carr
https://www.sothebys.com/en/artists/emily-carr

Emily Dickinson

https://www.poetryfoundation.org/poets/emily-dickinson

https://www.biography.com/writer/emily-dickinson

Emily Greene Balch

https://www.nobelprize.org/prizes/peace/1946/balch/biographical/

https://www.massmoments.org/moment-details/emily-greene-balch-born.html

https://www.fembio.org/english/biography.php/woman/biography/emily-greene-balch/

Emmeline Pankhurst

https://www.biography.com/activist/emmeline-pankhurst

https://www.independent.co.uk/life-style/women/emmeline-pankhurst-who-womens-suffrage-leader-suffragette-political-activist-statue-a8681901.html

https://www.thoughtco.com/emmeline-pankhurst-1779832

Empress Dowager Cixi

https://www.smithsonianmag.com/history/cixi-the-woman-behind-the-throne-22312071/

https://www.chinahighlights.com/travelguide/china-history/empress-cixi-facts.htm

Empress Wu Zetian

https://www.smithsonianmag.com/history/the-demonization-of-empress-wu-20743091/

https://www.ancient.eu/Wu_Zetian/

Enheduanna

https://www.ancient.eu/Enheduanna/

https://theconversation.com/hidden-women-of-history-enheduanna-princess-priestess-and-the-worlds-first-known-author-109185

https://en.wikipedia.org/wiki/Enheduanna

Eostre

https://thecelticjourney.wordpress.com/tag/eostre/

https://www.goddessandgreenman.co.uk/ostara/

Erzulie Freda

https://occult-world.com/ezili-freda-dahomey/

http://freesophia.com/erzulie-freda-the-goddess-projectmade-in-her-image/

Esther Martinez (aka P'oe Tsawa)

https://www.nmhistoricwomen.org/location/esther-martinez-poe-tsawa/

https://www.languagepolicy.org/post/esther-martinez-native-american-languages-program-passes-house

https://savingplaces.org/stories/esther-martinez-protecting-the-intangible-heritage-of-the-tewa-people#.YB3GqC1h3q0

Etheldred Benett

https://www.strangescience.net/ebenett.htm

https://www.encyclopedia.com/science/encyclopedias-almanacs-transcripts-and-maps/benett-etheldred-1776-1845

https://westcountrygeology.com/etheldred-benett/

Eva Peron

https://www.biography.com/political-figure/eva-peron

https://www.thoughtco.com/eva-peron-1779803

https://moderndiplomacy.eu/2020/12/19/eva-peron-the-legacy-and-the-contributions-to-the-feminist-movement-in-argentina/

Fannie Barrier Williams

https://www.blackpast.org/african-american-history/williams-fannie-barrier-1855-1944/

https://rrlc.org/winningthevote/biographies/fannie-barrier-williams/

Fanny Jackson Coppin

https://www.blackpast.org/african-american-history/coppin-fannie-jackson-1837-1913/

https://www.encyclopedia.com/women/encyclopedias-almanacs-transcripts-and-maps/coppin-fanny-jackson-1837-1913

https://searchblackandeducation.com/stories/2019/4/2/fanny-jackson-coppin

Fanny Lou Hamer

https://www.womenshistory.org/education-resources/biographies/fannie-lou-hamer

https://www.washingtonpost.com/news/retropolis/wp/2017/10/06/civil-rights-crusader-fannie-lou-hamer-defied-men-and-presidents-who-tried-to-silence-her/

Fanny Mendelssohn

https://www.loc.gov/item/ihas.200156440/

http://www.fannyhensel.de/hensel_eng/bio_frame.htm

Fatima al-Fihri

https://manchesteruniversitypress.co.uk/blog/2018/03/08/fatima-al-fihri-founder-worlds-first-university/

https://www.wisemuslimwomen.org/muslim-woman/fatima-al-fihri-6/

https://oxfordaasc.com/view/10.1093/acref/9780195301731.001.0001/acref-9780195301731-e-48736

Florence Beatrice Price

https://www.classicfm.com/discover-music/florence-price/

http://afrovoices.com/florence-price-biography/

Florence Nightingale OM, RRC, DStJ

https://www.history.com/topics/womens-history/florence-nightingale-1

https://www.womenshistory.org/education-resources/biographies/florence-nightingale

https://www.biography.com/scientist/florence-nightingale

Frances Burney

https://writersinspire.org/content/frances-burney-mother-english-fiction

https://en.wikipedia.org/wiki/Frances_Burney

Frances Dana Barker Gage

https://uudb.org/articles/francesgage.html

https://www.civilwarmed.org/surgeons-call/gage/

https://www.mariettatimes.com/news/202/influential-women-frances-dana-barker-gage

https://www.womenhistoryblog.com/2008/05/frances-dana-gage.html

Frances Densmore

http://collections.mnhs.org/mnauthors/10001192

http://siarchives.si.edu/research/sciservwomendensmore.html

http://news.minnesota.publicradio.org/features/199702/01_smiths_densmore/docs/1early.shtml

Frances Ellen Watkins Harper

https://www.womenshistory.org/education-resources/biographies/frances-ellen-watkins-harper

https://www.poetryfoundation.org/poets/frances-ellen-watkins-harper

Francesca Caccini

https://www.amodernreveal.com/francesca-caccini
https://www.lib.uchicago.edu/efts/IWW/BIOS/A0083.html

Frederika Bremer

Frederika Bremer, Swedish Feminist Writer
https://www.thoughtco.com/fredrika-bremer-biography-3530875
http://www.fredrikabremer.net/aboutbremer.html
https://en.wikipedia.org/wiki/Fredrika_Bremer

Frida Kahlo

https://www.fridakahlo.org
https://www.biography.com/artist/frida-kahlo
https://en.wikipedia.org/wiki/Frida_Kahlo

Frigga (Freya)

https://www.ancient-origins.net/myths-legends-europe/frigg-queen-asgard-beloved-norse-goddess-mother-009707
https://sites.psu.edu/miamidolphins/2017/02/23/freya-and-frigg/
https://mythopedia.com/norse-mythology/gods/freya/

Gabriela Mistral

https://www.nobelprize.org/prizes/literature/1945/mistral/biographical/
https://www.poetryfoundation.org/poets/gabriela-mistral

Gaia

https://www.theoi.com/Protogenos/Gaia.html
https://www.greeklegendsandmyths.com/gaia.html

Ganga

https://www.ancient.eu/Ganges/
https://www.iloveindia.com/spirituality/goddesses/ganga/index.html
https://journeyingtothegoddess.wordpress.com/2012/01/12/goddess-ganga/

Gaspara Stampa

https://www.poetryfoundation.org/poets/gaspara-stampa
https://mypoeticside.com/poets/gaspara-stampa-poems

Geertruida Wijsmuller-Meijer

https://www.fozmuseum.com/explore-foz/the-unknown-dutch-holocaust-hero-who-saved-over-10000-children/

https://righteous.yadvashem.org/index.html?language=en&itemId=4018228

https://www.timesofisrael.com/truus-wijsmuller-saved-1000s-of-jews-in-wwii-so-why-has-no-one-heard-of-her/

George Eliot

http://www.bbc.co.uk/history/historic_figures/eliot_george.shtml

https://www.notablebiographies.com/Du-Fi/Eliot-George.html

https://www.newworldencyclopedia.org/entry/George_Eliot

Georgia O'Keeffe

https://www.georgiaokeeffe.net

https://www.biography.com/artist/georgia-okeeffe

https://www.metmuseum.org/toah/hd/geok/hd_geok.htm

Germaine Tailleferre

https://www.wisemusicclassical.com/composer/1557/Germaine-Tailleferre/

https://www.billaudot.com/en/composer.php?p=Germaine&n=Tailleferre

https://www.allmusic.com/artist/germaine-tailleferre-mn0001866250/biography

Gerty Cori

https://www.jewishvirtuallibrary.org/gerty-theresa-radnitz-cori

https://jwa.org/encyclopedia/article/cori-gerty-theresa

Golda Meir

https://www.jewishvirtuallibrary.org/golda-meir

https://www.biography.com/political-figure/golda-meir

Grace Gallatin Seton

https://www.encyclopedia.com/women/encyclopedias-almanacs-transcripts-and-maps/seton-grace-gallatin-1872-1959

https://wednesdayswomen.com/grace-gallatin-seton-adventurer-and-champion-of-women-rights/

https://snaccooperative.org/ark:/99166/w6np4zq4

Grace Mary Crowfoot

https://journals.openedition.org/ema/3606

https://peoplepill.com/people/grace-crowfoot

Grandma Moses

https://www.biography.com/artist/grandma-moses
https://nmwa.org/art/artists/grandma-moses-anna-mary-robertson-moses/
https://en.wikipedia.org/wiki/Grandma_Moses

Gula

https://www.ancient.eu/Gula/
https://hekint.org/2018/12/06/from-the-goddess-of-healing-to-hair-of-the-dog-the-role-of-canines-in-health-myth-and-fact/

Gwendolyn Brooks

https://www.poetryfoundation.org/poets/gwendolyn-brooks
https://www.npr.org/sections/codeswitch/2017/05/29/530081834/remembering-the-great-poet-gwendolyn-brooks-at-100

Hallie M. Daggett

https://www.fs.usda.gov/detail/r2/learning/history-culture/?cid=stelprdb5360607
https://www.nnrg.org/women-in-the-woods-then-and-now/
https://history.denverlibrary.org/news/women-united-states-forest-service
https://foresthistory.org/wp-content/uploads/2017/01/Daggett.pdf

Hannah Arendt

https://www.newstatesman.com/culture/books/2019/03/hannah-arendt-resurgence-philosophy-relevance
https://www.jewishvirtuallibrary.org/hannah-arendt
https://plato.stanford.edu/entries/arendt/

Hanwi

https://www.tirzaschaefer.com/hanwi
https://www.crystalvaults.com/goddess-hanwi/?shape=144

Hanya Holm

https://www.copyright.gov/history/lore/pdfs/201502%20CLore_February2015.pdf
https://www.encyclopedia.com/humanities/encyclopedias-almanacs-transcripts-and-maps/holm-hanya

Harriet Beecher Stowe

https://www.history.com/topics/american-civil-war/harriet-beecher-stowe
https://www.biography.com/activist/harriet-beecher-stowe
https://connecticuthistory.org/the-most-famous-american-in-the-world/

https://en.wikipedia.org/wiki/Harriet_Beecher_Stowe

Harriet Forten Purvis

https://www.womenhistoryblog.com/2016/08/harriet-forten-purvis.html

https://en.wikipedia.org/wiki/Harriet_Forten_Purvis

https://www.encyclopedia.com/women/encyclopedias-almanacs-transcripts-and-maps/purvis-harriet-forten-1810-1875

Harriet Jacobs

https://www.pbs.org/wgbh/aia/part4/4p2923.html

https://docsouth.unc.edu/fpn/jacobs/bio.html

https://www.ncpedia.org/biography/jacobs-harriet

Harriet Tubman

https://www.biography.com/activist/harriet-tubman

https://www.womenshistory.org/education-resources/biographies/harriet-tubman

https://www.battlefields.org/learn/biographies/harriet-tubman

Hathshepsut

https://www.history.com/topics/ancient-history/hatshepsut

https://www.ancient.eu/hatshepsut/

https://www.nationalgeographic.com/culture/people/reference/hatshepsut/

Hecate

https://www.ancient.eu/Hecate/

https://www.greekmythology.com/Other_Gods/Hecate/hecate.html

https://occult-world.com/hecate/

Helen of Anjou

http://www.serbia.com/visit-serbia/natural-beauties/unique-nature/the-valley-of-lilacs-a-proof-of-love/

https://www.serbianorthodoxmonastery.org/st-helen-of-anjou-fellowship/

https://www.geni.com/people/Helen-of-Anjou/5114171182350103651

https://www.serbianmonitor.com/en/tag/helen-of-anjou/

Herma Albertson Baggley

https://www.nps.gov/parkhistory/online_books/sontag/baggley.htm

https://www.nps.gov/yell/blogs/a-wildflower-in-yellowstone-herma-albertson-baggley.htm

https://awomantoknow.substack.com/p/a-woman-to-know-herma-baggley

Hestia

https://www.greekmythology.com/Olympians/Hestia/hestia.html

https://greekgodsandgoddesses.net/goddesses/hestia/

https://www.ancient.eu/Hestia/

Hilda Doolittle

https://poets.org/poet/h-d

https://biography.yourdictionary.com/hilda-doolittle

https://www.poetryfoundation.org/poets/h-d

Hildegard of Bingen

https://www.ancient.eu/Hildegard_of_Bingen/

https://www.encyclopedia.com/people/literature-and-arts/music-history-composers-and-performers-biographies/hildegard-bingen

Huda Sha'arawi

https://amazingwomeninhistory.com/huda-shaarawi-egyptian-feminist/

https://scholarblogs.emory.edu/postcolonialstudies/2014/06/12/shaarawi-huda/

https://en.wikipedia.org/wiki/Huda_Sha%27arawi

Hypatia

https://scientificwomen.net/women/hypatia--47

https://www.ancient.eu/Hypatia_of_Alexandria/

https://www.famousscientists.org/hypatia/

Ida B Wells

https://www.blackpast.org/african-american-history/barnett-ida-wells-1862-1931/

https://www.biography.com/activist/ida-b-wells

https://www.nps.gov/people/idabwells.htm

https://en.wikipedia.org/wiki/Ida_B._Wells

Ida Halpern CBE, OC

https://www.academia.edu/4668685/Ida_Halpern_and_First_Nations_music_art_or_law

https://en.wikipedia.org/wiki/Ida_Halpern

Ida Tarbell

https://www.smithsonianmag.com/history/the-woman-who-took-on-the-tycoon-651396/

https://www.pbs.org/wgbh/americanexperience/features/ida-tarbell-pioneering-journalist/

https://en.wikipedia.org/wiki/Ida_Tarbell

Ina Boyle

https://www.wrti.org/post/classical-album-week-irish-composer-ina-boyles-musical-voice-past-now-shines

https://journalofmusic.com/focus/making-case-ina-boyle

https://en.wikipedia.org/wiki/Ina_Boyle

Inanna

https://www.ancient.eu/Inanna/

https://journeyingtothegoddess.wordpress.com/2012/08/20/goddess-inanna/

https://en.wikipedia.org/wiki/Inanna

Indira Gandhi

https://www.biography.com/news/indira-gandhi-biography-facts

https://www.history.com/topics/india/indira-gandhi

https://en.wikipedia.org/wiki/Indira_Gandhi

Ines Maria Mendoza

http://www.paralanaturaleza.org/en/ines-maria-mendoza-eng/

https://www.tropicalinnspr.com/natural-reserve-ines-mendoza

Irena Sendler

https://irenasendler.org/facts-about-irena/

https://www.yadvashem.org/yv/en/exhibitions/righteous-women/sendler.asp

https://www.jewishvirtuallibrary.org/irena-sendler

Irene Joliet-Curie

https://www.nobelprize.org/prizes/chemistry/1935/joliot-curie/biographical/

https://www.famousscientists.org/irene-joliot-curie/

https://biography.yourdictionary.com/irene-joliot-curie

Isabelle de Charriere

https://www.dbnl.org/tekst/_low001199401_01/_low001199401_01_0021.php\

https://en.wikipedia.org/wiki/Isabelle_de_Charrière

https://www.encyclopedia.com/women/encyclopedias-almanacs-transcripts-and-maps/charriere-isabelle-de-1740-1805

Isis

https://www.ancient-egypt-online.com/isis.html

http://egyptian-gods.org/egyptian-gods-isis/

Janaki Ammal

https://www.smithsonianmag.com/science-nature/pioneering-female-botanist-who-sweetened-nation-and-saved-valley-180972765/

Jane Addams

https://www.womenshistory.org/education-resources/biographies/jane-addams

https://www.nobelprize.org/prizes/peace/1931/addams/biographical/

https://plato.stanford.edu/entries/addams-jane/

Jane Colden

https://www.sierracollege.edu/ejournals/jscnhm/v6n1/colden.html

https://www.encyclopedia.com/history/encyclopedias-almanacs-tran-scripts-and-maps/colden-jane

https://massivesci.com/articles/jane-colden-botany-colonial-america-new-york-marsh-st-johns-wort/

Jane Johnston Schoolcraft

https://plato.stanford.edu/entries/addams-jane/

https://www.womenhistoryblog.com/2012/07/jane-johnston-schoolcraft.html

https://www.upenn.edu/pennpress/book/14292.html

Jane Marcet

https://www.famousscientists.org/jane-marcet/

https://www.encyclopedia.com/science/dictionaries-thesauruses-pic-tures-and-press-releases/marcet-jane-haldimand

Jeanne Baret

https://www.npr.org/2010/12/26/132265308/a-female-explorer-discovered-on-the-high-seas

https://exploration.marinersmuseum.org/subject/jeanne-baret/

Jeannette Rankin

https://history.house.gov/People/Listing/R/RANKIN,-Jeannette-(R000055)/

https://www.biography.com/political-figure/jeannette-rankin

https://www.thoughtco.com/jeannette-rankin-biography-3528695

Jessie Redmon Fauset

https://poets.org/poet/jessie-redmon-fauset
http://www.myblackhistory.net/Jessie_Fauset.htm
https://www.brynmawr.edu/bulletin/bryn-mawrs-loss

Joan D'Arc

https://www.history.com/topics/middle-ages/saint-joan-of-arc
https://www.biography.com/military-figure/joan-of-arc

Josefina Fierro de Bright

https://oac.cdlib.org/findaid/ark:/13030/c8416wc2/entire_text/
https://en.wikipedia.org/wiki/Josefina_Fierro_de_Bright
https://damianogirona.wordpress.com/hispaniclatino-2/josephina-fierro-de-bright/

Josephine Baker

https://www.womenshistory.org/education-resources/biographies/josephine-baker
https://www.thoughtco.com/josephine-baker-biography-3528473
https://en.wikipedia.org/wiki/Josephine_Baker
https://www.biography.com/performer/josephine-baker

Josephine St. Pierre Ruffin

https://www.womenofthehall.org/inductee/josephine-st-pierre-ruffin/
https://www.blackpast.org/african-american-history/ruffin-josephine-st-pierre-1842-1924/
http://www.pbs.org/blackpress/news_bios/newbios/nwsppr/Biogrphs/josephruff/joseph.html

Jovita Idar

https://www.womenshistory.org/education-resources/biographies/jovita-idar
https://www.womenintexashistory.org/biographies/jovita-idar/

Juno

https://www.ancient.eu/Juno/
https://mythopedia.com/roman-mythology/gods/juno/

Kassia

https://blogs.bl.uk/digitisedmanuscripts/2016/03/kassia.html
https://www.mezzocammin.com/timeline/timeline.php?vol=timeline&iss=800&cat=10&page=kassia
https://en.wikipedia.org/wiki/Kassia

Kate Chopin

https://americanliterature.com/author/kate-chopin

https://www.pbs.org/katechopin/program.html

https://www.newworldencyclopedia.org/entry/Kate_Chopin

https://en.wikipedia.org/wiki/Kate_Chopin

https://www.mentalfloss.com/article/527341/15-facts-about-kate-chopins-awakening

Kate Warne

https://pinkerton.com/our-insights/blog/unsung-heroes-first-female-detective-kate-warne

https://www.mentalfloss.com/article/606901/kate-warne-first-female-detective

Katherine Dunham

http://kdcah.org/katherine-dunham-biography/

https://www.loc.gov/collections/katherine-dunham/articles-and-essays/katherine-dunham-timeline/

https://www.britannica.com/biography/Katherine-Dunham

La Mulatresse Solitude

http://slaveryandremembrance.org/people/person/?id=PP015

https://goodblacknews.org/2018/08/09/history-meet-solitude-the-great-warrior-woman-of-guadeloupe-who-fought-against-french-troops-in-1802-while-pregnant/

Lakshmi Bai

https://www.historynet.com/who-is-marnikarnika-legendary-hindu-queen-lakshmi-bai.htm

https://biography.yourdictionary.com/lakshmi-bai

Leizu

https://www.ancient-origins.net/history/legend-leizu-and-origins-luxurious-chinese-silk-005475

https://searchinginhistory.blogspot.com/2014/01/goddess-of-silk-leizu.html

Lena Horne

https://www.notablebiographies.com/Ho-Jo/Horne-Lena.html

https://www.nytimes.com/2010/05/10/arts/music/10horne.html

https://en.wikipedia.org/wiki/Lena_Horne

Lili Boulanger

https://seattlesymphony.org/watch-listen/beyondthestage/lili-boulanger

https://www.pcmsconcerts.org/composer/lili-boulanger/

https://insidestory.org.au/the-talent-of-lili-boulanger/

Lilith

https://www.newworldencyclopedia.org/entry/lilith

https://www.myjewishlearning.com/article/lilith-lady-flying-in-darkness/

https://www.learnreligions.com/legend-of-lilith-origins-2076660

Lillian Moller Gilbreth

https://www.womenshistory.org/lillian-moller-gilbreth

https://www.sdsc.edu/ScienceWomen/gilbreth.html

https://www.thefamouspeople.com/profiles/lillian-moller-gilbreth-7079.php

https://www.womenofthehall.org/inductee/lillian-moller-gilbreth/

Lise Meitner

https://www.sdsc.edu/ScienceWomen/meitner.html

https://www.famousscientists.org/lise-meitner/

https://www.smithsonianmag.com/science-nature/ten-historic-female-scientists-you-should-know-84028788/?page=6

https://jwa.org/encyclopedia/article/meitner-lise

Loie Fuller

https://dance.washington.edu/people/loie-fuller

https://archive.nytimes.com/www.nytimes.com/books/first/c/current-loie.html?module=inline

http://www.artsalive.ca/en/dan/meet/bios/artistDetail.asp?artistID=168

Lois Weber

https://wfpp.columbia.edu/pioneer/ccp-lois-weber/

https://www.bbc.com/culture/article/20190318-lois-weber-the-trailblazing-director-who-shocked-the-world

Lorena Hickok

https://www.nps.gov/people/lorena-hickok.htm

https://legacyprojectchicago.org/person/lorena-hickok

Louisa May Alcott

https://www.womenshistory.org/education-resources/biographies/louisa-may-alcott

https://www.biography.com/news/meet-the-real-life-family-behind-little-women

Louise Bogan

https://poets.org/poet/louise-bogan

https://poetryarchive.org/poet/louise-bogan/

https://www.loc.gov/item/n50010084/louise-bogan/

Louise Farrenc

https://www.classicfm.com/discover-music/louise-farrenc-story/

https://www.notablebiographies.com/supp/Supplement-Ca-Fi/Farrenc-Louise.html

Lucretia Mott

https://www.nps.gov/wori/learn/historyculture/lucretia-mott.htm

https://www.history.com/topics/womens-history/lucretia-mott

https://www.smithsonianmag.com/smithsonian-institution/modesty-isnt-weakness-1809755207

Lucy Bakewell Audubon

https://www.womenhistoryblog.com/2015/09/lucy-bakewell-audubon.html

https://www.sdnhm.org/blog/blog_details/lucy-audubon-a-womans-story-behind-audubons-birds/120/

Lucy Burns

https://www.nps.gov/people/lucy-burns.htm

http://vcencyclopedia.vassar.edu/alumni/lucy-burns.html

Lucy Craft Laney

https://www.blackpast.org/african-american-history/laney-lucy-craft-1854-1933/

https://lucylaney.mpls.k12.mn.us/history_of_lucey_craft_laney

https://en.wikipedia.org/wiki/Lucy_Craft_Laney

Lucy Maud Montgomery OBE

https://www.lmmontgomery.ca/about/lmm/her-life

https://www.thecanadianencyclopedia.ca/en/article/montgomery-lucy-maud

Lucy Stone

https://www.womenshistory.org/education-resources/biographies/lucy-stone

https://www.nps.gov/people/lucy-stone.htm

https://www.biography.com/activist/lucy-stone

Ma Rainey

https://www.biography.com/musician/ma-rainey

https://www.theguardian.com/music/2020/dec/15/ma-rainey-black-bottom-netflix-mother-of-the-blues

https://en.wikipedia.org/wiki/Ma_Rainey

Ma'at

https://www.ancient.eu/Ma%27at/

https://www.ancient-origins.net/history-ancient-traditions/maat-ancient-egyptian-goddess-truth-justice-and-morality-003131

Madam Yoko

http://www.sierra-leone.org/Heroes/heroes5.html

https://www.encyclopedia.com/women/encyclopedias-almanacs-transcripts-and-maps/yoko-c-1849-1906

Madame C. J. Walker

https://www.history.com/topics/black-history/madame-c-j-walker

https://www.biography.com/inventor/madam-cj-walker

Madame Montour

http://www.native-americans.org/madame-montour/

https://en.wikipedia.org/wiki/Madame_Montour

https://www.departments.bucknell.edu/environmental_center/sunbury/website/MadameMontour.shtml

https://b-womeninamericanhistory18.blogspot.com/2019/12/biography-madame-montour-c-1684-c-1752.html

Maddalena Casulana

https://www.amodernreveal.com/maddalena-casulana

https://musictheoryexamplesbywomen.com/composers/maddalena-casulana-c-1544-c-1590/

https://www.vpr.org/post/timeline-014-maddalena-casulana-first-female-composer-be-printed-and-published#stream/0

Maeve (Medb, Meadb)

https://journeyingtothegoddess.wordpress.com/2012/05/04/goddess-maeve/

https://www.ireland-information.com/irish-mythology/maeve-irish-legend.html

http://themotherhouseofthegoddess.com/2014/05/01/52-goddesses-bealtaine-and-the-goddess-meadb-maeve/

Maggie Lena Walker

https://www.biography.com/scholar/maggie-lena-walker

https://www.womenshistory.org/education-resources/biographies/maggie-le-na-walker

Margaret Bancroft

https://njwomenshistory.org/discover/biographies/margaret-bancroft/

https://www.bancroft.org/about/history/

https://www.ncu.edu/blog/national-women's-history-month-female-leaders-educa-tion#gref

Margaret Fuller

https://www.poetryfoundation.org/poets/margaret-fuller

https://www.encyclopedia.com/people/social-sciences-and-law/social-reformers/margaret-fuller

Margaret Mead

http://www.interculturalstudies.org/Mead/biography.html

https://www.history.com/topics/womens-history/margaret-mead

Margaret Thomas Murie

https://wilderness.net/learn-about-wilderness/olaus-mardy-murie.php

https://www.wilderness.org/articles/blog/happy-birthday-mardy-murie-grand-mother-conservation-movement

https://www.britannica.com/biography/Margaret-Murie

Maria Mitchell

https://www.biography.com/scientist/maria-mitchell

https://scientificwomen.net/women/mitchell-maria-70

https://www.famousscientists.org/maria-mitchell/

https://www.womenshistory.org/education-resources/biographies/maria-mitchell

Maria Montessori

https://amshq.org/About-Montessori/History-of-Montessori/Who-Was-Maria-Mon-tessori

https://montessori.org.au/biography-dr-maria-montessori

Maria Sabina

https://www.faena.com/aleph/maria-sabina-a-most-fascinating-mexican-healer

https://psychedelicreview.com/person/maria-sabina/

https://www.ucpress.edu/book/9780520239531/maria-sabina

Maria Sibylla Merian

https://www.botanicalartandartists.com/about-maria-sibylla-merian.html

https://www.nytimes.com/2017/01/23/science/maria-sibylla-merian-metamorphosis-insectorum-surinamensium.html

http://www.sibyllamerian.com/biography.html

Maria Stewart

https://www.nps.gov/people/maria-w-stewart.htm

https://www.cwhf.org/inductees/maria-miller-stewart

https://www.thoughtco.com/maria-stewart-biography-3530406

Maria Teresa Ferrari

https://peoplepill.com/people/maria-teresa-ferrari-1

https://adb.anu.edu.au/biography/ferrari-maria-teresa-9274

Marian Anderson

https://www.pbs.org/wgbh/americanexperience/features/eleanor-anderson/

https://www.smithsonianmag.com/smithsonian-institution/how-marian-anderson-became-iconic-symbol-equality-180972898/

Marianna Martines

https://www.amodernreveal.com/marianna-martines

https://www.notablebiographies.com/supp/Supplement-Ka-M/Martinez-Marianne.html

https://saskatoonsymphony.org/the-renaissance-of-marianna-martines/

Marianne North

https://www.kew.org/read-and-watch/marianne-north-botanical-artist

https://www.plantexplorers.com/explorers/botanical-artists/marianne-north.htm

https://en.wikipedia.org/wiki/Marianne_North

Marie Curie

https://www.nobelprize.org/prizes/physics/1903/marie-curie/biographical/

https://www.biography.com/scientist/marie-curie

https://www.famousscientists.org/marie-curie/

Marie Laveaux

https://64parishes.org/entry/marie-laveau-2

https://www.atlasobscura.com/places/marie-laveaus-tomb

https://www.womenhistoryblog.com/2012/07/marie-laveau.html

Marie Popelin

https://focusonbelgium.be/en/Do%20you%20know%20these%20Belgians/marie-popelin-feminist-icon

https://www.lawgazette.co.uk/commentary-and-opinion/engaging-with-the-history-of-women-lawyers/5104736.article

Marion Bauer

https://jwa.org/encyclopedia/article/bauer-marion-eugenie

https://musictheoryexamplesbywomen.com/composers/marion-bauer-1882-1955/

Marion Dickerman

https://erpapers.columbian.gwu.edu/marion-dickerman-1890-1983

https://www.nps.gov/people/mariondickerman.htm

Marjorie Stoneman Douglas

https://www.womenofthehall.org/inductee/marjory-stoneman-douglas/

https://www.theriverofgrass.com/marjory-stoneman-douglas/

https://www.everglades.org/about-marjory/

Mary Adelaide Nutting

https://www.womenshistory.org/education-resources/biographies/mary-adelaide-nutting

https://www.encyclopedia.com/women/encyclopedias-almanacs-transcripts-and-maps/nutting-mary-adelaide-1858-1948

https://en.wikipedia.org/wiki/Mary_Adelaide_Nutting

Mary Ann Shadd Cary

https://www.nps.gov/nr/travel/underground/dc2.htm

https://www.biography.com/activist/mary-ann-shadd-cary

https://www.nytimes.com/2018/06/06/obituaries/mary-ann-shadd-cary-abolitionist-overlooked.html

Mary Anning

https://www.nhm.ac.uk/discover/mary-anning-unsung-hero.html

https://ucmp.berkeley.edu/history/anning.html

https://www.famousscientists.org/mary-anning/

Mary Bowser

https://www.history.com/news/female-spies-civil-war-mary-bowser-elizabeth-van-lew

https://time.com/5609045/misremembering-mary-bowser/
https://www.newworldencyclopedia.org/entry/Mary_Elizabeth_Bowser
https://en.wikipedia.org/wiki/Mary_Bowser

Mary Buckland

https://trowelblazers.com/mary-buckland/
https://scientificwomen.net/women/buckland-mary-171
https://www.geolsoc.org.uk/Library-and-Information-Services/Exhibitions/Women-and-Geology/Mary-Buckland

Mary Carpenter

https://www.jstor.org/stable/41971151?seq=1
https://www.encyclopedia.com/women/encyclopedias-almanacs-transcripts-and-maps/carpenter-mary-1807-1877
https://archives.history.ac.uk/history-in-focus/Migration/articles/dresser.html

Mary Carson Breckenridge

https://nursing-theory.org/famous-nurses/Mary-Carson-Breckinridge.php
https://wednesdayswomen.com/the-mother-of-american-midwifery-mary-carson-breckinridge/
https://peoplepill.com/people/mary-carson-breckinridge/

Mary Cassatt

https://www.biography.com/artist/mary-cassatt
https://www.artsy.net/artist/mary-cassatt
https://www.moma.org/artists/1016

Mary Mahoney

https://www.womenshistory.org/education-resources/biographies/mary-mahoney
https://nursing-theory.org/famous-nurses/Mary-Mahoney.php
https://www.biography.com/activist/mary-mahoney

Mary Jane Seacole

https://www.nationalgeographic.org/article/mary-seacole/
https://www.blackpast.org/global-african-history/seacole-mary-jane-1805-1881/
https://nursing-theory.org/famous-nurses/Mary-Jane-Seacole.php

Mary Kawena Pukui

https://hanahou.com/10.4/kawenas-legacy

https://wams.nyhistory.org/confidence-and-crises/great-depression/mary-kawe-na-pukui/

Mary Lyon
https://www.mtholyoke.edu/175/gallery/mary-lyon
https://biography.yourdictionary.com/mary-lyon
https://www.mtholyoke.edu/marylyon

Mary McCleod Bethune
https://www.womenshistory.org/education-resources/biographies/mary-mcleod-bethune
https://www.biography.com/activist/mary-mcleod-bethune
https://www.nationalww2museum.org/war/articles/mary-mcleod-bethune

Mary Prince
https://www.encyclopedia.com/women/encyclopedias-almanacs-tran-scripts-and-maps/prince-mary-c-1788-after-1833
http://www.bbc.co.uk/history/british/abolition/abolitionists_gallery_04.shtml
https://womenshistorynetwork.org/black-history-month-witness-against-slavery-the-story-of-mary-prince/

Mary Sommerville
https://mathshistory.st-andrews.ac.uk/Biographies/Somerville/
http://adsabs.harvard.edu/full/1996JBAA..106..201B
https://www.famousscientists.org/mary-somerville/

Mary Edwards Walker
https://www.ausa.org/dr-mary-e-walker
https://www.nps.gov/people/mary-walker.htm
https://www.biography.com/activist/mary-walker

Mary Wigman
https://www.fembio.org/english/biography.php/woman/biography/mary-wigman/
https://www.encyclopedia.com/people/literature-and-arts/dance-biographies/mary-wigman
https://www.haaretz.com/israel-news/culture/.premium-the-german-dancer-who-stepped-too-close-to-the-nazis-1.5413894

Mary Wollstonecraft
https://plato.stanford.edu/entries/wollstonecraft/

https://www.thoughtco.com/mary-wollstonecraft-early-years-3530791

https://www.feministsforlife.org/herstory-mary-wollstonecraft/

Mary-Cooke Branch Munford

https://thedrakeharper.medium.com/education-activist-mary-cooke-branch-munford-and-the-equal-suffrage-league-of-virginia-853b873a8d45

https://www.virginiahistory.org/collections-and-resources/virginia-history-explorer/mary-cooke-branch-munford

Mata Hari

https://www.theguardian.com/lifeandstyle/2016/dec/05/the-real-mata-hari-executed-abused-woman

http://www.eyewitnesstohistory.com/matahari.htm

https://www.bbc.com/culture/article/20171020-who-was-the-real-mata-hari

Maud Lewis

https://www.thecanadianencyclopedia.ca/en/article/paying-tribute-to-painter-maud-lewis

https://www.npr.org/2017/06/19/532816482/home-is-where-the-art-is-the-unlikely-story-of-folk-artist-maud-lewis

https://www.artsy.net/article/artsy-editorial-joyous-overlooked-canadian-folk-artist-maud-lewis

May Sarton

https://digital.library.upenn.edu/women/sarton/blouin-biography.html

https://www.britannica.com/biography/May-Sarton

Mercy Otis Warren

https://www.womenshistory.org/education-resources/biographies/mercy-otis-warren

https://biography.yourdictionary.com/mercy-otis-warren

Mileva Maric Einstein

https://scientificwomen.net/women/maric-einstein-mileva-62

https://www.independent.co.uk/news/long_reads/mileva-maric-albert-einsten-physics-science-history-women-a8396411.html

https://www.fembio.org/english/biography.php/woman/biography/mileva-maric-einstein/

Minerva

https://www.ancient.eu/trans/tr/1-12417/minerva/

https://mythopedia.com/roman-mythology/gods/minerva/

https://www.ancient-origins.net/myths-legends-europe/minerva-0011221

Minnie Cox

https://postalmuseum.si.edu/research-articles/the-history-and-experience-of-african-americans-in-america's-postal-service/minnie

http://www.mshistorynow.mdah.ms.gov/articles/421/minnie-geddings-cox-and-the-indianola-affair

Modjadji

https://nationalmuseumpublications.co.za/modjadji-the-rain-queen/

https://www.downtoearth.org.in/news/young/all-hail-the-rain-queen-of-south-africa-71209

Molly Brant (Konwatsi'tsiaienni)

https://www.nps.gov/people/molly-brant-konwatsi-tsiaienni.htm

https://www.encyclopedia.com/people/history/historians-miscellaneous-biographies/molly-brant

Morana

https://www.slavorum.org/morena-and-legends-of-this-ancient-slavic-goddess-of-winter/

https://www.ancient-origins.net/myths-legends/cycle-life-and-death-slavic-goddesses-morana-and-vesna-006984

https://www.thoughtco.com/marzanna-4774267

Morgan le Fay

https://encyclopedia2.thefreedictionary.com/Morgan+Le+Fay

https://occult-world.com/morgan-le-fay/

Mother Jones

Mary Harris Jones (1837-1930)
https://www.womenshistory.org/education-resources/biographies/mary-harris-jones

National Women's Hall of Fame—Mary "Mother" Harris Jones.
https://www.womenofthehall.org/inductee/mary-mother-harris-jones/

MumBett

https://www.womenshistory.org/education-resources/biographies/elizabeth-freeman

https://www.encyclopedia.com/history/encyclopedias-almanacs-transcripts-and-maps/freeman-elizabeth-mum-bett-mumbet

https://www.masshist.org/endofslavery/index.php?id=54

Nadia Boulanger

https://www.bbc.com/culture/article/20170308-the-greatest-music-teacher-who-ever-lived

https://www.classicfm.com/discover-music/women-in-music/nadia-boulanger-composer-conductor-music-teacher/

https://daily.redbullmusicacademy.com/2017/02/nadia-boulanger-feature

https://www.nytimes.com/1979/10/23/archives/nadia-boulanger-teacher-of-top-composers-dies-onewoman-graduate.html

Nana Asma'u

https://oxfordre.com/africanhistory/view/10.1093/acrefore/9780190277734.001.0001/acrefore-9780190277734-e-468

https://chnm.gmu.edu/wwh/p/214.html

Nana Buluku

https://face2faceafrica.com/article/nana-buluku-the-revered-goddess-and-supreme-deity-of-west-africa-and-the-caribbean

http://www.elementdance.co.uk/Orixas/Nana.html

Nannie Helen Burroughs

https://www.nps.gov/people/nannie-helen-burroughs.htm

https://kinginstitute.stanford.edu/encyclopedia/burroughs-nannie-helen

Nanyehi

https://wams.nyhistory.org/settler-colonialism-and-revolution/the-american-revolution/nanyehi-nancy-ward/

https://www.smliv.com/stories/nanyehi-nancy-ward/

Nisaba

https://www.ancient.eu/Nisaba/

https://journeyingtothegoddess.wordpress.com/2012/11/01/goddess-nisaba/

https://en.wikipedia.org/wiki/Nisaba

Nongqawuse

https://www.sahistory.org.za/people/nongqawuse

https://freshwriting.nd.edu/volumes/2017/essays/examining-the-unseen-reasons-behind-the-xhosa-cattle-killing

http://www.siyabona.com/eastern-cape-xhosa-cattle-killing.html

Nora Zeale Hurston

https://www.womenshistory.org/education-resources/biographies/zora-hurston
https://www.loc.gov/collections/zora-neale-hurston-plays/about-this-collection/
https://www.biography.com/writer/zora-neale-hurston

Nur Jahan

http://www.womeninworldhistory.com/heroine11.html
https://www.bbc.com/news/world-asia-india-45319055
https://medium.com/@W.W.NortonUK/empress-nur-jahan-55fe163478b

Nuwa

https://www.newworldencyclopedia.org/entry/nuwa
https://mythopedia.com/chinese-mythology/gods/nuwa/
http://www.mythencyclopedia.com/Ni-Pa/Nu-Wa.html

Nzinga Mbande

https://www.blackpast.org/global-african-history/queen-nzinga-1583-1663/
https://www.thoughtco.com/queen-anna-nzinga-3529747

Olivia Hooker

https://www.apa.org/monitor/2012/11/history
https://www.rochester.edu/2020-celebration/olivia-hooker/
http://www.uncrownedcommunitybuilders.com/person/olivia-2

Ona Simaite

https://www.yadvashem.org/odot_pdf/Microsoft%20Word%20-%206025.pdf
http://www.lituanus.org/2008/08_2_01%20Sukys.html

Oodgeroo Noonuccal

https://www.poetrylibrary.edu.au/poets/noonuccal-oodgeroo
https://ia.anu.edu.au/biography/noonuccal-oodgeroo-18057

Oshun

https://www.ancient-origins.net/myths-legends-africa/oshun-african-goddess-love-and-sweet-waters-002908
https://journeyingtothegoddess.wordpress.com/2012/01/21/goddess-oshun/

Pandita Ramabai

https://www.bu.edu/missiology/ramabai-dongre-medhavi/
https://www.nytimes.com/2018/11/14/obituaries/pandita-ramabai-overlooked.html

Parvati

https://www.learnreligions.com/goddess-parvati-or-shakti-1770367

https://www.newworldencyclopedia.org/entry/Parvati

https://goddessgift.com/goddess-info/meet-the-goddesses/parvati/

Paula Modersohn-Becker

https://www.moma.org/artists/4037

https://awarewomenartists.com/en/artiste/paula-modersohn-becker/

Paulina Luisi

https://en.wikipedia.org/wiki/Paulina_Luisi

https://www.rd.com/list/amazing-women-in-history/

https://www.bustle.com/life/11-overlooked-women-from-history-according-to-10-female-historians-15961727

Pauline Viardot

https://digitalcommons.lsu.edu/cgi/viewcontent.cgi?article=4923&context=gradschool_dissertations

https://bonjourparis.com/history/pauline-viardot-a-forgotten-woman-of-musical-genius/

https://www.paulineviardot.de/Komponistin_englisch.htm

https://www.britannica.com/biography/Pauline-Viardot

Pearl S. Buck (aka Sai Zhenzhu)

https://www.english.upenn.edu/Projects/Buck/biography.html

https://www.biography.com/writer/pearl-s-buck

Pele

https://www.hawaii.com/discover/culture/pele/

http://www.coffeetimes.com/pele.htm

Pilar Barbosa

https://www.encyclopedia.com/women/encyclopedias-almanacs-transcripts-and-maps/barbosa-pilar-1898-1997

https://www.nytimes.com/1997/01/24/us/pilar-barbosa-99-puerto-rican-political-mentor-dies.html

Princess Kartini

https://www.encyclopedia.com/women/encyclopedias-almanacs-transcripts-and-maps/kartini-1879-1904

https://en.wikipedia.org/wiki/Kartini
https://medium.com/@moroseparsnip/raden-adjeng-kartini-letters-of-a-javanese-princess-c40caeb9c928
https://www.biography.com/activist/raden-adjeng-kartini

Quan Yin (Guanyin)
https://www.holymtn.com/homepage/gods-goddesses/quan-yin-goddess-mercy/
https://en.wikipedia.org/wiki/Guanyin

Queen Amina
http://www.africanfeministforum.com/queen-amina-of-zaria-nigeria/
https://www.encyclopedia.com/history/news-wires-white-papers-and-books/queen-amina

Queen Anacaona
https://www.rejectedprincesses.com/princesses/anacaona
https://culturacolectiva.com/history/anacaona-haitian-queen

Queen Yaa Asantewaa
https://www.blackpast.org/global-african-history/yaa-asantewaa-mid-1800s-1921/
http://nanayaaasantewaa.de/who-is-nana-yaa-asantewaa/

Queen Emma of Hawaii
https://www.aloha-hawaii.com/big-island/queen-emma/
https://www.crownofhawaii.com/queen-emma-rs

Queen Himiko
https://www.ancient.eu/Queen_Himiko/
https://www.historyofroyalwomen.com/japan/who-was-queen-himiko/
https://www.tofugu.com/japan/queen-himiko/

Queen Lili'uokalani
https://www.nps.gov/articles/000/liliuokalani-hawaii-s-last-queen.htm
https://www.biography.com/royalty/liliuokalani

Queen Nanny of the Maroons
https://www.blackpast.org/global-african-history/queen-nanny-maroons-1733/
https://jis.gov.jm/information/heroes/nanny-of-the-maroons/
https://jamaicans.com/queennanny/

Queen Ndate Yalla

https://face2faceafrica.com/article/ndate-yalla-mbodj-the-last-queen-of-senegal-who-fought-off-the-french-arabs-and-moors

https://blackwomenworldhistory.tumblr.com/post/30501841386/afrikanwomen-queen-ndaté-yalla-mbodj-she-was

Queen Seon-deok of Silla

https://www.ancient.eu/Queen_Seondeok/

https://www.thoughtco.com/queen-seondeok-of-koreas-silla-kingdom-195722

Queen Tiye

https://www.ancient.eu/tiye/

https://face2faceafrica.com/article/queen-tiye-an-influential-royal-wife-and-adviser-of-pharaoh-amenhotep-iii-whose-death-ended-the-18th-dynasty-of-ancient-egypt

https://www.historyofroyalwomen.com/egypt/queen-tiye-elder-lady/

Queen Victoria

https://www.biography.com/royalty/queen-victoria

https://www.thoughtco.com/queen-victoria-biography-3530656

Queen Wilhelmina

Wilhelmina of the Netherlands
https://www.newworldencyclopedia.org/entry/Wilhelmina_of_the_Netherlands

Wilhelmina (1880-1962)
https://www.encyclopedia.com/women/encyclopedias-almanacs-transcripts-and-maps/wilhelmina-1880-1962

Rachel Carson

https://www.fws.gov/refuge/Rachel_Carson/about/rachelcarson.html

https://www.womenshistory.org/education-resources/biographies/rachel-carson

https://www.biography.com/scientist/rachel-carson

Rebecca Clarke

https://www.newworldencyclopedia.org/entry/Rebecca_Clarke

https://www.seattlechambermusic.org/composers/rebecca-clarke/

https://interlude.hk/us-whipped-rebecca-clarke/

Rebecca Lee Crumpler

https://www.nps.gov/people/dr-rebecca-lee-crumpler.htm

https://www.pbs.org/newshour/health/celebrating-rebecca-lee-crumpler-first-african-american-physician

https://en.wikipedia.org/wiki/Rebecca_Lee_Crumpler

Recha Sternbuch
https://www.amimagazine.org/2018/06/27/the-secret-deal/

https://www.accidentaltalmudist.org/heroes/2017/12/06/a-woman-of-valor/

Rhiannon
https://sacredwicca.com/rhiannon

https://www.rhiannon.ie/myths.htm

https://journeyingtothegoddess.wordpress.com/2012/09/18/goddess-rhiannon/

Rosa Ponselle
https://www.britannica.com/biography/Rosa-Ponselle

https://www.fembio.org/english/biography.php/woman/biography/rosa-ponselle/

https://www.encyclopedia.com/women/encyclopedias-almanacs-transcripts-and-maps/ponselle-rosa-1897-1981

Rosalie Barrow Edge
https://wednesdayswomen.com/rosalie-edge-champion-of-womens-suffrage-and-environmental-activism/

https://milliontrees.me/2014/09/12/rosalie-edge-conservation-hero/

https://en.wikipedia.org/wiki/Rosalie_Edge

Ruby Dee
https://www.biography.com/actor/ruby-dee

https://www.nytimes.com/2014/06/13/arts/ruby-dee-actress-dies-at-91.html

Rufaida al-Aslamia
https://saudigazette.com.sa/article/175811

https://muslimheritage.com/people/scholars/rufaida-al-aslamia/

http://sohabih.blogspot.com/2017/02/saidatuna-rufaida-al-aslamia-ra.html

Ruth St. Denis
https://www.britannica.com/biography/Ruth-St-Denis

http://www.pitt.edu/~gillis/dance/ruth.html

https://www.newworldencyclopedia.org/entry/Ruth_St._Denis

Sappho of Lesbos

https://www.ancient.eu/Sappho_of_Lesbos/

https://www.ancient-literature.com/greece_sappho.html

https://poets.org/poet/sappho

https://www.britannica.com/biography/Sappho-Greek-poet

Sarah E. Goode

https://www.biography.com/inventor/sarah-e-goode

https://www.blackpast.org/african-american-history/goode-sarah-e-c-1855-1905/

Sarah Jane Woodson Early

https://www.monticello.org/getting-word/people/sarah-woodson-early

https://goodblacknews.org/2013/02/04/black-female-pioneers-sarah-jane-woodson-early-paves-way-for-black-educators/

https://www.womenhistoryblog.com/2015/03/sarah-jane-woodson-early.html

Sarah Winnemucca

https://biography.yourdictionary.com/sarah-winnemucca

https://www.smithsonianmag.com/history/sarah-winnemucca-devoted-life-protecting-lives-native-americans-face-expanding-united-states-180959930/

https://www.womenofthehall.org/inductee/sarah-winnemucca/

Savitribai Phule

https://www.indiatoday.in/education-today/gk-current-affairs/story/how-savitribai-phule-india-s-first-female-teacher-dealt-with-abusers-hell-bent-on-preventing-her-from-educating-girls-1633725-2020-01-03

https://feminisminindia.com/2016/09/05/essay-life-savitribai-phule/

https://www.hindustantimes.com/ht-school/savitribai-phule-india-s-first-female-teacher/story-uEto1oUyhgcftvyuzD8waO.html

Sedna

https://www.thecanadianencyclopedia.ca/en/article/the-goddess-of-the-sea-the-story-of-sedna

https://journeyingtothegoddess.wordpress.com/2012/06/26/goddess-sedna/

http://www.mythencyclopedia.com/Sa-Sp/Sedna.html

Sekhmet

https://ancientegyptonline.co.uk/sekhmet/

http://egyptian-gods.org/egyptian-gods-sekhmet/

Selene/Luna Selene

https://www.thoughtco.com/greek-mythology-selene-1526204

https://www.theoi.com/Titan/Selene.html

https://www.greek-gods.info/ancient-greek-gods/selene/#selene-chariot

Semiramis

https://www.ancient.eu/Semiramis/

https://www.nationalgeographic.com/history/magazine/2017/09-10/searching-for-semiramis-assyrian-legend/

https://www.encyclopedia.com/women/encyclopedias-almanacs-transcripts-and-maps/sammuramat-fl-8th-c-bce

Septima Poinsette Clark

https://kinginstitute.stanford.edu/encyclopedia/clark-septima-poinsette

https://www.biography.com/activist/septima-poinsette-clark

https://www.nps.gov/people/septimapoinsetteclark.htm

Simone de Beauvoir

https://plato.stanford.edu/entries/beauvoir/

https://www.biography.com/scholar/simone-de-beauvoir

https://www.the-tls.co.uk/articles/simone-de-beauvoir-freedom-forgiveness/

Sissieretta Joyner Jones

https://www.blackpast.org/african-american-history/jones-sissieretta-1869-1933/

https://afrovoices.com/sissieretta-jones-biography/

https://www.encyclopedia.com/people/history/historians-miscellaneous-biographies/m-sissieretta-jones

https://www.pbs.org/wnet/americanmasters/first-black-woman-headline-concert-carnegie-hall-wtx97f/14930/

Sister Nivedita

https://www.english-heritage.org.uk/visit/blue-plaques/sister-nivedita/

https://www.livehistoryindia.com/history-daily/2020/04/07/sister-nivedita-calcuttas-angel-of-mercy

https://www.encyclopedia.com/women/encyclopedias-almanacs-transcripts-and-maps/nivedita-sister-1867-1911

Sojourner Truth

https://www.womenshistory.org/education-resources/biographies/sojourner-truth

https://www.nps.gov/people/sojourner-truth.htm

https://en.wikipedia.org/wiki/Sojourner_Truth

Sol

https://mythology.net/norse/norse-gods/sol/

https://journeyingtothegoddess.wordpress.com/2012/05/14/goddess-sol/

http://ydalir.ca/norsegods/sol/

Sophia

https://www.crystalinks.com/sophia.html

https://goddessgift.com/goddess-info/meet-the-goddesses/sophia/

Sophie Germain

https://www.agnesscott.edu/lriddle/women/germain.htm

https://mathshistory.st-andrews.ac.uk/Biographies/Germain/

https://www.sdsc.edu/ScienceWomen/germain.html

Sophinisba Breckinridge

https://www.newworldencyclopedia.org/entry/Sophonisba_Breckinridge

https://spartacus-educational.com/USAWbreckinridge.htm

Sor Juana Ines de la Cruz

https://www.biography.com/writer/sor-juana-ines-de-la-cruz

https://poets.org/poet/sor-juana-ines-de-la-cruz

https://daily.jstor.org/sor-juana-founding-mother-of-mexican-literature/

Spider Woman

https://www.crystalinks.com/mayanspiderwomen.html

https://www.ancient-origins.net/myths-legends-americas/spider-woman-0014386

Sucheta Kripalani

https://feminisminindia.com/2018/03/05/sucheta-kripalani-first-woman-chief-minister/

https://www.constitutionofindia.net/constituent_assembly_members/sucheta_kripalini

Susan Fenimore Cooper

http://earlywomeninscience.biodiversityexhibition.com/en/card/susan-fenimore-cooper

https://www.audubon.org/news/meet-susan-fenimore-cooper-americas-first-recognized-female-nature-writer

https://en.wikipedia.org/wiki/Susan_Fenimore_Cooper

https://blogs.loc.gov/inside_adams/2017/04/susan-fenimore-cooper-the-first-american-woman-to-publish-nature-writing/

Susan La Flesche Picotte

https://www.smithsonianmag.com/history/incredible-legacy-susan-la-flesche-first-native-american-earn-medical-degree-180962332/

https://sitn.hms.harvard.edu/flash/2021/susan-la-flesche-picotte-leader-in-tribal-health-with-eye-toward-sovereignty/

https://en.wikipedia.org/wiki/Susan_La_Flesche_Picotte

Susanne K. Langer

https://www.newworldencyclopedia.org/p/index.php?title=Susanne_Langer&oldid=1030571

https://www.nytimes.com/1985/07/19/nyregion/susanne-k-langer-philosopher-is-dead-at-89.html

https://en.wikipedia.org/wiki/Susanne_Langer

Susan B. Anthony

https://www.womenshistory.org/education-resources/biographies/susan-b-anthony

https://www.biography.com/activist/susan-b-anthony

https://www.historynet.com/susan-b-anthony

Susie King Taylor

https://www.georgiaencyclopedia.org/articles/history-archaeology/susie-king-taylor-1848-1912

https://www.georgiawomen.org/susie-baker-king-taylor

https://www.nps.gov/people/susie-king-taylor.htm

https://www.blackpast.org/african-american-history/taylor-susan-susie-baker-king-1848-1912/

Susie Walking Bear Yellowtail

http://montanawomenshistory.org/susie-walking-bear-yellowtail-our-bright-morning-star/

https://nursingclio.org/2020/11/19/susie-walking-bear-yellowtail-and-histories-of-native-american-nursing/

Sybil Ludington

https://www.womenshistory.org/education-resources/biographies/sybil-ludington

https://www.thoughtco.com/sybil-ludington-biography-3530671

Tacumwah

https://archfw.org/heritagetrail/kekionga/tacumwah-and-the-old-apple-tree/

https://muse.jhu.edu/article/192180/summary

http://historycenterfw.blogspot.com/2012/08/tacumwah-18th-century-people-magazine.html

Touran Mirhadi

https://women.ncr-iran.org/2018/12/18/touran-mirhadi-educator-childrens-book-author/

https://en.wikipedia.org/wiki/Touran_Mirhadi

https://www.iranwire.com/en/special-features/7017?ref=special

Toypurina

https://www.kcet.org/history-society/toypurina-a-legend-etched-in-the-landscape-of-los-angeles

https://www.girlboss.com/read/2018-3-13-toypurina-history

https://en.wikipedia.org/wiki/Toypurina

Trota of Salerno

https://scientificwomen.net/women/trota_of_salerno--91

https://www.encyclopedia.com/history/encyclopedias-almanacs-transcripts-and-maps/trota-salerno

https://womenyoushouldknow.net/trota-salerno-medieval-womens-medicine/

Tsuda Umeko

https://www.learningtogive.org/resources/tsuda-umeko

https://pubmed.ncbi.nlm.nih.gov/20533730/

https://en.wikipedia.org/wiki/Tsuda_Umeko

Tuba Azmudeh

http://www.midooni.org/midooni-blog/celebrating-iranian-women-tuba-azmudeh

https://iranwire.com/en/features/7384

Vanessa Bell

https://www.britannica.com/biography/Vanessa-Bell

https://www.theartstory.org/artist/bell-vanessa/life-and-legacy/

https://awarewomenartists.com/en/artiste/vanessa-bell/

Vernie Merze Tate

https://www.blackpast.org/african-american-history/tate-vernie-merze-1905-1996/

https://wednesdayswomen.com/from-one-room-school-to-international-renown-vernie-merze-tate/

Victoria Claflin Woodhull

https://ehistory.osu.edu/biographies/victoria-woodhull
https://www.history.com/news/9-things-you-should-know-about-victoria-woodhull
https://www.biography.com/activist/victoria-woodhull

Virginia Woolf

https://www.notablebiographies.com/We-Z/Woolf-Virginia.html
https://www.bl.uk/people/virginia-woolf
https://www.biography.com/writer/virginia-woolf

Vigdis Finnbogadottir GCMG

https://www.britannica.com/explore/100women/profiles/vigdis-finnbogadottir
https://en.wikipedia.org/wiki/Vigd%C3%ADs_Finnbogadóttir
https://amazingwomeninhistory.com/vigdis-finnbogadottir-worlds-first-female-president/
https://www.smu.ca/academics/archives/vigdis-finnbogadottir.html
http://www.clubmadrid.org/miembro/vigdis-finnbogadottir/

Vijaya Lakshmi Pandit

https://biography.yourdictionary.com/vijaya-lakshmi-pandit
https://www.un.org/en/ga/president/bios/bio08.shtml

Wane Roonseraw

https://edu.lva.virginia.gov/changemakers/items/show/190
http://www.nottowayindians.org/edithedyturner.html

White Buffalo Calf Woman

https://www.legendsofamerica.com/na-whitebuffalo/
https://www.pipekeepers.org/buffalo-white-calf-woman.html
https://www.ancient-origins.net/history-ancient-traditions/white-buffalo-calf-woman-healer-teacher-and-inspirational-spirit-lakota-021067

Zinaida Serebriakova

https://musings-on-art.org/serebryakova-zinaida
http://artroots.com/ra/bio/serebryakova/zinaidaserebryakovabio.htm
https://moscsp.ru/en/biografiya-zinaidy-evgenevny-serebryakovoi-hudozhnik-zinaida.html

https://en.wikipedia.org/wiki/Zinaida_Serebriakova

Zitkala-Sa

https://www.nps.gov/people/zitkala-sa.htm
https://wams.nyhistory.org/modernizing-america/xenophobia-and-racism/zitkala-sa/
https://en.wikipedia.org/wiki/Zitkala-Sa

Zofia Kossak-Szczucka

https://www.facinghistory.org/holocaust-and-human-behavior/chapter-9/speaking-out-face-murder
https://www.accidentaltalmudist.org/heroes/2020/02/19/the-anti-semite-who-saved-jews/
https://en.wikipedia.org/wiki/Zofia_Kossak-Szczucka
https://www.encyclopedia.com/women/encyclopedias-almanacs-transcripts-and-maps/kossak-zofia-1890-1968